Taking SIDES

Clashing Views on Controversial Psychological Issues

Tenth Edition

Edited, Selected, and with Introductions by

Brent Slife
Brigham Young University

Dushkin/McGraw-Hill
A Division of The McGraw-Hill Companies

To my three garrulous sons, Conor, Nathan, and Jacob

Photo Acknowledgments

Cover image: © 1997 by PhotoDisc, Inc.

Cover Art Acknowledgment

Charles Vitelli

Library of Congress Cataloging-in-Publication Data

Main entry under title:
    Taking sides: clashing views on controversial psychological issues/edited, selected, and
with introductions by Brent Slife.—10th ed.
    Includes bibliographical references and index.
    1. Psychology. 2. Human behavior. I. Slife, Brent, *comp.*

150

0-697-39112-4

Printed on Recycled Paper

PREFACE

Critical thinking skills are a significant component of a meaningful education, and this book is specifically designed to stimulate critical thinking and initiate lively and informed dialogue on psychological issues. In this book I present 36 selections, arranged in pro and con pairs, that address a total of 18 different controversial issues in psychology. The opposing views demonstrate that even experts can derive conflicting conclusions and opinions from the same body of information.

A dialogue approach to learning is certainly not new. The ancient Greek philosopher Socrates engaged in it with his students some 2,400 years ago. His point-counterpoint procedure was termed a *dialectic*. Although Socrates and his companions hoped eventually to know the "truth" by this method, they did not see the dialectic as having a predetermined end. There were no right answers to know or facts to memorize. The emphasis in this learning method is on how to evaluate information—on developing reasoning skills.

It is in this dialectical spirit that *Taking Sides: Clashing Views on Controversial Psychological Issues* was originally compiled, and it has guided me through this 10th edition as well. To encourage and stimulate discussion and to focus the debates in this volume, each issue is expressed in terms of a single question and answered with two points of view. But certainly the reader should not feel confined to adopt only one or the other of the positions presented. There are positions that fall between the views expressed, or totally outside them, and I encourage you to fashion your own conclusions.

Some of the questions raised in this volume go to the very heart of what psychology as a discipline is all about and the methods and manner in which psychologists work. Others address newly emerging concerns. In choosing readings I was guided by the following criteria: the readings had to be understandable to newcomers to psychology; they had to have academic substance; and they had to express markedly different points of view.

Plan of the book   Each issue in this volume has an issue *introduction*, which defines each author's position and sets the stage for debate. Also provided is a set of point-counterpoint statements that pertain to the issue and that should help to get the dialogue off the ground. Each issue concludes with *challenge questions* to provoke further examination of the issue. The introduction and challenge questions are designed to assist the reader in achieving a critical and informed view on important psychological issues. At the back of the book is a listing of all the *contributors to this volume*, which gives information on the psychologists, psychiatrists, philosophers, professors, and social critics whose views are debated here.

In the interest of space, the reference lists of many of the original articles have been omitted or severely curtailed. Although I welcome further scholarly investigations on these issues, I assume that readers who engage in such investigation will want to look up the original articles (with the original reference lists) anyway. Furthermore, many of the articles have been heavily edited.

Changes to this edition   This edition represents a considerable revision. There are 6 completely new issues: *Is the* Consumer Reports *Conclusion That "Psychotherapy Helps" Valid?* (Issue 1); *Classic Dialogue: Was Stanley Milgram's Study of Obedience Unethical?* (Issue 2); *Is There a Racial Difference in Intelligence?* (Issue 8); *Is Schizophrenia a Biological Disorder?* (Issue 10); *Are There Valid Psychological Reasons for Physician-Assisted Suicide?* (Issue 11); and *Are Women Violent Toward Their Male Partners?* (Issue 17). In addition, for the issues on the origins of homosexuality (Issue 4) and prescription privileges for psychologists (Issue 12), both the YES and NO readings have been replaced to bring a fresh perspective to each debate. In all, there are 16 new selections. The issues that were dropped from the previous edition were done so on the recommendation of professors who let me know what worked and what could be improved.

A word to the instructor   An *Instructor's Manual With Test Questions* (multiple-choice and essay) is available through the publisher for the instructor using *Taking Sides* in the classroom. A general guidebook, *Using Taking Sides in the Classroom*, which discusses methods and techniques for integrating the pro-con approach into any classroom setting, is also available. An online version of *Using Taking Sides in the Classroom* and a correspondence service for *Taking Sides* adopters can be found at www.cybsol.com/usingtakingsides/. For students, we offer a field guide to analyzing argumentative essays, *Analyzing Controversy: An Introductory Guide*, with exercises and techniques to help them to decipher genuine controversies.

Taking Sides: Clashing Views on Controversial Psychological Issues is only one title in the Taking Sides series. If you are interested in seeing the table of contents for any of the other titles, please visit the Taking Sides Web site at http://www.dushkin.com/takingsides/.

Acknowledgments   In working on this revision I received useful suggestions from many of the users of the previous edition, and I was able to incorporate many of their recommendations for new issues and new readings. I particularly wish to thank the following professors:

Cyrus Azimi   Frank L. Collins
Columbia College   Oklahoma State University

Edward Crothers
University of
  Colorado–Boulder

Janet Dizinno
Saint Mary's University

Margo Elliott
Columbia College

Leta F. Fennell
Chesapeake College

George W. Handley
Ohio State University–Lima
  Campus

Harold Herzog
Western Carolina University

Louis Manza
Lebanon Valley College

Jean-Louis G. Marchand
Chesapeake College

Lyla S. Maynard
Des Moines Area Community
  College

Marc Reiss
Middlebury College

R. Erik Seastedt
Jamestown Community
  College

Rita Wolpert
Caldwell College

Tiffney Yeager
University of North Dakota

In addition, special thanks go to David Dean, list manager for the Taking Sides series at Dushkin/McGraw-Hill, for his support and perspective.

Brent Slife
Brigham Young University

CONTENTS IN BRIEF

CONTENTS

Psychotherapy researcher Martin E. P. Seligman defends the conclusion of *Consumer Reports* that psychotherapy is effective. Psychotherapy researchers Neil S. Jacobson and Andrew Christensen contend that the *Consumer Reports* study is essentially the same as 40-year-old studies that have long been rejected as inadequate.

Psychologist Diana Baumrind argues that Stanley Milgram's study of obedience did not meet ethical standards for research, because participants were subjected to a research design that caused undue psychological stress that was not resolved after the study. Social psychologist Stanley Milgram asserts that the study was well designed and the participants' anguish dissipated after a thorough debriefing.

Elizabeth Baldwin, a research ethics officer for the American Psychological Association's Science Directorate, maintains that the benefits of behavioral research with animals are substantial. Professor of educational psychology Alan D. Bowd and Kenneth J. Shapiro, executive director of Psychologists for the Ethical Treatment of Animals, argue that the "benefits" of animal research do not make up for the cruel treatment of the animals.

Psychologist J. Michael Bailey and psychiatrist Richard C. Pillard argue that studies of homosexual twin pairs indicate a substantial genetic influence on homosexuality. Terry R. McGuire, a professor of biological sciences, counters that studies that indicate a genetic basis for human homosexuality omit methodological practices that are needed to give credence to the findings.

Robert Wright, a senior editor of *The New Republic*, claims that sexual behavior is determined by people's genes. Theoretical psychologist Richard N. Williams argues that the philosophy underlying genetic explanations of human behavior is dangerous.

Brandon S. Centerwall, an epidemiologist, argues that children who see a
lot of violence on television display more violent behaviors in adulthood.
Brian Siano, a writer and researcher, argues that parental neglect and lack of
nurturance are better predictors of aggression than television viewing habits.

Clinician Judith S. Wallerstein contends that children of divorced parents are
at greater risk of developing mental and physical problems than are children
of intact families. Sociologists David H. Demo and Alan C. Acock argue that
any negative effects of divorce are short-lived.

Professor of psychology J. Philippe Rushton argues that there is irrefutable
scientific evidence of racial differences in intelligence. Teacher and psychologist Zack Z. Cernovsky argues that Rushton's data is based on racial prejudice
that is reflective of Nazi dogma.

Ellen Bass and Laura Davis, both counselors of victims of child sexual abuse, assert that even a faint or vague memory of sexual abuse is prime evidence that sexual abuse has occurred. Psychiatrist Lee Coleman argues that "memories" of sexual abuse that never occurred can be created in therapy with the encouragement of mental health professionals.

Clinical psychiatrist Nancy C. Andreasen asserts that although schizophrenia is a disease that manifests itself in the mind, it arises from the brain. Clinical psychologist Victor D. Sanua contends that the assumption that schizophrenia is a biological disorder is not supported by research.

Dutch physician H. S. Cohen argues that control over one's death allows for a healthier outlook on one's life, particularly when one has a terminal illness. Psychiatrists Herbert Hendin and Gerald Klerman assert that those who wish to die are probably suffering from a variety of treatable mental illnesses.

Psychologist Patrick H. DeLeon and Jack G. Wiggins, Jr., former president of the American Psychological Association, argue that giving prescription privileges to psychologists will allow them to address society's pressing needs. Psychologists Steven C. Hayes and Elaine Heiby maintain that prescription privileges will cost psychologists their unique professional identity.

Psychiatrist Peter D. Kramer argues that antidepressant drugs benefit depressed patients with almost no side effects. Professors of psychology Seymour Fisher and Roger P. Greenberg maintain that there is no reliable evidence that antidepressants are safe and effective.

Psychologist D. L. Rosenhan argues that patients labeled as schizophrenic are seen as such by mental health workers regardless of the true state of the patients' mental health. Psychiatrist Robert L. Spitzer argues that diagnostic labels are necessary and valuable.

Victor Cline, a professor emeritus of psychology, argues that pornography poses a great harm to viewers because it degrades women. Professor of philosophy F. M. Christensen contends that there is little evidence that pornography is harmful.

David B. Larson, president of the National Institute for Healthcare, maintains that religious commitment improves mental health. Albert Ellis, president of the Institute for Rational-Emotive Therapy, asserts that extreme religious commitment, or fanaticism, is mentally unhealthy.

Sociologist Murray A. Straus contends that women are just as physically violent toward their partners as men are. Feminist researcher Demie Kurz contends that family violence researchers like Straus misunderstand the context of inequality and male dominance in marriage.

Psychotherapists Anne C. Speckhard and Vincent M. Rue argue that abortion has serious psychological consequences for women. Psychologists Nancy E. Adler et al. contend that severe negative psychological reactions following abortion are infrequent.

INTRODUCTION

Unresolved Issues in Psychology

Brent Slife
Stephen C. Yanchar

Eminent psychologist Edward Bradford Titchener (1867–1927) once stated that although psychology has a short history, it has a long past. He meant that even though the science of psychology is of relatively recent origin, the subject matter of psychology extends back to ancient history. Unfortunately, this dual history—the short and the long—is rarely treated in psychology texts; most texts focus almost exclusively on the shorter history. This shorter history is thought to be guided by the scientific method, so texts are generally filled with the scientific facts of the discipline. However, we cannot fully understand psychology without also understanding its longer intellectual history, a history of age-old questions that have recently been addressed by science but rarely been completely answered. Some history texts portray this longer intellectual history, but they do not deal with its contemporary implications. *Taking Sides: Clashing Views on Controversial Psychological Issues* is dedicated to the unresolved issues that still plague psychologists from this longer history.

WHY ARE THERE UNRESOLVED ISSUES?

The subject matter of psychology is somewhat different from the subject matter of the natural sciences. In fact, psychology has been termed a "soft" science because it deals with neither the "hard" world of observable entities and physical elements—like zoology, biology, physiology, and chemistry—nor the rigorous computational analyses of mathematics, physics, and astronomy. These hard sciences are disciplines in which the crucial questions can usually be answered through scientific observation and experimentation.

Psychologists, on the other hand, deal with the warm, "soft" world of human beings—the thoughts, attitudes, emotions, and behaviors of people interacting with other people. Psychologists are therefore concerned with many of the philosophical questions that seem so central and unique to humanity. These questions have no quick and simple answers. Indeed, these questions have occupied thinkers—scientists and philosophers alike—since at least the time of the ancient Greeks.

For example, psychologists regularly deal with the topic of mind and matter, or what is sometimes referred to as the mind-body problem. The mind-body problem essentially asks, Does the mind (which is often viewed as *not* being entirely composed of matter) control the body (which *is* entirely composed of matter), or does the brain control the mind? Yet the essence of what we mean by the mind-body problem has been a topic of debate since at least the time of the Greek philosopher Aristotle (Robinson, 1989). Aristotle (384–322 B.C.) believed that the human mind had to be distinct from the crude matter of the human body. While the human body would eventually die and decay, the human mind (or soul) was imperishable. Aristotle accounted for much of human psychology on biological grounds (i.e., in terms of matter), but he still considered the higher rational activities of a human to be aspects of a mind that are independent of the body (Robinson, 1986). However, what is left out of his and other accounts is a precise explanation of how mind and body are connected. That is, if we assume that the mind is *not* composed of matter and is thus intangible, then how can it connect or interact with something material and tangible like the body? If, on the other hand, we decide that the mind *is* tangible and material, then we inherit a host of other problems associated with reductionism (see Slife & Williams, 1995, for details).

The point is that these and other such questions may not be resolved merely through scientific observation and experimentation. Scientific method is helpful for answering certain empirical questions, but its benefits are limited for many philosophical questions. And, for better or worse, psychology is infused with philosophical questions as well as empirical questions. There are basically two reasons for this infusion: the complexity of psychology's subject matter and the methods that psychologists use to study their subject matter.

Human beings—the primary subject matter of psychology—appear to operate with wills of their own within a hopelessly complex network of situations and relationships. This, it would seem, hinders the ability of scientists to attain the kind of certainty with people that they can attain with inanimate objects. Perhaps more important, it is difficult to know *why* people act in a particular manner because we cannot directly observe their intentions, thoughts, and desires. Thus, there are some aspects of human beings that elude the traditional methods of natural science.

The scientific method itself provides no irrefutable verification of an explanation. This is because data alone do not provide answers. Scientists sometimes talk as if the data from their experiments "tell" them what to believe or "give" them results, but this is somewhat misleading. Data are meaningless until they have been interpreted by the scientist (Slife & Williams, 1995). That is, scientists have a lot to do with their findings. Because there are a number of possible interpreters, there are, in principle, a number of possible interpretations. As some of the issues in this volume show, results that seem to supply indubitable proof for one interpreter might appear quite dubious to another. The reason for this is that the scientific method is set up in a manner that requires interpretation. As many who have studied this method have noted (e.g., Popper, 1959; Rychlak, 1988), the scientific method basically takes the form of a logical if-then statement: *If* my theory is correct, *then* my data will come out as I predict. However, problems can occur when we use this logic inappropriately. What if we know, for example, that we have the "then" portion of our statement, that the data did come out as I predicted? Do we then know that my theory is correct? Of course we cannot know this, because there can be an alternative theory (or many alternatives) that could explain the same data.

Unfortunately, however, this is the way in which science is conducted. We do not know the "if" portion of our logical statement—that my theory is correct; we can only know the "then" portion—that my data came out as I predicted. And our knowledge of our data cannot tell us that our theory is correct. All we can ever do is *interpret* what our data mean because our data can always mean something else.[1]

So, as a little logic has shown, data from human subjects can always be interpreted in different ways. In fact, because of these possible interpretations, there can never be a final and definitive experiment to determine what is really true about human beings (Slife & Williams, 1995). This is what scientists mean when they say that they cannot *prove* a theory but can only *support* it. Unfortunately, this simple distinction leaves many important questions unresolved, such as the mind-body problem. Still, this lack of resolution does not mean that scientists can ignore these issues. Just because certain issues are not amenable to scientific methods does not mean they go away. The issue of whether or not the mind controls matter, for example, is vital to cancer patients who wonder whether or not positive mental attitudes will alter the course of their disease. Such issues require exploration and debate regardless of the state of scientific knowledge. Whatever scientific information is available is important, and the lack of a complete scientific answer cannot prevent us from debating what information we do have, particularly when we may never get a complete scientific answer.

A DIALECTICAL APPROACH

This volume introduces some of the most important contemporary debates in psychology as well as some classical issues that remain unresolved. As mentioned, this volume is different from texts that focus exclusively on what is known scientifically. Most texts with an exclusive scientific focus adopt a "banking conception" of education.

The banking conception of education assumes that students are essentially "banks" in which scientific facts are "deposited." Because psychology is considered a science, there are presumably many scientific psychological facts, derived from experiments, that need to be deposited in students' minds. The banking conception makes teachers and textbooks fact distributors or information transmitters. Lectures are monologues through which the facts of experiments or the findings of method are distributed and transmitted into the mental "banks" of students. At test time, then, teachers make information "withdrawals" to discern how well students have maintained the deposits of educational currency referred to as knowledge.

Since the time of the Greek philosopher Socrates (470–399 B.C.), the banking conception of education has not been considered effective for learning about unresolved conceptual issues. One reason for this is that nestled within the banking conception lies the assumption that knowledge is above reasonable criticism and that the facts of a scholarly discipline are approximations of truth—distilled and ready for distribution to students. This is the notion of education that considers knowledge to be strictly objective. Students are thought to acquire a clear and objective picture of reality—the way things really are. As we have observed, however, it is questionable whether teachers of the "soft" sciences have access to clear and objective facts only. In many cases, the "facts" are not so clear and objective but rather puzzling and debatable. Indeed, interpretations of data are always debatable, in principle.

An alternative to the banking tradition of education is the *dialectical* tradition of education. In this tradition, there can be no meaning (and thus no knowledge) without opposition. For example, there is no way to understand what "beauty" or "upness" means without implicitly understanding what "ugliness" or "downness" is, respectively. To judge the beauty of a work of art, one must have some notion of the contrast to beauty. In other words, opposing notions only make sense when considered at the same time, one complementing the other and together forming a complete concept. In this Greek conception of the dialectic, there are no quick and easy answers to difficult questions, and there are few incontestable facts to present. Instead, there are at least two sides to every issue.

Socrates taught his students that we may begin in error or falsity, but we will eventually arrive at truth if we continue our dialectical conversation. This is because truth, for Socrates, involves uncovering what is already there. Because all conceptions—true or false—supposedly have their dialectical complements implicit within them, truth is itself already implicit and waiting to be revealed. Truth, then, according to Socrates, is uncovered by a rational analysis of the relevant (and perhaps even false) ideas and arguments already under discussion.

The discipline of psychology is often considered to be dialectical, at least in part. Any student who has studied the many different theories of human behavior (e.g., humanism, behaviorism, psychoanalysis) can attest to this. Psychology frequently consists of two or more voices on the same psychological issue. Consequently, many of the ideas of psychology develop through conversation that takes place among psychologists or among the students of psychology. Although this is understandable when we consider the complexity of psychology's subject matter, it can create problems for the banking approach to education. What can be deposited in a mental bank when two or more voices are possible and the conversation among the voices is ongoing? Some information distribution is certainly important. However, information distribution alone cannot capture this type of knowledge in the discipline, because that knowledge is dialectical in nature.

BENEFITS OF A DIALECTICAL APPROACH

The dialectical approach is the focus of this volume: Psychological issues are presented in true dialectical fashion, with two distinct sides. Students are asked to familiarize themselves with both sides of an issue, look at the supporting evidence on both sides, and engage in constructive conversation about possible resolutions. This approach to education requires students to take an active role in making sense of the issues. In so doing, students benefit in several ways.

First, students come to a richer understanding of the subject matter of psychologists. It is important to understand that there is a dialectical, or humanities, side of psychology as well as an informational, or scientific, side of psychology. As necessary as data may be, there will always be a human interpreter of the data that will never permit psychology to dispense with humanities entirely.

Second, students develop a healthy respect for both sides of a debate. There is a natural tendency to underestimate reasonable arguments on one side or the other of a debate. Often, of course, the side one favors is the "most reasonable." Without exception, the issues in this book have reasonable people and reasonable arguments *on both sides*. That is, these issues are issues in psychology precisely because they have reasonable arguments and evidence on either side. This is not to say that both sides are correct (although this too is possible). It is to say, rather, that a proper appreciation of both sides is necessary to understanding what is at issue and thus to begin to find a resolution.

A third benefit of this dialectical approach is that students better understand the nature of psychological knowledge in general. Although contemporary psychologists have taken up the scientific challenge of exploring behavior and mind, many questions are still far from being answered. Psychology's parent, like all sciences, is philosophy. Hence, philosophical (or theoretical) issues always lurk behind the activities of psychologists. Issues such as mind versus body, free will versus determinism, nature versus nurture, and the philosophy of science are both philosophical and psychological questions. Students will necessarily have to entertain and explicate these types of issues as they learn about and advance the discipline.

Fourth, students become more aware of alternative views on controversial psychological issues. People often do not even realize that there is another point of view to an issue or evidence to the contrary. This realization, however, can help students to be more cautious in their knowledge. As the dialectician Socrates once noted, this caution is sometimes the first step toward true wisdom—knowing what it is that you don't know.

Finally, the dialectical approach promotes critical thinking skills. As authorities on critical thinking have noted (e.g., Brookfield, 1987), thinking skills require an awareness of what one *does* believe and a knowledge of alternatives regarding what one *could* believe. *Taking Sides: Clashing Views on*

Controversial Psychological Issues provides both elements. Finely honed critical skills give students a better position from which to examine the psychological literature critically and to select or develop their own positions on important psychological issues.

NOTES

1. Unfortunately, falsifying the consequent—the "then" portion of our logical statement—does not prevent us from needing to interpret either, as Slife and Williams (1995) have shown.

REFERENCES

Brookfield, S. (1987). *Developing critical thinkers: Challenging adults to explore alternative ways of thinking.* San Francisco: Jossey-Bass.

Popper, K. (1959). *The logic of scientific discovery.* New York: Basic Books.

Robinson, D. (1986). *An intellectual history of psychology.* Madison, WI: University of Wisconsin Press.

Robinson, D. (1989). *Aristotle's psychology.* New York: Columbia University Press.

Rychlak, J. F. (1988). *The psychology of rigorous humanism* (2d ed.). New York: New York University Press.

Slife, B. D., & Williams, R. N. (1995). *What's behind the research: Discovering hidden assumptions in the behavioral sciences.* Thousand Oaks, CA: Sage Publications.

On the Internet . . .

Abraham A. Brill Library
The Abraham A. Brill Library, perhaps the largest psycho-analytic library in the world, contains data on over 40,000 books, periodicals, and reprints in psychoanalysis and related fields. Its holdings span the literature of psychoanalysis from its beginning to the present day.
http://plaza.interport.net/nypsan/service.html

Psychnet
Information on psychology may be obtained at this Web site through the site map or by using the search engine. You can access the American Psychological Association's newspaper, the *APA Monitor,* APA books on a wide range of topics, PsychINFO—an electronic database of abstracts on over 1,350 scholarly journals—and the Help Center for information on dealing with modern life problems.
http://www.apa.org/psychnet/

Psychology Departments Around the World
Connections to psychology departments and other related psychology sites can be found at this site, which was organized by the University of California at San Diego.
http://psy.ucsd.edu/otherpsy.html

Psychology Research on the Net
Psychologically related experiments on the Internet can be found at this site. Biological psychology/neuropsychology, clinical psychology, cognition, developmental psychology, emotions, health psychology, personality, sensation/perception, and social psychology are just some of the areas addressed.
http://psych.hanover.edu/APS/exponnet.html

PART 1

Research Issues

Research methods allow psychologists to investigate their ideas and subject matter. How psychologists perform their research is often a subject of controversy. For example, sometimes animals are used to test experimental procedures before they are applied to humans. Is this right? Should animals be experimented upon—and sometimes sacrificed—in the service of humans? Similarly, what limits, if any, should be set on psychological research that is conducted on humans? Are there some experiments that are so potentially psychologically harmful to people that they should not be performed?

■ Is the *Consumer Reports* Conclusion That "Psychotherapy Helps" Valid?

■ Classic Dialogue: Was Stanley Milgram's Study of Obedience Unethical?

■ Should Animals Be Used in Psychological Research?

1

ISSUE 1

Is the *Consumer Reports* Conclusion That "Psychotherapy Helps" Valid?

YES: Martin E. P. Seligman, from "The Effectiveness of Psychotherapy: The *Consumer Reports* Study," *American Psychologist* (December 1995)

NO: Neil S. Jacobson and Andrew Christensen, from "Studying the Effectiveness of Psychotherapy: How Well Can Clinical Trials Do the Job?" *American Psychologist* (October 1996)

ISSUE SUMMARY

YES: Psychotherapy researcher Martin E. P. Seligman defends the conclusion of *Consumer Reports* that psychotherapy is effective by pointing to the importance of client satisfaction in the actual settings in which the clients are treated.

NO: Psychotherapy researchers Neil S. Jacobson and Andrew Christensen contend that the *Consumer Reports* study is essentially the same as 40-year-old studies that have long been rejected as inadequate.

In 1994 *Consumer Reports* (CR), the well-known evaluator of appliances and automobiles (among other things), decided to evaluate something it had never evaluated before—the effectiveness of psychotherapy. True to its own philosophy, CR surveyed the consumers of psychotherapy to determine how these consumers felt about their treatment. Twenty-six questions about people's experiences with mental health professionals were asked, including questions about presenting problems, therapist competence, type of therapy, and satisfaction with treatment.

In the November 1995 issue CR published its controversial but seemingly clear-cut findings. Perhaps the most noteworthy finding was that over 90 percent of the people who responded to the survey found psychotherapy to be beneficial. Although this specific percentage can be disputed, other research has supported the overall conclusion that psychotherapy is generally helpful. (See, for example, Allen E. Bergin and Sol L. Garfield, eds., *Handbook of Psychotherapy and Behavior Change*, John Wiley, 1994). This general conclusion is not the root of the controversy. The root of the controversy is the methods that CR used to reach its conclusion. Most mainstream psychotherapy researchers favor experimental methods—with control groups and manipulated variables—to evaluate psychotherapy's effectiveness. CR's conclusions were reached without such methods. Were CR's methods valid?

If they were not, then the conclusion that "psychotherapy helps" would itself be in question.

In the following selections, Martin E. P. Seligman defends CR's methods by making a distinction between efficacy research and effectiveness research. Efficacy research pertains to the experimental type of design that most researchers favor. Although Seligman believes that these designs have some advantages, he contends that they also have many disadvantages, which he feels the CR type of study (effectiveness research) can complement. The types of studies that CR conducts have their own problems, Seligman admits, but they can reveal whether or not people feel that psychotherapy is effective. In this case, the answer is yes.

Neil S. Jacobson and Andrew Christensen, on the other hand, compare the CR survey to outmoded studies that therapy researchers rejected long ago. Jacobson and Christensen point to "two fundamental problems" with retrospective surveys, or surveys based on participants' recollections of previous experiences. They admit that "consumer satisfaction is far from trivial." However, such ratings of satisfaction are "uncorrelated with... general [client] functioning." These authors contend that psychotherapy researchers were initially correct in rejecting these types of studies long ago.

POINT	COUNTERPOINT
• There are two types of therapy research—efficacy and effectiveness—that complement one another.	• The "effectiveness" type of research was found to be inadequate many years ago.
• CR's survey type of study has many advantages, such as greater realism and comprehensiveness.	• Surveys have two fundamental problems that disallow their use as serious studies of effectiveness.
• CR's study is large in scale and cost-effective.	• If such a study is not valid, its scale and minimal cost mean little.
• The CR study has several clear-cut results.	• Some of the results of the CR study are strikingly different from the results of more highly controlled studies.
• CR has pioneered a whole new type of therapy outcome study.	• The CR study is essentially the same as studies that were performed and subsequently rejected many years ago.

YES

Martin E. P. Seligman

THE EFFECTIVENESS OF PSYCHOTHERAPY: THE *CONSUMER REPORTS* STUDY

How do we find out whether psychotherapy works? To answer this, two methods have arisen: the *efficacy study* and the *effectiveness study*. An efficacy study is the more popular method. It contrasts some kind of therapy to a comparison group under well-controlled conditions....

The high praise "empirically validated" is now virtually synonymous with positive results in efficacy studies, and many investigators have come to think that an efficacy study is the "gold standard" for measuring whether a treatment works....

But my belief has changed about what counts as a "gold standard." And it was a study by *Consumer Reports* (1995, November) that singlehandedly shook my belief. I came to see that deciding whether one treatment, under highly controlled conditions, works better than another treatment or a control group is a different question from deciding what works in the field (Muñoz, Hollon, McGrath, Rehm, & VandenBos, 1994). I no longer believe that efficacy studies are the only, or even the best, way of finding out what treatments actually work in the field. I have come to believe that the "effectiveness" study of how patients fare under the actual conditions of treatment in the field, can yield useful and credible "empirical validation" of psychotherapy and medication. This is the method that *Consumer Reports* pioneered....

CONSUMER REPORTS SURVEY

Consumer Reports (CR) included a supplementary survey about psychotherapy and drugs in one version of its 1994 annual questionnaire, along with its customary inquiries about appliances and services. CR's 180,000 readers received this version, which included approximately 100 questions about automobiles and about mental health. CR asked readers to fill out the mental health section "if at any time over the past three years you experienced stress or other emotional problems for which you sought help from any of the following: friends, relatives, or a member of the clergy; a mental health professional like a psychologist or a psychiatrist; your family doctor; or a support group." Twenty-two thousand readers responded. Of these, approximately 7,000 subscribers responded to the mental health questions. Of these 7,000 about 3,000 had just talked to friends, relatives, or clergy, and 4,100 went to some combination of mental health professionals, family doctors, and support groups. Of these 4,100, 2,900 saw a mental health professional: Psychologists (37%) were the most frequently seen mental health professional, followed by psychiatrists (22%), social workers (14%), and marriage counselors 9(%). Other mental health professionals made up 18%. In addition, 1,300 joined self-help groups, and about 1,000 saw family physicians. The respondents as a whole were highly educated, predominantly middle class; about half were women, and the median age was 46....

There were a number of clear-cut results, among them:

- Treatment by a mental health professional usually worked. Most respondents got a lot better. Averaged over all mental health professionals, of the 426 people who were feeling *very poor* when they began therapy, 87% were feeling *very good, good,* or at least *so-so* by the time of the survey. Of the 786 people who were feeling *fairly poor* at the outset, 92% were feeling *very good, good,* or at least *so-so* by the time of the survey. These findings converge with meta-analyses of efficacy (Lipsey & Wilson, 1993; Shapiro & Shapiro, 1982, Smith, Miller, & Glass, 1980).

- Long-term therapy produced more improvement than short-term therapy.

This result was very robust, and held up over all statistical models....

- There was no difference between psychotherapy alone and psychotherapy plus medication for any disorder (very few respondents reported that they had medication with no psychotherapy at all).

- While all mental health professionals appeared to help their patients, psychologists, psychiatrists, and social workers did equally well and better than marriage counselors. Their patients' overall improvement scores (0–300 scale) were 220, 226, 225 (not significantly different from each other), and 208 (significantly worse than the first three), respectively.

- Family doctors did just as well as mental health professionals in the short term, but worse in the long term. Some patients saw both family doctors and mental health professionals, and those who saw both had more severe problems. For patients who relied solely on family doctors, their overall improvement scores when treated for up to six months was 213, and it remained at that level (212) for those treated longer than six months. In contrast, the overall improvement scores for patients of mental health professionals was 211 up to six months, but climbed to 232 when treatment went on for more than six months. The advantages of long-term treatment by a mental health professional held not only for the specific problems that led to treatment, but for a variety of general functioning scores as well: ability to relate to others, coping with everyday stress, enjoying life more, personal growth and understanding, self-esteem and confidence.

- Alcoholics Anonymous (AA) did especially well, with an average improvement score of 251, significantly bettering mental health professionals. People who went to non-AA groups had less severe problems and did not do as well as those who went to AA (average score = 215).

- Active shoppers and active clients did better in treatment than passive recipients (determined by responses to "Was it mostly your idea to seek therapy? When choosing this therapist, did you discuss qualifications, therapist's experience, discuss frequency, duration, and cost, speak to someone who was treated by this therapist, check out other therapists? During therapy, did you try to be as open as possible, ask for explanation of diagnosis and unclear terms, do homework, not cancel sessions often, discuss negative feelings toward therapist?").

- No specific modality of psychotherapy did any better than any other for any problem. These results confirm the "dodo bird" hypothesis, that all forms of psychotherapies do about equally well (Luborsky, Singer, & Luborsky, 1975). They come as a rude shock to efficacy researchers, since the main theme of efficacy studies has been the demonstration of the usefulness of specific techniques for specific disorders.

- Respondents whose choice of therapist or duration of care was limited by their insurance coverage did worse,... (determined by responses to "Did limitations on your insurance coverage affect any of the following choices you made? Type of therapist I chose; How often I met with my therapist; How long I stayed in therapy").

These findings are obviously important, and some of them could not be included in the original *CR* article because of space limitations. Some of these findings were quite contrary to what I expected, but it is not my intention to discuss their substance here. Rather, I want to explore the methodological adequacy of this survey. My underlying questions are "Should we believe the findings?" and "Can the method be improved to give more authoritative answers?"

CONSUMER REPORTS SURVEY: METHODOLOGICAL VIRTUES

Sampling. This survey is, as far as I have been able to determine, the most extensive study of psychotherapy effectiveness on record. The sample is not representative of the United States as a whole, but my guess is that it is roughly representative of the middle class and educated population who make up the bulk of psychotherapy patients. It is important that the sample represents people who choose to go to treatment for their problems, not people who do not "believe in" psychotherapy or drugs. The *CR* sample, moreover, is probably weighted toward "problem solvers," people who actively try to do something about what troubles them.

Treatment duration. *CR* sampled all treatment durations from one month or less through two years or more. Because the study was naturalistic, treatment, it can be supposed, continued until the patient (a) was better, (b) gave up unimproved, or (c) had his or her coverage run out. This, by definition, mirrors what actually happens in the field. In contrast to all efficacy studies, which are of fixed treatment duration regardless of how the patient is progressing, the CR study informs us about treatment effectiveness under the duration constraints of actual therapy.

Self-correction. Because the CR study was naturalistic, it informs us of how treatment works as it is actually performed—without manuals and with self-correction when a technique falters. This also contrasts favorably to efficacy studies, which are manualized and not self-correcting when a given technique or modality fails.

Multiple problems. The large majority of respondents in the CR study had more than one problem. We can also assume that a good-sized fraction were "subclinical" in their problems and would not meet *DSM-IV* [Diagnostic and Statistical Manual of Mental Disorders, 4th Ed.] criteria for any disorder. No patients were discarded because they failed exclusion criteria or because they fell one symptom short of a full-blown "disorder." Thus the sample more closely reflected people who actually seek treatment than the filtered and single-disordered patients of efficacy studies.

General functioning. The CR study measured self-reported changes in productivity at work, interpersonal relations, well-being, insight, and growth, in addition to improvement on the presenting problem.... Importantly, more improvement on the presenting problem occurred for treatments which lasted longer than six months. In addition, more improvement occurred in work, interpersonal relations, enjoyment of life, and personal growth domains in treatments which lasted longer than six months. Since im-

provements in general functioning, as well as symptom relief, is almost always a goal of actual treatment but rarely of efficacy studies, the CR study adds to our knowledge of how treatment does beyond the mere elimination of symptoms.

Clinical significance. There has been much debate about how to measure the "clinical significance" of a treatment. Efficacy studies are designed to detect statistically significant differences between a treatment and control groups, and an "effect size" can be computed. But what degree of statistical significance is clinical significance? How large an effect size is meaningful? The CR study leaves little doubt about the human significance of its findings, since respondents answered directly about how much therapy helped the problem that led them to treatment—from *made things a lot better* to *made things a lot worse*. Of those who started out feeling *very poor*, 54% answered treatment *made things a lot better*, and another one third answered it made things *somewhat better*.

Unbiased. Finally, it cannot be ignored that CR is about as unbiased a scrutinizer of goods and services as exists in the public domain. They have no axe to grind for or against medications, psychotherapy, managed care, insurance companies, family doctors, AA, or long-term treatment. They do not care if psychologists do better or worse than psychiatrists, marriage and family counselors, or social workers. They are not pursuing government grants or drug company favors. They do not accept advertisements. They have a track record of loyalty only to consumers. So this study comes with higher credibility than studies that issue from drug houses, from either APA [American Psychiatric Association], from consensus conferences of the National Institute of Mental Health, or even from the halls of academe....

THE IDEAL STUDY

The CR study, then, is to be taken seriously—not only for its results and its credible source, but for its method. It is large-scale; it samples treatment as it is actually delivered in the field; it samples without obvious bias those who seek out treatment; it measures multiple outcomes including specific improvement and more global gains such as growth, insight, productivity, mood, enjoyment of life, and interpersonal relations; it is statistically stringent and finds clinically meaningful results. Furthermore, it is highly cost-effective.

Its major advantage over the efficacy method for studying the effectiveness of psychotherapy and medications is that it captures how and to whom treatment is actually delivered and toward what end. At the very least, the CR study and its underlying survey method provides a powerful addition to what we know about the effectiveness of psychotherapy and a pioneering way of finding out more.

The study is not without flaws, the chief one being the limited meaning of its answer to the question "Can psychotherapy help?" This question has three possible kinds of answers. The first is that psychotherapy does better than something else, such as talking to friends, going to church, or doing nothing at all. Because it lacks comparison groups, the CR study only answers this question indirectly. The second possible answer is that psychotherapy returns people to normality or more liberally to within, say, two standard deviations of the average. The CR study, lacking an untroubled group and lacking measures of how people were before they became troubled, does not answer this question. The third answer is "Do people have fewer symptoms and a better life after therapy than they did before?" This is the question that the CR study answers with a clear "yes."

NO

Neil S. Jacobson and
Andrew Christensen

STUDYING THE EFFECTIVENESS
OF PSYCHOTHERAPY

[T]here is considerable debate about the merits of a recent *Consumer Reports (CR)* survey (1995).... This survey has received a great deal of attention within psychology and has been publicized in the popular press. Seligman (1995) suggested that this is the best study ever conducted on the effectiveness of psychotherapy.

Much like Freud's case studies, the report by *CR* (1995) is very persuasive and will probably have a great deal of influence on the public perception of psychotherapy. However, the purpose of this article is to show that most of what the *CR* study says has already been proven to the satisfaction of both practitioners and psychotherapy researchers. Moreover, those findings from the *CR* study that have not been previously established are highly questionable because of the study's methodological shortcomings. Finally, controlled experiments that avoid the methodological pitfalls of the *CR* study can answer virtually all of the questions considered by Seligman (1995) to be beyond the scope of clinical trials. In fact, it would be unfortunate if the field of psychotherapy research abandoned the controlled experiment when attempting to answer questions regarding the effectiveness of psychotherapy. Although clinical trials have their limitations and may need to be supplemented by other types of methodologies, they are far superior to the type of design reflected in the *CR* study, a design that has already been debated and rejected by both practitioners and researchers. ...

A CRITIQUE OF THE NEW FINDINGS FROM THE
CONSUMER REPORTS SURVEY

The methodological shortcomings of the *CR* (1995) survey greatly limit their evidentiary value. Seligman (1995) mentioned some of these shortcomings but not others; the ones he did mention tended to be minimized. Here are a sample of these shortcomings.

From Neil S. Jacobson and Andrew Christensen, "Studying the Effectiveness of Psychotherapy: How Well Can Clinical Trials Do the Job?" *American Psychologist*, vol. 51, no. 10 (October 1996). Copyright © 1996 by The American Psychological Association. Reprinted by permission. Notes and references omitted.

A Retrospective Survey Is Not an Ideal Prototype for Effectiveness Research

Seligman (1995) suggested that the CR (1995) study is a well-done effectiveness study and was careful to distinguish this study from an efficacy study—a randomized clinical trial. However, in fact, the CR survey is not necessarily a good model for an effectiveness study as that term is typically used. The main virtue of the CR survey, according to Seligman, is its "realism"; that is, it is a report about real therapy, conducted by real therapists, with real clients, in the real world. The retrospective biases that are impossible to rule out are not seen as fatal flaws but simply as aspects of the design that need to be refined.

There are two fundamental problems with retrospective surveys. The first is that, because they are retrospective, there is no opportunity to corroborate respondents' reports. When participants are reporting on their own previous experiences, whether in therapy or otherwise, there is no way of assessing their accuracy. Various biases may contaminate their responses, ranging from demand characteristics to memory distortion. With a prospective study, some of these biases can be minimized, whereas others can be evaluated, using corroborative measures coming from different modalities. For example, self-report data can be supplemented with observational data. With retrospective surveys, such validation is impossible, and thus the responses are hard to interpret.

The second problem with retrospective surveys is the possibility that an unrepresentative subsample of those surveyed returned their questionnaires. Although it cannot be proven that those who benefited from psychotherapy were more likely to complete the survey than were those who did not, neither can that possibility be disproven. With a prospective study, one doesn't have to guess. This additional problem makes the improvement rates reported in the CR (1995) survey hard to interpret.

The most striking example of this selectivity problem is in the findings pertaining to Alcoholics Anonymous (AA), which had the highest mean improvement rate of any treatment category reported by Seligman (1995). In fact, as a treatment, AA significantly outperformed other mental health professionals. This finding can be contrasted with the lack of evidence supporting the efficacy of AA in prospective studies (McCrady & Delaney, 1995). Seligman acknowledged the strong possibility of sampling bias in AA and offered some speculations on why one might expect AA to be particularly susceptible to such biases. However, he then inexplicably minimized the likelihood of similarly extensive biases operating in the sample as a whole, suggesting that

> a similar kind of sampling bias, *to a lesser degree*, [italics added] cannot be overlooked for other kinds of treatment failures. At any rate, it is quite possible that there was a *large* [italics added] oversampling of successful AA cases and a *smaller* [italics added] oversampling of successful treatment for problems other than alcoholism. (p. 971)

Is it not possible that the oversampling of successful cases was as large for other problems as it was for AA? Is there any evidence to the contrary?

In addition to contaminating the overall estimates of treatment gains, sampling bias could easily explain the apparent superiority of long-term therapy reported by the respondents in the CR (1995) study.

Unlike Howard et al. (1986), who found a negatively accelerated dose–response relationship, the CR survey found a linear relationship: the more therapy, the better the outcome. This would indeed be an important finding if it were interpretable; unfortunately, it is not interpretable. Seligman (1995) argued against the possibility of sampling bias by focusing on one potential source. He suggested that, if early dropouts are treatment failures and those who remain in treatment are beneficiaries, then earlier dropouts should have lower rates of "problem resolution" than later dropouts. In fact, the rates are uniform: About two thirds of dropouts quit because the problem is resolved, whether they quit therapy one month or two years after they started.

The problem with Seligman's (1995) refutation is that it fails to rule out the primary source of interpretive ambiguity —spontaneous remission. The longer people stay in therapy, the greater the opportunity for factors other than therapy to produce improvement. There is no way of knowing whether the superiority of long-term therapy is due to the treatment itself or simply to increased opportunities for other factors to produce improvements.

Seligman (1995) argued that the main virtue of the CR (1995) study is its realism. If one thinks of realism using the metaphor of a snapshot, the implication is that the CR survey provides a snapshot of what psychotherapy is really like. But, because the study is retrospective, the snapshot may be out of focus. With a prospective study, one can take a snapshot of psychotherapy whose focus is indisputable. But, with a retrospective survey, the negatives are gone forever.

The Absence of Control Groups of Any Kind Constitutes an Additional Fatal Flaw

Seligman (1995) fully acknowledged the problems introduced by the uncontrolled nature of the study but suggested that there are "internal controls" that can be used as surrogates. Unfortunately, none of Seligman's internal controls can be considered adequate substitutes for control groups.

First, he suggested that the inferior performance of marriage counselors allowed them to serve as a reference group because they controlled for various nonspecific factors such as the presence of an attentive listener. However, because marriage counselors may have differed systematically from other professionals in the client population with whom they worked, their performance cannot be compared with that of other mental health professionals who may have treated more mental health problems that were not primarily related to marital distress. In other words, there may have been a systematic confounding between type of problem treated and profession, which rendered marriage counselors useless as an internal control.

Second, Seligman (1995) noted that long-term treatment worked better than short-term treatment, thus allowing the use of the first point in the dose–response curve as a control group. As we have already suggested, this internal control is useless because of the confound with greater opportunity for spontaneous remission in long-term therapy.

Third, according to Seligman (1995), because it is known that drugs outperform placebos, and because psychotherapy did as well as psychotherapy plus drugs in the CR (1995) study, one can infer that psychotherapy would have outperformed an adequate placebo if one had been included in the CR study. This argument is specious for a number of reasons: It is not known what drugs were used for which problems in the CR study; it is not known whether the pharmacotherapy performed was adequate (compliance, dosage, etc.); and most importantly, it is not known whether the sample of patients in the CR study was similar to those in which drugs typically outperform placebos.

Fourth, family doctors did not perform as well as mental health professionals when treatment continued beyond six months, thus suggesting family doctors as an internal control. However, family doctors saw clients for a fewer number of sessions than did mental health professionals, creating a confound that Seligman (1995) himself acknowledged.

Seligman (1995) concluded that spontaneous remission is an unlikely explanation for the high improvement rates reported by respondents in the CR (1995) study. We come to a different conclusion, because none of the proposed internal controls are adequate. We conclude that factors other than psychotherapy might very well have accounted for the improvement rates reported by the respondents. We come to this conclusion for several reasons. First, there is no adequate control to rule it out, thus no compelling reason to reject the null hypothesis. Second, because the 4,000 respondents in the CR study were, to use Seligman's (1995) terminology, "middle class and educated" (p. 969) and "a good-sized fraction were 'subclinical'... and would not meet DSM-IV [Diagnostic and Statistical Manual of Mental Disorders, 4th Edition; American Psychiatric Association, 1994] criteria for any disorder" (p. 970), we have the kind of sample that is most

likely to spontaneously remit, or to benefit from any treatment, specific or nonspecific (Jacobson & Hollon, 1996). As Seligman noted, in most clinical trials, the single largest basis for exclusion is that the client is not sufficiently distressed or dysfunctional to be included.

For example, in research on depression, by far the most common basis for exclusion is that not enough symptoms are present for the patient to meet criteria for major depressive disorder; even if DSM-IV criteria are met, participants are often excluded because the major depressive disorder is not severe enough (Jacobson et al., 1996). In efficacy studies, there is a good reason to exclude these participants: They seem to get better no matter what they receive. Even the less severe patients who make it into these trials tend to respond as well to placebos as they do to active treatments (cf. Jacobson & Hollon, 1996). Thus, it is a fair assumption that many of the respondents to the CR (1995) survey who improved would have improved without therapy.

The Measures in the *Consumer Reports* Survey Were Not Only Unreliable but Unrevealing

The CR (1995) survey measured little more than consumer satisfaction. Consumer satisfaction is far from trivial. However, consumer satisfaction ratings are uncorrelated with symptomatic outcome and general functioning. In the CR survey, three questions were asked in the assessment of improvement, one pertaining to "satisfaction with therapist," a second pertaining to "improvement in the presenting problem," and a third pertaining to "improvement in overall functioning." The latter measure was a change score, derived by subtracting posttest scores from pretest scores (both obtained retrospectively); the other two measures were simply posttest scores. Seligman (1995) seized on these three questions to argue that three different constructs are being measured: consumer satisfaction, symptom relief, and general functioning. However, since all three questions are global and retrospective and have method variance in common, they cannot be considered independent assessments of functioning or to be measuring different constructs. Furthermore, the three questions were combined into a multivariate composite for the calculation of improvement rates, thus making it impossible to separate out consumer satisfaction from the other items.

The Specificity Question Revisited: The *Consumer Reports* Survey Did Not Assess Which Therapies Led to Improvement in Which Problems

Researchers are long past the stage of referring to psychotherapy as if it were uniform, without specifying the nature of the problem being treated or the treatment used. Yet, the *CR* (1995) study failed to inform the public about any particular treatment for any particular problem and thus provides little information that advances knowledge about psychotherapy. The data may be available to answer more specific questions. But even if they were available, and were released, they would be based on respondent reports: Respondents would be reporting what their presenting problem was and the kind of treatment they received (we have already seen some data on this latter question), and they would be defining both the profession and the theoretical orientation of the therapist. How reliable are survey respondents at describing the theoretical orientation of their therapist or at fitting their presenting problem into one of a series of choices on a survey, especially in retrospect? Both of us have small private practices, and a large proportion of our clients are couples. We have heard ourselves referred to as marriage counselors, psychologists, and even, on occasion, psychiatrists. We doubt whether the number of our clients who could correctly identify our theoretical orientation would much exceed chance.

Even Assuming Methodological Adequacy, the Results as Reported by *Consumer Reports* and by Seligman Are Misleading

Although the sound bite coming out of both the *CR* (1995) report and Seligman's (1995) article says that 90% of the respondents found psychotherapy beneficial, it is worth noting that this figure comes from combining those who were helped "a great deal," "a lot," and "somewhat." Only 54% reported that they were helped "a great deal." This is not a very impressive figure from the standpoint of clinical significance, especially when one takes into account the number of subclinical respondents in the sample and the possibility that the respondents may be overrepresented by those who found treatment to be helpful.

The Eysenck Evaluation Revisited

The *CR* (1995) survey bears remarkable resemblance to the controversial evaluation of psychotherapy reported by Eysenck (1952). In this report, Eysenck summarized the results of 24 reports of psychoanalytic and eclectic psychotherapy with more than 7,000 neurotic patients treated in naturalistic settings. Using therapist ratings of improvement, Eysenck reported a 44% improvement rate for psychoanalytic therapy and a

64% improvement rate for eclectic psychotherapy. Unlike the CR survey, however, these reports were prospective in that the therapist evaluations occurred at the time of termination. Also unlike the CR survey, Eysenck used control groups: One consisted of all improved patients who had been discharged from hospitals in New York between 1917 and 1934 for "neurotic" conditions, receiving nothing but custodial care; the other consisted of 500 disability claimants who were periodically evaluated by general practitioners without receiving psychotherapy, so it could be determined whether they were improved enough to go back to work. Improvement for this latter control group was defined as their ability to return to work, which was decided by the general practitioner. Eysenck reported, on the basis of these two control groups, that the spontaneous remission rate for these minimally treated patients was 72% and that psychotherapy was therefore ineffective.

The merits of these findings and the methodology supporting them were debated vigorously for 20 years. Initially, Luborsky (1954) criticized the study on the grounds that the measures of improvement were flawed, the control groups were inadequate, and the treatments were lacking on both uniformity and representativeness. Similar critiques were registered by Rosenzweig (1954) and De Charrus, Levy, and Wertheimer (1954). These and more recent critiques (e.g., Bergin, 1971) argued, with considerable merit, that Eysenck (1952) had underestimated the success of therapy and overestimated the spontaneous remission rate. As recently as the mid-1970s,

Eysenck's study was subject to refutation by more optimistic appraisals and interpretations of psychotherapy's impact (Luborsky et al., 1975; Meltzoff & Kornreich, 1970). Now, the controversy has largely subsided, and Eysenck's study has been rejected by clinical scientists. In fact, in the most recent edition of Bergin and Garfield's (1994) *Handbook of Psychotherapy and Behavioral Change* the study is not even cited. When it is referenced nowadays, it is primarily for its historical impact and its heuristic value.

What is interesting about examining Eysenck's (1952) study in light of the CR (1995) survey is that virtually all of the criticisms leveled at Eysenck's evaluation also apply to the CR survey, even though Eysenck's evaluation was more sophisticated from a methodological perspective. Eysenck had a sample that was almost twice as large as the sample reported in the CR survey; he did at least include control groups, however inadequate they might have been; the measures of improvement were concurrent rather than retrospective; and the measures were obtained from trained therapists rather than from the clients themselves. Given Seligman's (1995) assumptions that therapists are able to self-correct their therapeutic work and cannily select which clients need drugs and psychotherapy, therapists should also be better judges of when clients have made genuine improvement versus transitory symptom change. However, the field was correct in rejecting Eysenck's evaluation: The control groups and the measures of outcome were inadequate. We don't see any reason to revert to a methodology that was rejected for its methodological inadequacies 20 years ago.

CHALLENGE QUESTIONS

Is the *Consumer Reports* Conclusion That "Psychotherapy Helps" Valid?

1. You have probably learned about the difference between correlation and causation in research and methods. How does this difference pertain to the controversy over the *Consumer Reports* study?

2. Do you think that psychotherapy is effective? Assert your own conclusion and support it with scientific research.

3. Jacobson and Christensen discuss the parallels between Hans Eysenck's 1952 study of psychotherapy and *CR*'s study. Look up Eysenck's original study and describe how it is also different from the *CR* study.

4. Why are "experimental" designs favored by not only therapy researchers but also psychological researchers in general?

5. How important do you feel "consumer satisfaction" should be in the evaluation of psychotherapy? Support your answer.

ISSUE 2

Classic Dialogue: Was Stanley Milgram's Study of Obedience Unethical?

YES: Diana Baumrind, from "Some Thoughts on Ethics of Research: After Reading Milgram's 'Behavioral Study of Obedience,'" *American Psychologist* (vol. 19, 1964)

NO: Stanley Milgram, from "Issues in the Study of Obedience: A Reply to Baumrind," *American Psychologist* (vol. 19, 1964)

ISSUE SUMMARY

YES: Psychologist Diana Baumrind argues that Stanley Milgram's study of obedience did not meet ethical standards for research, because participants were subjected to a research design that caused undue psychological stress that was not resolved after the study.

NO: Social psychologist Stanley Milgram, in responding to Baumrind's accusations, asserts that the study was well designed, the stress caused to participants could not have been anticipated, and the participants' anguish dissipated after a thorough debriefing.

Are there psychological experiments that should not be conducted? Is the psychological distress that participants experience in some studies too extreme to justify the experimental outcomes and knowledge gained? Or is it sometimes necessary to allow participants to experience some anguish so that a researcher can better understand important psychological phenomena? These questions lie at the heart of ethical considerations in psychological research. They have traditionally been answered by the researcher, who attempts to weigh the costs and benefits of conducting a given study.

The problem is that a researcher's ability to accurately anticipate the costs and benefits of a study is severely limited. Researchers are likely to have an investment in their studies, which may lead them to overestimate the benefits and underestimate the costs. For these and other reasons, in 1974 the United States Department of Health, Education, and Welfare established regulations for the protection of human subjects. These regulations include the creation of institutional review boards, which are responsible for reviewing research proposals and ensuring that researchers adequately protect research participants.

The establishment of these regulations can be traced to past ethical controversies, such as the one raised in the following selection by Diana Baumrind regarding Stanley Milgram's famous 1963 study of obedience. Baumrind's primary concern is that the psychological welfare of the study's participants was compromised not only through the course of the study but also through the course of their lives. She contends that participants were prone to obey the experimenter because of the atmosphere of the study and the participants' trust in the experimenter. As a result, participants behaved in ways that disturbed them considerably. Baumrind maintains that these disturbances could not be resolved through an after-study debriefing but rather remained with the participants.

In response to these accusations, Milgram argues that the atmosphere of a laboratory generalizes to other contexts in which obedience is prevalent and is thus appropriate to a study of obedience. Furthermore, he and a number of other professionals never anticipated the results of the study; they were genuinely surprised by its outcome. Milgram also asserts that the psychological distress experienced by some participants was temporary, not dangerous, and that it dissipated after the true nature of the study was revealed.

POINT	COUNTERPOINT
• Milgram's indifference toward distressed participants reveals his lack of concern for their well-being.	• Milgram made special efforts to assure participants that their behavior was normal.
• A study of obedience should not be conducted in the laboratory because subjects are particularly prone to behave obediently and to put trust in the researcher.	• The laboratory setting is well suited to a study of obedience because it is similar to other contexts in which obedience is prevalent.
• The psychological distress experienced by participants exceeded appropriate limits.	• The psychological distress was brief and not injurious.
• Participants experienced long-term, negative psychological consequences as a result of their participation in Milgram's experiment.	• Participants spoke positively about the experiment, indicating that it was psychologically beneficial.
• In planning and designing the study, Milgram ignored issues regarding the extreme psychological distress that was experienced by some participants.	• The extreme psychological tension experienced by some participants was unanticipated by Milgram and many other professionals.

YES
Diana Baumrind

SOME THOUGHTS ON ETHICS OF RESEARCH

Certain problems in psychological research require the experimenter to balance his career and scientific interests against the interests of his prospective subjects. When such occasions arise the experimenter's stated objective frequently is to do the best possible job with the least possible harm to his subjects. The experimenter seldom perceives in more positive terms an indebtedness to the subject for his services, perhaps because the detachment which his functions require prevents appreciation of the subject as an individual.

Yet a debt does exist, even when the subject's reason for volunteering includes course credit or monetary gain. Often a subject participates unwillingly in order to satisfy a course requirement. These requirements are of questionable merit ethically, and do not alter the experimenter's responsibility to the subject.

Most experimental conditions do not cause the subjects pain or indignity, and are sufficiently interesting or challenging to present no problem of an ethical nature to the experimenter. But where the experimental conditions expose the subject to loss of dignity, or offer him nothing of value, then the experimenter is obliged to consider the reasons why the subject volunteered and to reward him accordingly.

The subject's public motives for volunteering include having an enjoyable or stimulating experience, acquiring knowledge, doing the experimenter a favor which may some day be reciprocated, and making a contribution to science. These motives can be taken into account rather easily by the experimenter who is willing to spend a few minutes with the subject afterwards to thank him for his participation, answer his questions, reassure him that he did well, and chat with him a bit. Most volunteers also have less manifest, but equally legitimate, motives. A subject may be seeking an opportunity to have contact with, be noticed by, and perhaps confide in a person with psychological training. The dependent attitude of most subjects toward the experimenter is an artifact of the experimental situation as well as an expression of some subjects' personal need systems at the time they volunteer.

From Diana Baumrind, "Some Thoughts on Ethics of Research: After Reading Milgram's 'Behavioral Study of Obedience,'" *American Psychologist*, vol. 19 (1964). Copyright © 1964 by The American Psychological Association. Reprinted by permission.

The dependent, obedient attitude assumed by most subjects in the experimental setting is appropriate to that situation. The "game" is defined by the experimenter and he makes the rules. By volunteering, the subject agrees implicitly to assume a posture of trust and obedience. While the experimental conditions leave him exposed, the subject has the right to assume that his security and self-esteem will be protected.

There are other professional situations in which one member—the patient or client—expects help and protection from the other— the physician or psychologist. But the interpersonal relationship between experimenter and subject additionally has unique features which are likely to provoke initial anxiety in the subject. The laboratory is unfamiliar as a setting and the rules of behavior ambiguous compared to a clinician's office. Because of the anxiety and passivity generated by the setting, the subject is more prone to behave in an obedient, suggestible manner in the laboratory than elsewhere. Therefore, the laboratory is not the place to study degree of obedience or suggestibility, as a function of a particular experimental condition, since the base line for these phenomena as found in the laboratory is probably much higher than in most other settings. Thus experiments in which the relationship to the experimenter as an authority is used as an independent condition are imperfectly designed for the same reason that they are prone to injure the subjects involved. They disregard the special quality of trust and obedience with which the subject appropriately regards the experimenter.

Other phenomena which present ethical decisions, unlike those mentioned above, *can* be reproduced successfully in the laboratory. Failure experience, confor-mity to peer judgment, and isolation are among such phenomena. In these cases we can expect the experimenter to take whatever measures are necessary to prevent the subject from leaving the laboratory more humiliated, insecure, alienated, or hostile than when he arrived. To guarantee that an especially sensitive subject leaves a stressful experimental experience in the proper state sometimes requires special clinical training. But usually an attitude of compassion, respect, gratitude, and common sense will suffice, and no amount of clinical training will substitute. The subject has the right to expect that the psychologist with whom he is interacting has some concern for his welfare, and the personal attributes and professional skill to express his good will effectively.

Unfortunately, the subject is not always treated with the respect he deserves. It has become more commonplace in sociopsychological laboratory studies to manipulate, embarrass, and discomfort subjects. At times the insult to the subject's sensibilities extends to the journal reader when the results are reported. Milgram's (1963) study is a case in point. The following is Milgram's abstract of his experiment:

This article describes a procedure for the study of destructive obedience in the laboratory. It consists of ordering a naive S to administer increasingly more severe punishment to a victim in the context of a learning experiment. Punishment is administered by means of a shock generator with 30 graded switches ranging from Slight Shock to Danger: Severe Shock. The victim is a confederate of E. The primary dependent variable is the maximum shock the S is willing to administer before he refuses to continue further. 26 Ss obeyed the experimental commands fully, and administered the highest shock on the generator. 14 Ss broke off the experiment at some point after the victim protested and refused to provide further answers. The procedure created extreme levels of nervous tension in some Ss. Profuse sweating, trembling, and stuttering were typical expressions of this emotional disturbance. One unexpected sign of tension—yet to be explained—was the regular occurrence of nervous laughter, which in some Ss developed into uncontrollable seizures. The variety of interesting behavioral dynamics observed in the experiment, the reality of the situation for the S, and the possibility of parametric variation within the framework of the procedure, point to the fruitfulness of further study [p. 371].

The detached, objective manner in which Milgram reports the emotional disturbance suffered by his subject contrasts sharply with his graphic account of that disturbance. Following are two other quotes describing the effects on his subjects of the experimental conditions:

I observed a mature and initially poised businessman enter the laboratory smiling and confident. Within 20 minutes he was reduced to a twitching, stuttering wreck, who was rapidly approaching a point of nervous collapse. He constantly pulled on his earlobe, and twisted his hands. At one point he pushed his fist into his forehead and muttered: "Oh, God, let's stop it." And yet he continued to respond to every word of the experimenter, and obeyed to the end [p. 377].

In a large number of cases the degree of tension reached extremes that are rarely seen in sociopsychological laboratory studies. Subjects were observed to sweat, tremble, stutter, bite their lips, groan, and dig their fingernails into their flesh. These were characteristic rather than exceptional responses to the experiment.

One sign of tension was the regular occurrence of nervous laughing fits. Fourteen of the 40 subjects showed definite signs of nervous laughter and smiling. The laughter seemed entirely out of place, even bizarre. Full-blown, uncontrollable seizures were observed for 3 subjects. On one occasion we observed a seizure so violently convulsive that it was necessary to call a halt to the experiment... [p. 375].

Milgram does state that,

After the interview, procedures were undertaken to assure that the subject would leave the laboratory in a state of well being. A friendly reconciliation was arranged between the subject and the victim, and an effort was made to reduce any tensions that arose as a result of the experiment [p. 374].

It would be interesting to know what sort of procedures could dissipate the type of emotional disturbance just described. In view of the effects on subjects, traumatic to a degree which Milgram himself considers nearly unprecedented in sociopsychological experiments, his casual assurance that these tensions were dissipated before the subject left the laboratory is unconvincing.

What could be the rational basis for such a posture of indifference? Perhaps Milgram supplies the answer himself when he partially explains the subject's destructive obedience as follows, "Thus they assume that the discomfort caused the victim is momentary, while the scientific gains resulting from the experiment are enduring [p. 378]." Indeed such a rationale might suffice to justify the means used to achieve his end if that end were of inestimable value to humanity or were not itself transformed by the means by which it was attained.

The behavioral psychologist is not in as good a position to objectify his faith in the significance of his work as medical colleagues at points of breakthrough. His experimental situations are not sufficiently accurate models of real-life experience; his sampling techniques are seldom of a scope which would justify the meaning with which he would like to endow his results; and these results are hard to reproduce by colleagues with opposing theoretical views.... [T]he concrete benefit to humanity of his particular piece of work, no matter how competently handled, cannot justify the risk that real harm will be done to the subject. I am not speaking of physical discomfort, inconvenience, or experimental deception per se, but of permanent harm, however slight. I do regard the emotional disturbance described by Milgram as potentially harmful because it could easily effect an alteration in the subject's self-image or ability to trust adult authorities in the future. It is potentially harmful to a subject to commit, in the course of an experiment, acts which he himself considers unworthy, particularly when he has been entrapped into committing such acts by an individual he has reason to trust. The subject's personal responsibility for his actions is not erased because the experimenter reveals to him the means which he used to stimulate these actions. The subject realizes that he would have hurt the victim if the current were on. The realization that he also made a fool of himself by accepting the experimental set results in additional loss of self-esteem. Moreover, the subject finds it difficult to express his anger outwardly after the experimenter in a self-acceptant but friendly manner reveals the hoax.

A fairly intense corrective interpersonal experience is indicated wherein the subject admits and accepts his responsibility for his own actions, and at the same time gives vent to his hurt and anger at being fooled. Perhaps an experience as distressing as the one described by Milgram can be integrated by the subject, provided that careful thought is given to the matter. The propriety of such experimentation is still in question even if such a reparational experience were forthcoming. Without it I would expect a naive, sensitive subject to remain deeply hurt and anxious for some time, and a sophisticated, cynical subject to become even more alienated and distrustful.

In addition the experimental procedure used by Milgram does not appear suited to the objectives of the study because it does not take into account the special quality of the set which the subject has in the experimental situation. Milgram is concerned with a very important problem, namely, the social consequences of destructive obedience. He says, .

> Gas chambers were built, death camps were guarded, daily quotas of corpses were produced with the same efficiency as a manufacture of appliances. These inhumane policies may have originated in the mind of a single person, but they could only be carried out on a massive scale if a very large number of persons obeyed orders [p. 371].

But the parallel between authority-subordinate relationships in Hitler's Germany and in Milgram's laboratory is unclear. In the former situation the SS man or member of the German Officer Corps, when obeying orders to slaughter, had no reason to think of his superior officer as benignly disposed towards himself or their victims. The victims were perceived as subhuman and not worthy of consideration. The subordinate officer was an agent in a great cause. He did not need to feel guilt or conflict because within his frame of reference he was acting rightly.

It is obvious from Milgram's own descriptions that most of his subjects were concerned about their victims and did trust the experimenter, and that their stressful conflict was generated in part by the consequences of these two disparate but appropriate attitudes. Their distress may have resulted from shock at what the experimenter was doing to them as well as from what they thought they were doing to their victims. In any case there is not a convincing parallel between the phenomena studied by Milgram and destructive obedience as that concept would apply to the subordinate-authority relationship demonstrated in Hitler Germany. If the experiments were conducted "outside of New Haven [Connecticut] and without any visible ties to [Yale University]," I would still question their validity on similar although not identical grounds. In addition, I would question the representativeness of a sample of subjects who would voluntarily participate within a noninstitutional setting.

In summary, the experimental objectives of the psychologist are seldom incompatible with the subject's ongoing state of well being, provided that the experimenter is willing to take the subject's motives and interests into consideration when planning his methods and correctives. Section 4b in *Ethical Standards of Psychologists* (APA, undated) reads in part:

Only when a problem is significant and can be investigated in no other way, is the psychologist justified in exposing human subjects to emotional stress or other possible harm. In conducting such research, the psychologist must seriously consider the possibility of harmful aftereffects, and should be prepared to remove them as soon as permitted by the design of the experiment. Where the danger of serious aftereffects exists, research should be conducted only when the subjects or their responsible agents are fully informed of this possibility and volunteer nevertheless [p. 12].

From the subject's point of view procedures which involve loss of dignity, self-esteem, and trust in rational authority are probably most harmful in the long run and require the most thoughtfully planned reparations, if engaged in at all. The public image of psychology as a profession is highly related to our own actions, and some of these actions are changeworthy. It is important that as research psychologists we protect our ethical sensibilities rather than adapt our personal standards to include as appropriate the kind of indignities to which Milgram's subjects were exposed. I would not like to see experiments such as Milgram's proceed unless the subjects were fully informed of the dangers of serious aftereffects and his correctives were clearly shown to be effective in restoring their state of well being.

REFERENCES

AMERICAN PSYCHOLOGICAL ASSOCIATION. Ethical Standards of Psychologists: A summary of ethical principles. Washington, D.C.: APA, undated.

MILGRAM, S. Behavioral study of obedience. *J. abnorm. soc. Psychol.*, 1963, 67, 371–378.

NO

Stanley Milgram

ISSUES IN THE STUDY OF OBEDIENCE: A REPLY TO BAUMRIND

Obedience serves numerous productive functions in society. It may be ennobling and educative and entail acts of charity and kindness. Yet the problem of destructive obedience, because it is the most disturbing expression of obedience in our time, and because it is the most perplexing, merits intensive study.

In its most general terms, the problem of destructive obedience may be defined thus: If X tells Y to hurt Z, under what conditions will Y carry out the command of X, and under what conditions will he refuse? In the concrete setting of a laboratory, the question may assume this form: If an experimenter tells a subject to act against another person, under what conditions will the subject go along with the instruction, and under what conditions will he refuse to obey?

A simple procedure was devised for studying obedience (Milgram, 1963). A person comes to the laboratory, and in the context of a learning experiment, he is told to give increasingly severe electric shocks to another person. (The other person is an actor, who does not really receive any shocks.) The experimenter tells the subject to continue stepping up the shock level, even to the point of reaching the level marked "Danger: Severe Shock." The purpose of the experiment is to see how far the naive subject will proceed before he refuses to comply with the experimenter's instructions. Behavior prior to this rupture is considered "obedience" in that the subject does what the experimenter tells him to do. The point of rupture is the act of disobedience. Once the basic procedure is established, it becomes possible to vary conditions of the experiment, to learn under what circumstances obedience to authority is most probable, and under what conditions defiance is brought to the fore (Milgram, in press).

The results of the experiment (Milgram, 1963) showed, first, that it is more difficult for many people to defy the experimenter's authority than was generally supposed. A substantial number of subjects go through to the end of the shock board. The second finding is that the situation often places a person in considerable conflict. In the course of the experiment, subjects fidget,

From Stanley Milgram, "Issues in the Study of Obedience: A Reply to Baumrind," *American Psychologist*, vol. 19 (1964). Copyright © 1964 by The American Psychological Association. Reprinted by permission.

sweat, and sometimes break out into nervous fits of laughter. On the one hand, subjects want to aid the experimenter; and on the other hand, they do not want to shock the learner. The conflict is expressed in nervous reactions.

In a recent issue of *American Psychologist*, Diana Baumrind (1964) raised a number of questions concerning the obedience report. Baumrind expressed concern for the welfare of subjects who served in the experiment, and wondered whether adequate measures were taken to protect the participants. She also questioned the adequacy of the experimental design.

Patently, "Behavioral Study of Obedience" did not contain all the information needed for an assessment of the experiment. But... this was only one of a series of reports on the experimental program, and Baumrind's article was deficient in information that could have been obtained easily....

At the outset, Baumrind confuses the unanticipated outcome of an experiment with its basic procedure. She writes, for example, as if the production of stress in our subjects was an intended and deliberate effect of the experimental manipulation. There are many laboratory procedures specifically designed to create stress (Lazarus, 1964), but the obedience paradigm was not one of them. The extreme tension induced in some subjects was unexpected. Before conducting the experiment, the procedures were discussed with many colleagues, and none anticipated the reactions that subsequently took place. Foreknowledge of results can never be the invariable accompaniment of an experimental probe. Understanding grows because we examine situations in which the end is unknown. An investigator unwilling to accept this degree of risk must give up the idea of scientific inquiry.

Moreover, there was every reason to expect, prior to actual experimentation, that subjects would refuse to follow the experimenter's instructions beyond the point where the victim protested; many colleagues and psychiatrists were questioned on this point, and they virtually all felt this would be the case. Indeed, to initiate an experiment in which the critical measure hangs on disobedience, one must start with a belief in certain spontaneous resources in men that enable them to overcome pressure from authority.

It is true that after a reasonable number of subjects had been exposed to the procedures, it became evident that some would go to the end of the shock board, and some would experience stress. That point, it seems to me, is the first legitimate juncture at which one could even start to wonder whether or not to abandon the study. But momentary excitement is not the same as harm. As the experiment progressed there was no indication of injurious effects in the subjects; and as the subjects themselves strongly endorsed the experiment, the judgment I made was to continue the investigation.

Is not Baumrind's criticism based as much on the unanticipated findings as on the method? The findings were that some subjects performed in what appeared to be a shockingly immoral way. If, instead, every one of the subjects had broken off at "slight shock," or at the first sign of the learner's discomfort, the results would have been pleasant, and reassuring, and who would protest?

NO Stanley Milgram / 25

PROCEDURES AND BENEFITS

A most important aspect of the procedure occurred at the end of the experimental session. A careful post-experimental treatment was administered to all subjects. The exact content of the dehoax varied from condition to condition and with increasing experience on our part. At the very least all subjects were told that the victim had not received dangerous electric shocks. Each subject had a friendly reconciliation with the unharmed victim, and an extended discussion with the experimenter. The experiment was explained to the defiant subjects in a way that supported their decision to disobey the experimenter. Obedient subjects were assured of the fact that their behavior was entirely normal and that their feelings of conflict or tension were shared by other participants. Subjects were told that they would receive a comprehensive report at the conclusion of the experimental series. In some instances, additional detailed and lengthy discussions of the experiments were also carried out with individual subjects.

When the experimental series was complete, subjects received a written report which presented details of the experimental procedure and results. Again their own part in the experiments was treated in a dignified way and their behavior in the experiment respected. All subjects received a follow-up questionnaire regarding their participation in the research, which again allowed expression of thoughts and feelings about their behavior.

The replies to the questionnaire confirmed my impression that participants felt positively toward the experiment. In its quantitative aspect (see Table 1), 84% of the subjects stated they were glad to have been in the experiment; 15% indicated neutral feelings, and 1.3% indicated negative feelings. To be sure, such findings are to be interpreted cautiously, but they cannot be disregarded.

Further, four-fifths of the subjects felt that more experiments of this sort should be carried out, and 74% indicated that they had learned something of personal importance as a result of being in the study....

The debriefing and assessment procedures were carried out as a matter of course, and were not stimulated by any observation of special risk in the experimental procedure. In my judgment, at no point were subjects exposed to danger and at no point did they run the risk of injurious effects resulting from participation. If it had been otherwise, the experiment would have been terminated at once.

Baumrind states that, after he has performed in the experiment, the subject cannot justify his behavior and must bear the full brunt of his actions. By and large it does not work this way. The same mechanisms that allow the subject to perform the act, to obey rather than to defy the experimenter, transcend the moment of performance and continue to justify his behavior for him. The same viewpoint the subject takes while performing the actions is the viewpoint from which he later sees his behavior, that is, the perspective of "carrying out the task assigned by the person in authority."

Because the idea of shocking the victim is repugnant, there is a tendency among those who hear of the design to say "people will not do it." When the results are made known, this attitude is expressed as "if they do it they will not be able to live with themselves afterward." These two forms of denying

Table 1

**Excerpt from Questionnaire Used in a Follow-up
Study of the Obedience Research**

Now that I have read the report and all things considered …	Defiant	Obedient	All
1. I am very glad to have been in the experiment	40.0%	47.8%	43.5%
2. I am glad to have been in the experiment	43.8%	35.7%	40.2%
3. I am neither sorry nor glad to have been in the experiment	15.3%	14.8%	15.1%
4. I am sorry to have been in the experiment	0.8%	0.7%	0.8%
5. I am very sorry to have been in the experiment	0.0%	1.0%	0.5%

Note—Ninety-two percent of the subjects returned the questionnaire. The characteristics of the nonrespondents were checked against the respondents. They differed from the respondents only with regard to age; younger people were overrepresented in the nonresponding group.

the experimental findings are equally inappropriate misreadings of the facts of human social behavior. Many subjects do, indeed, obey to the end, and there is no indication of injurious effects.

The absence of injury is a minimal condition of experimentation; there can be, however, an important positive side to participation. Baumrind suggests that subjects derived no benefit from being in the obedience study, but this is false. By their statements and actions, subjects indicated that they had learned a good deal, and many felt gratified to have taken part in scientific research they considered to be of significance. A year after his participation one subject wrote:

This experiment has strengthened my belief that man should avoid harm to his fellow man even at the risk of violating authority.

Another stated:

To me, the experiment pointed up … the extent to which each individual should have or discover firm ground on which to base his decisions, no matter how trivial they appear to be. I think people should think more deeply about themselves and their relation to their world and to other people. If this experiment serves to jar people out of complacency, it will have served its end.

These statements are illustrative of a broad array of appreciative and insightful comments by those who participated.

The 5-page report sent to each subject on the completion of the experimental series was specifically designed to enhance the value of his experience. It laid out the broad conception of the experimental program as well as the logic of its design. It described the results of a dozen of the experiments, discussed the causes of tension, and attempted to indicate the possible significance of the experiment. Subjects responded enthusiastically; many indicated a desire to be in further experimental research. This report was sent to all subjects several years ago. The care with which it was prepared does not support Baumrind's assertion that the experimenter was indifferent to the value subjects derived from their participation.

Baumrind's fear is that participants will be alienated from psychological experiments because of the intensity of experience associated with laboratory procedures. My own observation is that subjects more commonly respond with distaste to the "empty" laboratory hour, in which cardboard procedures are employed, and the only possible feeling upon emerging from the laboratory is that one has wasted time in a patently trivial and useless exercise.

The subjects in the obedience experiment, on the whole, felt quite differently about their participation. They viewed the experience as an opportunity to learn something of importance about themselves, and more generally, about the conditions of human action.

A year after the experimental program was completed, I initiated an additional follow-up study. In this connection an impartial medical examiner, experienced in outpatient treatment, interviewed 40 experimental subjects. The examining psychiatrist focused on those subjects he felt would be most likely to have suffered consequences from participation. His aim was to identify possible injurious effects resulting from the experiment. He concluded that, although extreme stress had been experienced by several subjects,

> none was found by this interviewer to show signs of having been harmed by his experience.... Each subject seemed to handle his task [in the experiment] in a manner consistent with well established patterns of behavior. No evidence was found of any traumatic reactions.

Such evidence ought to be weighed before judging the experiment.

OTHER ISSUES

Baumrind's discussion is not limited to the treatment of subjects, but diffuses to a generalized rejection of the work.

Baumrind feels that obedience cannot be meaningfully studied in a laboratory setting: The reason she offers is that "The dependent, obedient attitude assumed by most subjects in the experimental setting is appropriate to that situation [p. 421]." Here, Baumrind has cited the very best reason for examining obedience in this setting, namely that it possesses "ecological validity." Here is one social context in which compliance occurs regularly. Military and job situations are also particularly meaningful settings for the study of obedience precisely because obedience is natural and appropriate to these contexts. I reject Baumrind's argument that the observed obedience does not count because it occurred where it is appropriate. That is precisely why it *does* count. A soldier's obedience is no less meaningful because it occurs in a pertinent military context. A subject's obedience is no less problematical because it occurs within a social institution called the psychological experiment.

Baumrind writes: "The game is defined by the experimenter and he makes the rules [p. 421]." It is true that for disobedience to occur the framework of the experiment must be shattered. That, indeed, is the point of the design. That is why obedience and disobedience are genuine issues for the subject. *He must really assert himself as a person against a legitimate authority.*

Further, Baumrind wants us to believe that outside the laboratory we could not find a comparably high expression of obedience. Yet, the fact that ordinary citizens are recruited to military service and, on command, perform far harsher acts against people is beyond dispute. Few of them know or are concerned with the complex policy issues underlying martial action; fewer still become conscientious objectors. Good soldiers do as they are told, and on both sides of the battle line. However, a debate on whether a higher level of obedience is represented by (a) killing men in the service of one's country, or (b) merely shocking them in the service of Yale science, is largely unprofitable. The real question is: What are the forces underlying obedient action?

Another question raised by Baumrind concerns the degree of parallel between obedience in the laboratory and in Nazi Germany. Obviously, there are enormous differences: Consider the disparity in time scale. The laboratory experiment takes an hour; the Nazi calamity unfolded in the space of a decade. There is a great deal that needs to be said on this issue, and only a few points can be touched on here.

1. In arguing this matter, Baumrind mistakes the background metaphor for the precise subject matter of investigation. The German event was cited to point up a serious problem in the human situation: the potentially destructive effect of obedience. But the best way to tackle the problem of obedience, from a scientific standpoint, is in no way restricted by "what happened exactly" in Germany. What happened exactly can *never* be duplicated in the laboratory or anywhere else. The real task is to learn more about the general problem of destructive obedience using a workable approach. Hopefully, such inquiry will stimulate insights and yield general propositions that can be applied to a wide variety of situations.

2. One may ask in a general way: How does a man behave when he is told by a legitimate authority to act against a third individual? In trying to find an answer to this question, the laboratory situation is one useful starting point—and for the very reason stated by Baumrind—

namely, the experimenter does constitute a genuine authority for the subject. The fact that trust and dependence on the experimenter are maintained, despite the extraordinary harshness he displays toward the victim, is itself a remarkable phenomenon.

3. In the laboratory, through a set of rather simple manipulations, ordinary persons no longer perceived themselves as a responsible part of the causal chain leading to action against a person. The means through which responsibility is cast off, and individuals become thoughtless agents of action, is of general import. Other processes were revealed that indicate that the experiments will help us to understand why men obey. That understanding will come, of course, by examining the full account of experimental work and not alone the brief report in which the procedure and demonstrational results were exposed.

At root, Baumrind senses that it is not proper to test obedience in this situation, because she construes it as one in which there is no reasonable alternative to obedience. In adopting this view, she has lost sight of this fact: A substantial proportion of subjects do disobey. By their example, disobedience is shown to be a genuine possibility, one that is in no sense ruled out by the general structure of the experimental situation.

Baumrind is uncomfortable with the high level of obedience obtained in the first experiment. In the condition she focused on, 65% of the subjects obeyed to the end. However, her sentiment does not take into account that within the general framework of the psychological experiment obedience varied enormously from one condition to the next. In some variations, 90% of the subjects *dis*obeyed. It seems to be *not* only the fact of an experiment, but the particular structure of elements within the experimental situation that accounts for rates of obedience and disobedience. And these elements were varied systematically in the program of research.

A concern with human dignity is based on a respect for a man's potential to act morally. Baumrind feels that the experimenter *made* the subject shock the victim. This conception is alien to my view. The experimenter tells the subject to do something. But between the command and the outcome there is a paramount force, the acting person who may obey or disobey. I started with the belief that every person who came to the laboratory was free to accept or to reject the dictates of authority. This view sustains a conception of human dignity insofar as it sees in each man a capacity for *choosing* his own behavior. And as it turned out, many subjects did, indeed, choose to reject the experimenter's commands, providing a powerful affirmation of human ideals.

Baumrind also criticizes the experiment on the grounds that "it could easily effect an alteration in the subject's... ability to trust adult authorities in the future [p. 422]." But I do not think she can have it both ways. On the one hand, she argues the experimental situation is so special that it has no generality; on the other hand, she states it has such generalizing potential that it will cause subjects to distrust all authority. But the experimenter is not just any authority: He is an authority who tells the subject to act harshly and inhumanely against another man. I would consider it of the highest value if participation in the experiment could, indeed, inculcate a skepticism of this kind of authority. Here, perhaps, a difference in philosophy emerges most

clearly. Baumrind sees the subject as a passive creature, completely controlled by the experimenter. I started from a different viewpoint. A person who comes to the laboratory is an active, choosing adult, capable of accepting or rejecting the prescriptions for action addressed to him. Baumrind sees the effect of the experiment as undermining the subject's trust of authority. I see it as a potentially valuable experience insofar as it makes people aware of the problem of indiscriminate submission to authority.

CONCLUSION

My feeling is that viewed in the total context of values served by the experiment, approximately the right course was followed. In review, the facts are these: (a) At the outset, there was the problem of studying obedience by means of a simple experimental procedure. The results could not be foreseen before the experiment was carried out. (b) Although the experiment generated momentary stress in some subjects, this stress dissipated quickly and was not injurious. (c) Dehoax and follow-up procedures were carried out to insure the subjects' well-being. (d) These procedures were assessed through questionnaire and psychiatric studies and were found to be effective. (e) Additional steps were taken to enhance the value of the laboratory experience for participants, for example, submitting to each subject a careful report on the experimental program. (f) The subjects themselves strongly endorse the experiment, and indicate satisfaction at having participated.

If there is a moral to be learned from the obedience study, it is that every man must be responsible for his own actions. This author accepts full responsibility for the design and execution of the study. Some people may feel it should not have been done. I disagree and accept the burden of their judgment.

Baumrind's judgment, someone has said, not only represents a personal conviction, but also reflects a cleavage in American psychology between those whose primary concern is with *helping* people and those who are interested mainly in *learning* about people. I see little value in perpetuating divisive forces in psychology when there is so much to learn from every side. A schism may exist, but it does not correspond to the true ideals of the discipline. The psychologist intent on healing knows that his power to help rests on knowledge; he is aware that a scientific grasp of all aspects of life is essential for his work, and is in itself a worthy human aspiration. At the same time, the laboratory psychologist senses his work will lead to human betterment, not only because enlightenment is moredignified than ignorance, but because new knowledge is pregnant with humane consequences.

REFERENCES

BAUMRIND, D. Some thoughts on ethics of research: After reading Milgram's "Behavioral study of obedience." *Amer. Psychologist*, 1964, 19, 421–423.

LAZARUS, R. A laboratory approach to the dynamics of psychological stress. *Amer. Psychologist*, 1964, 19, 400–411.

MILGRAM, S. Behavioral study of obedience. *J. abnorm. soc. Psychol.*, 1963, 67, 371–378.

MILGRAM, S. Some conditions of obedience and disobedience to authority. *Hum. Relat.*, in press.

CHALLENGE QUESTIONS

Classic Dialogue: Was Stanley Milgram's Study of Obedience Unethical?

1. Investigate the role that your college's institutional review board (see the introduction to this issue) plays in protecting subjects from undue harm.

2. Sometimes people make the wrong decisions and end up hurting other people. Apart from utilizing institutional review boards, what can researchers do to avoid making wrong decisions regarding potentially harmful studies?

3. Imagine that you have just participated in Milgram's study. How would you feel about the deception that occurred? Is it ever appropriate to deceive participants in research studies? If so, when? If not, why not?

4. Both Baumrind and Milgram might agree that there are cases in which some low-level tension for research participants is allowable. Under what conditions might it be acceptable to allow participants to experience some distress? Under what conditions is it inappropriate to subject participants to any distress?

5. Baumrind raises the issue of trust. Do you think the participants in the Milgram study lost trust in psychological researchers or authority figures in general? Why, or why not?

6. If you were on an ethics review board and the Milgram study was brought before you, would you allow Milgram to run the study? Support your answer.

ISSUE 3

Should Animals Be Used in Psychological Research?

YES: Elizabeth Baldwin, from "The Case for Animal Research in Psychology," *Journal of Social Issues* (vol. 49, no. 1, 1993)

NO: Alan D. Bowd and Kenneth J. Shapiro, from "The Case Against Laboratory Animal Research in Psychology," *Journal of Social Issues* (vol. 49, no. 1, 1993)

ISSUE SUMMARY

YES: Elizabeth Baldwin, a research ethics officer for the American Psychological Association's Science Directorate, maintains that the benefits of behavioral research with animals are substantial and that the animals are being treated humanely.

NO: Professor of educational psychology Alan D. Bowd and Kenneth J. Shapiro, executive director of Psychologists for the Ethical Treatment of Animals, argue that the harm done to animals in this research is not widely known and that the "benefits" are not sufficient to balance this cruelty.

Until relatively recently, humans were thought to be distinctly different from lower animals. Only humans were considered to have self-consciousness, rationality, and language. Today, however, these distinctions appear to have been blurred by modern research. Many scientists, for example, believe that chimpanzees use language symbols and that many animals have some type of consciousness.

This apparent lack of hard and fast distinctions between humans and other animals has many implications. One of these concerns the use of animals in experimental research. For hundreds of years animals have been considered tools of research. In fact, research ethics has demanded that most experimental treatments be tested on animals before they are tested on humans. Another view, however, has come to the fore. Because there is no clear distinction between lower and higher animals, this view asserts that the lower animals should be accorded the same basic rights as humans. Animal experimentation, from this perspective, cannot be taken for granted; it must be justified on the same moral and ethical grounds as research on humans. This perspective has recently gained considerable momentum as supporters have become politically organized.

Elizabeth Baldwin disagrees with this perspective. She argues that animals should be used in psychological research and that although people should be held responsible for the humane treatment of animals, animals do not have the same rights as humans. Baldwin describes the important role that animals have played in improving the human condition through research and how animal research benefits the health and welfare of other animals. Baldwin argues that many people are not aware of the many federal regulations and laws that protect animals from inhumane treatment. Ultimately, she contends, humans and animals cannot be viewed as essentially the same, with the same ethics and rights.

Alan D. Bowd and Kenneth J. Shapiro do not concur with this view. Their case against the use of animals for psychological research hinges on the idea that animals are denied basic rights. Bowd and Shapiro have developed what they call a "scale of invasiveness," which is an index of the suffering and harm done to animals before, during, or after an experimental procedure. Unlike Baldwin, they argue that federal laws and regulations are not sufficient because they do not consider the animals. Bowd and Shapiro also maintain that the research revealing the harm done to animals is not being published and, in turn, is not being sufficiently recognized. Consequently, they suggest that alternatives to the use of animals in laboratory research be found.

POINT	COUNTERPOINT
• Animals do not have the same rights as humans, but people have a responsibility to ensure the humane treatment of animals.	• Those who accord rights to human beings and deny them to other species must show a morally relevant difference between these species.
• There are elaborate federal regulations protecting animals in research, as well as state laws and professional guidelines on the care of animals.	• Many species are not covered by the Animal Welfare Act and are therefore not reported as part of federally mandated inspections.
• Society has made a collective judgment that the benefits derived from animal research far outweigh the costs.	• In contrast to the uncertain benefits of laboratory animal research, the cost to animals is clear and real.
• Animals have played a pivotal role in improving the human condition and, in return, society should strive to treat them well.	• The benefits of animal research are indeterminate because they depend on unknowns, such as human welfare.

YES

Elizabeth Baldwin

THE CASE FOR ANIMAL RESEARCH IN PSYCHOLOGY

Animal liberationists do not separate out the human animal. A rat is a pig is a dog is a boy.

—Ingrid Newkirk, Director, People for the Ethical Treatment of Animals.

The shock value of this quote has made it a favorite of those defending the use of animals in research. It succinctly states the core belief of many animal rights activists who oppose the use of animals in research. Although some activists work for improved laboratory conditions for research animals, recent surveys suggest that most activists would like to eliminate animal research entirely (Plous, 1991). These activists believe animals have rights equal to humans and therefore should not be used as subjects in laboratory research.

The debate over animal research can be confusing unless one understands the very different goals of animal welfare organizations and animal rights groups. People concerned with animal welfare seek to improve laboratory conditions for research animals and to reduce the number of animals needed. These mainstream goals encompass traditional concerns for the humane treatment of animals, and most researchers share these goals. In contrast, the views of animal rights activists are *not* mainstream, since there are few people who would agree with the above quote from Ingrid Newkirk. Indeed, in a national poll conducted by the National Science Foundation, half the respondents answered the following question affirmatively: "Should scientists be allowed to do research that causes pain and injury to animals like dogs and chimpanzees if it produces new information about human health problems?" (National Science Board, 1991). These findings are particularly impressive given the explicit mention of "pain and injury" to popular animals such as dogs and chimpanzees. My own position is that animals do not have rights in the same sense that humans do, but that people have a responsibility to ensure the humane treatment of animals under their care. Animals have played a pivotal role in improving the human condition, and in return, society should strive to treat them well.

BACKGROUND

The modern animal rights movement is intellectual and spiritual heir to the Victorian antivivisection movement in Britain (Sperling, 1988). This 19th-century movement was a powerful force in Britain and arose in part from accelerating changes brought about by science and technology (and the resulting challenges to the prevailing view of humanity's relationship to nature).

The British movement peaked in 1876 with the passage of the Cruelty to Animals Act. This compromise legislation required licenses for conducting animal research, but recognized the societal value of continuing to use animals in research. It was about this time that the scientific community began to organize a defense of animal research. Several challenges to animal research were made in the ensuing 20 years, but in the end, the medical and scientific community were able to successfully protect their interests. The Victorian antivivisection movement, however, did bring about the regulation of research and helped prevent outright abuse (Sperling, 1988).

The beginning of the modern animal rights movement is generally dated to the 1975 publication of *Animal Liberation* by philosopher Peter Singer. Although Singer himself is not an advocate of animal "rights," he provided the groundwork for later arguments that animals have rights—including the right not to be used in research. Most animal rights activists believe animals have a right not to be used for research, food, entertainment, and a variety of other purposes. An inordinate amount of attention is devoted to animal research, however, even though far fewer animals are used for research than for other purposes (Nicoll & Russell, 1990).

There has been a phenomenal growth in the animal rights movement since the publication of Singer's book. People for the Ethical Treatment of Animals (PETA), the leading animal rights organization in the United States, has grown from 18 members in 1981 to more than 250,000 members in 1990. (McCabe, 1990). By any standard, the animal rights movement is a force to be reckoned with.

PHILOSOPHICAL ISSUES

There are two basic philosophies that support the animal rights movement, although activists are often unable to articulate them (Sperling, 1988). These two positions are summarized by Herzog (1990) as the *utilitarian* argument and the *rights* argument.

The utilitarian position is that the greatest good is achieved by maximizing pleasure and happiness, and by minimizing suffering and pain. Although traditionally applied only to humans, Singer argues that animals should be included when considering the greatest good. He states, "No matter what the nature of the being, the principle of equality requires that its suffering be counted equally with the like suffering—insofar as rough comparisons can be made—of any other being" (Singer, 1990, p. 8). Utilitarians would thus argue that animals have an interest equal to that of humans in avoiding pain and suffering, and should therefore not be used in experiments that could cause them harm. Two problems with this philosophy are that (1) it is hard to draw a line between creatures that suffer and creatures that do not, and (2) the argument does not address *qualitative* differences in pain and pleasure across species (Herzog, 1990).

The rights position states that animals possess certain rights based on their inherent value. This philosophy, first developed by Tom Regan (1983), argues that animals have a right not to be used by humans in research (and for many other purposes). Major problems with this position arise in deciding just what rights are and in determining who is entitled to hold them (Herzog, 1990).

While the above positions have been developed relatively recently, the alternative view of animals as qualitatively different from humans has a long history in Judeo-Christian thought. Traditionally, humans were believed to have been created in the image of God and to have dominion over animals. Robb (1988) uses this perspective in arguing that humans are unique by virtue of their capacity for moral choice. Because of this capacity, humans can be held responsible for their choices, and can therefore enter into contractual agreements with binding rights and responsibilities for *both* parties. Robb acknowledges that some animals have human capacities in certain areas, but he argues that this does not make them morally equal to humans or give them rights that take precedence over human needs.

The most persuasive argument for using animals in behavioral research, however, is the untold benefit that accrues to both humans and animals. The benefits of behavioral research with animals have been enumerated by such authors as Miller (1985) and King and Yarbrough (1985), and for most people, these benefits are the reason that they support the continued use of animals in research. This argument—which is basically utilitarian—is the one most often cited by the research community in defense of animal research. In contrast to Singer's utilitarianism, however, animals are not given the same degree of consideration as people.

In conclusion, both sides in the animal rights debate have philosophical underpinnings to support their position, but what often emerges in the rhetoric is not reasoned debate but emotion-laden charges and personal attacks. This is not surprising, given the strong passions aroused in the discussion.

FRAMING THE DEBATE

In the 1980s, activists targeted certain researchers or areas of research that they viewed as vulnerable to attack, and researchers were forced to assume a defensive posture. Unfortunately, activists were right about the vulnerability of individual scientists; little or no institutional defense was mounted against these early attacks. The prevailing attitude was to ignore the activists in hopes that they would go away, and thus attract less attention from the public and the press. This passivity left the early targets of animal rights activists in the position of a man asked, "Why do you beat your wife?" No matter how researchers responded, they sounded defensive and self-serving. It took several years for the research community to realize that animal rights activists were not going away, and that the activists' charges needed to be answered in a systematic and serious manner.

This early failure on the part of the research community to communicate its position effectively left the public with little information beyond what was provided by the animal rights activists. Framing the debate is half the battle, and the research community was left playing catch-up and answering the question, "Why do you abuse your research animals?"

The research community also faced the daunting task of explaining the use of animals in research to a public whose understanding of the scientific method was almost nil. The most difficult misconception to correct was the belief that every research project with animals should produce "useful" results (Orem, 1990). Social scientists who have received Senator William Proxmire's "Golden Fleece Award" are well aware of this line of thinking—a line of thinking that displays a complete misunderstanding of how science works, and ignores the vast amount of basic research that typically precedes each "useful" discovery.

It is difficult for scientific rationales to compete with shocking posters, catchy slogans, and soundbites from the animal rights movement. The most effective response from the scientific community has been to point out innumerable health advances made possible by the use of animals as research models. This approach is something that most people can relate to, since everyone has benefited from these advances.

The early defensive posture of scientists also failed to allay public concerns about the ability of researchers to self-regulate their care and use of research animals. Unlike the participation of humans in research (who are usually able to speak in their own defense and give consent), there seemed to be no one in the system able to "speak" for the animals. Or so people were encouraged to believe by animal rights activists. As discussed below, there are elaborate federal regulations on the use of animals in research, as well as state laws and professional guidelines on the care and use of animals in research.

RESTORING TRUST

Scientists, research institutions, and federal research agencies finally came to realize that the charges being leveled by animal rights activists needed to be publicly —and forcefully—rebutted. Dr. Frederick Goodwin, former Administrator of the Alcohol, Drug Abuse, and Mental Health Administration (ADAMHA), was one of the first federal officials to defend animal research publicly, and point out the difference between animal welfare and animal rights (Booth, 1989). Recently, many more federal officials and respected researchers have publicly spoken on the importance of animal research (Mervis, 1990).

Countering Misinformation

Animal rights literature often uses misleading images to depict animal research —images such as animals grimacing as they are shocked with electricity. These descriptions lead readers to believe animals are routinely subjected to high voltage shocks capable of producing convulsions (e.g., Singer, 1990, pp. 42–45). Such propaganda is far from the truth. In most cases, electric shock (when used at all) is relatively mild—similar to what one might feel from the discharge of static electricity on a cold, dry day. Even this relatively mild use of shock is carefully reviewed by Institutional Animal Care and Use Committees before being approved, and researchers must demonstrate that alternate techniques are not feasible. Stronger shock *is* used in animal research, but it is used to study medical problems such as epilepsy (a convulsive disorder). It is also used to test the effectiveness and side effects of drugs developed to control such disorders. It is not within the scope of this article to refute the myriad charges issued against animal research in general, specific projects, and individual researchers. Suffice it to say that such allegations have been persuasively refuted (Coile & Miller, 1984; Feeney, 1987; Johnson, 1990; McCabe, 1986).

Benefits to Animals

Animal rights activists often fail to appreciate the many benefits to animals that have resulted from animal research. Behavioral research has contributed to improvements in the environments of captive animals, including those used in research (Novak & Petto, 1991). The list of benefits also includes a host of veterinary procedures and the development of vaccines for deadly diseases such as rabies, Lyme disease, and feline leukemia. Research in reproductive biology and captive breeding programs are also the only hope for some animals on the brink of extinction (King et al., 1988).

Regulations and Guidelines

It is clear that many people concerned about the use of animals in research are not aware of the elaborate structure that exists to regulate the care and use of animals in research. This system includes federal regulations under the Animal Welfare Act (U.S. Department of Agriculture, 1989, 1990, 1991), Public Health Service (PHS) policy (Office for Protection from Research Risks, 1986), and state laws that govern the availability of pound animals for research.

The Animal Welfare Act, most recently amended in 1985, is enforced by the USDA's Animal and Plant Health Inspection Service (APHIS). The regulations connected with this law include 127 pages of guidelines governing the use of animals in research. It also includes unannounced inspections of animal research facilities by APHIS inspectors who do nothing but inspect research facilities. Their inspections are conducted to ensure compliance with regulations that include everything from cage size, feeding schedules, and lighting to exercise requirements for dogs and the promotion of psychological well-being among nonhuman primates.

In addition to APHIS inspectors who make unannounced inspections of animal research facilities, there are local Institutional Animal Care and Use Committees (IACUCs) that review each proposed research project using animals. Research proposals must include a justification for the species used and the number of animals required, an assurance that a thorough literature review has been conducted (to prevent unnecessary replication of research), and a consideration of alternatives if available. IACUCs are also responsible for inspecting local animal research facilities to check for continued compliance with state protocols.

Each grant proposal received by a PHS agency (National Institutes of Health, and the Centers for Disease Control) that proposes using animals must contain an assurance that it has been reviewed by an IACUC and been approved. IACUCs must have no less than five members and contain at least one veterinarian, one practicing scientist experienced in research involving animals, one member who is primarily concerned in nonscientific matters (e.g., a lawyer or ethicist), and one member who is not affiliated with the institution in any way and is not an immediate family member of anyone affiliated with the institution (Office for Protection from Research Risks, 1986; USDA, 1989).

Beyond federal animal welfare regulations, PHS policy, and the PHS Guidelines (National Research Council, 1985), there are professional guidelines for the care and use of research animals. Examples include the American Psychological Association's (APA) *Ethical Principles of Psychologists* (1990) and *Guidelines for Ethical Conduct in the Care and Use of Animals* (1993), and the Society for Neuroscience's Handbook (Society for Neuroscience, 1991).

The APA also has a Committee on Animal Research and Ethics (CARE) whose charge includes the responsibility to "review the ethics of animal experimentation and recommend guidelines for the ethical conduct of research, and appropriate care of animals in research." CARE wrote the APA's *Guidelines for Ethical Conduct in the Care and Use of Animals*, and periodically reviews it and makes revisions. These guidelines are widely used by psychologists and other scientists, and have been used in teaching research ethics at the undergraduate and graduate level. The APA's Science Directorate provided support for a conference on psychological well-being of nonhuman primates used in research, and published a volume of proceedings from that conference (Novak & Petto, 1991). The APA also helps promote research on animal welfare by membership in and support for such organizations as the American Association for the Accreditation of Laboratory Animal Care (AAALAC).

AAALAC is the only accrediting body recognized by the PHS, and sets the "gold standard" for animal research facilities. To receive AAALAC accreditation, an institution must go beyond what is required by federal animal welfare regula-tions and PHS policy. AAALAC accreditation is highly regarded, and those institutions that receive it serve as models for the rest of the research community.

Even with all these safeguards in place, some critics question the ability of the research community to self-regulate its use of animals in research. The system can only be considered self-regulating, however, if one assumes that researchers, institutional officials, members of IACUCs (which must include a member not affiliated with the institution), USDA inspectors, animal care and lab technicians, and veterinarians have identical interests. These are the individuals with the most direct access to the animals used in research, and these are the specialists most knowledgeable about the conditions under which animals are used in research.

In several states, animal rights activists have succeeded in gaining access to IACUC meetings where animal research proposals are discussed. On the whole, however, research institutions have fought—and are still fighting—to keep these meetings closed to the general public. There is a very real fear among researchers that information gleaned from such meetings will be used to harass and target individual researchers. Given the escalating nature of illegal break-ins by such organizations as the Animal Liberation Front, this is a legitimate concern. Indeed, on some campuses "reward posters" offer money to individuals who report the abuse of research animals.

Even though IACUC meetings are generally closed to the public, the elaborate system regulating animal research is by no means a closed one. The most recent animal welfare regulations were finalized after five years of proposals recorded in the *Federal Register;* comments from the public, research institutions, professional associations, animal welfare groups, and animal rights groups; the incorporation of these comments; republication of the revised rules; and so forth. Neither researchers nor animal rights groups were entirely pleased with the final document, but everyone had their say. Although certain elements of the regulatory system rely on researchers, it is hard to imagine a workable system that would fail to use their expertise. The unspoken assumption that researchers cannot be trusted to care for their research animals is not supported by the records of APHIS inspections. Good science demands good laboratory animal care, and it is in a researcher's best interest to ensure that laboratory animals are well cared for.

The Benefits of Behavioral Research With Animals

The use of animals in psychological and behavioral research was an early target of animal rights activists. This research was perceived as a more vulnerable target than biomedical research, which had more direct and easily explained links to specific human health benefits. Psychological and behavioral research also lacked the powerful backing of the medical establishment (Archer, 1986).

There is, of course, a long list of benefits derived from psychological research with animals. These include rehabilitation of persons suffering from stroke, head injury, spinal cord injury, and Alzheimer's disease; improved communication with severely retarded children; methods for the early detection of eye disorders in children (allowing preventive treatment to avoid permanent impairment); control of chronic anxiety without the use of drugs; and improved treatments for alcoholism, obesity, substance abuse, hypertension, chronic migraine headaches, lower back pain, and insomnia (Miller, 1985). Behavioral research with nonhuman primates also permits the investigation of complex behaviors such as social organization, aggression, learning and memory, communication, and growth and development (King et al., 1988).

The nature of psychological and behavioral research makes the development and use of alternatives difficult. It is the behavior of the whole organism, and the interaction among various body systems, that is examined. Computer models may be used, but "research with animals will still be needed to provide basic data for writing computer software, as well as to prove the validity and reliability of computer alternatives" (U.S. Congress, Office of Technology Assessment, 1986). The alternative of using nonliving systems may be possible with epidemiologic data bases for some behavioral research, but chemical and physical systems are not useful for modeling complex behaviors. Likewise, in vitro cultures of organs, tissues, and cells do not display the characteristics studied by psychologists.

CONCLUSION

Research psychologists have been asked to eschew emotionalism, and bring logic and reason to the debate over animal research (Bowd, 1990). This is certainly the style most researchers are comfortable with—yet they have also been advised to quit trying to "apply logic and reason in their responses [to animal rights activists]" (Culliton, 1991). Culliton warns that while "animal rights people go for the heart, the biologists go for the head" and are losing the public in the process.

Which path is best? A reasoned approach draws high marks for civility, but will it help scientists in their trench warfare with animal rights activists?

Do animals have rights that preclude their use in laboratory research? I, and the psychologists I help represent, would say no. But researchers do have responsibilities to the animals they use in their research. These responsibilities include ensuring the humane care of their research animals, using the minimum number of animals necessary, and seeing to it that all laboratory assistants are adequately trained and supervised. As stated in the APA's *Ethical Principles*, "Laws and regulations notwithstanding, an animal's immediate protection depends upon the scientist's own conscience" (APA, 1990).

Researchers and others concerned with animal welfare can engage in a useful dialogue as standards of care and use evolve. This dialogue has proven fruitless with animal rights activists, though, since they seem unwilling to compromise or consider other viewpoints. What is the middle ground for a discussion with someone whose goal is the elimination of all research on animals?

The collective decision society has made is that the benefits derived from animal research far outweigh the costs. As public opinion polls indicate, most people are willing to accept these costs but want assurances that animals are humanely cared for. Yes, I'm "speciesist" in the eyes of Ingrid Newkirk—I will never believe my son is a dog is a pig is a rat.

NO

Alan D. Bowd and
Kenneth J. Shapiro

THE CASE AGAINST LABORATORY ANIMAL RESEARCH IN PSYCHOLOGY

In this article, we will (1) present empirical evidence documenting several serious problems with the use of animals in psychology, (2) consider philosophical objections to the use of animals in invasive research, (3) give an overview of how the research community has responded to these concerns, and (4) suggest directions for change.

THE PROBLEM

The number of nonhuman animals used in psychological research in the United States is difficult to estimate. Many species are not covered by the Animal Welfare Act and are therefore not reported as part of federally mandated inspections (Rowan & Andrutis, 1990). The Animal Legal Defense Fund (a nonprofit animal protection group) is currently challenging this loophole, but at present, rats, mice, and birds—which comprise roughly 90% of all nonhuman research subjects—are not considered "animals" under the Animal Welfare Act. Attempts to arrive at estimates from departmental surveys, analyses of *Psychological Abstracts,* and extrapolations from countries where better records are kept all have their limitations, but integrating these sources of information, we estimate that roughly 1–2 million animals are used in psychological research each year.

Although some laboratory animals are obtained from shelters—a practice that is illegal in 14 states and is abhorred by a majority of the public—most laboratory animals are "purpose bred" for research. This method of procuring subjects is not without problems, however. For example, the legal office of the United States Department of Agriculture is currently investigating a major producer of animals for alleged abuse (Holden, 1990). Other problems with producing animals for laboratory research arise from selective breeding and genetic engineering. Producing animals that are susceptible to audiogenic seizures or cancerous tumors, or that adapt well to confinement, raises significant ethical questions (President's Commission, 1982).

From Alan D. Bowd and Kenneth J. Shapiro, "The Case Against Laboratory Animal Research in Psychology," *Journal of Social Issues,* vol. 49, no. 1 (1993), pp. 133–142. Copyright © 1993 by The Society for the Psychological Study of Social Issues. Reprinted by permission. References omitted.

Invasiveness in Research

In reviewing laboratory practices, it is important to distinguish between the experimental procedure itself and pre- or post-experimental care (i.e., "husbandry"). It is also critical to separate individual cases of abuse from customary practices. The case of the Silver Spring monkeys, for example, is an instance of individual abuse that became a cause célèbre of the animal rights movement. Charges against psychologist Edward Taub centered on abusive husbandry practices—inadequate veterinary care, food, ventilation, and cage space. However, much of the public outcry reflected objections to the experimental procedure (deafferentation) itself (Shapiro, 1989).

An example of a routine experimental procedure under scrutiny is the use of chair restraints. Primates that are chair restrained as part of a study spend a mean time of 5.7 hours confined in the chair each day (Bayne, 1991). An example of a customary husbandry practice under scrutiny is the housing of primates in individual cages. In one survey, 84% of the investigators housed their adult primates singly (Bayne, 1991), despite the importance of social interaction to these animals. Thus, quite apart from any trauma induced by experimental procedures, the animals suffered from routine husbandry practices.

Contrary to what defenders of animal research often say, a good deal of psychological research is highly invasive. Many studies involve stress, pain, punishment, social and environmental deprivation, and induced emotional and intellectual deficits. In their "scale of invasiveness," Field and Shapiro (1988) operationalized the term to encompass suffering and harm before, during, or after an experimental procedure. By this definition, most investigators targeted by the animal rights movement have conducted highly invasive research (e.g., maternal deprivation and drug addiction in macaques, physiology of taste in rats, visual deprivation in kittens). Beyond their invasiveness, these studies have been criticized for their nongeneralizability, redundancy, purely theoretical focus, parametric tinkering, and diversion of funds from treatment programs.

Areas of highly invasive research have shifted over time. In 1947, electroconvulsive shock and audiogenic seizures were prevalent, while in 1967 punishment, brain lesioning, and the administration of curare were more common (Field, 1988). The most frequently cited invasive studies in popular college introductory psychology textbooks (1984–1988 editions) are infant maternal deprivation, perceptual restriction in newborns, brain studies of the eating/satiety center, and learned helplessness (Field, 1990).

As a popular college major, psychology influences thousands of students each year. Typically, psychology coursework includes direct exposure to animal research in laboratories and/or indirect exposure through texts and audiovisual materials that feature animal research. Yet descriptions of invasive research in popular psychology textbooks are often sanitized (Field, 1989). For example, most discussions of Harlow's work on maternal deprivation—the most frequently cited invasive experiment—minimize the suffering involved, present pictures of "cute" animals, and omit reference to the subjective experience of the animals.

ETHICAL ISSUES

The animal rights movement began to have an impact on psychology shortly after the publication of Singer's *Animal Liberation* and Ryder's *Victims of Science* (both in 1975). Both books targeted behavioral research in particular for its painful and unnecessary experiments. The ethical foundation of the animal rights movement has since been broadened to include several other discourses: Regan (1983) provided a theory of rights to complement Singer's utilitarianism, Adams (1990) developed a feminist discourse that linked the subjugation of animals with patriarchy, and several authors provided theological perspectives on the use of animals (Linzey, 1987; McDaniel, 1989; Regenstein, 1991).

Experimental psychologists have been forced to defend their ethical positions with rational arguments. Many psychologists consider ethics a matter of personal preference, a view that exempts individuals from public scrutiny and justifies individual self-regulation. Others have attempted to reduce ethics to science, arguing that ethics is a naturally evolved phenomenon and that regulation from outside the field is inappropriate (e.g., Gallup & Suarez, 1980). However, the burgeoning field of moral philosophy suggests that ethical positions—like any other human beliefs—are subject to logical examination, and may be found to be ambiguous or contradictory.

Following Ryder (1989) and Rollin (1981), here we propose an ethic that draws upon the work of both Singer and Regan. To wit:

Interests and rights are not the sole preserve of the human species, and should be evaluated consistently and with due consideration to an animal's capacity to suffer. Our ethical obligations extend to individuals who are intellectually unable to reciprocate them, within and beyond our own species. Those who would accord rights to human beings but deny them to all other species must make the case that there is a morally relevant difference separating *Homo sapiens* from other creatures. We do not believe such a difference exists.

All creatures capable of experiencing pain and other forms of suffering have an interest in being spared it, and the rights that flow from this interest vary from individual to individual and species to species. Although this point may seem obvious, animal protectionists are often ridiculed for believing all animals are identical or for advocating that farm animals be given the right to vote. Such caricatures (usually based on quotations taken out of context) make easy targets and avoid serious discussion.

Many proponents of invasive research argue that the work is justified by morally relevant differences that exist between the human species and all others. However, by focusing on attributes such as intelligence, empathy, and a sense of moral responsibility (e.g., Fox, 1986; King, 1986), they exclude young children and developmentally delayed adults from moral consideration. Because humans and nonhumans overlap on some of these dimensions (e.g., intelligence, self-awareness), and because young or impaired humans wholly lack other characteristics (e.g., empathy, sense of moral responsibility), there is simply no morally relevant attribute that separates humans from nonhumans. To base ethical decisions on species membership alone in the absence of such an attribute is as arbitrary as relying on skin color or gender in hiring decisions.

The most morally relevant factor in a decision to cause suffering to others is their ability to experience it. Cognitive competence and related abilities are relevant to certain human rights (such as the right to vote), but not to other rights (such as the freedom to move one's limbs or to interact with others). Research justified by consequent human benefit abridges these rights. We feel methods involving inescapable pain, deprivation, or fear are unacceptable because each sentient being, regardless of its other capabilities, has an interest in being spared suffering. Modern-day society rejects the notion of performing painful experiments on humans who are incapable of granting consent, regardless of the benefits which might accrue to others. In the absence of morally relevant distinctions between ourselves and other animals, painful research on sentient nonhumans should be rejected for the same reasons.

THE RESPONSE FROM PSYCHOLOGISTS

Social constructionists and others have recently noted the Western, ethnocentric, and male-dominated agenda of traditional psychological research (Gergen, 1985; Hare-Mustin & Marecek, 1990; Irvine & Berry, 1988). The broad cultural changes represented by the women's movement, environmentalism, and the animal rights movement have been instrumental in fomenting the current debate within psychology regarding animal research, and many analysts now view the practice of invasive laboratory-based research as symptomatic of anthropocentrism in psychology.

Within the psychological community, a growing number of individuals have expressed reservations about animal research on both scientific and ethical grounds (Bowd, 1980, 1990; Fox, 1982; Giannelli, 1985; Segal, 1982; Shapiro, 1991;

Ulrich, 1991). Nonetheless, many psychologists have defended current practices. We will first examine organizational responses and then discuss responses within the professional literature. The focus will be on developments in the United States, though it should be noted that similar debates are taking place among psychologists in Canada, Great Britain, Australia, and other countries.

Organizational Responses

In 1981, the American Psychological Association (APA) amended its Ethics Code to include the treatment of animals (American Psychological Association [APA], 1981). However, the APA Ethics Committee considered only one animal welfare case from 1982 to 1990 (APA, 1991)—a period during which the animal rights movement charged several laboratories with specific animal welfare violations. The Ethics Committee considered the case of Edward Taub, a psychologist who studied deafferentation (the severing of sensory nerves) in macaque monkeys at the Institute for Behavioral Research in Maryland. This case came to light after Alex Pacheco, cofounder of People for the Ethical Treatment of Animals, documented several explicit violations of animal welfare regulations.

According to Principle 10 of the current Ethics Code, researchers must ensure that "The acquisition, care, use and disposal of all animals are in compliance of current Federal, state or provincial, and local laws and regulations" (APA, 1981). After reviewing Pacheco's evidence, the National Institutes of Health (NIH) suspended Taub's grant because of violations in NIH guidelines, and Taub was convicted of cruelty to animals under Maryland law (a verdict that he later appealed). Nevertheless, even though the suspension of funding and the conviction of animal cruelty were known by members of the APA Ethics Committee, the panel cleared Taub of any wrongdoing on a split vote.

A second APA body charged with overseeing animal welfare, the Committee on Animal Research and Ethics (CARE), was established in 1925 "to combat attempts to prevent or restrict [animal experimentation]" (Young, 1928). In fact, the two events that led to the formation of CARE were both legislative efforts, outside APA, to curtail animal research (Young, 1928; Young, 1930). For the first 50 years of its existence, CARE's stated purpose was to defend and protect animal *research*, not *animals*. It was not until the early 1980s that the task of protecting animals was added (CARE, 1980), and even then the meetings continued to focus on the protection of animal research and animal researchers (Bernstein, personal communication, 1990). Furthermore, Field, Shapiro, and Carr (1990) found that the animal research conducted by recent CARE chairs was more invasive than comparable research published in leading journals. Thus, the APA responded to ethical challenges by forming advocacy groups rather than impartial or balanced review panels.

Responses Within the Professional Literature

APA publications have discussed animal welfare with increasing frequency in recent years (Phillips & Sechzer, 1989). However, in its scientific and news publications, the APA often takes a one-sided position (Bowd, 1990). We examined issues of the *APA Monitor* from 1980 to 1986, and found 30 articles and 43 letters dealing with the ethics of animal research. By our estimate, roughly 60% supported animal research and only 10% opposed it explicitly. Similarly, the *American Psychologist* published 17 relevant articles or commentaries during the same period, 10 advocating animal research and 7 opposing it. Of the 5 full-length articles that appeared during this interval, 4 explicitly supported animal research.

A recent article in the *APA Monitor* typifies this slant in coverage. Moses (1991) described how psychology students were upset by a laboratory break-in, but failed to mention a much more widespread source of student concern about animal research—the refusal of faculty to provide alternatives to the laboratory study of animals. In a recent survey of 300 psychology departments, one of the authors (KJS) found that 50% of the departments used animals in education, and of these, only 40% had a policy to accommodate students who objected.

Indeed, not only do APA publications neglect to mention such problems—the APA actively discourages their discussion. For example, the APA refused to sell exhibit space at its 1991 convention to Psychologists for the Ethical Treatment of Animals for the purpose of displaying publications, although other organizations were provided with space to display animal research publications and catalogues of laboratory equipment (Shapiro, 1990).

Turning to the scientific literature, most accounts defend animal research with some version of the following arguments: (1) animal research leads to applications that improve human welfare; (2) the costs to animals are relatively small; (3) whatever harm the animals incur is necessary, because there are no viable alternatives to animal research (Gallup & Suarez, 1985; King, 1984; Miller, 1985).

The tenor of these articles tends to be indignant, adversarial, and defensive. In fact, in their survey of the scientific literature, Phillips and Sechzer (1989) found a marked increase in defensiveness between the 1960s and the 1980s. Gluck and Kubacki (1991) have also described a "strategic defensive posture" assumed by researchers, part of which is to trivialize the issue of animal protection. For example, some researchers trivialize the issue by pointing out that laboratory rats fare better than their uncaged city conspecifics (e.g., Gallup & Suarez, 1987). Typically, there is little empirical evidence offered to support such assertions, and in many cases, the arguments are specious (Shapiro, 1988). For example, Gallup and Suarez (1987) failed to provide evidence about the relative welfare of laboratory and feral rats, although data are available regarding invasiveness of procedures undergone by the former, and Hendrickson (1983) found that rats in urban nonlaboratory settings often proliferate and live quite well. Furthermore, the suffering of laboratory rats is additional; its cost must be added to whatever suffering other rats endure. The argument advanced by Gallup and Suarez (1987) is particularly ironic given their portrayal of scientists as rational and animal activists as illogical and emotional.

Assessment of Costs and Benefits

Miller (1985) and other authors have claimed that animal research generates applications that improve human welfare. However, Kelly (1986) found that in the 1984 volume of the *Journal of Consulting and Clinical Psychology* (a journal devoted to studies of the treatments Miller explicitly linked to animal research), only 0.3% of more than 3,000 citations were of laboratory animal studies. In addition, Giannelli (1985) found that only seven of the 118 citations selected by Miller to demonstrate the value of animal research were listed in the 1985 Association for Advanced Training in the Behavioral Sciences, a well-known and comprehensive course for national licensure in psychology. Even more problematically, the potential benefits of any animal research are indeterminate, for they depend on several unknowns: the applicability of the results to human welfare, the question of whether the study will get published (rejection rates for mainstream psychology journals are over 50%), and more subtly, the *missed benefits of studies not undertaken.* Any research program implies paths not taken.

In contrast to the uncertain benefits from laboratory animal research, the cost to animals is clear and real. Reliable measures of the cost to animals do exist (Field & Shapiro, 1988), yet virtually no published study—or study proposal—presents detailed analyses of the costs of husbandry conditions, experimental procedures, and disposition of the animals. In any case, any analysis of costs to animals presumes they are willing participants. In truth, in the current research enterprise they are commodities produced, confined, and harmed in a system in which they are only incidental beneficiaries. Yet in our Western tradition, individuals have rights that safeguard against their welfare being compromised for the benefit of others. Because of these operational and ethical problems, cost–benefit analyses are an unsatisfactory tool in the assessment of the use of animals in research.

SUGGESTED DIRECTIONS

As an interim strategy, we favor the following: (1) the development of alternatives to laboratory animal research; (2) the specification and prohibition of experimental procedures that are deemed "intrinsically objectionable" (Heim, 1978) —that is, procedures generally agreed to be so invasive that they are objectionable regardless of possible benefits; and (3) a reduced reliance on the search for animal models of complex, culturally generated human phenomena. These practices should replace the hollow, justificatory language of cost–benefit analyses. In the longer term, we favor a shift from laboratory-based invasive research to minimally manipulative research conducted in naturalistic and seminaturalistic settings.

We urge psychologists, individually and through professional societies such as the APA, to (1) establish advocacy committees charged solely with the protection of animals used in psychology-related settings, (2) develop alternatives for students who object to the use of laboratory animals, and (3) include balanced coverage of animal welfare issues and a discussion of ethical issues in professional and textbook publications. Such policies will not only contribute to animal welfare—they will contribute to *human* welfare by broadening the education of tomorrow's psychologists.

CHALLENGE QUESTIONS

Should Animals Be Used in Psychological Research?

1. How and where would you draw the line on the use of animals in research? Even if the use of animals is justified in research that saves human lives, is the use of animals justified in cosmetic or plastic surgery research? Why, or why not?

2. Assuming you were against all instances of animal research, would you turn down medical procedures for yourself or your children because they were developed at the expense of animals? Would there be exceptions, such as vaccinations for your children or a cure for a life-threatening illness?

3. Baldwin makes the case that experimentation with animals has produced many important medical and psychological findings. Are there other types of research that use animals? Is this other research justified? Why, or why not?

4. Baldwin claims that the use of animals in research has been beneficial to animals as well as to humans. Does this claim change the debate?

5. Locate the federal and state regulations on the use and care of animals in psychological research, and evaluate both authors' claims regarding the sufficiency of those regulations.

On the Internet . . .

Ask NOAH About: Mental Health

This enormous resource contains information about child and adolescent family problems, mental conditions and disorders, suicide prevention, and much more, all organized in a "clickable" outline form.
http://www.noah.cuny.edu/illness/mentalhealth/mental.html

Biological Changes in Adolescence

This site offers a discussion of puberty, sexuality and biological changes, cross-cultural differences, and nutrition for adolescents, including obesity and its effects on adolescent development.
http://www.personal.psu.edu/faculty/n/x/nxd10/biologic2.htm

Mental Health Risk Factors for Adolescents

This collection of Web resources is part of the Adolescence Directory On-Line (ADOL), an electronic guide to information on adolescent issues provided by the Center for Adolescent Studies at Indiana University. It covers a great deal of topics, including abuse, conduct disorders, stress, and support.
http://education.indiana.edu/cas/adol/mental.html

Serendip

Organized into five subject areas (brain and behavior, complex systems, genes and behavior, science and culture, and science education), Serendip contains interactive exhibits, articles, links to other resources, and a forum area for comments and discussion.
http://serendip.brynmawr.edu/serendip/

PART 2

Biological Issues

No behavioral or mental activity can take place without biology. Biological processes are fundamental to all mental functions, including emotion, perception, and mental health. Does this mean that differences in behavior are essentially the result of biological differences? Are differences between males and females or between thin people and fat people primarily biological?

■ Is Homosexuality Genetically Determined?

■ Do Evolutionary and Genetic Factors Determine Our Sexual Behaviors?

ISSUE 4

Is Homosexuality Genetically Determined?

YES: J. Michael Bailey and Richard C. Pillard, from "A Genetic Study of Male Sexual Orientation," *Archives of General Psychiatry* (December 1991)

NO: Terry R. McGuire, from "Is Homosexuality Genetic? A Critical Review and Some Suggestions," *Journal of Homosexuality* (vol. 28, no. 1/2, 1995)

ISSUE SUMMARY

YES: Psychologist J. Michael Bailey and psychiatrist Richard C. Pillard argue that studies of homosexual twin pairs indicate a substantial genetic influence on homosexuality.

NO: Terry R. McGuire, a professor of biological sciences, counters that studies that indicate a genetic basis for human homosexuality omit methodological practices that are needed to give credence to the findings.

Homosexuality has long been a controversial issue in psychology. Before 1973 homosexuality was considered abnormal or a sexual deviance. Homosexuals were thought to have an "arrested development" or interpersonal problems that resulted in their preference for sexual relations with the same sex. In 1973, however, psychologists endorsed changes in their diagnostic manual, intentionally omitting homosexuality from the list of possible abnormalities. In effect, homosexuality was now considered a normal variation of sexuality by many mental health professionals.

This diagnostic change, however, did not answer the deeper and perhaps more difficult question: Why are some people homosexual and some people heterosexual? Many psychological, theological, and political issues hinge on the answer to this question. If homosexuality were a learned behavior, then, presumably, homosexuals could *un*learn their sexual orientation. This would mean that a therapeutic change in sexual orientation would be possible if it were desired. On the other hand, if homosexuality were genetically determined, then no amount of psychotherapy could effect any change. Moreover, homosexuals could not change their sexual orientation even if they wanted to. Genetic origins, therefore, would imply a dramatically different set of psychological, political, and theological ramifications than environmental origins would.

The importance of this question has led to many psychological and biological investigations. The oft-cited work of J. Michael Bailey and Richard

C. Pillard has quickly become the standard for homosexuality research. In the following selection, Bailey and Pillard describe how they took samples of identical, fraternal, and adoptive brothers to examine the frequency of same-sex sibling homosexuality. Their rationale is that if homosexuality has a genetic component, then identical twins, who share all their genetic information, should exhibit a greater frequency of similar sexual preference. They report that they did find a greater frequency of homosexuality between identical twins than between fraternal twins or adoptive brothers. Bailey and Pillard contend that their research confirms their hypothesis.

In the second selection, Terry R. McGuire questions Bailey and Pillard's line of research. Citing his own studies on insects, McGuire argues that genetic studies of this nature require a precision that has never been reached in human studies. Without this precision, the data from human studies are almost meaningless. McGuire maintains that the studies of Bailey and Pillard have not come close in terms of the precision that is necessary for meaningful interpretation. Even if the precision were attained, he says, data that fit the genetic model may only deceptively support it. The problem is that twin studies are inherently flawed, according to McGuire. Furthermore, their flaws indicate that the nature-versus-nurture question is the wrong one to be asking.

POINT

- Increased frequency of homosexuality in identical twins supports a genetic link to homosexual behavior.

- If the sampling method of the twins study were corrected, the support for a genetic influence would be strengthened.

- Establishing the genetic basis of homosexuality has important political implications for increasing its acceptance as a natural state.

COUNTERPOINT

- There are substantial problems with genetic models in twin studies, including nonrandom selection and the assumed equality of the environments.

- Because subjects were recruited from homosexual publications and not all their siblings were contacted, the data of the study are severely compromised.

- Genetic explanations of behavior have been used to oppress others more often than they have been used to liberate them.

YES

J. Michael Bailey and Richard C. Pillard

A GENETIC STUDY OF MALE SEXUAL ORIENTATION

During the past decade, there has been a resurgence of interest in biological explanations of sexual orientation. This reflects several lines of scientific research, as well as sociological and historical factors.

First, several competitors to biological explanations have been tested and found wanting. The data testing the psychodynamic hypothesis that during childhood, male homosexuals tend to be distant from their fathers, show small effect size and are causally ambiguous. Anthropologic observations reported by Stoller and Herdt suggest that sexual orientation is not conditioned by sexual experiences in adolescence.

Second, a large literature on animal sexual behavior suggests that mating and other sex dimorphic behaviors are subject to the influence of sex steroid hormones acting on the brain during prenatal and early postnatal development. The sexual behavior of rodents can be altered by manipulating the testosterone level during sexual differentiation of the brain. Prenatally androgenized female monkeys play in a manner more typical of the opposite sex, as do human homosexuals in childhood.

A "neurohormonal" theory of sexual orientation has received direct support from at least four studies of humans. Ehrhardt et al found that women who had been prenatally exposed to diethylstilbestrol, a synthetic estrogen that can exert androgenlike effects during brain differentiation, were more likely to report homosexual feelings than were unexposed controls. Similarly, Money et al found that prenatally androgenized women had a higher incidence of homosexual feelings. Dörner et al and Gladue et al found that homosexual men showed a surge of luteinizing hormone in response to estradiol injections, intermediate to heterosexual women and men, which they interpreted as reflecting a partially female-differentiated brain in male homosexuals. Such research has led to the theory that human sexual orientation depends on variations in the degree of masculinization and behavioral defeminization of the brain that may occur during early periods of sexual differentiation....

A final factor that has increased interest in biological explanations of sexual orientation is the continuing tension between those who view homosexuality as an illness or a sign of moral weakness and those who see it simply as an alternative phenotype, without moral or pathological implications. It appears that one's etiological theory of homosexuality may contribute importantly to one's views on this larger issue. For instance, in American psychiatry, it has been those holding psychodynamic theories about the origin of homosexuality who have been most closely associated with the position that the homosexual is ill.... A recent survey found that those who believed that homosexuals are "born that way" held significantly more positive attitudes toward homosexuals than subjects who believed that homosexuals "choose to be that way" and/or "learn to be that way." ...

Given some evidence for genetic influence, there remains the question of what, exactly, is inherited. One possibility concerns childhood gender nonconformity (CGN), which has been strongly linked to adult homosexuality. In childhood male homosexuals are frequently perceived as "sissies," and female homosexuals are frequently perceived as "tomboys." However, a substantial minority of male and female homosexuals deny a history of CGN. Bell et al have suggested that homosexuals who were gender nonconforming as children may be more "constitutionally" homosexual than those who were more gender typical. A behavioral genetics translation of this hypothesis is that homosexuals with CGN should have a greater genetic loading, and hence should have a higher rate of homosexual relatives, or if twins, should be more likely to have homosexual cotwins.

The study... has two broad goals: first, to determine whether there is a genetic contribution to male sexual orientation; and second, to investigate the behavioral nature of this contribution. The study combines two methods from classical behavioral genetics: the twin method and the adoption method. Three groups of probands were recruited: male MZ [monozygotic] twins, male DZ [dizygotic] twins the same-sex cotwins, and male subjects with adoptively related brothers. We predicted that the rate of homosexuality would be higher for MZ than for DZ cotwins, and would be lowest for adoptive brothers of homosexual probands. We considered the degree to which ascertainment bias may have affected results. We then examined the possibility that CGN might be an indicator of genetic influence....

Fifty-two percent (29/56) of the MZ cotwins were either homosexual or bisexual,... compared with 22% (12/54) of the DZ cotwins and 11% (6/57) of the adoptive brothers. The proportion of bisexuals and homosexuals was significantly greater for MZ cotwins than for either DZ cotwins... or adoptive brothers.... The proportion of homosexuals and bisexuals was greater for DZ twins than for adoptive brothers; however, the difference was only marginally significant....

Focusing on those relatives for whom we have complete data, ie, confirmation by self-report, the picture was similar for the twin comparisons. The proportion of homosexuals among MZ cotwins exceeded that for DZ cotwins.... Similarly, the rate of homosexuality in MZ cotwins remained greater than that rate for adoptive brothers.... However, the rate of homosexuality among DZ cotwins was no longer significantly greater than that for adoptive brothers.... This was primarily due to the decreased likelihood that a proband with a heterosexual adoptive brother would consent to have him contacted: consent was given to contact 30 of 51 heterosexual adoptive brothers; for heterosexual cotwins, this figure was 59 of 67.... There was a high degree of cooperation in both groups when relatives were homosexual: twins allowed contact for 37 of 40 such cases; adoptive brothers allowed this in all six cases. Evidently, adoptive probands were particularly unwilling (or twins particularly willing) to involve their heterosexual adoptive brothers. The cooperation pattern was similar (uniformly high) for MZ and DZ twins: MZ probands authorized contact for 93% (25/27) of their heterosexual cotwins and 93% (26/28) of their homosexual cotwins; the corresponding figures for DZ twins were 85% (34/40) and 92% (11/12).

Heritability of Sexual Orientation

Results of the... analyses suggest that genetic factors are important in determining individual differences in sexual orientation. However, the mere finding that the rates of homosexuality in different types of relatives are consistent with some genetic influence does not provide an estimate of the *magnitude* of that influence. Assuming a multifactorial model of transmission (ie, genetic influence is polygenic and environmental events are many with each of small effect), one can calculate heritabilities from rates of homosexuality in relatives, provided that one has an estimate of the base rate of homosexuality in the general population....

Genetic model fitting capitalizes on the fact that phenotypic correlations between different types of relatives will reflect different degrees of genetic and/or environmental similarity. For example, MZ cotwins share all their genes, DZ cotwins share half (identical by descent), and adoptive brothers share none. Because all three types of relatives studied herein were reared together, they are all perfectly correlated for shared environment. Nonshared environment, by definition, must be uncorrelated for all types of relatives....

[E]stimated heritability remained substantial under a wide variety of assumptions. The estimate of variance attributed to shared environment... ranged from 0... to .23... and was in every case smaller than the estimated heritability. Estimated nonshared environmental variance... ranged from .17... to .69....

The Rate of Homosexuality in Nontwin Brothers

Twin probands reported 142 nontwin brothers about whose sexual orientation they were at least virtually certain. Of these, 13 (9.2%) were thought to be homosexual or bisexual. This percentage is considerably less than one would expect, given a simple model with only additive genetic, shared environmental, and nonshared environmental factors. Specifically, the rate of homosexuality and bisexuality in nontwin brothers was significantly less than the 22% rate found for DZ cotwins.... Furthermore, this rate failed to exceed the analogous rate for adoptive brothers....

CGN

If homosexuals who were gender nonconforming as children are more constitutionally homosexual, and if "constitutional" is taken to mean "heritable," then the twin probands who were most gender nonconforming should be most likely to have homosexual cotwins. Translated into the measures of our study, this hypothesis predicts that for both the MZ and DZ subsamples, probands with homosexual cotwins should have higher scores on the CGN composite than should probands with heterosexual cotwins. If such a pattern occurred due to genetic (and not shared environmental) factors, then there should be no difference in the CGN scores between probands with homosexual adoptive brothers vs those with heterosexual adoptive brothers. Table 1 shows that contrary to the hypothesis, probands with homosexual relatives were not significantly distinguishable from probands with heterosexual relatives on the basis of CGN in any of the three subsamples.... Thus, we found no evidence that the presence of gender nonconformity increases the likelihood of finding homosexual relatives.

A second question concerns the extent to which the different types of relatives resemble each other for CGN. For instance, do heterosexual cotwins of gender-nonconforming MZ probands also report having been gender nonconforming as children? Are homosexual MZ cotwins similar to their proband twins with respect to CGN? Table 1 also contains correlations between probands' and relatives' CGN, separately for homosexual and heterosexual relatives. The only significant correlation was for MZ probands with homosexual cotwins. This correlation ($r = .76$) exceeded the lower-bound reliability estimate of the composite scale. Thus, if twins were both homosexual, they reported a very similar degree of CGN. This contrasted with the correlation ($r = .10$) between MZ probands and their heterosexual cotwins, which is significantly lower ($z = 4.2; P < .001$). Thus, the CGN of MZ cotwins depended on the interaction between their own sexual orientation and the probands' CGN....

Implications for the Genetics of Sexual Orientation

Results of this study confirm the view that Kallmann's finding of perfect concordance for homosexuality for MZ pairs is too high. The 52% rate was similar to both the 50% rate estimated by Pillard et al and the 40% rate found by Heston and Shields, who reported the only systematically ascertained sample of homosexual twins to date. Nevertheless, the pattern of rates of homosexuality by type of relative was generally consistent with substantial genetic influence, with the exception of nontwin brothers, whose rate was lower than that of DZ cotwins and approximately equal to that of adoptive brothers....

Heritability varied according to assumptions regarding the base rate of homosexuality and the degree of ascertainment bias. However, all heritability estimates accounted for a substantial proportion of phenotypic variance. It is not clear that attempts to narrow the heritability estimates within the broad range of estimates obtained should be given high priority. Heritability is not informative regarding the development of sexual orientation (or, for that matter, of any trait). That is, given any heritability estimate, there are a variety of possible developmental mechanisms. For instance, these data are consistent with heritable variation in prenatal brain development or in some aspect of physical appearance that, by way of differential parental treatment, leads to differences in sexual orientation.

Nevertheless, there are at least two ways in which the finding of substantial heritability is important. First, the present study provided some support for the view that sexual orientation is influenced by constitutional factors. This contrasts with previous attempts to test psychodynamic and psychosocial theories, which have largely yielded negative findings, and emphasizes the necessity of considering causal factors arising within the individual, and not just his psychosocial environment.

Second, the demonstration of nonzero heritability for sexual orientation raises the question of how genes for homosexuality could persist despite presumed strong evolutionary counterselection. Bell and Weinberg, for instance, found that adult male homosexuals reported about one fifth the number of children as male heterosexuals....

Moreover, one assumption of the heritability analyses presented above is that there are no major genes for homosexuality, and that any discontinuity is at the phenotypic level. This is a multifactorial threshold model. One alternative to a major gene as an explanation for the bimodality is a developmental process in which factors that cause attraction to female subjects simultaneously inhibit the development of attraction to male subjects. Distinguishing between these possibilities will require further data.

Implications for the Development of Sexual Orientation

Contrary to prior speculation, we found no evidence that homosexuality associated with CGN is more heritable. Homosexuals who behaved like typical boys during childhood do not appear to have been influenced particularly by external events during and after childhood compared with homosexuals who behaved atypically from an early age. Monozygotic pairs concordant for homosexuality tended to be concordant for the degree of childhood gender nonconformity. This suggests that among homosexuals, individual differences in development are largely determined by genetic and/or shared environmental factors. To determine which of these factors is more important for the expression of CGN, it will be useful to study pairs of homosexual relatives, such as homosexual brothers, to see if they report similar levels of CGN. Furthermore and more generally, it would be desirable to focus more attention on the differences between homosexuals who report a history of CGN and those who do not.

NO

Terry R. McGuire

IS HOMOSEXUALITY GENETIC?
A CRITICAL REVIEW AND
SOME SUGGESTIONS

In the past few years there have been a number of studies of the familial nature of homosexuality with heavy emphasis on possible genetic origins. These studies have been carried out for a number of reasons. Bailey and Pillard (1991), for example, suggested that the search for biological explanations for homosexuality (1) reflects the failure of social and psychological explanations, (2) looks instead to neurohormonal mechanisms, and (3) could be politically useful. They write, "A final factor that has increased interest in biological explanations of sexual orientation is the continuing tension between those who view homosexuality as an illness or a sign of moral weakness, and those who see it simply as an alternative phenotype, without moral or pathological implications. It appears that one's etiological theory of homosexuality may contribute importantly to one's views on this larger issue" (p. 1089). These behavior-genetic studies have been widely reported in the popular press although the press often makes claims far beyond those intended by the investigators. For example, Wheeler (1992) reported that one scientist found the Bailey and Pillard (1991) evidence so compelling that he intended to search for the gene or genes that may cause homosexuality. Despite the "hype" of popular press articles, just how compelling is the evidence for a genetic factor in homosexuality?

I have worked extensively with insect behavior genetics. This allows a level of certainty since the implications of my research apply mostly to laboratory-reared insects. Still, I must be careful to use appropriate experimental designs, have adequate sample sizes and control groups, and use suitable genetic models. Even when all of these criteria have been met, in drawing conclusions I must be extremely cautious in generalizing from research on one strain of insects to other strains of the same species.

Genetic analyses of human behavioral differences also require careful experimental design and appropriate genetic models. Any behavior-genetic study must use (1) valid and precise measures of individual differences,

From Terry R. McGuire, "Is Homosexuality Genetic? A Critical Review and Some Suggestions," *Journal of Homosexuality*, vol. 28, no. 1/2 (1995). Copyright © 1995 by Haworth Press, Inc. Reprinted by permission. Notes and references omitted.

(2) appropriate methods to ascertain biological relationships, (3) research subjects that have been randomly recruited, (4) appropriate sample sizes, and (5) appropriate genetic models to interpret the data. In addition, the experimenters must exercise caution in attributing biosocial effects to the observed genetic and phenotypic correlations....

GENETIC MODELS

There is nothing mysterious or magical about genetic models. They are essentially sophisticated guesses about a particular set of phenotypes. Mathematical models are constructed using specific genetic theories....

Recent attention has focused on model fitting that is based on path analyses or path models (Wright, 1968). Path models use variance-covariance matrices to estimate genetic and environmental parameters. The underlying assumption of path models is that the resemblance between any two relatives is a linear sum of genetic and environmental variables. The models are generally quite simple but they require many presuppositions. For example, it is assumed that MZ [monozygotic or "identical"] and DZ [dizygotic or "fraternal"] twins have experienced equal environments (Heath, Neale, Hewitt, Eaves, & Fulker, 1989) and have been randomly selected. It is further assumed that the behavior of interest is either continuously or dichotomously variable. If the latter, it is assumed that the behavior must represent an underlying normal distribution. Generally only additive genetic values can be estimated. Genetic dominance, for example, cannot be estimated unless other parameters are removed. Complex interactions such as epistasis or effects of assortative mating can not be represented in the model.... Even a good fit to the data does not prove that the model is correct. As Neale et al. (p. 46) have stated, "On the contrary, the model could be completely and utterly false yet give a good account of the observed data." Researchers also often evaluate alternative models without actually determining if any of the parameters of that model are significantly different from zero. Exploring biometrical genetic models as a first step can be quite interesting. They are extremely limited, however, and one must be cautious in interpreting the results.

BEHAVIOR GENETICS STUDIES OF HOMOSEXUALITY

There are three methods available for human behavior genetics: family studies, twin studies, and adoption studies. Only the first two have been attempted with homosexuality. All of these studies share common problems, including nonrandom recruitment and small sample size.

Family Studies

The underlying presupposition of family studies is that behavioral resemblance between relatives should be a function of the number of genes (and interactions) that the relatives share. For example, parents and offspring share $1/2$ of their genes but none of their genetic interactions. Full sibs share $1/2$ of their genes as well as $1/4$ of their dominance and some of their epistatic interactions....

In a family study it is extremely important that family members have been reared in equivalent environments and that the same behavior is measured at the same age with the same tests. Determining equivalency of environments is especially difficult in multigenerational studies. Measuring all family members at the same age with the same test is nearly impossible for multigenerational studies and awkward for sibling studies. If one uses different tests, then it is difficult to interpret any correlations. Using individuals of different ages may or may not affect the results depending on the particular behavior studied. In family studies of homosexuality it is inappropriate to compare adults to adolescents.

There have been few systematic family studies of homosexuality; most are anecdotal. For example, Dank (1971) described six homosexual siblings who had a very abusive, alcoholic father. His findings paralleled those of Heston and Shields (1968), who studied a family of 14 siblings, with two sets of MZ twins who were both homosexual. Their family resembled Dank's family in the descriptions of the father and mother. These two reports, however, were case studies, not family studies. Henry (1948) studied family trees for a number of homosexuals. He collected his information from the subjects and lumped a variety of traits (e.g., artistic ability, venereal disease, alcoholism, psychopathology, homosexuality, promiscuity, and bisexuality). As such, his family trees are essentially useless....

Twin Studies

At first glance, using twins seem to be the ideal method of studying human behavior genetics. Price (1950, p. 293) has stated that "monozygotic twins are 'experiments' which nature has conducted for us, starting in each case with identical sets of genes and varying environmental factors." There are two ways of conducting twin studies. One is to find monozygotic twins (also called MZ twins, one-egg twins, or identical twins)

who have been separated at birth. If they are MZ twins and they had been randomly placed into families, then the behavioral trait for which they correlate is genetic.... The other twin method compares sets of MZ twins to sets of dizygotic twins (also known as DZ twins, two-egg twins, and fraternal twins). If MZ and DZ twins experience equal environments, and one makes a number of simplifying assumptions, then heritability can be estimated. Such heritability estimates are often the only goal of twin studies, including those of homosexuality.

Twin studies are often used to calculate heritability (h^2). MZ twins share all of their additive genetic variance (V_a), all of their dominance genetic variance (V_d), and all of their epistatic interaction variance (for only two genes V_{aa}, V_{ad}, V_{dd}). The usual method of calculating heritability is to calculate the intraclass correlations for MZ twins and DZ twins. If one assumes equal environments, no dominance variance, and no interaction variance, then the difference between the MZ and DZ correlations equals $1/2h^2$ (Falconer, 1981). If there is dominance and epistasis, the estimate of h^2 is widely biased. The heritability estimate includes not only additive variance, if any, but $3/2\ V_d$ and $3/2\ V_{aa} + 7/4\ V_{ad} + 15/8\ V_{dd}$. Even modest amounts of V_d, V_{aa}, V_{ad}, or V_{dd} would vastly overestimate the genetic contribution *even if there were absolutely no additive genetic variance*. In most models, the contribution of the environmental effects depend on the accurate estimate of heritability. Inflating the heritability term must necessarily deflate the environmental terms (see Haviland, McGuire, & Rothbaum, 1983, p. 638).

Twin Studies of Homosexuality

Most twin studies of homosexuality are anecdotal accounts of concordant (both twins are homosexual) or discordant (only one twin is homosexual) twin pairs....

Bailey and Pillard's (1991) study was widely reported in the popular press. As with other studies, Bailey and Pillard (1991) had the problem of non-random recruitment of subjects and uneven cooperation of family members. All subject recruitment was through gay publications in the Midwest and Southwest. They obtained 115 twins and 46 subjects with an adoptive brother. Subjects were interviewed either in person or by telephone. These 161 subjects had 174 qualified relatives. Permission was granted to contact only 135 of the relatives. Of these only 127 relatives returned the questionnaires. They also used the reports of the subject to identify the sexual orientation of their relatives (113 co-twins and 57 adoptive brothers). In addition, twin subjects were asked about non-twin brothers, although the latter were not contacted.

The researchers relied heavily on questionnaires. Zygosity was based entirely on a questionnaire. The relatives answered 5 questionnaire items about sexual preference.... Four different instruments were used to measure homosexuality: (1) personal interviews of index cases, (2) telephone interviews, (3) questionnaire answers, and (4) rating by co-twin.... Using ratings derived from questionnaire responses, the concordance rates of MZ twins was 50% (25 out of 50), DZ twins was 24% (11 out of 46), and adopted brothers was 19% (6 out of 31). Adopted brothers were not significantly different from DZ twins. Bailey and Pillard attributed this result to sampling error. That is, heterosexual adoptive brothers were not allowed to be contacted. Of non-twin biological brothers (13 out of 142), 9.2% were reported to be homosexual, a percentage no greater than that for adopted brothers.

Such results are problematic. The greater MZ vs. DZ correlations could be due to differential environmental effects, recruitment bias, substantially shared environments, additive genetic effects, or substantial non-additive genetic effects. The fact that biological brothers and adopted brothers show the same incidence of homosexuality strongly suggests that it is entirely environmental in origin. Bailey and Pillard downplay this comparison which seriously weakens their biological argument, by invoking the Pillard and Weinrich (1986) study. I have already shown that study has profound problems of its own and its results cannot rescue the weak results of this subsequent study.

Bailey and Pillard (1991) estimate heritability using tetrachoric correlations and model fitting. No standard errors of the heritability estimates are reported. It is quite possible that the heritability estimates are not significantly different from either zero or one since very large numbers of twins must be tested to get an accurate estimate. Rather than estimating heritability directly, Bailey and Pillard use model fitting. That is, they found an estimate of heritability that made their particular model work. However, it is inappropriate to try to fit alternative models without evaluating the significance of each parameter contained within that model.

King and McDonald (1992) investigated factors within a twin pair that might lead to homosexuality. They recruited 46 homosexual men and women who were twins through advertisements in local and national gay publications in Britain. These subjects completed a questionnaire about themselves and their co-twin. In addition, they answered questions about sexual attraction toward, and sexual interaction with, their co-twin. Information was not confirmed by the co-twins. Zygosity was determined by asking the subjects if they were monozygotic or dizygotic twins. This study shares all of the problems of the previous four twin studies.

King and McDonald did not find any evidence for a genetic basis of homosexuality. Only 9 of the co-twins were rated as homosexual or bisexual (5 out of 15 MZ twins and 3 out of 22 DZ twins). The researchers also reported that 7 of the twins (6 MZ, 1 DZ) had had sexual contact with their same-sex twin. In five of these seven cases, however, the co-twin was regarded as heterosexual. Obviously, the data in this study are no stronger than the data in the other four studies. King and McDonald suggest, however, that it is time to look at the dynamics of the twin relationship. They state a "more detailed exploration of the sexual relationships between twins and their later development may cast more light on the origins of sexuality than a narrow search for genetic factors" (p. 409).

SOCIAL IMPLICATIONS OF GENETIC MODELS

Research on humans is often used for political or social purposes. For example, some people want homosexuality to be biological or genetic because they then believe that because homosexuals are "born that way" they will somehow be tolerated. Others advocate environmental explanations since this justifies their belief that individuals "chose a gay lifestyle." I am all too conscious of the sordid history of eugenics in the United States where pseudogenetics has been used an an instrument of oppression. For example, studies of poor Southern whites who were characterized as "shiftless lazy white trash" tried to show that their behavior was genetic. We now know that their lethargy was due to chronic hookworm infection (Chase, 1980). More recently, people advocated incarcerating XYY males at birth because they were destined to become violent criminals (Reilly, 1977, pp. 238–248). The political decision to back a genetic explanation for homosexuality is a two-edged sword; it can alleviate discrimination or it might lead to another round of eugenics.

CONCLUSIONS

The evidence for a genetic component for homosexuality is hardly overwhelming. Numerous studies that purport to prove the existence of a genetic aspect to homosexuality are either anecdotal or seriously flawed. Homosexuality is often poorly defined and researchers use a variety of behavioral measures. The sample sizes are too small and recruitment of subjects is biased. As a result, only the simplest possible genetic models can be applied. At best, there might be a modest familial effect to account for populational variance, although the significance of such an effect is impossible to assess. It is very difficult to determine whether a hypothesized familial factor is due to additive genetic, emergent genetic, environmental, or random effects.

If researchers continue to pursue this type of investigation of homosexuality, then, at a minimum, they should be expected to adhere to scientific standards. The "glamour" of working on controversial behaviors must not be a substitute for scientific rigor. Researchers working with traits that are stigmatized must be even more rigorous in their methodology and extremely careful in generalizing their data.

Even if one could design a human-behavior genetic study that met all of the requisite criteria, one could ask, "What do you intend to learn from twin and family studies of homosexuality?" Partitioning the variance of a population tells us nothing about an individual's sexual orientation or about the etiology of any particular trait. There is no compelling reason to estimate heritability unless one is going to selectively breed for the trait. Heritability will not lead one to discover its etiology.

As a culture, the West is obsessed with causality and dichotomy. Just as many researchers persist in asserting a homosexual/heterosexual dichotomy, most people want to have homosexuality attributed either to a genetic or an environmental factor. At best, they wish to know *how much* of the trait is genetic and how much is environmental. This nature-nurture dichotomy can never be resolved because it is false. Genetically identical animals reared in identical laboratory environments are often very different. Such variation is generally attributed to unseen environmental differences. The variation, could just as easily be due to differences in the timing of developmental events. The process of growing from a single cell to a functional adult is chaotic and dynamic (Gleik, 1988). Even if we knew absolutely everything about genes and absolutely everything about environments, we still could not predict the final phenotype of any individual. It is very likely that behavior, in general, and sexual identity, in particular, are results of idiosyncratic processes. Minor events can be amplified to have major effects. The nature-nurture dichotomy should be retired once and for all.

CHALLENGE QUESTIONS

Is Homosexuality Genetically Determined?

1. What would be the implications for psychotherapy with homosexuals if homosexuality were proven to be biologically determined? What if homosexuality were proven to be a learned characteristic?

2. Psychological researchers often say, "Correlation does not mean causation." That is, a high or a significant correlational finding does not necessarily prove a causal relation. Do you think Bailey and Pillard make the assumption that correlational data indicate a causal relation? Why, or why not?

3. Scientists currently working on the Human Genome Project are learning how to perform gene therapy (which allows scientists to manipulate genetic sequences of DNA). Is it appropriate for such scientists to look for DNA sequence structures that account for homosexuality? Is it appropriate for scientists to alter the DNA of a fetus that might identify the individual as homosexual? Why, or why not?

4. McGuire claims that we are asking the wrong question when we look for either biological or environmental causes of behavior. Why does he make this claim? What alternative question does he offer?

ISSUE 5

Do Evolutionary and Genetic Factors Determine Our Sexual Behaviors?

YES: Robert Wright, from "Our Cheating Hearts," *Time* (August 15, 1994)

NO: Richard N. Williams, from "Science or Story Telling? Evolutionary Explanations of Human Sexuality," An Original Essay Written for this Volume (1995)

ISSUE SUMMARY

YES: Robert Wright, a senior editor of *The New Republic*, claims that it is natural for people to commit adultery because human sexual behavior is determined by their genes.

NO: Theoretical psychologist Richard N. Williams questions the evidence supporting Wright's claim and argues that the philosophy underlying genetic explanations of human behavior is dangerous.

There is perhaps no explanation that has more excited scientists in the last century than that of evolution. The main contribution of Charles Darwin (1809–1882) to this theory is a mechanism for the evolution of species—natural selection. In essence, Darwin proposed that nature, or the environment, "selects" the species that survive and the species that become extinct. Some species are better adapted for some environmental niches, so they thrive and even endow their offspring with genetic advantages that further their adaptability.

As history shows, this mechanism of natural selection allowed the popularity of evolutionary explanations to explode. Suddenly, all types of phenomena were explained as evolutionary processes, including psychological phenomena. For instance, immediate comparisons were made between the evolution of the species and the evolution of a person's behaviors and personality.

What accounts for the popularity of evolutionary explanations? Proponents of evolution will contend that the empirical evidence is strongly supportive of Darwin's theory. However, the evidence and its strength are somewhat in the eye of the beholder. Moreover, history has repeatedly shown that some popular explanations become overly extended to arenas that are inappropriate. Could the connections between evolutionary theory and psychological phenomena, such as human sexuality, be an instance of inappropriate theory extension?

In the following selection, Robert Wright asserts that the connections are appropriate. Indeed, he describes a new and growing subdiscipline called *evolutionary psychology* that argues for just such connection making. Wright argues that the natural, evolved characteristics of men and women determine marital fidelity and contends that lifelong monogamy is not as "natural" as many might think. He argues, instead, that natural selection favors genes that incline men and women to eventually sour on a mate. He suggests that evolution has invented romantic love and also corrupted it.

Richard N. Williams, in an original response, argues that evolutionary explanations have been overextended by Wright and others, perhaps dangerously so. Although Wright seems to be reporting the facts of human sexuality, claims Williams, his evidence is composed primarily of stories and analogies —not scientific data. In addition, a closer look at genetic evidence, according to Williams, shows that our genes are responsible for *physical* structures, not particular *mental* events or behaviors. Although evolutionary theory may make a good story, he says it does not make for good science, at least in this instance.

POINT	COUNTERPOINT
• By studying how natural selection shaped the mind, evolutionary psychologists are painting a new portrait of human nature.	• Evolutionary accounts of our behavior are not based on scientific findings; they are more storytelling than fact.
• Natural selection indicates that genes incline men and women to sour on a mate after long periods.	• Genes cannot be aware of "outside romantic opportunities" and motivate us to act on them.
• Human beings are designed to fall in love. Unfortunately, they are not designed to stay there.	• The consequence of such explanations is the loss of our very humanity, because without agency and relationships, there is no humanity in our lives.
• Evolutionary psychology can establish how evolution and genetic factors influence psychological factors.	• Science has never established that psychological or mental events are produced by genetic material.

YES

Robert Wright

OUR CHEATING HEARTS

The language of zoology used to be so reassuring. Human beings were called a "pair-bonding" species. Lasting monogamy, it seemed, was natural for us, just as it was for geese, swans and the other winged creatures that have filled our lexicon with such labels as "lovebirds" and "lovey-dovey." Family values, some experts said, were in our genes. In the 1967 best seller *The Naked Ape*, zoologist Desmond Morris wrote with comforting authority that the evolutionary purpose of human sexuality is "to strengthen the pair-bond and maintain the family unit."

This picture has lately acquired some blemishes. To begin with, birds are no longer such uplifting role models. Using DNA fingerprinting, ornithologists can now check to see if a mother bird's mate really is the father of her offspring. It turns out that some female chickadees (as in "my little chickadee") indulge in extramarital trysts with males that outrank their mates in the social hierarchy. For female barn swallows, it's a male with a long tail that makes extracurriculars irresistible. The innocent-looking indigo bunting has a cuckoldry rate of 40%. And so on. The idea that most bird species are truly monogamous has gone from conventional wisdom to punctured myth in a few short years. As a result, the fidelity of other pair-bonding species has fallen under suspicion.

Which brings us to the other problem with the idea that humans are by nature enduringly monogamous: humans. Of course, you don't need a Ph.D. to see that till-death-do-we-part fidelity doesn't come as naturally to people as, say, eating. But an emerging field known as evolutionary psychology can now put a finer point on the matter. By studying how the process of natural selection shaped the mind, evolutionary psychologists are painting a new portrait of human nature, with fresh detail about the feelings and thoughts that draw us into marriage—or push us out.

The good news is that human beings are designed to fall in love. The bad news is that they aren't designed to stay there. According to evolutionary psychology, it is "natural" for both men and women—at some times, under some circumstances—to commit adultery or to sour on a mate, to suddenly find a spouse unattractive, irritating, wholly unreasonable. (It may even be natural to *become* irritating and wholly unreasonable, and thus hasten the departure of a mate you've soured on.) It is similarly natural to find some attractive colleague superior on all counts to the sorry wreck of a spouse you're saddled with. When we see a couple celebrate a golden anniversary, one apt reaction is the famous remark about a dog walking on two legs: the point is not that the feat was done well but that it was done at all.

All of this may sound like cause for grim resignation to the further decline of the American family. But what's "natural" isn't necessarily unchangeable. Evolutionary psychology, unlike past gene-centered views of human nature, illuminates the tremendous flexibility of the human mind and the powerful role of environment in shaping behavior. In particular, evolutionary psychology shows how inhospitable the current social environment is to monogamy. And while the science offers no easy cures, it does suggest avenues for change.

* * *

The premise of evolutionary psychology is simple. The human mind, like any other organ, was designed for the purpose of transmitting genes to the next generation; the feelings and thoughts it creates are best understood in these terms. Thus the feeling of hunger, no less than the stomach, is here because it helped keep our ancestors alive long enough to reproduce and rear their young. Feelings of lust, no less than the sex organs, are here because they aided reproduction directly. Any ancestors who lacked stomachs or hunger or sex organs or lust—well, they wouldn't have become ancestors, would they? Their traits would have been discarded by natural selection.

This logic goes beyond such obviously Darwinian feelings as hunger and lust. According to evolutionary psychologists, our everyday, ever shifting attitudes toward a mate or prospective mate —trust, suspicion, rhapsody, revulsion, warmth, iciness—are the handiwork of natural selection that remain with us today because in the past they led to behaviors that helped spread genes.

How can evolutionary psychologists be so sure? In part, their faith rests on the whole data base of evolutionary biology. In all sorts of species, and in organs ranging from brains to bladders, nature's attention to the subtlest aspects of genetic transmission is evident. Consider the crafting of primate testicles—specifically, their custom tailoring to the monogamy, or lack thereof, of females. If you take a series of male apes and weigh their testicles (not recommended, actually), you will find a pattern. Chimpanzees and other species with high "relative testes weight" (testes weight in comparison to body weight) feature quite promiscuous females. Species with low relative testes weight are either fairly monogamous (gibbons, for example) or systematically polygynous (gorillas), with one male monopolizing a harem of females. The explanation is simple. When females breed with many males, male genes can profit by producing lots of semen for their own transportation. Which male succeeds in getting his genes into a given egg may be a question of sheer volume, as competing hordes of sperm do battle.

THE TROUBLE WITH WOMEN

Patterns like these, in addition to showcasing nature's ingenuity, allow a kind of detective work. If testicles evolved to match female behavior, then they are clues to the natural behavior of females. Via men's testicles, we can peer through the mists of prehistory and see how women behaved in the social environment of our evolution, free from the influence of modern culture; we can glimpse part of a pristine female mind.

The relative testes weight of humans falls between that of the chimpanzee and the gorilla. This suggests that women, while not nearly so wild as chimpanzee females (who can be veritable sex machines), are by nature somewhat adventurous. If they were not, why would natural selection divert precious resources to the construction and maintenance of weighty testicles?

There is finer evidence, as well, of natural female infidelity. You might think that the number of sperm cells in a husband's ejaculate would depend only on how long it has been since he last had sex. Wrong. What matters more, according to a recent study, is how long his mate has been out of sight. A man who hasn't had sex for, say, a week will have a higher sperm count if his wife was away on a business trip than if she's been home with the flu. In short, what really counts is whether the woman has had the opportunity to stray. The more chances she has had to collect sperm from other males, the more profusely her mate sends in his own troops. Again: that natural selection designed such an elaborate weapon is evidence of something for the weapon to combat—female faithlessness.

So here is problem No. 1 with the pair-bond thesis: women are not by nature paragons of fidelity. Wanderlust is an innate part of their minds, ready to surface under propitious circumstances. Here's problem No. 2: if you think women are bad, you should see men.

THE TROUBLE WITH MEN

With men too, clues from physiology help uncover the mind. Consider "sexual dimorphism"—the difference between average male and female body size. Extreme sexual dimorphism is typical of a polygynous species, in which one male may impregnate several females, leaving other males without offspring. Since the winning males usually secure their trophies by fighting or intimidating other males, the genes of brawny, aggressive males get passed on while the genes of less formidable males are deposited in the dust-bin of history. Thus male gorillas, who get a whole haremful of mates if they win lots of fights and no mates if they win none, are twice as big as females. With humans, males are about 15% bigger—sufficient to suggest that male departures from monogamy, like female departures, are not just a recent cultural invention.

Anthropology offers further evidence. Nearly 1,000 of the 1,154 past or present human societies ever studied—and these include most of the world's "hunter-gatherer" societies—have permitted a man to have more than one wife. These are the closest things we have to living examples of the "ancestral environment" —the social context of human evolution, the setting for which the mind was designed. The presumption is that people reared in such societies—the !Kung San of southern Africa, the Ache of Paraguay, the 19th century Eskimo—behave fairly "naturally." More so, at least, than people reared amid influences that weren't part of the ancestral environment: TVs, cars, jail time for bigamy.

There are vanishingly few anthropological examples of systematic female polygamy, or polyandry—women monopolizing sexual access to more than one man at once. So, while both sexes are prone under the right circumstances to infidelity, men seem much more deeply inclined to actually acquire a second or third mate—to keep a harem.

They are also more inclined toward the casual fling. Men are less finicky about sex partners. Prostitution—sex with someone you don't know and don't care to know—is a service sought overwhelmingly by males the world round. And almost all pornography that relies sheerly on visual stimulation—images of anonymous people, spiritless flesh—is consumed by males.

Many studies confirm the more discriminating nature of women. One evolutionary psychologist surveyed men and women about the minimal level of intelligence they would accept in a person they were "dating." The average response for both male and female: average intelligence. And how smart would the potential date have to be before they would consent to sex? Said the women: Oh, in that case, markedly above average. Said the men: Oh, in that case, markedly below average.

There is no dispute among evolutionary psychologists over the basic source of this male open-mindedness. A woman, regardless of how many sex partners she has, can generally have only one offspring a year. For a man, each new mate offers a real chance for pumping genes into the future. According to the *Guinness Book of Records,* the most prolific human parent in world history was Moulay ("The Bloodthirsty") Ismail, the last Sharifian Emperor of Morocco, who died in 1727. He fathered more than 1,000 children.

This logic behind undiscerning male lust seems obvious now, but it wasn't always. Darwin had noted that in species after species the female is "less eager than the male," but he never figured out why. Only in the late 1960s and early 1970s did biologists George Williams and Robert Trivers attribute the raging libido of males to their nearly infinite potential rate of reproduction.

WHY DO WOMEN CHEAT?

Even then the female capacity for promiscuity remained puzzling. For women, more sex doesn't mean more offspring. Shouldn't they focus on quality rather than quantity—look for a robust, clever mate whose genes may bode well for the offspring's robustness and cleverness? There's ample evidence that women are drawn to such traits, but in our species genes are not all a male has to offer. Unlike our nearest ape relatives, we are a species of "high male-parental investment." In every known hunter-gatherer culture, marriage is the norm—not necessarily monogamous marriage, and not always lasting marriage, but marriage of some sort; and via this institution, fathers help provide for their children.

In our species, then, a female's genetic legacy is best amplified by a mate with two things: good genes and much to invest. But what if she can't find one man who has both? One solution would be to trick a devoted, generous and perhaps wealthy but not especially brawny or brainy mate into raising the offspring of another male. The woman need not be aware of this strategy, but at some level, conscious or unconscious, deft timing is in order. One study found that women who cheat on mates tend to do so around ovulation, when they are most likely to get pregnant.

For that matter, cheating during the infertile part of the monthly cycle might have its own logic, as a way (unconsciously) to turn the paramour into a dupe; the woman extracts goods or services from him in exchange for his fruitless conquest. Of course the flowers he buys may not help her genes, but in the ancestral environment, less frivolous gifts—notably food—would have. Nisa, a woman in a !Kung San hunter-gatherer village, told an anthropologist that "when you have lovers, one brings you something and another brings you something else. One comes at night with meat, another with money, another with beads. Your husband also does things and gives them to you."

Multiple lovers have other uses too. The anthropologist Sarah Blaffer Hrdy has theorized that women copulate with more than one man to leave several men under the impression that they might be the father of particular offspring. Then, presumably, they will treat the offspring kindly. Her theory was inspired by langur monkeys. Male langurs sometimes kill infants sired by others as a kind of sexual icebreaker, a prelude to pairing up with the (former) mother. What better way to return her to ovulation—by putting an emphatic end to her breast-feeding—and to focus her energies on the offspring to come?

Anyone tempted to launch into a sweeping indictment of langur morality should first note that infanticide on grounds of infidelity has been acceptable in a number of human societies. Among the Yanomamö of South America and the Tikopia of the Solomon Islands, men have been known to demand, upon marrying women with a past, that their babies be killed. And Ache men sometimes collectively decide to kill a newly fatherless child. For a woman in the ancestral environment, then, the benefits of multiple sex partners could have ranged from their sparing her child's life to their defending or otherwise investing in her youngster.

Again, this logic does not depend on a conscious understanding of it. Male langurs presumably do not grasp the concept of paternity. Still, genes that make males sensitive to cues that certain infants may or may not carry their genes have survived. A gene that says, "Be nice to children if you've had lots of sex with their mothers," will prosper over the long haul.

THE INVENTION AND CORRUPTION OF LOVE

Genes don't talk, of course. They affect behavior by creating feelings and thoughts—by building and maintaining the brain. Whenever evolutionary psychologists talk about some evolved behavioral tendency—a polygamous or monogamous bent, say, or male parental investment—they are also talking about an underlying mental infrastructure.

The advent of male parental investment, for example, required the invention of a compelling emotion: paternal love. At some point in our past, genes that inclined a man to love his offspring began to flourish at the expense of genes that promoted remoteness. The reason, presumably, is that changes in circumstance —an upsurge in predators, say—made it more likely that the offspring of undevoted, unprotective fathers would perish.

Crossing this threshold meant love not only for the child; the first step toward becoming devoted parents consists of the man and woman developing a mutual attraction. The genetic payoff of having two parents committed to a child's welfare seems to be the central reason men and women can fall into swoons over one another.

Until recently, this claim was heresy. "Romantic love" was thought to be the unnatural invention of Western culture. The Mangaians of Polynesia, for instance, were said to be "puzzled" by references to marital affection. But lately anthropologists have taken a second look at purportedly loveless cultures, including the Mangaians, and have discovered what nonanthropologists already knew: love between man and woman is a human universal.

In this sense the pair-bonding label is apt. Still, that term—and for that matter the term love—conveys a sense of permanence and symmetry that is wildly misleading. Evolution not only invented romantic love but from the beginning also corrupted it. The corruption lies in conflicts of interest inherent in male parental investment. It is the goal of maximizing male investment, remember, that sometimes leads a woman to infidelity. Yet it is the preciousness of this investment that makes her infidelity lethal to her mate's interests. Not long for this world are the genes of a man who showers time and energy on children who are not his.

Meanwhile, male parental investment also makes the man's naturally polygynous bent inimical to his wife's reproductive interests. His quest for a new wife could lead him to withdraw, or at least dilute, investment in his first wife's children. This reallocation of resources may on balance help his genes but certainly not hers.

The living legacy of these long-running genetic conflicts is human jealousy— or, rather, human jealousies. In theory, there should be two kinds of jealousy —one male and one female. A man's jealousy should focus on sexual infidelity, since cuckoldry is the greatest genetic threat he faces. A woman, though she'll hardly applaud a partner's strictly sexual infidelity (it does consume time and divert some resources), should be more concerned with emotional infidelity—the sort of magnetic commitment to another woman that could lead to a much larger shift in resources.

David Buss, an evolutionary psychologist at the University of Michigan, has confirmed this prediction vividly. He placed electrodes on men and women and had them envision their mates doing various disturbing things. When men imagined sexual infidelity, their heart rates took leaps of a magnitude typically induced by three cups of coffee. They sweated. Their brows wrinkled. When they imagined a budding emotional attachment, they calmed down, though not quite to their normal level. For women, things were reversed: envisioning emotional infidelity—redirected love, not supplementary sex—brought the deeper distress.

That jealousy is so finely tuned to these forms of treachery is yet more evidence that they have a long evolutionary history. Still, the modern environment has carried them to new heights, making marriage dicier than ever. Men and women have always, in a sense, been designed to make each other miserable, but these days they are especially good at it.

MODERN OBSTACLES TO MONOGAMY

To begin with, infidelity is easier in an anonymous city than in a small hunter-gatherer village. Whereas paternity studies show that 2% of the children in a !Kung San village result from cuckoldry, the rate runs higher than 20% in some modern neighborhoods.

Contraceptive technology may also complicate marriage. During human evolution, there were no condoms or birth-control pills. If an adult couple slept together for a year or two and produced no baby, the chances were good that one of them was not fertile. No way of telling which one, but from their genes' point of view, there was little to lose and much to gain by ending the partnership and finding a new mate. Perhaps, some have speculated, natural selection favored genes inclining men and women to sour on a mate after long periods of sex without issue. And it is true that barren marriages are especially likely to break up.

Another possible challenge to monogamy in the modern world lies in movies, billboards and magazines. There was no photography in the long-ago world that shaped the human male mind. So at some deep level, that mind may respond to glossy images of pinups and fashion models as if they were viable mates —alluring alternatives to dull, monogamous devotion. Evolutionary psychologist Douglas Kenrick has suggested as much. According to his research, men who are shown pictures of *Playboy* models later describe themselves as less in love with their wives than do men shown other images. (Women shown pictures from *Playgirl* felt no such attitude adjustment toward spouses.)

Perhaps the largest modern obstacle to lasting monogamy is economic inequality. To see why, it helps to grasp a subtle point made by Donald Symons, author of the 1979 classic *The Evolution of Human Sexuality*. Though men who leave their wives may be driven by "natural" impulses, that does not mean men have a natural impulse designed expressly to make them leave their wives. After all, in the ancestral environment, gaining a second wife didn't mean leaving the first. So why leave her? Why not stay near existing offspring and keep giving some support? Symons believes men are designed less for opportune desertion than for opportune polygyny. It's just that when polygyny is illegal, a polygynous impulse will find other outlets, such as divorce.

If Symons is right, the question of what makes a man feel the restlessness that leads to divorce can be rephrased: What circumstances, in the ancestral environment, would have permitted the acquisition of a second wife? Answer: possessing markedly more resources, power or social status than the average Joe.

Even in some "egalitarian" hunter-gatherer societies, men with slightly more status or power than average are slightly more likely to have multiple wives. In less egalitarian pre-industrial societies, the anthropologist Laura Betzig has shown, the pattern is dramatic. In Incan society, the four political offices from petty chief to chief were allotted ceilings of seven, eight, 15 and 30 women. Polygyny reaches its zenith under the most despotic regimes. Among the Zulu, where coughing or sneezing at the king's dinner table was punishable by death, his highness might monopolize more than 100 women.

To an evolutionary psychologist, such numbers are just extreme examples of a simple fact: the ultimate purpose of the wealth and power that men seek so ardently is genetic proliferation. It is only natural that the exquisitely flexible human mind should be designed to capitalize on this power once it is obtained.

Thus it is natural that a rising corporate star, upon getting a big promotion, should feel a strong attraction to women other than his wife. Testosterone —which expands a male's sexual appetite —has been shown to rise in nonhuman primates following social triumphs, and there are hints that it does so in human males too. Certainly the world is full of triumphant men—Johnny Carson, Donald Trump—who trade in aging wives for younger, more fertile models. (The multi-wived J. Paul Getty said, "A lasting relationship with a woman is only possible if you are a business failure.")

A man's exalted social status can give his offspring a leg up in life, so it's natural that women should lust after the high-status men who lust after them. Among the Ache, the best hunters also have more extramarital affairs and more illegitimate children than lesser hunters. In modern societies, contraception keeps much of this sex appeal from translating into offspring. But last year a study by Canadian anthropologist Daniel Pérusse found that single men of high socioeconomic status have sex with more partners than lower-status men.

One might think that the appeal of rich or powerful men is losing its strength. After all, as more women enter the work force, they can better afford to premise their marital decisions on something other than a man's income. But we're dealing here with deep romantic attractions, not just conscious calculation, and these feelings were forged in a different environment. Evolutionary psychologists have shown that the tendency of women to place greater emphasis than men on a mate's financial prospects remains strong regardless of the income or expected income of the women in question.

The upshot of all this is that economic inequality is monogamy's worst enemy. Affluent men are inclined to leave their aging wives, and young women —including some wives of less affluent men—are inclined to offer themselves as replacements.

Objections to this sort of analysis are predictable: "But people leave marriages for emotional reasons. They don't add up their offspring and pull out their calculators." True. But emotions are just evolution's executioners. Beneath the thoughts and feelings and temperamental differences marriage counselors spend their time sensitively assessing are the stratagems of the genes—cold, hard equations composed of simple variables: social status, age of spouse, number of children, their ages, outside romantic opportunities and so on. Is the wife really duller and more nagging than she was 20 years ago? Maybe, but maybe the husband's tolerance for nagging has dropped now that she is 45 and has no reproductive future. And the promotion he just got, which has already drawn some admiring glances from a young woman at work, has not helped.

Similarly, we might ask the young, childless wife who finds her husband intolerably insensitive why the insensitivity wasn't so oppressive a year ago, before he lost his job and she met the kindly, affluent bachelor who seems to be flirting with her. Of course, maybe her husband's abuses are quite real, in which case they signal his disaffection and perhaps his impending departure—and merit just the sort of pre-emptive strike the wife is now mustering.

THE FALLOUT FROM MONOGAMY'S DEMISE

Not only does male social inequality favor divorce. Divorce can also reinforce male social inequality; it is a tool of class exploitation. Consider Johnny Carson. Like many wealthy, high-status males, he spent his career dominating the reproductive years of a series of women. Somewhere out there is a man who wanted a family and a pretty wife and, if it hadn't been for Johnny Carson, would have married one of these women. And if this man has managed to find another woman, she was similarly snatched from the clutches of some other man. And so on—a domino effect: a scarcity of fertile females trickles down the social scale.

As theoretical as this sounds, it cannot help happening. There are only about 25 years of fertility per woman. When some men dominate more than 25 years' worth, some man somewhere must do with less. And when, in addition to all the serial husbands, you count the men who live with a woman for five years before deciding not to marry her, and then do it again (perhaps finally at 35 marrying a 28-year-old), the net effect is not trivial. As some Darwinians have put it, serial monogamy is tantamount to polygyny. Like polygyny, it lets powerful men grab extra sexual resources (a.k.a. women), leaving less fortunate men without mates —or at least without mates young enough to bear children. Thus rampant divorce not only ends the marriages of some men but also prevents the marriage of others. In 1960, when the divorce rate was around 25%, the portion of the never married population age 40 or older was about the same for men and women. By 1990, with the divorce rate running at 50%, the portion for men was larger by 20% than for women.

Viewing serial monogamy as polygyny by another name throws a kink into the family-values debate. So far, conservatives have got the most political mileage out of decrying divorce. Yet lifelong monogamy—one woman per man for rich and poor alike—would seem to be a natural rallying cry for liberals.

One other kind of fallout from serial monogamy comes plainly into focus through the lens of evolutionary psychology: the toll taken on children. Martin Daly and Margo Wilson of McMaster University in Ontario, two of the field's seminal thinkers, have written that one of the "most obvious" Darwinian predictions is that stepparents will "tend to care less profoundly for children than natural parents." After all, parental investment is a precious resource. So natural selection should "favor those parental psyches that do not squander it on nonrelatives"—who after all do not carry the parent's genes.

Indeed, in combing through 1976 crime data, Daly and Wilson found that an American child living with one or more substitute parents was about 100 times as likely to be fatally abused as a child living with biological parents. In a Canadian city in the 1980s, a child age two or younger was 70 times as likely to be killed by a parent if living with a stepparent and a natural parent than if living with two natural parents.

Of course, murdered children are a tiny fraction of all children living with stepparents; divorce and remarriage hardly amount to a child's death warrant. But consider the more common problem of nonfatal abuse. Children under 10 were, depending on their age and the study in question, three to 40 times as likely to suffer parental abuse if living with a stepparent and a biological parent instead of two biological parents.

There are ways to fool Mother Nature, to induce parents to love children who are not theirs. (Hence cuckoldry.) After all, people cannot telepathically sense that a child is carrying their genes. Instead they rely on cues that in the ancestral environment would have signaled as much. If a woman feeds and cuddles an infant day after day, she may grow to love the child, and so may the woman's mate. This sort of bonding is what makes adopted children lovable (and is one reason relationships between stepparent and child are often harmonious). But the older a child is when first seen, the less profound the attachment will probably be. Most children who acquire stepfathers are past infancy.

Polygynous cultures, such as the 19th century Mormons, are routinely dismissed as cruelly sexist. But they do have at least one virtue: they do not submit children to the indifference or hostility of a surrogate father. What we have now—serial monogamy, quasi-polygyny—is in this sense worse than true polygyny. It massively wastes the most precious evolutionary resource: love.

IS THERE HOPE?

Given the toll of divorce—on children, on low-income men, and for that matter on mothers and fathers—it would be nice to come up with a magic monogamy-restoration plan. Alas, the importance of this task seems rivaled only by its difficulty. Lifelong monogamous devotion just isn't natural, and the modern environment makes it harder than ever. What to do?

As Laura Betzig has noted, some income redistribution might help. One standard conservative argument against antipoverty policies is their cost: taxes burden the affluent and thus, by lowering work incentive, reduce economic output. But if one goal of the policy is to bolster monogamy, then making the affluent less so would help. Monogamy is threatened not just by poverty in an absolute sense but also by the relative wealth of the rich. This is what lures a young woman to a wealthy married or formerly married man. It is also what makes the man who attracts her feel too good for just one wife.

As for the economic consequences, the costs of soaking the rich might well be outweighed by the benefits, financial and otherwise, of more stable marriages, fewer divorces, fewer abused children and less loneliness and depression.

There are other levers for bolstering monogamy, such as divorce law. In the short run, divorce brings the average man a marked rise in standard of living, while his wife, along with her children, suffers the opposite. Maybe we should not lock people into unhappy marriages with financial disincentives to divorce, but surely we should not reward men for leaving their wives either.

A MORAL ANIMAL

The problem of divorce is by no means one of public policy alone. Progress will also depend on people using the explosive insight of evolutionary psychology in a morally responsible way. Ideally this insight would lead people to subject their own feelings to more acute scrutiny. Maybe for starters, men and women will realize that their constantly fluctuating perceptions of a mate are essentially illusions, created for the (rather absurd, really) purpose of genetic proliferation, and that these illusions can do harm. Thus men might beware the restlessness designed by natural selection to encourage polygyny. Now that it brings divorce, it can inflict great emotional and even physical damage on their children.

And men and women alike might bear in mind that impulses of wanderlust, or marital discontent, are not always a sign that you married the "wrong person." They may just signify that you are a member of our species who married another member of our species. Nor, as evolutionary psychiatrist Randolph L. Nesse has noted, should we believe such impulses are a sign of psychopathology. Rather, he writes, they are "expected impulses that must, for the most part, be inhibited for the sake of marriage."

The danger is that people will take the opposite tack: react to the new knowledge by surrendering to "natural" impulses, as if what's "in our genes" were beyond reach of self-control. They may even conveniently assume that what is "natural" is good.

This notion was common earlier in this century. Natural selection was thought of almost as a benign deity, constantly "improving" our species for the greater good. But evolutionary psychology rests on a quite different world view: recognition that natural selection does not work toward overall social welfare, that much of human nature boils down to ruthless genetic self-interest, that people are naturally oblivious to their ruthlessness.

George Williams, whose 1966 book *Adaptation and Natural Selection* helped dispel the once popular idea that evolution often works for "the good of the group," has even taken to calling natural selection "evil" and "the enemy." The moral life, in his view, consists largely of battling human nature.

Darwin himself believed the human species to be a moral one—in fact, the only moral animal species. "A moral being is one who is capable of comparing his past and future actions or motives, and of approving or disapproving of them," he wrote.

In this sense, yes, we are moral. We have at least the technical capacity to lead an examined life: self-awareness, memory, foresight and judgment. Still, chronically subjecting ourselves to moral scrutiny and adjusting our behavior accordingly is hardly a reflex. We are potentially moral animals—which is more than any other animal can say—but we are not naturally moral animals. The first step to being moral is to realize how thoroughly we aren't.

NO

Richard N. Williams

SCIENCE OR STORY TELLING? EVOLUTIONARY EXPLANATIONS OF HUMAN SEXUALITY

Robert Wright's article, "Our Cheating Hearts," provides a good example of how genetic explanations of behavior (derived from evolutionary theory) have become popular in the social sciences, and thus, how they have found their way into the mainstream of our culture. Wright introduces his audience to the new field of environmental psychology, which attempts to explain some of our most important and meaningful human behaviors, like sexuality and marital fidelity, in terms of evolutionary and genetic processes. However, a careful analysis of Wright's article illuminates the problems and conceptual gaps found in attempts to explain human behavior as being caused by evolutionary forces or genes.

On the surface of his article, Wright seems to be simply reporting scientific facts that have been discovered about how and why animals engage in sexual behaviors, and how they have evolved in ways that facilitate such behaviors. Wright's article is similar to a great many other articles and books all trying to make the point that human behaviors are governed by genes, and by evolutionary processes, and, therefore, humans are essentially like animals in their sexual and other behaviors. However, the kind of data used to support this kind of explanation is not scientific in the usual sense. It is composed mostly of stories and analogies. On the surface, Wright seems to be merely pointing out the truths of the similarities of animal to human behavior, and then offering the obvious explanation for these similarities—that evolution, through the workings of our genes, has guided, and continues to control our behaviors. A closer look at the so-called evidence that evolutionary psychology uses to explain our sexual behaviors reveals that it is not at all convincing. It is more story telling than it is science.

IS THERE COMPELLING EVIDENCE THAT OUR INTIMATE OR SEXUAL BEHAVIORS ARE DETERMINED BY EVOLUTION OR GENES?

The idea that human sexual behaviors and intimate relationships are governed by biological structures or evolutionary forces is not scientific in the sense in which we usually use that term. We usually consider scientific facts to be those that are discovered through careful experimentation giving rise to unambiguous results. Scientific work on which evolutionary psychology bases its explanations of human behavior is of quite a different sort. To make this point clear, it is important to distinguish between what we might call "evolutionary theory," and genetic biology.

Scientific studies in the field of genetic biology are very sophisticated and careful. They have provided us a convincing picture of what genes are and how they work. Studies in genetics have resulted in hybrid strains of plants and animals, and in new, and even patented, life forms. However, all this work demonstrates only that genetic material is responsible for a number of *physical* structures and attributes. There is little argument that our genetic material plays a major role in such things as eye color, physical stature, and certain diseases. These are physical characteristics and have a recognizably physical and/or chemical foundation. However, the claims of evolutionary psychology are quite different.

There are several important ideas that Wright, and the evolutionary psychologists, take for granted that are not established by hard scientific evidence. What is not established by careful scientific work is: (a) that psychological or mental events and behaviors (such as human intimacy and sexual attraction) can be produced by genetic material; and (b) that *evolution* controls these events and governs their development and their manifestation.[1] Wright, and the evolutionary psychologists, assume that these two points are true. However, before we are willing to accept them, and Wright's explanations for our sexual behavior, these two points need to be clarified and examined more carefully. Because Wright simply accepts these two claims as true, he is able to tell an evolutionary story about us and our sexual behavior. I argue that Wright's account is a creative story about human sexuality and not a report of scientific facts of human sexuality.

Evolutionary Explanation as Story

Evolutionary theory is convincing to many people chiefly because the living world we experience seems to be like evolutionary theory would predict it should be. In other words, evolutionary theory seems to be true because it fits the data. Evolutionary theorists have offered an account or story of the origin of life, how it developed, and how it regulates itself that makes sense. It seems reasonable, and we can think of very few examples of phenomena that evolutionary theory could not explain. However, it should be kept in mind that because a theory or story can be shown to fit the world and explain it reasonably well, it is not necessarily the case that the story is true. Certainly this is not enough to establish the story as scientific fact. To see why this is the case, we need only ask ourselves what people used to think about the world before evolutionary theories became popular. Did they live in a world they could not explain? Did the world not make sense to them? Certainly a study of history reveals that before evolutionary theories as we know them came into vogue as explanations, people had other stories that made sense of the living world, its origins, and its development. The truth or falsity of evolutionary explanations is not a scientific question because it would be impossible to formulate a properly scientific test of these explanations in contrast to other nonevolutionary explanations. Instead, evidence for evolutionary theory is philosophical and conceptual. Evolutionary theorists observe the world and the nature and behavior of various species and then offer a story of what might be the case. Wright's notion of evolutionary psychology thus rests on conceptual and philosophical rather than scientific grounds.

For example, evolutionary theory suggests that humans are motivated above all to insure the survival of their own genes in succeeding generations. This, in turn, suggests that the best way to do this would be to make sure our offspring survive. And this, in turn, suggests that humans will take better care of their own biological children than stepchildren who do not share their genes. Statistics are reported in Wright's article that show that children who live with one or more stepparents are much more likely to be abused than are children who live with both of their biological parents. Evolutionary theorists will claim that this statistic supports evolutionary theory because it is consistent with what an evolutionary story would predict. However, it seems clear that there are more obvious and immediate factors that might explain why children living with stepparents are more likely to be abused. It seems obvious that children living with stepparents are doing so because of some trouble in their birth family. The factors that contributed to the breakup of the birth family in the

first place are likely to continue with both parents and children into subsequent family arrangements. These factors include unsatisfactory relationships between parents, stresses from the breakup of the original family, economic troubles, and any number of other social and cultural factors. It seems that the evolutionary account of the abuse of these children is quite far removed from the immediate and compelling circumstances of the case. Evolutionary forces do not seem—even by common sense—to be the most direct or obvious source of the problem of abused stepchildren. There does not seem to be anything obvious that would argue that the evolutionary explanation of the statistics of abuse is the best, or most sensible one. Rather, the evolutionary account of this tragedy seems rather contrived. It should also be noted that there is no scientific test that could possibly separate evolutionary causes from the host of social and personal causes of this sort of child abuse.

Wright's account of the evolutionary origins of human intimacy provides many good illustrations of this sort of story telling. For example, he points out that the size of the testicles (relative to body weight) in various primate species is correlated with the extent to which the species tend to be monogamous or polygynous. The story of evolutionary biology is consistent with this bit of data, however, there is nothing about these data that suggest in the least that some evolutionary process is the *cause* of the correlation. Similarly, Wright reports that nearly 1,000 of 1,154 past or present human societies have at one time or another permitted the practice of polygamy. This is also consistent with evolutionary theory —or, rather, evolutionary theory can fit this bit of information into its story. However, there are many other reasons for which cultures might practice polygamy besides evolutionary forces. Some societies practice it for religious reasons, some for seemingly pragmatic reasons, and some, perhaps, for purely social reasons. The point is that these alternative stories can also "make sense" of this bit of data. The datum itself (i.e., the practice of polygamy) does not demand an evolutionary explanation. Which story we prefer is not based on scientific evidence but on our historical prejudices, and current preferences for some kinds of explanations over others. Evolutionary explanations are currently very popular.

In summary then, evolutionary explanations of our behavior rest not on sound scientific demonstration but on our perceptions that evolutionary accounts, like the one Wright gives, make sense, and fit the data. Support for the story of evolution is grounded in how well the story can be used to make sense of the data of the world.

The Logical Fallacy of Affirming the Consequent

We will leave the specifics of Wright's evolutionary analysis in order to make an important but more general point and then show how this general point applies to Wright's argument. From the analysis of evolutionary theories just given, it can be concluded that the truth or falsity of evolutionary theory as an explanation of human behavior is not a genuinely scientific question because it depends for support not on hard scientific data but on reason and argument and a certain degree of cleverness in making the story fit. Since evolutionary accounts of our behavior stand or fall on the basis of reason and argument, we should be very careful about the kind of reasoning and

arguments that are used to support the evolutionary explanation of our actions. From the very beginnings of our Western intellectual tradition, scholars have spent much effort detailing what kinds of reasoning and arguments were valid and trustworthy and what kinds were not. Rules have been established for logical analysis so that we can be confident of the conclusions we reach from our arguments. Likewise, certain kinds of errors have been identified which make our arguments and conclusions invalid —or illogical. This is not the forum to fully discuss the nature of human reason itself, and the power of logic. We need only point out that by the rules scholars have traditionally accepted certain forms of argument are considered invalid, and do not bring us to valid necessary conclusions.[2]

One of the most common and well known logical fallacies is *affirming the consequent*. To see what this fallacy looks like, let us consider one common type of logical argument. It has the following form:

1. *If* Socrates is a man, *then* he is mortal.
2. Socrates is a man.
3. Therefore, he is mortal.

Note that this whole argument hangs on the validity of a very important assumption that is not even stated in the argument—that *all men really are mortal.* If this is not true, then the argument, while still valid according to the rules of logic, is not sensible. Many theoretical arguments, including many of those supporting evolutionary explanations of human behavior, have assumptions that are presumed to be true but are almost never stated, much less examined.

Whenever an argument is presented in the form just presented, it is considered, by the rules of logic, to be valid. That is, the conclusion is reasonable, and we should agree with it and comprehend that it is true. The part of the argument (in statement 1) that follows the word *if* is called the antecedent of the argument. The part following the word *then* is the consequent. In statement 2 the antecedent is restated. That is, it is shown to be true —Socrates really is a man. Whenever we can show that the antecedent is true, then, as we see in statement 3, the consequent follows—it is taken to be true. If he *is* a man—we can show or accept that he is—then he *is* mortal. This classical type of arguing is called affirming the antecedent.

What would have happened, however, if the argument had been made in the following form?

1. *If* Socrates is a man, *then* he is mortal.
2. Socrates *is* mortal.
3. Therefore, he is (must be) a man.

Notice that in this argument we have stated that the consequent is true in statement 2, rather than the antecedent. Then we try to conclude that the antecedent must also be true in statement 3. A moment's reflection is sufficient to show that our conclusion is not valid. Socrates could be a dog—since dogs are mortal. Just because he is mortal, we do not know that he is a man. The conclusion is not valid because the form of the argument is not valid. This is an illustration of a classical logical fallacy called affirming the consequent. Even though this is a commonly understood logical fallacy, it is a commonly employed strategy in arguing for the validity of theories.

In Wright's exposition of the evolutionary basis of human sexuality, there are numerous examples of this fallacy of af-

firming the consequent. For example, as I noted above, Wright uses evidence of sexual dimorphism—the difference in the average size of human males and females —to argue for the validity of his evolutionary account. The argument has the following form:

1. *If* evolution makes humans prone to polygyny, *then* we will find sexual dimorphism in humans (because there is dimorphism in polygynous animals).
2. We do find sexual dimorphism in humans. (The consequent is true.)
3. Therefore, evolution makes humans prone to polygyny. (The antecedent supposedly follows.)

This is, of course, a classic example of affirming the consequent.

Wright's article offers a long string of similar but unsound arguments. In its general form the foundational argument for evolutionary explanations of human behavior is:

1. *If* evolutionary theory is true, *then* we should observe that humans do X (some phenomenon).
2. We observe that humans do X (this phenomenon).
3. Therefore, evolutionary theory is true.

In summary, it should be noted that this style of reasoning by affirming the consequent is not sound scientific practice. Thus, the evidence generally marshalled in favor of evolutionary accounts of human behavior, such as evolutionary psychology, is not genuinely scientific. Rather, it is argument and deduction. And, as has been shown, most often it is not sound argument.

The Criterion of Falsifiability

At least since the publication of the influential work of Karl Popper (1959), a philosopher of science, it has been accepted in most scientific circles that a good theory—a genuinely scientific theory—must be of the type that can be proven false. That is, sound scientific practice demands that a theory must be capable of being tested in such a way that if the results don't turn out to be consistent with the predictions of the theory, then it can be concluded that the theory is false. Theories that cannot be shown to be false are not to be considered genuinely scientific theories. I have already argued in the previous sections of this essay that evolutionary explanations of human behavior are not falsifiable in this sense. There is no experimental test that can settle the question of the validity of these explanations.

However, most proponents of evolutionary theories of human behavior do not even attempt to formulate or explain their theories in a way that can be falsified.[3] While it should be acknowledged that Wright's article is written more for a popular audience than for a professional scientific audience, it nonetheless is illustrative of the approach taken even in more technical and scientific presentations of evolutionary theory. Thus it provides a good example of how the theories are generally presented in unfalsifiable form.

In order to see how evolutionary theories are presented in unfalsifiable form let us pay attention to the way in which Wright reassures his readers that the new evolutionary psychology does not subscribe to the strict and fatalistic theories of previous evolutionary and genetic explanations. He points out that "what's 'natural' isn't necessarily unchangeable."

This is because of the "tremendous flexibility of the human mind and the powerful role of the environment in shaping behavior." Two important points are illustrated in this quotation. The first is that most proponents of evolutionary or genetic explanations of human behavior allow for some determining influence from the environment. However, being caused to behave by our environment does not make for a much better image of our humanity than does being caused by our biology. Acknowledging the causal role of the environment is not much of a corrective to the strict fatalism of biological explanations of our behavior.

The other point, more relevant to the present discussion, is that Wright suggests that the flexibility of the human mind is a source of power to counteract some of the natural processes that might otherwise control us. The problem, however, is that according to Wright's own account of the evolutionary perspective, the human mind is "built and maintained" by genes to serve their (reproductive) purposes. For example, evolutionary theory might predict that since our overriding concern is to get our genes into the next generation, we (especially males) would not care much for one another, especially, for reproductive rivals. We would expect males to be aggressive with all other males. However, as we study societies throughout history, we notice that humans, even males, have tended to be rather civilized and caring, even altruistic. On the surface, this seems to counter evolutionary explanations. However, many evolutionary accounts would claim that our minds (or brains) evolved the capacity to care for others and be kind because being kind and caring had survival value, and actually would help us make sure our genes survived into the next generation, because if we care for others, they are likely to care for us and our children. So, no matter what we observe about the behavior of human males—aggression or cooperation—evolutionary theory can claim the observation as evidence that it is true.

If we take this kind of argument seriously, then, when we see people behaving in accordance with the predictions of evolutionary theory, it is evidence that evolutionary theory is true. And when we see people behaving in a way that seems not to be consistent with evolutionary theory, it is because of the influence of a "tremendously flexible" mind—which, in turn, has evolved according to the dictates of evolutionary theory to serve the ends of evolution itself. So when evolutionary theory seems to work as an explanation we can assume it is true. When it does not seem to work so well it is still true because it is merely *appearing to* work against itself via the evolved human mind. Evolutionary theory is thus unfalsifiable because both observations that confirm predictions, and observations that do not, are counted as evidence for the validity of evolution as an explanation.

Myths of Magic Genes

There is one aspect of evolutionary theory that has a firm foundation of scientific research. This is the structure and function of genes and their role in determining important characteristics of organisms. These are, for the most part, physical characteristics. Very sophisticated research assures us that many important characteristics of organisms have their origins in genetic codes contained in the chromosomes of the tissues of the organism. However, even though we know much about the structure and function of genes, the picture is not at all clear when we turn attention to the relationship between genes and *psychological*—rather than strictly physical—characteristics and behaviors of organisms, especially humans.[4]

We find in Wright's essay the following:

> Genes don't talk, of course. They affect behavior by creating feelings and thoughts—by building and maintaining... an underlying mental infrastructure.

The claim here is quite clear: genes create mental phenomena. Wright also speaks of "genes that inclined a man to love his offspring," and suggests that the purposes of the genes required "the invention of a compelling emotion: parental love." Not only are genes sophisticated enough to invent emotions, but, according to Wright, also to contradict them. "Evolution not only invented romantic love but from the beginning also corrupted it."

According to evolutionary theory, not only are genes capable of producing particular emotions, they are also capable of predicting and monitoring behavioral outcomes. This portrayal of genes and their activities is problematic for a number of reasons. The description of genes as intelligent and possessing "stratagems" is problematic in that it seems to overlook what genes really are. We need to remind ourselves as we read evolutionary and genetic accounts of our behavior that genes are simply molecules—chemicals —locked away in the nuclei of the cells of our bodies. How, we might ask, could genes as molecules of chemicals be aware of such things as "outside romantic opportunities" in order to motivate us to take advantage of them? The orthodox evolutionary answer, of course, is that the genes are not aware of such things (that would be silly). Rather, the genes give rise to minds, thoughts, feelings, and sophisticated mental capacities for monitoring all of these social factors and deciding what should be done. But here we run headlong into the fundamental and perpetually vexing question of evolutionary and genetic theories of our behavior. The response to this question determines the adequacy and believability of the accounts of our behavior these theories offer. The question is this: How do chemical compounds locked within the nuclei of the cells of the tissues of our bodies give rise to nonchemical and intelligent things like particular ideas, feelings, emotions, and stratagems? Ideas, feelings, emotions, and stratagems are not simply and strictly chemical or physical. "Stratagems," and "romantic opportunities" are not chemical substances, nor substances at all. It is not at all clear how they might arise from molecules of chemicals that compose our genes. There seems to be no answer to this essential question in all the literature on evolutionary and genetic accounts of human behavior. It is simply assumed that it can happen and does because then the theory "fits."

CONCLUSION

This response to "evolutionary psychology" and Wright's treatment of it has centered on the argument that evolutionary and genetic explanations of human behaviors are not based on hard scientific data and that they are really more like story telling than science. However, much more is at stake than a mere disagreement about how certain observations should be interpreted. Simply making the case that there are other and simpler explanations for our behaviors than the evolutionary explanation, or that such evolutionary explanations are not truly scientific, is not in itself a strong enough refutation and is hardly sufficient grounds for rejecting them. The larger issues need to be made clear.

Evolutionary and genetic explanations of human behavior are not just stories about us; they are stories that pretend not to be stories. Furthermore, they ask us to reduce our most human and most meaningful behaviors to the level of simple animal behaviors. They ask us to accept that the same fundamental processes are at work to determine our intimate relationships as determine "mating behaviors" in animal species. Evolutionary psychologists accomplish this reduction subtly by using the same terms to describe both animal and human behaviors. This reduction of the human to the animal and the application of a common vocabulary destroys the meaning of human behavior. If, as evolutionary psychology declares, human and animal sexuality have the same roots, then human intimacy is no more meaningful than the copulatory acts of common breeding stock. Proponents of evolution claim that we are recompensed for the loss of meaning in our lives by scientific credibility. But if, as I argue, there is no convincing scientific base for the evolutionary account of our behaviors, then we are being asked to sacrifice the meaning of human intimacy for nothing.

The end result of evolutionary and genetic accounts of human behavior is a moral vacuum in which we do not engage one another as moral agents at all but as organisms controlled by biological forces beyond our control. Until such time as there is overwhelming scientific evidence that chemicals in our cells can produce morality and human affections, we are morally obligated to resist explanations that destroy the meaning and morality of our lives. The evolutionary story exacts too great a price both in credulity and in humanity.

NOTES

1. Some evolutionary theorists might argue that at some future date when technology has advanced and when they are given permission to manipulate human genes, genuine scientific validation will be available. It is axiomatic in science, however, that one does not rely on nor claim credibility from what might someday be done. To argue in this way moves one from science to science fiction.

2. The interested reader is referred to Slife & Williams (1995) for a fuller account of how logic plays a role in scientific and theoretical work, and how both scientists and theorists too easily fall into the practice of affirming the consequent.

3. The work of most experimental geneticists is sophisticated and scientifically sound. Their experiments are routinely set up so that their *predictions can* be falsified. However, to falsify a prediction derived from a theory such as evolution is not at all the same thing as to falsify the theory itself. Even though it has generated much credible scientific work, evolutionary theory as a world view has never been at risk. Because of the way it is formulated and promulgated it is unfalsifiable.

4. Some would argue that some behavioral characteristics can also be shown to be genetically determined. Whether this is the case depends in large part on how the term "behavior" is defined. For example, is a plant's "growing" a behavior?

REFERENCES

James, W. (1897/1956). The dilemma of determinism. In W. James, *The will to believe and other essays in popular philosophy* (pp. 145–184). New York: Dover.

Popper, K. (1959). *The logic of scientific discovery.* New York: Basic Books.

Slife, B. D., & Williams, R. N. (1995). *What's behind the research? Discovering hidden assumptions in the behavioral sciences.* Newbury Park, CA: Sage Publications.

CHALLENGE QUESTIONS

Do Evolutionary and Genetic Factors Determine Our Sexual Behaviors?

1. Is Williams correct that there is no specified process for nor evidence that genetic materials produce psychological factors? Interview a geneticist to investigate this.

2. Explore the implications of an evolutionary/genetic account of sexuality for your own life. If it were proved true, how would it affect your current and future relationships?

3. Williams describes the importance of falsifiability in scientific explanations. After reading the selections by Wright and Williams, do you believe that the evolutionary theory described by Wright is falsifiable? Why, or why not?

4. Is there evidence other than that cited by Wright that supports claims about the importance of the new field of evolutionary psychology?

5. Wright claims that it is natural for both men and women to commit adultery "at some times, under some circumstances." Under what circumstances is it *not* natural for adultery, according to Wright? How is it that evolutionary theory only operates under certain circumstances?

On the Internet . . .

American Psychological Association's Division 20, Adult Development and Aging

At this site Division 20, which is dedicated to studying the psychology of adult development and aging, provides links to research guides, laboratories, instructional resources, and other related areas.
http://www.iog.wayne.edu/APADIV20/lowdiv20.htm

Behavior Analysis Resources

Those who are interested in the behaviorist approach to human development should check out the links at this site.
http://www.coedu.usf.edu/behavior/bares.htm

Seven Developmental Needs of Young Adolescents

This article discusses the developmental diversity of early adolescence and the wide range of differences that are generally encountered within a group of 13- or 14-year-olds.
http://sunsite.unc.edu/youthlink/needs.html

The Jean Piaget Society: Society for the Study of Knowledge and Development

This is the home page of the Jean Piaget Society: Society for the Study of Knowledge and Development. From here you can link to information on the society, symposia, conferences, and publications, as well as links to related sites.
http://www.sunnyhill.bc.ca/Lalonde/JPS/

PART 3

Human Development

The goal of developmental psychologists is to document the course of our physical, social, and intellectual changes over a life span. Considerable attention has been paid to the childhood part of that life span because this period of development seems to set the stage for later periods. Two potential influences on childhood are debated here: television and parental divorce.

■ Does Viewing Television Increase a Child's Aggression?

■ Are Children of Divorced Parents at Greater Risk?

ISSUE 6

Does Viewing Television Increase a Child's Aggression?

YES: Brandon S. Centerwall, from "Television and Violent Crime," *The Public Interest* (Spring 1993)

NO: Brian Siano, from "Frankenstein Must Be Destroyed: Chasing the Monster of TV Violence," *The Humanist* (January/February 1994)

ISSUE SUMMARY

YES: Brandon S. Centerwall, an epidemiologist, argues that children act out the violence they see on television and carry the violent behaviors into adulthood.

NO: Brian Siano, a writer and researcher, believes that children with nonnurturing parents, regardless of the children's television viewing habits, tend to be more aggressive than children who closely identify with either parent.

Survey after survey shows that one of the primary concerns of contemporary society is violence. The popular perception is that violence is on the rise. Indeed, some people believe that violence is like some contagious disease that has spread to epidemic proportions. What is the reason for this seeming "epidemic"? Why does the current generation appear to be more prone to violence than previous generations? How is today different from the "good old days"?

Many people would sum up that difference in one word—television. Television now occupies a place (or two or three) in almost every home in the United States, regardless of the inhabitants' race or level of income. And television has been cited time and again by the U.S. surgeon general, by members of the U.S. Congress, and by psychological researchers as a medium filled with many kinds of violence. It seems only natural for parents to wonder about television's impact on small children, who average over 20 hours of television viewing per week. Indeed, some have suggested that a child witnesses over 100,000 acts of violence on television before graduating from elementary school. How do these acts of violence affect a child's development?

In the following selection, Brandon S. Centerwall asserts that televised violence leads to an increase in a child's aggression, referring to numerous published studies to support this assertion. He theorizes that children have an instinctive desire to imitate behavior. Unfortunately, however, children are not born with an instinct for evaluating the appropriateness of certain actions. This means that children naturally model what they see on television and do not typically think about whether or not they *should* model what they see. Consequently, even when clearly antisocial behaviors are depicted on television, children are still likely to learn and imitate them. Centerwall believes that the danger to a child's development is so great that he advocates making television violence a part of the public health agenda.

In contrast, Brian Siano contends that factors other than television are more influential on a child's tendency for violent actions. He points to research that contradicts Centerwall's views. For example, one study found that boys who watch nonviolent shows tend to be more aggressive than boys who watch violent television. Siano argues that style of parenting is a better indicator of the development of violent behavior. Children of nonnurturing parents and children who do not identify with their parents are the ones most likely to exhibit violence. Although Siano is an advocate of quality programming, he is reluctant to indiscriminately censor all violence from television, particularly when effective parenting can counter any possible ill effects.

POINT	COUNTERPOINT
• Research indicates that parents who watched more television as children punished their own children more severely.	• Boys who watch nonviolent shows tend to be more aggressive than boys who watch violent shows.
• Children are incapable of discriminating between what they should and should not imitate.	• Good parents teach children how to discriminate among their behaviors.
• Limiting all children's exposure to television violence should become part of the public health agenda.	• Violence can be used in television shows for pro-social reasons.
• Many studies demonstrate a positive relationship between television exposure and physical aggression.	• Parental identification can change the way children interpret physical punishment on television.
• For children to be safe, television violence must be eliminated.	• Indiscriminate censorship of all violence is too high a price to pay for the minimal influence of television.

YES
<span></span>
Brandon S. Centerwall

TELEVISION AND VIOLENT CRIME

Children are born ready to imitate adult behavior. That they can, and do, imitate an array of adult facial expressions has been demonstrated in newborns as young as a few hours old, before they are even old enough to know that they have facial features. It is a most useful instinct, for the developing child must learn and master a vast repertoire of behavior in short order.

But while children have an instinctive desire to imitate, they do not possess an instinct for determining whether a behavior ought to be imitated. They will imitate anything, including behavior that most adults regard as destructive and antisocial. It may give pause for thought, then, to learn that infants as young as fourteen months demonstrably observe and incorporate behavior seen on television.

The average American preschooler watches more than twenty-seven hours of television per week. This might not be bad if these young children understood what they were watching. But they don't. Up through ages three and four, most children are unable to distinguish fact from fantasy on TV, and remain unable to do so despite adult coaching. In the minds of young children, television is a source of entirely factual information regarding how the world works. There are no limits to their credulity. To cite one example, an Indiana school board had to issue an advisory to young children that, no, there is no such thing as Teenage Mutant Ninja Turtles. Children had been crawling down storm drains looking for them.

Naturally, as children get older, they come to know better, but their earliest and deepest impressions are laid down at an age when they still see television as a factual source of information about the outside world. In that world, it seems, violence is common and the commission of violence is generally powerful, exciting, charismatic, and effective. In later life, serious violence is most likely to erupt at moments of severe stress—and it is precisely at such moments that adolescents and adults are most likely to revert to their earliest, most visceral sense of the role of violence in society and in personal behavior. Much of this sense will have come from television.

From Brandon S. Centerwall, "Television and Violent Crime," *The Public Interest*, no. 111 (Spring 1993), pp. 56–71. Copyright © 1993 by National Affairs, Inc. Reprinted by permission.

THE SEEDS OF AGGRESSION

In 1973, a remote rural community in Canada acquired television for the first time. The acquisition of television at such a late date was due to problems with signal reception rather than any hostility toward TV. As reported in *The Impact of Television* (1986), Tannis Williams and her associates at the University of British Columbia investigated the effect of television on the children of this community (which they called "Notel"), taking for comparison two similar towns that already had television.

The researchers observed forty-five first- and second-graders in the three towns for rates of inappropriate physical aggression before television was introduced into Notel. Two years later, the same forty-five children were observed again. To prevent bias in the data, the research assistants who collected the data were kept uninformed as to why the children's rates of aggression were of interest. Furthermore, a new group of research assistants was employed the second time around, so that the data gatherers would not be biased by recollections of the children's behavior two years earlier.

Rates of aggression did not change in the two control communities. By contrast, the rate of aggression among Notel children increased 160 percent. The increase was observed in both boys and girls, in those who were aggressive to begin with and in those who were not. Television's enhancement of noxious aggression was entirely general and not limited to a few "bad apples."

In another Canadian study, Gary Granzberg and his associates at the University of Winnipeg investigated the impact of television upon Indian communities in northern Manitoba. As described in *Television and the Canadian Indian* (1980), forty-nine third-, fourth-, and fifth-grade boys living in two communities were observed from 1973, when one town acquired television, until 1977, when the second town did as well. The aggressiveness of boys in the first community increased after the introduction of television. The aggressiveness of boys in the second community, which did not receive television then, remained the same. When television was later introduced in the second community, observed levels of aggressiveness increased there as well.

In another study conducted from 1960 to 1981, Leonard Eron and L. Rowell Huesmann (then of the University of Illinois at Chicago) followed 875 children living in a semirural U.S. county. Eron and Huesmann found that for both boys and girls, the amount of television watched at age eight predicted the seriousness of criminal acts for which they were convicted by age thirty. This remained true even after controlling for the children's baseline aggressiveness, intelligence, and socioeconomic status. Eron and Huesmann also observed second-generation effects. Children who watched much television at age eight later, as parents, punished their own children more severely than did parents who had watched less television as children. Second- and now third-generation effects are accumulating at a time of unprecedented youth violence.

All seven of the U.S. and Canadian studies of prolonged childhood exposure to television demonstrate a positive relationship between exposure and physical aggression. The critical period is preadolescent childhood. Later exposure does not appear to produce any additional effect. However, the aggression-enhancing effect of exposure in pre-adolescence extends into adolescence and adulthood. This suggests that any interventions should be designed for children and their caregivers rather than for the general adult population.

These studies confirmed the beliefs of most Americans. According to a Harris poll at the time of the studies, 43 percent of American adults believe that television violence "plays a part in making America a violent society." An additional 37 percent think it might. But how important is television violence? What is the effect of exposure upon entire populations? To address this question, I took advantage of an historical accident—the absence of television in South Africa prior to 1975.

THE SOUTH AFRICAN EXPERIENCE

White South Africans have lived in a prosperous, industrialized society for decades, but they did not get television until 1975 because of tension between the Afrikaner- and English-speaking communities. The country's Afrikaner leaders knew that a South African television industry would have to rely on British and American shows to fill out its programming schedule, and they felt that this would provide an unacceptable cultural advantage to English-speaking South Africans. So, rather than negotiate a complicated compromise, the government simply forbade television broadcasting. The entire population of two million whites—rich and poor, urban and rural, educated and uneducated—was thus excluded from exposure to television for a quarter century after the medium was introduced in the United States.

In order to determine whether exposure to television is a cause of violence, I compared homicide rates in South Africa,

Canada, and the United States. Since blacks in South Africa live under quite different conditions than blacks in the United States, I limited the comparison to white homicide rates in South Africa and the United States, and the total homicide rate in Canada (which was 97 percent white in 1951).[1] I chose the homicide rate as a measure of violence because homicide statistics are exceptionally accurate.

From 1945 to 1974, the white homicide rate in the United States increased 93 percent. In Canada, the homicide rate increased 92 percent. In South Africa, where television was banned, the white homicide rate declined by 7 percent.

CONTROLLING FOR OTHER FACTORS

Could there be some explanation other than television for the fact that violence increased dramatically in the U.S. and Canada while dropping in South Africa? I examined an array of alternative explanations. None is satisfactory:

- **Economic growth.** Between 1946 and 1974, all three countries experienced substantial economic growth. Per capita income increased by 75 percent in the United States, 124 percent in Canada, and 86 percent in South Africa. Thus differences in economic growth cannot account for the different homicide trends in the three countries.
- **Civil unrest.** One might suspect that anti-war or civil-rights activity was responsible for the doubling of the homicide rate in the United States during this period. But the experience of Canada shows that this was not the case, since Canadians suffered a doubling of the homicide rate without similar civil unrest.

Other possible explanations include changes in age distribution, urbanization, alcohol consumption, capital punishment, and the availability of firearms. As discussed in *Public Communication and Behavior* (1989), none provides a viable explanation for the observed homicide trends.

In the United States and Canada, there was a lag of ten to fifteen years between the introduction of television and a doubling of the homicide rate. In South Africa, there was a similar lag. Since television exerts its behavior-modifying effects primarily on children, while homicide is primarily an adult activity, this lag represents the time needed for the "television generation" to come of age.

The relationship between television and the homicide rate holds *within* the United States as well. Different regions of the U.S., for example, acquired television at different times. As we would expect, while all regions saw increases in their homicide rates, the regions that acquired television first were also the first to see higher homicide rates.

Similarly, urban areas acquired television before rural areas. As we would expect, urban areas saw increased homicide rates several years before the occurrence of a parallel increase in rural areas.

The introduction of television also helps explain the different rates of homicide growth for whites and minorities. White households in the U.S. began acquiring television sets in large numbers approximately five years before minority households. Significantly, the white homicide rate began increasing in 1958, four years before a parallel increase in the minority homicide rate.

Of course, there are many factors other than television that influence the amount of violent crime. Every violent act is the result of a variety of forces coming together—poverty, crime, alcohol and drug abuse, stress—of which childhood TV exposure is just one. Nevertheless, the evidence indicates that if, hypothetically, television technology had never been developed, there would today be 10,000 fewer homicides each year in the United States, 70,000 fewer rapes, and 700,000 fewer injurious assaults. Violent crime would be half what it is.

THE TELEVISION INDUSTRY TAKES A LOOK

The first congressional hearings on television and violence were held in 1952, when not even a quarter of U.S. households owned television sets. In the years since, there have been scores of research reports on the issue, as well as several major government investigations. The findings of the National Commission on the Causes and Prevention of Violence, published in 1969, were particularly significant. This report established what is now the broad scientific consensus: Exposure to television increases rates of physical aggression.

Television industry executives were genuinely surprised by the National Commission's report. What the industry produced was at times unedifying, but physically harmful? In response, network executives began research programs that collectively would cost nearly a million dollars.

CBS commissioned William Belson to undertake what would be the largest and most sophisticated study yet, an investigation involving 1,565 teenage boys. In *Television Violence and the Adolescent Boy* (1978), Belson controlled for one hundred variables, and found that teenage boys who had watched above-average quantities of television violence before adolescence were committing acts of serious violence (e.g., assault, rape, major vandalism, and abuse of animals) at a rate 49 percent higher than teenage boys who had watched below-average quantities of television violence. Despite the large sum of money they had invested, CBS executives were notably unenthusiastic about the report.

ABC commissioned Melvin Heller and Samuel Polsky of Temple University to study young male felons imprisoned for violent crimes (e.g, homicide, rape, and assault). In two surveys, 22 and 34 percent of the young felons reported having consciously imitated crime techniques learned from television programs, usually successfully. The more violent of these felons were the most likely to report having learned techniques from television. Overall, the felons reported that as children they had watched an average of six hours of television per day—approximately twice as much as children in the general population at that time.

Unlike CBS, ABC maintained control over publication. The final report, *Studies in Violence and Television* (1976), was published in a private, limited edition that was not released to the general public or the scientific community.

NBC relied on a team of four researchers, three of whom were employees of NBC. Indeed, the principal investigator, J. Ronald Milavsky, was an NBC vice president. The team observed some 2,400 schoolchildren for up to three years to see if watching television violence increased their levels of physical aggressiveness. In *Television and Aggression* (1982), Milavsky and his associates reported that television violence had no effect upon the children's behavior. However, every independent investigator who has examined their data has concluded that, to the contrary, their data show that television violence did cause a modest increase of about 5 percent in average levels of physical aggressiveness. When pressed on the point, Milavsky and his associates conceded that their findings were consistent with the conclusion that television violence increased physical aggressiveness "to a small extent." They did not concede that television violence actually caused an increase, but only that their findings were consistent with such a conclusion.

The NBC study results raise an important objection to my conclusions. While studies have repeatedly demonstrated that childhood exposure to television increases physical aggressiveness, the increase is almost always quite minor. A number of investigators have argued that such a small effect is too weak to account for major increases in rates of violence. These investigators, however, overlook a key factor.

Homicide is an extreme form of aggression—so extreme that only one person in 20,000 committed murder each year in the United States in the mid-1950s. If we were to rank everyone's degree of physical aggressiveness from the least aggressive (Mother Theresa) to the most aggressive (Jack the Ripper), the large majority of us would be somewhere in the middle and murderers would be virtually off the chart. It is an intrinsic property of such "bell curve" distributions that small changes in the average imply major changes at the extremes. Thus, if exposure to television causes 8 percent of the population to shift from below-average aggression to above-average aggression, it follows that the homicide rate will double. The findings of the NBC study and the doubling of the homicide rate are two sides of the same coin.

After the results of these studies became clear, television industry executives lost their enthusiasm for scientific research. No further investigations were funded. Instead, the industry turned to political management of the issue.

THE TELEVISION INDUSTRY AND SOCIAL RESPONSIBILITY

The television industry routinely portrays individuals who seek to influence programming as un-American haters of free speech. In a 1991 letter sent to 7,000 executives of consumer product companies and advertising agencies, the president of the Network Television Association explained:

> Freedom of expression is an inalienable right of all Americans vigorously supported by ABC, CBS, and NBC. However, boycotts and so-called advertiser "hit lists" are attempts to manipulate our free society and democratic process.

The letter went on to strongly advise the companies to ignore all efforts by anyone to influence what programs they choose to sponsor. By implication, the networks themselves should ignore all efforts by anyone to influence what programs they choose to produce.

But this is absurd. All forms of public discourse are attempts to "manipulate" our free society and democratic process. What else could they be? Consumer boycotts are no more un-American than are strikes by labor unions. The Network Television Association is attempting to systematically shut down all discourse between viewers and advertisers, and between viewers and the television industry. Wrapping itself in patriotism,

the television industry's response to uppity viewers is to put them in their place. If the industry and advertisers were to actually succeed in closing the circle between them, the only course they would leave for concerned viewers would be to seek legislative action.

In the war against tobacco, we do not expect help from the tobacco industry. If someone were to call upon the tobacco industry to cut back production as a matter of social conscience and concern for public health, we would regard that person as simple-minded, if not frankly deranged. Oddly enough, however, people have persistently assumed that the television industry is somehow different—that it is useful to appeal to its social conscience. This was true in 1969 when the National Commission on the Causes and Prevention of Violence published its recommendations for the television industry. It was equally true in 1989 when the U.S. Congress passed an anti-violence bill that granted television industry executives the authority to hold discussions on the issue of television violence without violating antitrust laws. Even before the law was passed, the four networks stated that there would be no substantive changes in their programming. They have been as good as their word.

For the television industry, issues of "quality" and "social responsibility" are peripheral to the issue of maximizing audience size—and there is no formula more tried and true than violence for generating large audiences. To television executives, this is crucial. For if advertising revenue were to decrease by just 1 percent, the television industry would stand to lose $250 million in revenue annually. Thus, changes in audience size that appear trivial to most of us are regarded as catastrophic by the industry. For this reason, industry spokespersons have made innumerable protestations of good intent, but nothing has happened. In the more than twenty years that levels of television violence have been monitored, there has been no downward movement. There are no recommendations to make to the television industry. To make any would not only be futile but could create the false impression that the industry might actually do something constructive.

On December 11, 1992, the networks finally announced a list of voluntary guidelines on television violence. Curiously, reporters were unable to locate any network producers who felt the new guidelines would require changes in their programs. That raises a question: Who is going to bell the cat? Who is going to place his or her career in jeopardy in order to decrease the amount of violence on television? It is hard to say, but it may be revealing that when Senator Paul Simon held the press conference announcing the new inter-network agreement, no industry executives were present to answer questions.

MEETING THE CHALLENGE

Television violence is everybody's problem. You may feel assured that your child will never become violent despite a steady diet of television mayhem, but you cannot be assured that your child won't be murdered or maimed by someone else's child raised on a similar diet.

The American Academy of Pediatrics recommends that parents limit their children's television viewing to one to two hours per day. But why wait for a pediatrician to say it? Limiting children's exposure to television violence should become part of the public health agenda, along with safety seats, bicycle helmets, immunizations, and good nutrition. Part of the public health approach should be to promote child-care alternatives to the electronic babysitter, especially among the poor.

Parents should also guide what their children watch and how much. This is an old recommendation that can be given new teeth with the help of modern technology. It is now feasible to fit a television set with an electronic lock that permits parents to preset the channels and times for which the set will be available; if a particular program or time of day is locked, the set will not operate then. Time-channel locks are not merely feasible; they have already been designed and are coming off the assembly line.

The model for making them widely available comes from closed-captioning circuitry, which permits deaf and hard-of-hearing persons access to television. Market forces alone would not have made closed-captioning available to more than a fraction of the deaf and hard-of-hearing. To remedy this problem, Congress passed the Television Decoder Circuitry Act in 1990, which requires that virtually all new television sets be manufactured with built-in closed-captioning circuitry. A similar law should require that all new television sets be manufactured with built-in time-channel lock circuitry—and for a similar reason. Market forces alone will not make this technology available to more than a fraction of households with children and will exclude most poor families, the ones who suffer the most from violence. If we can make television technology available to benefit twenty-four million deaf and hard-of-hearing Americans, surely we can do no less for the benefit of fifty million American children.

A final recommendation: Television programs should be accompanied by a violence rating so that parents can judge how violent a program is without having to watch it. Such a rating system should be quantitative, leaving aesthetic and social judgments to the viewers. This approach would enjoy broad popular support. In a *Los Angeles Times* poll, 71 percent of adult Americans favored the establishment of a TV violence rating system. Such a system would not impinge on artistic freedom since producers would remain free to produce programs with high violence ratings. They could even use high violence ratings in the advertisements for their shows.

None of these recommendations would limit freedom of speech. That is as it should be. We do not address the problem of motor vehicle fatalities by calling for a ban on cars. Instead, we emphasize safety seats, good traffic signs, and driver education. Similarly, to address the problem of television-inspired violence, we need to promote time-channel locks, program rating systems, and viewer education about the hazards of violent programming. In this way we can protect our children and our society.

NOTES

1. The "white homicide rate" refers to the rate at which whites are the victims of homicide. Since most homicide is intra-racial, this closely parallels the rate at which whites commit homicide.

REFERENCES

William A. Belson, *Television Violence and the Adolescent Boy.* Westmead, England: Saxon House (1978).

Brandon S. Centerwall, "Exposure to Television as a Cause of Violence," *Public Communication and Behavior,* Vol. 2. Orlando, Florida: Academic Press (1989), pp. 1–58.

Leonard D. Eron and L. Rowell Huesmann, "The Control of Aggressive Behavior by Changes in Attitudes, Values, and the Conditions of Learning," *Advances in the Study of Aggression.* Orlando, Florida: Academic Press (1984), pp. 139–171.

Gary Granzberg and Jack Steinbring (eds.), *Television and the Canadian Indian.* Winnipeg, Manitoba: University of Winnipeg (1980).

L. Rowell Huesmann and Leonard D. Eron, *Television and the Aggressive Child.* Hillsdale, New Jersey: Lawrence Erlbaum Associates (1986), pp. 45–80.

Candace Kruttschnitt, et al., "Family Violence, Television Viewing Habits, and Other Adolescent Experiences Related to Violent Criminal Behavior," *Criminology,* Vol. 24 (1986), pp. 235–267.

Andrew N. Meltzoff, "Memory in Infancy," *Encyclopedia of Learning and Memory.* New York: Macmillan (1992), pp. 271–275.

J. Ronald Milavsky, et al., *Television and Aggression.* Orlando, Florida: Academic Press (1982).

Jerome L. Singer, et al., "Family Patterns and Television Viewing as Predictors of Children's Beliefs and Aggression," *Journal of Communication,* Vol. 34, No. 2 (1984), pp. 73–89.

Tannis M. Williams (ed.), *The Impact of Television.* Orlando, Florida: Academic Press (1986).

NO

Brian Siano

FRANKENSTEIN MUST BE DESTROYED: CHASING THE MONSTER OF TV VIOLENCE

Here's the scene: Bugs Bunny, Daffy Duck, and a well-armed Elmer Fudd are having a stand-off in the forest. Daffy the rat-fink has just exposed Bugs' latest disguise, so Bugs takes off the costume and says, "That's right, Doc, I'm a wabbit. Would you like to shoot me now or wait until we get home?"

"Shoot him now! Shoot him now!" Daffy screams.

"You keep out of this," Bugs says. "He does not have to shoot you now."

"He does *so* have to shoot me now!" says Daffy. Full of wrath, he storms up to Elmer Fudd and shrieks, "And I *demand* that you shoot me now!"

Now, if you *aren't* smiling to yourself over the prospect of Daffy's beak whirling around his head like a roulette wheel, stop reading right now. This one's for a very select group: those evil degenerates (like me) who want to corrupt the unsullied youth of America by showing them violence on television.

Wolves' heads being conked with mallets in Tex Avery's *Swing Shift Cinderella*. Dozens of dead bodies falling from a closet in *Who Killed Who?* A sweet little kitten seemingly baked into cookies in Chuck Jones' *Feed the Kitty*. And best of all, Wile E. Coyote's unending odyssey of pain in *Fast and Furrious* and *Hook, Line, and Stinker*. God, I love it. The more explosions, crashes, gunshots, and defective ACME catapults there are, the better it is for the little tykes.

Shocked? Hey, I haven't even gotten to "The Three Stooges" yet.

* * *

The villagers are out hunting another monster—the Frankenstein of TV violence. Senator Paul Simon's hearings in early August 1993 provoked a fresh round of arguments in a debate that's been going on ever since the first round of violent kids' shows—"Sky King," "Captain Midnight," and "Hopalong Cassidy"—were on the air. More recently, Attorney General Janet Reno has taken a hard line on TV violence. "We're fed up with excuses," she told

From Brian Siano, "Frankenstein Must Be Destroyed: Chasing the Monster of TV Violence," *The Humanist*, vol. 54, no. 1 (January/February 1994). Copyright © 1994 by Brian Siano. Reprinted by permission.

the Senate, arguing that "the regulation of violence is constitutionally permissible" and that, if the networks don't do it, "government should respond."...

Simon claims to have become concerned with this issue because, three years ago, he turned on the TV in his hotel room and was treated to the sight of a man being hacked apart with a chainsaw.... This experience prompted him to sponsor a three-year antitrust exemption for the networks, which was his way of encouraging them to voluntarily "clean house." But at the end of that period, the rates of TV violence hadn't changed enough to satisfy him, so Simon convened open hearings on the subject in 1993.

If Simon was truly concerned with the content of television programming, the first question that comes to mind is why he gave the networks an antitrust exemption in the first place. Thanks to Reagan-era deregulation, ownership of the mass media has become steadily more concentrated in the hands of fewer and fewer corporations. For example, the Federal Communications Commission used to have a "seven-and-seven" rule, whereby no company was allowed to own more than seven radio and seven television stations. In 1984, this was revised to a "12-and-12-and-12" rule: 12 FM radio stations, 12 AM radio stations, and 12 TV stations. It's a process outlined by Ben Bagdikian in his fine book *The Media Monopoly*. The net result is a loss of dissident, investigative, or regional voices; a mass media that questions less; and a forum for public debate that includes only the powerful.

This process could be impeded with judicious use of antitrust laws and stricter FCC controls—a return to the "seven-and-seven" rule, perhaps. But rather than hold hearings on this subject—a far greater threat to the nation's political well-being than watching *Aliens* on pay-per-view—Simon gave the networks a three-year *exemption* from antitrust legislation....

The debate becomes even more impassioned when we ask how children might be affected. The innocent, trusting little tykes are spending hours bathed in TV's unreal colors, and their fantasy lives are inhabited by such weirdos as Wolverine and Eek the Cat. Parents usually want their kids to grow up sharing their ideals and values, or at least to be well-behaved and obedient. Tell parents that their kids are watching "Beavis and Butt-head" in their formative years and you set off some major alarms.

There are also elitist, even snobbish, attitudes toward pop culture that help to rationalize censorship. One is that the corporate, mass-market culture of TV isn't important enough or "art" enough to deserve the same free-speech protection as James Joyce's *Ulysses* or William Burrough's *Naked Lunch*. The second is that rational, civilized human beings are supposed to be into Shakespeare and Scarlatti, not Pearl Jam and "Beavis and Butt-head." Seen in this "enlightened" way, the efforts of Paul Simon are actually for *our own good*. And so we define anything even remotely energetic as "violent," wail about how innocent freckle-faced children are being defiled by such fare as "NYPD Blue," and call for a Council of Certified Nice People who will decide what the rest of us get to see. A recent *Mother Jones* article by Carl Cannon (July/August 1993) took just this hysterical tone, citing as proof "some three thousand research studies of this issue."

Actually, there aren't 3,000 studies. In 1984, the *Psychological Bulletin* published an overview by Jonathan Freedman of research on the subject. Referring to the "2,500 studies" figure bandied about at the time (it's a safe bet that 10 years would inflate this figure to 3,000), Freedman writes:

> The reality is more modest. The large number refers to the complete bibliography on television. References to television and aggression are far fewer, perhaps around 500.... The actual literature on the relation between television violence and aggression consists of fewer than 100 independent studies, and the majority of these are laboratory experiments. Although this is still a substantial body of work, it is not vast, and there are only a small number of studies dealing specifically with the effects of television violence outside the laboratory.

The bulk of the evidence for a causal relationship between television violence and violent behavior comes from the research of Leonard Eron of the University of Illinois and Rowell Huesmann of the University of Michigan. Beginning in 1960, Eron and his associates began a large-scale appraisal of how aggression develops in children and whether or not it persists into adulthood. (The question of television violence was, originally, a side issue to the long-term study.) Unfortunately, when the popular press writes about Eron's work, it tends to present his methodology in the simplest of terms: *Mother Jones* erroneously stated that his study "followed the viewing habits of a group of children for twenty-two years." It's this sort of sloppiness, and overzealousness to prove a point, that keeps people from understanding the issues or raising substantial criticisms. Therefore, we must discuss Eron's work in some detail.

* * *

The first issue in Eron's study was how to measure aggressiveness in children. Eron's "peer-nominated index" followed a simple strategy: asking each child in a classroom questions about which kids were the main offenders in 10 different categories of classroom aggression (that is, "Who pushes or shoves children?"). The method is consistent with other scales of aggression, and its one-month test/retest reliability is 91 percent. The researchers also tested the roles of four behavioral dimensions in the development of aggression: *instigation* (parental rejection or lack of nurturance), *reinforcement* (punishment versus reward), *identification* (acquiring the parents' behavior and values), and *sociocultural norms*.

Eron's team selected the entire third-grade population of Columbia County, New York, testing 870 children and interviewing about 75 to 80 percent of their parents. Several trends became clear almost immediately. Children with less nurturing parents were more aggressive. Children who more closely identified with either parent were less aggressive. And children with low parental identification who were punished tended to be *more* aggressive (an observation which required revision of the behavioral model).

Ten years later, Eron and company tracked down and re-interviewed about half of the original sample. (They followed up on the subjects in 1981 as well.) Many of the subjects—now high-school seniors—demonstrated a persistence in aggression over time. Not only were the "peer-nominated" ratings roughly consistent with the third-grade ratings, but the more aggressive kids were three times as likely to have a police record by adulthood.

Eron's team also checked for the influences on aggression which they had previously noted when the subjects were eight. The persistent influences were parental identification and socioeconomic variables. Some previously important influences (lack of nurturance, punishment for aggression) didn't seem to affect the subjects' behavior as much in young adulthood. Eron writes of these factors:

> Their effect is short-lived and other variables are more important in predicting later aggression. Likewise, contingencies and environmental conditions can change drastically over 10 years, and thus the earlier contingent response becomes irrelevant.

It's at this stage that Eron mentions television as a factor:

> One of the best predictors of how aggressive a young man would be at age 19 was the violence of the television programs he preferred when he was 8 years old. Now, because we had longitudinal data, we could say with more certainty, on the basis of regression analysis, partial correlation, path analysis, and so forth, that there indeed was a cause-and-effect relation. *Continued research, however, has indicated that the causal effect is probably bidirectional: Aggressive children prefer violent television, and the violence on television causes them to be more aggressive.* [italics added]

Before we address the last comment, I should make one thing clear. Eron's research is sound. The methods he used to measure aggression are used by social scientists in many other contexts. His research does not ignore such obvious factors as the parents' socioeconomic status. And, as the above summary makes clear, Eron's own work makes a strong case for the positive or negative influence of parents in the development of their children's aggressiveness.

Now let's look at this "causal effect" business. Eron's data reveals that aggressive kids who turn into aggressive adults like aggressive television. But this is a correlation; it is not proof of a causal influence. If aggressive kids liked eating strawberry ice cream more often than the class wusses did, that too would be a predictor, and one might speculate on some anger-inducing chemical in strawberries.

Of course, the relation between representational violence and its influence on real life isn't as farfetched as that. The problem lies in determining precisely the nature of that relation, as we see when we look at the laboratory studies conducted by other researchers. Usually, the protocol of these experiments involves providing groups of individuals with entertainment calibrated for violent content, and studying some aspect of behavior after exposure—response to a behavioral test, which toys the children choose to play with, and so forth. But the results of these tests have been somewhat mixed. Sometimes the results are at variance with other studies, and many have methodological problems. For example, which "violent" entertainment is chosen? Bugs Bunny and the "Teenage Mutant Ninja Turtles" present action in very different contexts, and in one study, the Adam West "Batman" series was deemed nonviolent, despite those *Pow! Bam! Sock!* fistfights that ended every episode.

Many of the studies report that children do demonstrate higher levels of interpersonal aggression shortly after watching violent, energetic entertainment. But a 1971 study by Feshbach and Singer had boys from seven schools watch preassigned violent and nonviolent shows for six weeks. The results were not constant from school to school—and the boys watching the *nonviolent* shows tended to be more aggressive. Another protocol, carried out in Belgium as well as the United States, separated children into cottages at an institutional school and exposed certain groups to violent films. Higher aggression was noted in *all* groups after the films were viewed, but it returned to a near-baseline level after a week or so. (The children also rated the less violent films as less exciting, more boring, and sillier than the violent films —indicating that maybe kids *like* a little rush now and then.) Given the criticisms of the short-term-effects studies, and the alternate interpretations of the longitudinal studies, is this matter really settled?

Eron certainly thinks so. Testifying before Simon's committee in August, he declared that "the scientific debate is over" and called upon the Senate to reduce TV violence. His statement did not include any reference to such significant factors as parental identification—which, as his own research indicates, can change the way children interpret physical punishment. And even though Rowell Huesmann concurred with Eron in similar testimony before a House subcommittee, Huesmann's 1984 study of 1,500 youths in the United States, Finland, Poland, and Australia argued that, assuming a causal influence, television might be responsible for 5 percent of the violence in society. At *most*.

This is where I feel one has to part company with Leonard Eron. He is one of the most respected researchers in his field, and his work points to an imperative for parents in shaping and sharing their children's lives. But he has lent his considerable authority to such diversionary efforts as Paul Simon's and urged us to address, by questionable means, what only *might* be causing a tiny portion of real-life violence.

Some of Eron's suggestions for improving television are problematic as well. In his Senate testimony, Eron proposed restrictions on televised violence from 6:00 AM to 10:00 PM—which would exclude pro football, documentaries about World War II, and even concerned lawperson Janet Reno's proudest moments. Or take Eron's suggestion that, in televised drama, "perpetrators of violence should not be rewarded for violent acts." I don't know what shows Eron's been watching, but all of the cop shows I remember usually ended with the bad guys getting caught or killed. And when Eron suggests that "gratuitous violence that is not necessary to the plot should be reduced or abandoned," one has to ask just *who* decides that it's "not necessary"? Perhaps most troubling is Eron's closing statement:

> For many years now Western European countries have had monitoring of TV and films for violence by government agencies and have *not* permitted the showing of excess violence, especially during child viewing hours. And I've never heard complaints by citizens of those democratic countries that their rights have been violated. If something doesn't give, we may have to institute some such monitoring by government agencies here in the U.S.A. If the industry does not police itself, then there is left only the prospect of official censorship, distasteful as this may be to many of us.

* * *

The most often-cited measure of just how violent TV programs are is that of George Gerbner, dean of the Annenberg School of Communications at the University of

Pennsylvania. Few of the news stories about TV violence explain how this index is compiled, the context in which Gerbner has conducted his studies, or even some criticisms that could be raised.

Gerbner's view of the media's role in society is far more nuanced than the publicity given the violence profile may indicate. He sees television as a kind of myth-structure/religion for modern society. Television dramas, situation comedies, news shows, and all the rest create a shared culture for viewers, which "communicates much about social norms and relationships, about goals and means, about winners and losers." One portion of Gerbner's research involves compiling "risk ratios" in an effort to discern which minority groups—including children, the aged, and women—tend to be the victims of the aggressors in drama. This provides a picture of a pecking order within society (white males on top, no surprise there) that has remained somewhat consistent over the 20-year history of the index.

In a press release accompanying the 1993 violence index, Gerbner discusses his investigations of the long-term effects of television viewing. Heavy viewers were more likely to express feelings of living in a hostile world. Gerbner adds, "Violence is a demonstration of power. It shows who can get away with what against whom."

In a previous violence index compiled for cable-television programs, violence is defined as a "clear-cut and overt episode of physical violence—hurting or killing or the threat of hurting and/or killing —in any context." An earlier definition reads: "The overt expression of physical force against self or other compelling action against one's will on pain of being hurt or killed, or actually hurting or killing." These definitions have been criticized for being too broad; they encompass episodes of physical comedy, depiction of accidents in dramas, and even violent incidents in documentaries. They also include zany cartoon violence; in fact, the indexes for Saturday-morning programming tend to be substantially higher than the indexes for prime-time programming. Gerbner argues that, since he is analyzing cultural norms and since television entertainment is a deliberately conceived expression of these norms, his definition serves the purposes of his study.

The incidents of violence (total number $= R$) in a given viewing period are compiled by Gerbner's staff. Some of the statistics are easy to derive, such as the percentage of programs with violence, the number of violent scenes per hour, and the actual duration of violence, in minutes per hour. The actual violence index is calculated by adding together the following stats:

%P—the *percentage* of programs in which there is violence;

$2(R/P)$—twice the number of violent episodes per program;

$2(R/H)$—twice the number of violent episodes per *hour*;

%V—percentage of *leading characters* involved in violence, either as victim or perpetrator; and

%K—percentage of leading characters involved in an actual *killing*, either as victim or perpetrator.

But if these are the factors used to compile the violence profile, it's difficult to see how they can provide a clear-cut mandate for the specific content of television drama. For example, two of the numbers used are averages; why are they arbitrarily doubled and then added to percentages? Also, because the numbers are determined by a definition which explicitly separates violence from dramatic context, the index says little about actual television content outside of a broad, overall gauge. One may imagine a television season of nothing but slapstick comedy with a very high violence profile.

This is why the violence profile is best understood within the context of Gerbner's wider analysis of media content. It does not lend itself to providing specific conclusions or guidelines of the sort urged by Senator Paul Simon. (It is important to note that, even though Simon observed little change in prime-time violence levels during his three-year antitrust exemption, the index for all three of those years was *below* the overall 20-year score.)

* * *

Finally, there's the anecdotal evidence—loudly trumpeted as such by Carl Cannon in *Mother Jones*—where isolated examples of entertainment-inspired violence are cited as proof of its pernicious influence. Several such examples have turned up recently. A sequence was edited out of the film *The Good Son* in which McCaulay Culkin drops stuff onto a highway from an overhead bridge. (As we all know, nobody ever did this before the movie came out.) The film *The Program* was re-edited when some kids were killed imitating the film's characters, who "proved their courage" by lying down on a highway's dividing line. Perhaps most notoriously, in October 1993 a four-year-old Ohio boy set his family's trailer on fire, killing his younger sister; the child's mother promptly blamed MTV's "Beavis and Butt-head" for setting a bad example. But a neighbor interviewed on CNN reported that the family didn't even have cable television and that the kid had a local rep as a pyromaniac months before. This particular account was not followed up by the national media, which, if there were no enticing "Beavis and Butt-head" angle, would never have mentioned this fire at a low-income trailer park to begin with.

Numerous articles about media-inspired violence have cited similar stories—killers claiming to be Freddy Kreuger, kids imitating crimes they'd seen on a cop show a few days before, and so forth. In many of these cases, it is undeniably true that the person involved took his or her inspiration to act from a dramatic presentation in the media—the obvious example being John Hinckley's fixation on the film *Taxi Driver*.... But stories of media-inspired violence are striking mainly because they're so *atypical* of the norm; the vast majority of people don't take a movie or a TV show as a license to kill. Ironically, it is the *abnormality* of these stories that ensures they'll get widespread dissemination and be remembered long after the more mundane crimes are forgotten.

Of course, there are a few crazies out there who will be unfavorably influenced by what they see on TV. But even assuming that somehow the TV show (or movie or record) shares some of the blame, how does one predict what future crazies will take for inspiration? What guidelines would ensure that people write, act, or produce something that *will not upset a psychotic*? Not only is this a ridiculous demand, it's insulting to the public as well. We would all be treated as potential murderers in order to gain a hypothetical 5 percent reduction in violence.

* * *

In crusades like this—where the villagers pick up their torches and go hunting after Frankenstein—people often lose sight of what they're defending. I've read reams of statements from people who claim to know what television does to kids; but what do *kids* do with television? Almost none of what I've read gives kids any credit for thinking. None of these people seems to remember what being a kid is like.

When *Jurassic Park* was released, there was a huge debate over whether or not children should be allowed to see it. Kids like to see dinosaurs, people argued, but this movie might scare them into catatonia.... These objections were actually taken seriously. But kids like dinosaurs because they're big, look really weird, and scare the hell out of everything around them. Dinosaurs *kick ass.* What parent would tell his or her child that dinosaurs were *cute?...*

Along the same lines, what kid hasn't tried to gross out everyone at the dinner table by showing them his or her chewed-up food? Or tried using a magnifying glass on an anthill on a hot day? Or clinically inspected the first dead animal he or she ever came across? Sixty years ago, adults were terrified of *Frankenstein* and fainted at the premiere of *King Kong.* But today, *Kong* is regarded as a fantasy story, *Godzilla* can be shown without the objections of child psychologists, and there are breakfast cereals called Count Chocula and Frankenberry. Sadly, there are few adults who seem to remember how they identified more with the monsters. Who wanted to be one of those stupid villagers waving torches at Frankenstein? That's what our *parents* were like.

But it's not just an issue of kids liking violence, grossness, or comic-book adventure. About 90 percent of the cartoon shows I watched as a child were the mass-produced sludge of the Hanna-Barbera Studios—like "Wacky Races," "The Jetsons," and "Scooby Doo, Where Are You?" I can't remember a single memorable moment from any of them. But that Bugs Bunny sequence at the beginning of this article (from *Rabbit Seasoning,* 1952, directed by Chuck Jones) was done from memory, and I have no doubt that it's almost verbatim.

I know that, even at the age of eight or nine, I had some rudimentary aesthetic sense about it all. There was something hip and complex about the Warner Bros. cartoons, and some trite, insulting *sameness* to the Hanna-Barbera trash, although I couldn't quite understand it then. Bugs Bunny clearly wasn't made for kids according to some study on social-interaction development. Bugs Bunny was meant to make adults laugh as much as children. Kids can also enjoy entertainment ostensibly created for adults—in fact, that's often the most rewarding kind. I had no trouble digesting *Jaws,* James Bond, and Clint Eastwood "spaghetti westerns" in my preteen years. And I'd have no problems with showing a 10-year-old *Jurassic Park,* because I know how much he or she would love it....

I don't enjoy bad television with lots of violence, but I'd rather not lose *decent* shows that use violence for good reason. Shows like "Star Trek," "X-Men," or the spectacular "Batman: The Animated Series" can give kids a sense of adventure while teaching them about such qualities as courage, bravery, and heroism. Even better, a healthy and robust spirit of irreverence can be found in Bugs Bunny, "Ren and Stimpy," and "Tiny Toons." Some of these entertainments—like adventure stories and comic books of the past—can teach kids how to be really *alive*.

Finally, if we must have a defense against the pernicious influence of the mass media, it cannot be from the Senate's legislation or the pronouncements of social scientists. It must begin with precisely the qualities I described above—especially irreverence. One good start is Comedy Central's "Mystery Science Theater 3000," where the main characters,

forced to watch horrendous movies, fight back by heckling them. Not surprisingly, children love the show, even though most of the jokes go right over their curious little heads. They recognize a kindred spirit in "MST 3000." Kids want to stick up for themselves, maybe like Batman, maybe like Bugs Bunny, or even like Beavis and Butt-head—but always against a world made by adults.

You know, *adults*—those doofuses with the torches, trying to burn up Frankenstein in the old mill.

CHALLENGE QUESTIONS

Does Viewing Television Increase a Child's Aggression?

1. Pretend that you have two young children, ages 5 and 7. After reading the selections by Centerwall and Siano, how would you handle television for your youngsters, and why?

2. Centerwall seems to imply that children have no choice but to imitate adults; imitation is instinctive. How does this explanation involve the issues of free choice and determinism? If children are truly determined by their environments and their instincts, can they be held responsible for their actions? Why, or why not?

3. Whose view does most of the research on this issue support, Centerwall's or Siano's? Review the research at your library to help you form a judgment.

4. There is considerable research on children who watch television with their parents. One set of findings indicates that parents who actively comment upon and engage their children in discussions about television programs minimize the impact of television's ill effects. How might such research affect the debate between Centerwall and Siano?

ISSUE 7

Are Children of Divorced Parents at Greater Risk?

YES: Judith S. Wallerstein, from "Children of Divorce: The Dilemma of a Decade," in Elam W. Nunnally, Catherine S. Chilman, and Fred M. Cox, eds., *Troubled Relationships* (Sage Publications, 1988)

NO: David H. Demo and Alan C. Acock, from "The Impact of Divorce on Children," *Journal of Marriage and the Family* (August 1988)

ISSUE SUMMARY

YES: Judith S. Wallerstein, a clinician, researcher, and the senior consultant to the Marin County Community Mental Health Center, contends that children of divorced parents are at greater risk of developing mental and physical problems than are children of intact families.

NO: Sociologists David H. Demo and Alan C. Acock question the idea that intact, two-parent families are always best for children. They argue that any negative effects of divorce are short-lived and that divorce often produces many positive changes.

Over half of all marriages now end in divorce. What effect do these divorces have on the young children involved? Many people assume that the changes involved in divorce would naturally lead to some emotional problems, with potentially permanent ramifications. Hidden in this view, however, is the assumption that the traditional, two-parent family is the most appropriate environment in which to raise children. Indeed, most research on children of divorce has been based on this assumption.

Several developmental psychologists have begun to question this assumption. They suggest that nontraditional families—single-parent families, for example—can also produce happy, emotionally stable children. This could mean that divorce is not always negative. In fact, the effects of living in a highly conflictual environment—such as the environment of a couple contemplating divorce—could be more damaging than the actual act of divorce itself. In this sense, the level of family conflict would have more to do with a child's adjustment than would the number of parents he or she has.

Judith S. Wallerstein, while acknowledging certain limitations on the relevant research, contends that children of divorce are at great risk of developing problems. She argues that increased attention to education, treatment, and prevention programs is needed for this special population of children. She identifies three broad stages in the divorcing process along with the effects each stage has on the children. Wallerstein also chronicles changes in the parent-child relationship that occur during the divorce process. These include a diminished capacity of adults to parent their children, a decline in emotional sensitivity and support for the children, decreased pleasure in the parent-child relationship, and less interaction with the children. All these changes, she concludes, have a negative impact on the development of the children. She asserts that for most children, divorce is "the most stressful period of their lives."

David H. Demo and Alan C. Acock, on the other hand, argue that "it is simplistic and inaccurate to think of divorce as having uniform consequences for children." They contend that most current research is based upon Freudian or social learning concepts, which emphasize that both parents are necessary for a child to develop normally. Demo and Acock, however, question the necessity of the traditional, two-parent family. They cite evidence showing that parental separation is actually beneficial for children when the alternative is continued familial conflict. Other studies reveal that factors such as maternal employment and social support are more important than the actual divorce in determining how successfully a child develops following a family breakup. Unfortunately, most studies do not distinguish between the effects of family structure (one- versus two-parent families, for example) and the effects of divorce. Demo and Acock maintain that studies that make this distinction are required before any final conclusions can be drawn about the effects of divorce on children.

POINT	COUNTERPOINT
• Children of divorce are at greater risk of developing problems than are children in traditional, two-parent families.	• Nontraditional families can also produce healthy, emotionally stable children.
• Children experience parental separation and its aftermath as the most stressful period of their lives.	• Children who experience divorce indicate that it is preferable to living in conflict.
• There are significant negative changes in the parent-child relationship during the divorce process.	• There are positive outcomes of divorce, such as greater assumption of responsibility and internal locus of control.
• A child's age and developmental stage appear to be the most important factors affecting his or her response to divorce.	• These factors are not as important as family characteristics in understanding the effects of divorce.

YES

Judith S. Wallerstein

CHILDREN OF DIVORCE: THE DILEMMA OF A DECADE

It is now estimated that 45% of all children born in 1983 will experience their parents' divorce, 35% will experience a remarriage, and 20% will experience a second divorce (A. J. Norton, Assistant Chief, Population Bureau, United States Bureau of the Census, personal communication, 1983)....

Although the incidence of divorce has increased across all age groups, the most dramatic rise has occurred among young adults (Norton, 1980). As a result, children in divorcing families are younger than in previous years and include more preschool children. ...

Although many children weather the stress of marital discord and family breakup without psychopathological sequelae, a significant number falter along the way. Children of divorce are significantly overrepresented in outpatient psychiatric, family agency, and private practice populations compared with children in the general population (Gardner, 1976; Kalter, 1977; Tessman, 1977; Tooley, 1976). The best predictors of mental health referrals for school-aged children are parental divorce or parental loss as a result of death (Felner, Stolberg, & Cowen, 1975). A national survey of adolescents whose parents had separated and divorced by the time the children were seven years old found that 30% of these children had received psychiatric or psychological therapy by the time they reached adolescence compared with 10% of adolescents in intact families (Zill, 1983).

A longitudinal study in northern California followed 131 children who were age 3 to 18 at the decisive separation. At the 5-year mark, the investigators found that more than one-third were suffering with moderate to severe depression (Wallerstein & Kelly, 1980a). These findings are especially striking because the children were drawn from a nonclinical population and were accepted into the study only if they had never been identified before the divorce as needing psychological treatment and only if they were performing at age-appropriate levels in school. Therefore, the deterioration observed in these children's adjustment occurred largely following the family breakup....

Divorce is a long, drawn-out process of radically changing family relationships that has several stages, beginning with the marital rupture and its immediate aftermath, continuing over several years of disequilibrium, and finally coming to rest with the stabilization of a new postdivorce or remarried family unit. A complex chain of changes, many of them unanticipated and unforeseeable, are set into motion by the marital rupture and are likely to occupy a significant portion of the child or adolescent's growing years. As the author and her colleague have reported elsewhere, women in the California Children of Divorce study required three to three-and-one-half years following the decisive separation before they achieved a sense of order and predictability in their lives (Wallerstein & Kelly, 1980a). This figure probably underestimates the actual time trajectory of the child's experience of divorce. A prospective study reported that parent–child relationships began to deteriorate many years prior to the divorce decision and that the adjustment of many children in these families began to fail long before the decisive separation (Morrison, 1982). This view of the divorcing process as long lasting accords with the perspective of a group of young people who reported at a 10-year follow-up that their entire childhood or adolescence had been dominated by the family crisis and its extended aftermath (Wallerstein, 1978).

Stages in the Process

The three broad, successive stages in the divorcing process, while they overlap, are nevertheless clinically distinguishable. *The acute phase* is precipitated by the decisive separation and the decision to divorce. This stage is often marked by steeply escalating conflict between the adults, physical violence, severe distress, depression accompanied by suicidal ideation, and a range of behaviors reflecting a spilling of aggressive and sexual impulses. The adults frequently react with severe ego regression and not unusually behave at odds with their more customary demeanor. Sharp disagreement in the wish to end the marriage is very common, and the narcissistic injury to the person who feels rejected sets the stage for rage, sexual jealousy, and depression. Children are generally not shielded from this parental conflict or distress. Confronted by a marked discrepancy in images of their parents, children do not have the assurance that the bizarre or depressed behaviors and moods will subside. As a result, they are likely to be terrified by the very figures they usually rely on for nurturance and protection.

As the acute phase comes to a close, usually within the first 2 years of the divorce decision, the marital partners gradually disengage from each other and pick up the new tasks of reestablishing their separate lives. *The transitional phase* is characterized by ventures into new, more committed relationships; new work, school, and friendship groups; and sometimes new settings, new lifestyles, and new geographical locations. This phase is marked by alternating success and failure, encouragement and discouragement, and it may also last for several years. Children observe and participate in the many changes of this period. They share the trials and errors and the fluctuations in mood. For several years life may be unstable, and home may be unsettled.

Finally, *the postdivorce phase* ensues with the establishment of a fairly stable single-parent or remarried household. Eventually three out of four divorced women and four out of five divorced men reenter wedlock (Cherlin, 1981). Unfortunately, though, remarriage does not bring immediate tranquility into the lives of the family members. The early years of the remarriage are often encumbered by ghostly presences from the earlier failed marriages and by the actual presences of children and visiting parents from the prior marriage or marriages. Several studies suggest widespread upset among children and adolescents following remarriage (Crohn, Brown, Walker, & Beir, 1981; Goldstein, 1974; Kalter, 1977). A large-scale investigation that is still in process reports long-lasting friction around visitation (Jacobson, 1983).

Changes in Parent–Child Relationships

Parents experience a diminished capacity to parent their children during the acute phase of the divorcing process and often during the transitional phase as well (Wallerstein & Kelly, 1980a). This phenomenon is widespread and can be considered an expectable, divorce-specific change in parent–child relationships. At its simplest level this diminished parenting capacity appears in the household disorder that prevails in the aftermath of divorce, in the rising tempers of custodial parent and child, in reduced competence and a greater sense of helplessness in the custodial parent, and in lower expectations of the child for appropriate social behavior (Hetherington, Cox, & Cox, 1978; 1982). Diminished parenting also entails a sharp decline in emotional sensitivity and support for the child; decreased pleasure in the parent–child relationship; decreased attentiveness to the child's needs and wishes; less talk, play, and interaction with the child; and a steep escalation in inappropriate expression of anger. One not uncommon component of the parent–child relationship coincident with the marital breakup is the adult's conscious or unconscious wish to abandon the child and thus to erase the un-

happy marriage in its entirety. Child neglect can be a serious hazard.

In counterpoint to the temporary emotional withdrawal from the child, the parent may develop a dependent, sometimes passionate, attachment to the child or adolescent, beginning with the breakup and lasting throughout the lonely postseparation years (Wallerstein, 1985). Parents are likely to lean on the child and turn to the child for help, placing the child in a wide range of roles such as confidante, advisor, mentor, sibling, parent, caretaker, lover, concubine, extended conscience or ego control, ally within the marital conflict, or pivotal supportive presence in staving off depression or even suicide. This expectation that children should not only take much greater responsibility for themselves but also should provide psychological and social support for the distressed parent is sufficiently widespread to be considered a divorce-specific response along with that of diminished parenting. Such relationships frequently develop with an only child or with a very young, even a preschool, child. Not accidentally, issues of custody and visitation often arise with regard to the younger children. While such disputes, of course, reflect the generally unresolved anger of the marriage and the divorce, they may also reflect the intense emotional need of one or both parents for the young child's constant presence (Wallerstein, 1985).

Parents may also lean more appropriately on the older child or adolescent. Many youngsters become proud helpers, confidantes, and allies in facing the difficult postdivorce period (Weiss, 1979b). Other youngsters draw away from close involvement out of their fears of engulfment, and they move precipitously out of the family orbit, sometimes before they are developmentally ready....

CHILDREN'S REACTIONS TO DIVORCE

Initial Responses

Children and adolescents experience separation and its aftermath as the most stressful period of their lives. The family rupture evokes an acute sense of shock, intense anxiety, and profound sorrow. Many children are relatively content and even well-parented in families where one or both parents are unhappy. Few youngsters experience any relief with the divorce decision, and those who do are usually older and have witnessed physical violence or open conflict between their parents. The child's early responses are governed neither by an understanding of issues leading to the divorce nor by the fact that divorce has a high incidence in the community. To the child, divorce signifies the collapse of the structure that provides support and protection. The child reacts as to the cutting of his or her lifeline.

The initial suffering of children and adolescents in response to a marital separation is compounded by realistic fears and fantasies about catastrophes that the divorce will bring in its wake. Children suffer with a pervasive sense of vulnerability because they feel that the protective and nurturant function of the family has given way. They grieve over the loss of the noncustodial parent, over the loss of the intact family, and often over the multiple losses of neighborhood, friends, and school. Children also worry about their distressed parents. They are concerned about who will take care of the parent who has left and whether the custodial parent will be able to manage alone. They experience intense anger toward one or both parents whom they hold responsible for disrupting the family. Some of their anger is reactive and defends them against their own feelings of powerlessness, their concern about being lost in the shuffle, and their fear that their needs will be disregarded as the parents give priority to their own wishes and needs. Some children, especially young children, suffer with guilt over fantasied misdeeds that they feel may have contributed to the family quarrels and led to the divorce. Others feel that it is their responsibility to mend the broken marriage (Wallerstein & Kelly, 1980a).

The responses of the child also must be considered within the social context of the divorce and in particular within the loneliness and social isolation that so many children experience. Children face the tensions and sorrows of divorce with little help from anybody else. Fewer than 10% of the children in the California Children of Divorce study had any help at the time of the crisis from adults outside the family although many people, including neighbors, pediatricians, ministers, rabbis, and family friends, knew the family and the children (Wallerstein & Kelly, 1980a). Thus, another striking feature of divorce as a childhood stress is that it occurs in the absence of or falling away of customary support.

Developmental factors are critical to the responses of children and adolescents at the time of the marital rupture. Despite significant individual differences in the child, in the family, and in parent–child relations, the child's age and developmental stage appear to be the most important factors governing the initial response. The child's dominant needs, his or her capacity to perceive and understand family events, the central psychological preoccupation and conflict, the available repertoire of defense and coping strategies, and the dominant patterning of relationships and expectations all reflect the child's age and developmental stage.

A major finding in divorce research has been the common patterns of response within different age groups (Wallerstein & Kelly, 1980a). The age groups that share significant commonalities in perceptions, responses, underlying fantasies, and behaviors are the preschool ages 3 to 5, early school age or early latency ages 5 1/2 to 8, later school age or latency ages 8 to 11, and, finally, adolescent ages 12 to 18 (Kelly & Wallerstein, 1976; Wallerstein, 1977; Wallerstein & Kelly, 1974; 1975; 1980a). These responses, falling as they do into age-related groupings, may reflect children's responses to acute stress generally, not only their responses to marital rupture.

Observations about preschool children derived from longitudinal studies in two widely different regions, namely, Virginia and northern California, are remarkably similar in their findings (Hetherington, 1979; Hetherington et al., 1978; 1982; Wallerstein & Kelly, 1975, 1980a). Preschool children are likely to show regression following one parent's departure from the household, and the regression usually occurs in the most recent developmental achievement of the child. Intensified fears are frequent and are evoked by routine separations from the custodial parent during the day and at bedtime. Sleep disturbances are also frequent, with preoccupying fantasies of many of the little children being fear of abandonment by both parents. Yearning for the departed parent is intense. Young children are likely to become irritable and demanding and to behave aggressively with parents, with younger siblings, and with peers.

Children in the 5- to 8-year-old group are likely to show open grieving and are preoccupied with feelings of concern and longing for the departed parent. Many share the terrifying fantasy of replacement. "Will my daddy get a new dog, a new mommy, a new little boy?" were the comments of several boys in this age group. Little girls wove elaborate Madame Butterfly fantasies, asserting that the departed father would some day return to them, that he loved them "the best." Many of the children in this age group could not believe that the divorce would endure. About half suffered a precipitous decline in their school work (Kelly & Wallerstein, 1979).

In the 9- to 12-year-old group the central response often seems to be intense anger at one or both parents for causing the divorce. In addition, these children suffer with grief over the loss of the intact family and with anxiety, loneliness, and the humiliating sense of their own powerlessness. Youngsters in this age group often see one parent as the "good" parent and the other as "bad," and they appear especially vulnerable to the blandishments of one or the other parent to engage in marital battles. Children in later latency also have a high potential for assuming a helpful and empathic role in the care of a needy parent. School performances and peer relationships suffered a decline in approximately one-half of these children (Wallerstein & Kelly, 1974).

Adolescents are very vulnerable to their parents' divorce. The precipitation of acute depression, accompanied by suicidal preoccupation and acting out, is frequent enough to be alarming. Anger can be intense. Several instances have been reported of direct violent attacks on custodial parents by young adolescents who had not previously shown such behavior (Springer & Wallerstein, 1983). Preoccupied with issues of morality, adolescents may judge the parents' conduct during the marriage and the divorce, and they may identify with one parent and do battle against the other. Many become anxious about their own future entry into adulthood, concerned that they may experience marital failure like their parents (Wallerstein & Kelly, 1974). By way of contrast, however, researchers have also called attention to the adolescent's impressive capacity to grow in maturity and independence as they respond to the family crisis and the parents' need for help (Weiss, 1979a)....

Long-Range Outcomes

The child's initial response to divorce should be distinguished from his or her long-range development and psychological adjustment. No single theme appears among all of those children who enhance, consolidate, or continue their good development after the divorce crisis has finally ended. Nor is there a single theme that appears among all of those who deteriorate either moderately or markedly. Instead, the author and her colleague (Wallerstein & Kelly, 1980a) have found a set of complex configurations in which the relevant components appear to include (a) the extent to which the parent has been able to resolve and put aside conflict and anger and to make use of the relief from conflict provided by the divorce (Emery, 1982; Jacobson, 1978 a, b, c); (b) the course of the custodial parent's handling of the child and the resumption or improvement of parenting within the home (Hess & Camara, 1979); (c) the extent to which the

child does not feel rejected by the noncustodial or visiting parent and the extent to which this relationship has continued regularly and kept pace with the child's growth; (d) the extent to which the divorce has helped to attenuate or dilute a psychopathological parent–child relationship; (e) the range of personality assets and deficits that the child brought to the divorce, including both the child's history in the predivorce family and his or her capacities in the present, particularly intelligence, the capacity for fantasy, social maturity, and the ability to turn to peers and adults; (f) the availability to the child of a supportive human network (Tessman, 1977); (g) the absence in the child of continued anger and depression; and (h) the sex and age of the child....

FUTURE DIRECTIONS

Despite the accumulating reports of the difficulties that many children in divorced families experience, society has on the whole been reluctant to regard children of divorce as a special group at risk. Notwithstanding the magnitude of the population affected and the widespread implications for public policy and law, community attention has been very limited; research has been poorly supported; and appropriate social, psychological, economic, or preventive measures have hardly begun to develop. Recently the alarm has been sounded in the national press about the tragically unprotected and foreshortened childhoods of children of divorce and their subsequent difficulties in reaching maturity (Winn, 1983). Perhaps this reflects a long-overdue awakening of community concern.

The agenda for research on marital breakdown, separation, divorce, and remarriage and the roads that families travel between each of these way stations [are] long and [have] been cited repeatedly in this [article]. The knowledge that we have acquired is considerable but the knowledge that we still lack is critical. More knowledge is essential in order to provide responsible advice to parents; to consult effectively with the wide range of other professionals whose daily work brings them in contact with these families; to design and mount education, treatment, or prevention programs; and to provide guidelines for informed social policy.

AUTHOR'S NOTE: The Center for the Family in Transition, of which the author is the Executive Director, is supported by a grant from the San Francisco Foundation. The Zellerback Family Fund supported the author's research in the California Children of Divorce Project, one of the sources for this [article]. A slightly different version of this paper has been published in *Psychiatry Update: The American Psychiatric Association Annual Review, Vol. III.* L. Grinspoon (Ed.), pp. 144–158, 1984.

REFERENCES

Cherlin, A. J. (1981). *Marriage, divorce, remarriage.* Cambridge, MA: Harvard University Press.

Crohn, H., Brown, H., Walker, L., & Beir, J. (1981). Understanding and treating the child in the remarried family. In I. R. Stuart & L. E. Abt (Eds.), *Children of separation and divorce: Management and treatment.* New York: Van Nostrand Reinhold.

Emery, R. E. (1982). Interparental conflict and children of discord and divorce. *Psychological Bulletin, 92,* 310–330.

Felner, R. D., Stolberg, A. L., & Cowen, E. L. (1975). Crisis events and school mental health referral patterns of young children. *Journal of Consulting and Clinical Psychology, 43,* 303–310.

Gardner, R. A. (1976). *Psychotherapy and children of divorce.* New York: Jason Aronson.

Goldstein, H. S. (1974). Reconstructed families: The second marriage and its children. *Psychiatric Quarterly, 48,* 433–440.

Hess, R. D., & Camara, K. A. (1979). Post-divorce relationships as mediating factors in the consequences of divorce for children. *Journal of Social Issues, 35,* 79–96.

Hetherington, E. (1979). Divorce: A child's perspective. *American Psychology, 34,* 79–96.

Hetherington, E., Cox, M., & Cox, R. (1978). The aftermath of divorce. In H. Stevens & M. Mathews (Eds.), *Mother–child relations.* Washington, DC: National Association for the Education of Young Children.

Hetherington, E. M., Cox, M., & Cox, R. (1982). Effects of divorce on parents and children. In M. E. Lamb (Ed.), *Nontraditional families: Parenting and child development.* Hillsdale, NJ: Lawrence Erlbaum Associates.

Jacobson, D. (1978a). The impact of marital separation/divorce on children: I. Parent–child separation and child adjustment. *Journal of Divorce, 1,* 341–360.

Jacobson, D. (1978b). The impact of marital separation/divorce on children: II. Interparent hostility and child adjustment. *Journal of Divorce, 2,* 3–20.

Jacobson, D. (1978c). The impact of marital separation/divorce on children: III. Parent–child communication and child adjustment, and regression analysis of findings from overall study. *Journal of Divorce, 2,* 175–194.

Jacobson, D. S. (1983). *Conflict, visiting and child adjustment in the stepfamily: A linked family system.* Paper presented at annual meeting of the American Orthopsychiatric Association, Boston.

Kalter, N. (1977). Children of divorce in an outpatient psychiatric population. *American Journal of Orthopsychiatry, 47,* 40–51.

Kelly, J. B., & Wallerstein, J. S. (1976). The effects of parental divorce: Experiences of the child in early latency. *American Journal of Orthopsychiatry, 46,* 20–32.

Kelly, J. B., & Wallerstein, J. S. (1979). The divorced child in the school. *National Principal, 59,* 51–58.

Morrison, A. L. (1982). *A prospective study of divorce: Its relation to children's development and parental functioning.* Unpublished dissertation, University of California at Berkeley.

Norton, A. J. (1980). The influence of divorce on traditional life cycle measures. *Journal of Marriage and the Family, 42,* 63–69.

Springer, C., & Wallerstein, J. S. (1983). Young adolescents' responses to their parents' divorces. In L. A. Kurdek (Ed.), *Children and divorce.* San Francisco: Jossey-Bass.

Tessman, L. H. (1977). *Children of parting parents.* New York: Jason Aronson.

Tooley, K. (1976). Antisocial behavior and social alienation post divorce: The "man of the house" and his mother. *American Journal of Orthopsychiatry, 46,* 33–42.

Wallerstein, J. S. (1977). Responses of the pre-school child to divorce: Those who cope. In M. F. McMillan & S. Henao (Eds.), *Child psychiatry: Treatment and research.* New York: Brunner/Mazel.

Wallerstein, J. S. (1978). Children of divorce: Preliminary report of a ten-year follow-up. In J. Anthony & C. Chilland (Eds.), *The child in his family* (Vol. 5). New York: Wiley.

Wallerstein, J. S. (1985). Parent–child relationships following divorce. In E. J. Anthony & G. Pollock (Eds.), *Parental influences in health and disease* (pp. 317–348). Boston: Little, Brown.

Wallerstein, J. S., & Kelly, J. B. (1974). The effects of parental divorce: The adolescent experience. In J. Anthony & C. Koupernik (Eds.), *The child in his family: Children at psychiatric risk* (Vol. 3). New York: Wiley.

Wallerstein, J. S., & Kelly, J. B. (1975). The effects of parental divorce: The experiences of the preschool child. *American Journal of Orthopsychiatry, 46,* 256–269.

Wallerstein, J. S., & Kelly, J. B. (1980a). *Surviving the breakup: How children and parents cope with divorce.* New York: Basic Books.

Weiss, R. S. (1979a). *Going it alone: The family life and social situation of the single parent.* New York: Basic Books.

Weiss, R. S. (1979b). Growing up a little faster. *Journal of Social Issues, 35,* 97–111.

Winn, M. (8 May 1983). The loss of childhood. *The New York Times Magazine.*

Zill, N. (22 March 1983). *Divorce, marital conflict, and children's mental health: Research findings and policy recommendations.* Testimony before Subcommittee on Family and Human Services, United States Senate Subcommittee on Labor and Human Resources.

NO

David H. Demo and
Alan C. Acock

THE IMPACT OF DIVORCE ON CHILDREN

With the acceleration of the divorce rate from the mid-1960s to the early 1980s, the number of nontraditional families (such as single-parent families and reconstituted families) have increased relative to intact, first-time nuclear families. This article reviews empirical evidence addressing the relationship between divorce, family composition, and children's well-being. Although not entirely consistent, the pattern of empirical findings suggests that children's emotional adjustment, gender-role orientation, and antisocial behavior are affected by family structure, whereas other dimensions of well-being are unaffected. But the review indicates that these findings should be interpreted with caution because of the methodological deficiencies of many of the studies on which these findings are based. Several variables, including the level of family conflict, may be central variables mediating the effect of family structure on children.

The purpose of this article is to review and assess recent empirical evidence on the impact of divorce on children, concentrating on studies of nonclinical populations published in the last decade. We also direct attention to a number of important theoretical and methodological considerations in the study of family structure and youthful well-being. We begin by briefly describing some of the theoretical propositions and assumptions that guide research in this area.

THEORETICAL UNDERPINNINGS

Consistent with the Freudian assumption that a two-parent group constitutes the minimal unit for appropriate sex-typed identification, anthropologists, sociologists, and social psychologists have long maintained the necessity of such a group for normal child development. Representative of structural-functional theorizing, Parsons and Bales argued that one of the basic functions of the family is to serve as a stable, organically integrated "factory" in which human personalities are formed.

From David H. Demo and Alan C. Acock, "The Impact of Divorce on Children," *Journal of Marriage and the Family*, vol. 50, no. 3 (August 1988). Copyright © 1988 by The National Council on Family Relations, 3989 Central Avenue, NE, Suite #550, Minneapolis, MN 55421. Reprinted by permission. Notes and references omitted.

Similarly, social learning theory emphasizes the importance of role models, focusing on parents as the initial and primary reinforcers of child behavior (Bandura and Walters, 1963). Much of the research adopting this perspective centers on parent-child similarities, analyzing the transmission of response patterns and the inhibitory or disinhibitory effect of parental models. The presence of the same-sex parent is assumed to be crucial in order for the child to learn appropriate sex-typed behavior. This assumption is shared by developmental and symbolic interactionist theories, various cognitive approaches to socialization, and confluence theory, as well as anthropological theories.

It logically follows that departures from the nuclear family norm are problematic for the child's development, especially for adolescents, inasmuch as this represents a crucial stage in the developmental process. Accordingly, a large body of research literature deals with father absence, the effects of institutionalization, and a host of "deficiencies" in maturation, such as those having to do with cognitive development, achievement, moral learning, and conformity. This focus has pointed to the crucial importance of both parents' presence but also has suggested that certain causes for parental absence may accentuate any negative effects....

Divorce and Family Structure

In examining [the] research, ... it is important to distinguish between studies investigating the effects of family structure and those investigating the effects of divorce. Most studies compare intact units and single-parent families, guided by the assumption that the latter family structure is precipitated by divorce. Of course, this is not always the case. Single-parent families consist of those with parents who have never married, those formed by the permanent separation of parents, and those precipitated by the death of a parent. Simple comparisons between one- and two-parent families are also suspect in that *two*-parent families are not monolithic. First-time or nondivorced units differ from divorced, remarried units in which stepparents are involved. In addition, little recognition has been given to the fact that families of different types may exhibit varying levels of instability or conflict, a potentially confounding variable in establishing the effects of family structure. In short, most investigations of the linkage between family structure and youthful well-being have failed to recognize the complexity of present-day families....

Bearing in mind these conceptual distinctions, we now move to a systematic review of recent evidence on the impact of divorce on children and adolescents.

EXISTING RESEARCH

A substantial amount of research has examined the effects of family structure on children's social and psychological well-being. Many studies document negative consequences for children whose parents divorce and for those living in single-parent families. But most studies have been concerned with limited dimensions of a quite complex problem. Specifically, the research to date has typically (a) examined the effects of divorce or father absence on children, ignoring the effects on adolescents; (b) examined only selected dimensions of children's well-being; (c) compared intact units and single-parent families but not recognized important variations (e.g., levels of marital instability and conflict) within these structures;

and (d) relied on cross-sectional designs to assess developmental processes.

Social and psychological well-being includes aspects of personal adjustment, self-concept, interpersonal relationships, antisocial behavior, and cognitive functioning....

Personal Adjustment

Personal adjustment is operationalized in various ways by different investigators but includes such variables as self-control, leadership, responsibility, independence, achievement orientation, aggressiveness, and gender-role orientation....

On the basis of her review of research conducted between 1970 and 1980, Cashion (1984: 483) concludes: "The evidence is overwhelming that after the initial trauma of divorce, the children are as emotionally well-adjusted in these [female-headed] families as in two-parent families." Investigations of long-term effects (Acock and Kiecolt, 1988; Kulka and Weingarten, 1979) suggest that, when socioeconomic status is controlled, adolescents who have experienced a parental divorce or separation have only slightly lower levels of adult adjustment....

While their findings are not definitive, Kinard and Reinherz speculate that either "the effects of parental divorce on children diminish over time; or that the impact of marital disruption is less severe for preschool-age children than for school-age children" (1986: 291). Children's age at the time of disruption may also mediate the impact of these events on other dimensions of their well-being (e.g., self-esteem or gender-role orientation) and thus will be discussed in greater detail below.... But two variables that critically affect children's adjustment to divorce are marital discord and children's gender.

Marital discord. ... [E]xtensive data on children who had experienced their parents' divorce indicated that, although learning of the divorce and adjusting to the loss of the noncustodial parent were painful, children indicated that these adjustments were preferable to living in conflict. Many studies report that children's adjustment to divorce is facilitated under conditions of low parental conflict—both prior to *and* subsequent to the divorce (Guidubaldi, Cleminshaw, Perry, Nastasi, and Lightel, 1986; Jacobson, 1978; Lowenstein and Koopman, 1978; Porter and O'Leary, 1980; Raschke and Raschke, 1979; Rosen, 1979).

Children's gender. Children's gender may be especially important in mediating the effects of family disruption, as most of the evidence suggests that adjustment problems are more severe and last for longer periods of time among boys (Hess and Camara, 1979; Hetherington, 1979; Hetherington, Cox, and Cox, 1978, 1979, 1982; Wallerstein, 1984; Wallerstein and Kelly, 1980b). Guidubaldi and Perry (1985) found, controlling for social class, that boys in divorced families manifested significantly more maladaptive symptoms and behavior problems than boys in intact families. Girls differed only on the dimension of locus of control; girls in divorced households scored significantly higher than their counterparts in intact households....

While custodial mothers provide girls with same-sex role models, most boys have to adjust to living without same-sex parents. In examining boys and girls living in intact families and in different custodial arrangements, Santrock and Warshak (1979) found that few effects could be attributed to family structure per se, but that children living with opposite-sex parents (mother-custody boys and father-custody girls) were not as well adjusted on measures of competent social behavior....

Along related lines, a number of researchers have examined gender-role orientation and, specifically, the relation of father absence to boys' personality development. Most of the evidence indicates that boys without adult male role models demonstrate more feminine behavior (Biller, 1976; Herzog and Sudia, 1973; Lamb, 1977a), except in lower-class families (Biller, 1981b). A variety of studies have shown that fathers influence children's gender role development to be more traditional because, compared to mothers, they more routinely differentiate between masculine and feminine behaviors and encourage greater conformity to conventional gender roles (Biller, 1981a; Biller and Davids, 1973; Bronfenbrenner, 1961; Heilbrun, 1965; Lamb, 1977b; Noller, 1978).... But it should be reiterated that these effects have been attributed to father absence and thus would be expected to occur among boys in all female-headed families, not simply those that have experienced divorce....

[M]ost of the research on boys' adjustment fails to consider the quality or quantity of father-child contact or the availability of alternative male role models (e.g., foster father, grandfather, big brother, other male relatives, coach, friend, etc.), which makes it difficult to assess the impact of changing family structure on boys' behavior. There are also limitations imposed by conceptualizing and measuring masculinity-femininity as a bipolar construct (Bem, 1974; Constantinople, 1973; Worell, 1978), and there is evidence that boys and girls in father-absent families are better described as androgynous (Kurdek and Siesky, 1980a).

Positive outcomes of divorce. ... [T]he tendency of children in single-parent families to display more androgynous behavior may be interpreted as a beneficial effect. Because of father absence, children in female-headed families are not pressured as strongly as their counterparts in two-parent families to conform to traditional gender roles. These children frequently assume a variety of domestic responsibilities to compensate for the absent parent (Weiss, 1979), thereby broadening their skills and competencies and their definitions of gender-appropriate behavior. Divorced parents also must broaden their behavioral patterns to meet increased parenting responsibilities, thereby providing more androgynous role models. Kurdek and Siesky (1980a: 250) give the illustration that custodial mothers often "find themselves needing to acquire and demonstrate a greater degree of dominance, assertiveness, and independence while custodial fathers may find themselves in situations eliciting high degrees of warmth, nurturance, and tenderness."

Aside from becoming more androgynous, adolescents living in single-parent families are characterized by greater maturity, feelings of efficacy, and an internal locus of control (Guidubaldi and Perry, 1985; Kalter, Alpern, Spence, and Plunkett, 1984; Wallerstein and Kelly, 1974; Weiss, 1979). For adolescent girls this maturity stems partly from the status and responsibilities they acquire in peer and confidant relationships with custodial mothers....

There is evidence (Kurdek et al., 1981) that children and adolescents with an internal locus of control and a high level of interpersonal reasoning adjust more easily to their parents' divorce and that children's divorce adjustment is related to their more global personal adjustment.

Self-Concept...

Marital discord. ... [F]amily structure is unrelated to children's self-esteem (Feldman and Feldman, 1975; Kinard and Reinherz, 1984; Parish, 1981; Parish, Dostal, and Parish, 1981), but parental discord is negatively related (Amato, 1986; Berg and Kelly, 1979; Cooper, Holman, and Braithwaite, 1983; Long, 1986; Raschke and Raschke, 1979; Slater and Haber, 1984). Because this conclusion is based on diverse samples of boys and girls of different ages in different living arrangements, the failure to obtain effects of family structure suggests either that family composition really does not matter for children's self-concept or that family structure alone is an insufficient index of familial relations. Further, these studies suggest that divorce per se does not adversely affect children's self-concept. Cashion's (1984) review of the literature indicates that children living in single-parent families suffer no losses to self-esteem, except in situations where the child's family situation is stigmatized (Rosenberg, 1979)....

Cognitive Functioning
... Many ... studies find that family conflict and disruption are associated with inhibited cognitive functioning (Blanchard and Biller, 1971; Feldman and Feldman, 1975; Hess and Camara, 1979; Kinard and Reinherz, 1986; Kurdek, 1981; Radin, 1981).... In this section we summarize the differential effects of family disruption on academic performance by gender and social class and offer some insights as to the mechanisms by which these effects occur.

Children's gender. Some studies suggest that negative effects of family disruption on academic performance are stronger for boys than for girls (Chapman, 1977; Werner and Smith, 1982), but most of the evidence suggests similar effects by gender (Hess and Camara, 1979; Kinard and Reinherz, 1986; Shinn, 1978). While females traditionally outscore males on standardized tests of verbal skills and males outperform females on mathematical skills, males who have experienced family disruption generally score higher on verbal aptitude (Radin, 1981). Thus, the absence of a father may result in a "feminine" orientation toward education (Fowler and Richards, 1978; Herzog and Sudia, 1973). But an important and unresolved question is whether this pattern results from boys acquiring greater verbal skills in mother-headed families or from deficiencies in mathematical skills attributable to father absence. The latter explanation is supported by evidence showing that father-absent girls are disadvantaged in mathematics (Radin, 1981).

Children's race. ... [M]ost studies show academic achievement among black children to be unaffected by family structure (Hunt and Hunt, 1975, 1977; Shinn, 1978; Solomon, Hirsch, Scheinfeld, and Jackson, 1972). Svanum, Bringle, and McLaughlin (1982) found, controlling for social class, that there are no significant effects of father absence on cognitive performance for white or black children. Again, these investigations focus on family composition and demonstrate that the effects of family structure on academic performance do not vary as much by race as by social class, but race differences in the impact of divorce remain largely unexplored....

Family socioeconomic status. ... When social class is controlled, children in female-headed families fare no worse than children from two-parent families on measures of intelligence (Bachman, 1970; Kopf, 1970), academic achievement (Shinn, 1978; Svanum et al., 1982), and educational attainment (Bachman, O'Malley, and Johnston, 1978).... In order to disentangle the intricate effects of family structure and SES [socioeconomic status] on children's cognitive performance, family researchers need to examine the socioeconomic history of intact families and those in which disruption occurs, to examine the economic resources available to children at various stages of cognitive development, and to assess changes in economic resources and family relationships that accompany marital disruption.

Family processes. ... First, family disruption alters daily routines and work schedules and imposes additional demands on adults and children living in single-parent families (Amato, 1987; Furstenberg and Nord, 1985; Hetherington et al., 1983; Weiss, 1979). Most adolescents must assume extra domestic and child care responsibilities, and financial conditions require some to work part-time. These burdens result in greater absenteeism, tardiness, and truancy among children in single-parent households (Hetherington et al., 1983). Second, children in recently disrupted families are prone to experience emotional and behavioral problems such as aggression, distractibility, dependency, anxiety, and withdrawal (Hess and Camara, 1979; Kinard and Reinherz, 1984), factors that may help to explain problems in school conduct and the propensity of teachers to label and stereotype children from broken families (Hess and Camara, 1979; Hetherington et al., 1979, 1983). Third, emotional problems may interfere with study patterns, while demanding schedules reduce the time available for single parents to help with homework....

Interpersonal Relationships ...

Peer relations. Studies of preschool children (Hetherington et al., 1979) and preadolescents (Santrock, 1975; Wyman, Cowen, Hightower, and Pedro-Carroll, 1985) suggest that children in disrupted families are less sociable: they have fewer close friends, spend less time with friends, and participate in fewer shared activities. Stolberg and Anker (1983) observe that children in families disrupted by divorce exhibit psychopathology in interpersonal relations, often behaving in unusual and inappropriate ways. Other studies suggest that the effects are temporary. Kinard and Reinherz (1984) found no differences in peer relations among children in intact and disrupted families, but those in recently disrupted families displayed greater hostility. Kurdek et al. (1981) conducted a two-year follow-up of children whose parents had divorced and showed that relationships with peers improved after the divorce and that personal adjustment was facilitated by opportunities to discuss experiences with peers, some of whom had similar experiences....

Dating patterns. Hetherington (1972) reported that adolescent girls whose fathers were absent prior to age 5 had difficulties in heterosexual relations, but Hainline and Feig's (1978) analyses of female college students indicated that early and later father-absent women could not be distinguished on measures of romanticism and heterosexual attitudes.

An examination of dating and sexual behavior among female college students found that women with divorced parents began dating slightly later than those in intact families, but women in both groups were socially active (Kalter, Riemer, Brickman, and Chen, 1985). Booth, Brinkerhoff, and White (1984) reported that, compared to college students with intact families, those whose parents were divorced or permanently separated exhibited higher levels of dating activity, and this activity increased further if parental or parent-child conflict persisted during and after the divorce. . . . Regarding adolescent sexual behavior, the findings consistently demonstrate that males and females not living with both biological parents initiate coitus earlier than their counterparts in intact families (Hogan and Kitagawa, 1985; Newcomer and Udry, 1987). But Newcomer and Udry propose that, because parental marital status is also associated with a broad range of deviant behaviors, these effects may stem from general loss of parental control rather than simply loss of control over sexual behavior. Studies of antisocial behavior support this interpretation.

Antisocial Behavior

Many studies over the years have linked juvenile delinquency, deviancy, and antisocial behavior to children living in broken homes (Bandura and Walters, 1959; Glueck and Glueck, 1962; Hoffman, 1971; McCord, McCord, and Thurber, 1962; Santrock, 1975; Stolberg and Ank-

er, 1983; Tooley, 1976; Tuckman and Regan, 1966). Unfortunately, these studies either relied on clinical samples or failed to control for social class and other factors related to delinquency. However, . . . a number of studies involving large representative samples and controlling for social class provide similar findings (Dornbusch, Carlsmith, Bushwall, Ritter, Leiderman, Hastorf, and Gross, 1985; Kalter et al., 1985; Peterson and Zill, 1986; Rickel and Langner, 1985). Kalter et al. (1985) studied 522 teenage girls and found that girls in divorced families committed more delinquent acts (e.g., drug use, larceny, skipping school) than their counterparts in intact families. Dornbusch et al. (1985) examined a representative national sample of male and female youth aged 12–17 and found that adolescents in mother-only households were more likely than their counterparts in intact families to engage in deviant acts, partly because of their tendency to make decisions independent of parental input. The presence of an additional adult (a grandparent, an uncle, a lover, a friend) in mother-only households increased control over adolescent behavior and lowered rates of deviant behavior, which suggests that "there are functional equivalents of two-parent families—nontraditional groupings that can do the job of parenting" (1985: 340). . . .

A tentative conclusion based on the evidence reviewed here is that antisocial behavior is less likely to occur in families where two adults are present, whether as biological parents, stepparents, or some combination of biological parents and other adults. Short-term increases in antisocial behavior may occur during periods of disruption, however, as children adjust to restructured relationships and parents struggle to maintain consistency in disciplining (Rickel and Langner, 1985).... Peterson and Zill (1986) demonstrated that, when social class was controlled, behavior problems were as likely to occur among adolescents living in intact families characterized by persistent conflict as among those living in disrupted families.... Peterson and Zill found that "poor parent-child relationships lead to more negative child behavior, yet maintaining good relationships with parents can go some way in reducing the effects of conflict and disruption" (1986: 306). Hess and Camara's (1979) analyses of a much smaller sample yielded a similar conclusion: aggressive behavior in children was unrelated to family type but was more common in situations characterized by infrequent or low-quality parent-child interaction and parental discord....

CONCLUSIONS

There is reason to question the validity of the family composition hypothesis. Theoretically, it has been assumed that the nuclear family is the norm and, by implication, that any departure from it is deviant and therefore deleterious to those involved. Even if this were the case, no theoretical perspective recognizes that these effects may be short-lived or otherwise mitigated by compensatory mechanisms and alternative role models. In the absence of a parent, it is possible that developmental needs are met by other actors.

It is simplistic and inaccurate to think of divorce as having uniform consequences for children. The consequences of divorce vary along different dimensions of well-being, characteristics of children (e.g., predivorce adjustment, age at the time of disruption) and charac-teristics of families (e.g., socioeconomic history, pre- and postdivorce level of conflict, parent-child relationships, and maternal employment). Most of the evidence reviewed here suggests that some sociodemographic characteristics of children, such as race and gender, are not as important as characteristics of families in mediating the effects of divorce. Many studies report boys to be at a greater disadvantage, but these differences usually disappear when other relevant variables are controlled. At present, there are too few methodologically adequate studies comparing white and black children to conclude that one group is more damaged by family disruption than the other.

Characteristics of families, on the other hand, are critical to youthful well-being. Family conflict contributes to many problems in social development, emotional stability, and cognitive skills (Edwards, 1987; Kurdek, 1981), and these effects continue long after the divorce is finalized. Slater and Haber (1984) report that ongoing high levels of conflict, whether in intact or divorced homes, produce lower self-esteem, increased anxiety, and a loss of self-control. Conflict also reduces the child's attraction to the parents (White, Brinkerhoff, and Booth, 1985). Rosen (1979) concludes that parental separation is more beneficial for children than continued conflict.... Such conflict and hostility may account for adolescent adjustment problems whether the family in question goes through divorce or remains intact (Hoffman, 1971). The level of conflict is thus an important dimension of family interaction that can precipitate changes in family structure and affect children's well-being.

Maternal employment is another variable mediating the consequences of divorce for children. Divorced women often find the dual responsibilities of provider and parent to be stressful (Bronfenbrenner, 1976). But studies indicate that women who work prior to the divorce do not find continued employment problematic (Kinard and Reinherz, 1984); the problem occurs for women who enter the labor force after the divorce and who view the loss of time with their children as another detriment to the children that is caused by the divorce (Kinard and Reinherz, 1984). As a practical matter, the alternative to employment for single-parent mothers is likely to be poverty or, at best, economic dependency. The effects of maternal employment on children's well-being need to be compared to the effects of nonemployment and consequent poverty.

Other bases of social support for single-parent mothers and their children must also be examined. The presence of strong social networks may ease the parents' and, presumably, the child's adjustment after a divorce (Milardo, 1987; Savage et al., 1978). However, women who are poor, have many children, and must work long hours are likely to have limited social networks and few friends. Typically, the single mother and her children are also isolated from her ex-husband's family (Anspach, 1976). By reuniting with her family of origin, the mother may be isolated from her community and new social experiences for herself and her children (McLanahan, Wedemeyer, and Adelberg, 1981). Kinship ties are usually strained, as both biological parents and parents-in-law are more critical of the divorce than friends are (Spanier and Thompson, 1984). Little has been done to relate these considerations about kinship relations and social networks of divorced women to the well-being of children and adolescents. We believe that these social relations are important, but empirical verification is needed.

CHALLENGE QUESTIONS

Are Children of Divorced Parents at Greater Risk?

1. How should parents help their children to adjust to divorce? What types of educational and treatment programs should be established to support children of divorce?

2. Which do you feel is more damaging to children, divorce or living in a conflictual environment? Give reasons (and possibly research) to support your stance.

3. What do you feel is the most significant factor affecting children's adjustment following divorce? Why? How would this affect treatment strategies for children?

4. Demo and Acock list several positive outcomes of divorce. Why do you think these occur, and can you think of other possible positive outcomes?

On the Internet . . .

Basic Neural Processes
A highly interactive site tutorial on brain structures by Dr. John H. Krantz, Hanover College.
http://psych.hanover.edu/Krantz/neurotut.html

Cognitive Science Society, Inc.
This is the home page for the Cognitive Science Society, Inc. *http://www.pitt.edu/~cogsci95/*

Max Planck Institute for Psychological Research
Several behavioral and cognitive development research projects are available at this site.
http://www.mpipf-muenchen.mpg.de/BCD/bcd_e.htm

Psychology Tutorials
A collection of interactive tutorials and simulations, primarily in the areas of sensation and perception, is available at this site.
http://psych.hanover.edu/Krantz/tutor.html

Shinshu University, Japan, Starting Points for Psychology and Cognitive Sciences
This page contains a large collection of psychology and cognitive science sites.
http://sasuke.shinshu-u.ac.jp/psych/

The Wonders of the Mind
At this site 12 world-class psychologists, neuroscientists, roboticists, and psychiatrists present the big picture on how the mind works in the brain.
http://www.hypermind.com/mind/MIND.HTM

Your Mind's Eye
This site is a multimedia museum exhibit on illusions, which is a natural teaching device that will inform and delight the user about something that is most central to us: how we think and perceive.
http://illusionworks.com/YME001.htm

PART 4

Cognitive Processes

The nature and limitations of our mental (or cognitive) processes pose fundamental questions for psychologists. Are mental capacities, such as intelligence, determined at birth? And if so, could there be innate differences in intelligence between racial groups? Also, how reliable is memory? For example, are memories of early sexual abuse always reliable? Can they be trusted enough to bring alleged abusers to trial?

■ Is There a Racial Difference in Intelligence?

■ Are Memories of Sex Abuse Always Real?

ISSUE 8

Is There a Racial Difference in Intelligence?

YES: J. Philippe Rushton, from "The Equalitarian Dogma Revisited," *Intelligence* (vol. 19, 1994)

NO: Zack Z. Cernovsky, from "On the Similarities of American Blacks and Whites: A Reply to J. P. Rushton," *Journal of Black Studies* (July 1995)

ISSUE SUMMARY

YES: Professor of psychology J. Philippe Rushton argues that there is irrefutable scientific evidence of racial differences in intelligence that are attributable to genetic differences.

NO: Teacher and psychologist Zack Z. Cernovsky argues that Rushton's data is based not on contemporary scientific research standards but on racial prejudice that is reflective of Nazi dogma.

One of the most heated controversies in psychology concerns the issue of race and intelligence. No psychologist wants to be considered a racist, but research findings that seem to show racial differences in intelligence continue to pop up. If we give credence to these findings, do we support racism? Traditionally, psychological researchers have resisted racism by denying the existence of innate differences between the races, such as differences in innate intelligence. This denial is sometimes referred to as *equalitarianism*—the assumption that all races are essentially equal. The problem is that equalitarian assumptions do not always seem to fit with the research findings on intelligence.

Some claim that equalitarian assumptions are themselves biasing scientific findings. In other words, scientists do not find racial differences in their research, because it is politically incorrect to do so. This is why the publication of *The Bell Curve: Intelligence and Class Structure in American Life* (Free Press, 1994) sent shock waves through the psychological community. The authors of this book, Richard J. Herrnstein and Charles Murray, claimed that genetically determined factors lead to the racial differences often seen in intelligence research. They argued that blacks consistently score lower on IQ tests than whites do. Perhaps more controversial, Herrnstein and Murray held that differences in test scores could not be attributed to cultural biases or environmental factors.

The author of the following selection, J. Philippe Rushton, essentially agrees with the authors of *The Bell Curve*. He argues that his research shows that there are undeniable racial differences in intelligence. He begins by contending that blacks, on average, have smaller skulls and brains than many other races. He then asserts that there is a link between brain size and intelligence. His conclusion from this line of reasoning is that there is a genetic and evolutionary origin for lower levels of intelligence among black populations. Rushton also claims that because his conclusion is unpopular, his research is routinely censored. He points to dire consequences for scientific and psychological scholarship if it bases validity on political agendas rather than objective results.

The author of the second selection, Zack Z. Cernovsky, vigorously disagrees with Rushton. Cernovsky considers the research that links brain size and intelligence to be faulty, and he claims that some of Rushton's own data contradict his position. Part of Rushton's problem, according to Cernovsky, is that he is biased by a genetic model of human nature and intelligence. Cernovsky contends that this model tends to ignore the plasticity of human beings, which is itself highly supported by empirical data. In this sense, Rushton is looking at his data through a biased lens, supported only by similarly biased and flawed research. According to Cernovsky, Rushton's research has been censored not because of its political incorrectness but because of its poor scholarship.

POINT

- On average, blacks have smaller skulls and brains than whites do.

- Brain size can be shown to correlate with intelligence; therefore, blacks are genetically predetermined to have lower intelligence levels.

- Black males have greater levels of testosterone, leading to their exhibiting more sexual activity and violent behavior than white males.

- Corruption in scholarship has lead to the suppression of views that are politically incorrect.

COUNTERPOINT

- The science used by Rushton rests on the same foundation that Nazi "scientists" used to show that Jews were less intelligent and thus inferior.

- The correlation between brain size and intelligence is weak and poorly conceived.

- Rushton uses nonscientific and methodologically inadequate sources to support his claims about racial differences in behavior.

- Rushton's work is unacceptable because of its poor scholarship.

YES

J. Philippe Rushton

THE EQUALITARIAN DOGMA REVISITED

RACE DIFFERENCES

The historical record shows that an African cultural disadvantage has existed, relative to Europeans and Asians, ever since Europeans first made contact 2,000 years ago (Baker, 1974; Rushton, 1995). However, until recently, it was not possible to be certain about the cause of the Black–White difference. Today the evidence has increased so much that it is almost certain that only evolutionary (and thereby genetic) theories can explain it. Surveys show that a plurality of experts in psychological testing and behavioral genetics think that a portion of the Black–White difference in IQ scores is genetic in origin (Snydermann & Rothman, 1987, 1988).

The IQ debate became international in scope when research showed that Asians scored higher on tests of mental ability than did Whites, whereas Africans and Caribbeans scored lower (Lynn, 1982, 1991; Vernon, 1982). The debate was also widened by data showing the same worldwide racial ordering in activity level, personality, speed of maturation, crime, family structure, and health (Rushton, 1995). I explored these and other variables and found that East Asians consistently averaged at one end of a continuum, Africans consistently at the other, and Caucasians consistently in between. There is, of course, enormous overlap in the distributions and thus, it is highly problematic to generalize from a group average to an individual.

The central theoretical questions are: Why should Caucasoids average so consistently between Negroids and Mongoloids on so many different dimensions? And, why is there an inverse relation between brain size and gamete production across the races? . . .

Brain Size

Rushton (1995) reviewed 100 years of scientific literature and found that across a triangulation of procedures, brains of Mongoloids average about 17 cm³ (1 in.³) larger than those of Caucasoids, whose brains average about 80 cm³ (5 in.³) larger than those of Negroids. For example, using brain mass at autopsy, Ho, Roessmann, Straumfjord, and Monroe (1980) summarized data for 1,261 Americans aged 25 to 80 after excluding obviously damaged brains. They reported a significant sex-combined difference between 811 Whites with a mean of 1,323 g (SD = 146) and 450 Blacks with a mean of 1,223 g (SD = 144). Using endocranial volume, Beals, Smith, and Dodd (1984, p. 307, Table 5) analyzed 20,000 crania and found sex-combined brain cases differed by continental area. Excluding Caucasoid areas of Asia (e.g., India) and Africa (e.g., Egypt), 19 Asian populations averaged 1,415 cm³ (SD = 51), 10 European groups averaged 1,362 cm³ (SD = 35), and 9 African groups averaged 1,268 cm³ (SD = 85). Using external head measurements, Rushton (1992b) found, in a stratified random sampling of 6,325 U.S. Army personnel measured in 1988 to determine head size for fitting helmets, Asian Americans, White Americans, and Black Americans averaged 1,416 cm³, 1,380 cm³, and 1,359 cm³, respectively. With data on tens of thousands of men and women collated by the International Labor Office in Geneva, Asians, Europeans, and Africans averaged, respectively, 1,308 cm³, 1,297 cm³, and 1,241 cm³ (Rushton, 1994)....

Intelligence

The global literature on cognitive ability was reviewed by Lynn (1991). Caucasoids in North American, Europe, and Australasia had mean IQs of around 100. Mongoloids, measured in North America and in Pacific Rim countries, had higher means, in the range of 101 to 111. Africans living south of the Sahara, African Americans, and African Caribbeans (including those living in Britain), had mean IQs from 70 to 90. However, the question remains whether test scores are valid measures of group differences in mental ability. Basically, the answer hinges on whether the tests are culture bound. Doubts about validity linger in many quarters, although considerable technical work has disposed of this problem among those with psychometric expertise (Jensen, 1980; Syndermann & Rothman, 1987, 1988; Wigdor & Garner, 1982). This is because the tests show similar patterns of internal item consistency and predictive validity for all groups, and the same differences are found on relatively culture-free tests....

The Brain Size–IQ Link

A positive correlation between mental ability and brain size has been established in studies using magnetic resonance imaging, which in vivo, construct three-dimensional pictures of the brain (Andreasen et al., 1993; Raz et al., 1993; Wickett, Vernon, & Lee, 1994; Willerman, Schultz, Rutledge, & Bigler, 1991). These confirm correlations, reported since the turn of the century, from measurements of head perimeter (Wickett et al., 1994). The brain size–cognitive ability correlations range from .10 to .40.

Two studies imply that brain size differences underlie the Black–White difference in mental ability. In an adolescent sample, Jensen (1994) found that the greater the difference between White and Black children on 17 tests, the higher was the tests' correlation with head size.... In a study of 14,000 4-7-year-olds, when the White and Black children were matched on IQ, they no longer differed in head size (Jensen & Johnson, 1994).

Other Variabels

... [T]he Asian–White–Black racial matrix occurs on a surprisingly wide range of dimensions. For example, the racial pattern in violent crime found within the U.S. holds internationally. I averaged several years of international police statistics to find rates of murder, rape, and serious assault to be three times higher in African and Caribbean countries than in Pacific Rim countries, again with European countries intermediate (Rushton, 1990). These results make it clear that whatever the causes of violent crime turn out to be, they must lie beyond U.S. particulars.

One neurohormonal contributor to crime is testosterone. As I review in *Race, Evolution and Behavior* (Rushton, 1995), studies show 3% to 19% more testosterone in Black college students and military veterans than in their White counterparts (e.g., Ellis & Nyborg, 1991), with the Japanese showing lower amounts than Whites. Sex hormones go everywhere in the body and have been shown to activate many brain-behavior systems involving crime, personality, and reproduction. As another example, around the world, the rate of dizygotic twinning per 1,000 births, caused by a double ovulation, is less than 4 among Mongoloids, 8 among Caucasoids, and 16 or greater among Negroids (Bulmer, 1970; Imaizumi, 1991).

Worldwide surveys show more sexual activity in Negroids compared to Caucasoids and especially to Mongoloids. Differences in sexual activity translate into consequences. International fertility rates show the racial pattern; so does the pattern of AIDS. As of January 1, 1994, World Health Organization and Centers for Disease Control and Prevention statistics showed infection rates, per hundred thousand population, for (a) Asian Americans and Asians in the Pacific Rim of less than 1, (b) European Americans and Europeans in Europe, Canada, and Australasia of 86, and (c) African Americans and Africans south of the Sahara and in the Caribbean of 355....

De Facto Censorship

It is important to draw attention to what sociologist Robert Gordon refers to as "one-party science." Irrespective of religious background, or political affiliation, virtually all American intellectuals adhere to what Linda Gottfredson (1994) called the "egalitarian fiction." For example, only politically correct hypotheses centering on cultural disadvantage are postulated to explain the differential representation of minorities in science. Analyses of aptitude test scores and behavioral genetics are taboo. Moralizing is so fierce that most sensible people avoid the taboo. This encourages vicious attacks on those who are convinced that there is a genetic basis underlying individual and group differences.

The high-placed pervasiveness of the egalitarian fiction is worrying. In an annual feature in *Science* (e.g., November 13, 1991, November 12, 1993 issues), the underrepresentation of minority scientists is documented. Unflinching statistics are accompanied by muddled analysis. First, the word *minority* is too inclusive. Only Blacks, Hispanics and American Indians are underrepresented in science: Several other minorities are overrepresented. Adopting the criterion of being listed in *American Men and Women of Science*, and using Weyl's (1989) ethnic classification of surnames, Chinese are overrepresented relative to their numbers in the population by 620%, Japanese by 351%, and Jews by 424%. These figures cast doubt on an explanation based on prejudice and, instead, suggest factors intrinsic to the various groups. The one-party line was forcefully presented in a lead editorial in *Nature* against my work (Maddox, 1992), which likened the possibility of finding significant group differences in brain size to contradicting accepted views of an ellipsoid earth, continental drift, and relativity theory.[1] ...

Many of my colleagues tell me, privately, that they agree with my views, not just about brain size and intelligence but also about the genetic basis of race differences in crime and other variables. I have even known senior African American police administrators who have told me that they believe biological factors underlie racial differences in crime. But, of course, my informants go on to say, "Please don't quote me." ...

In conclusion, I suggest that it is a dereliction of duty for us to continue to put up with the egalitarian dogma. It is immoral to know, or even suspect, the truth and to remain silent. Although rational people are not immune to data, they are also influenced by the judgment of their peers. If more scientists would speak openly about the views they now voice only in private, our world would become not only a safer place, but a more enlightened one as well.

NOTES

1. Special sections on "Women in Science" (*Science*, April 16, 1993, March 11, 1994), as well as the editorial in *Nature* by John Maddox (1992) also ignored or denigrated sex differences in aptitudes and brain size.

NO

Zack Z. Cernovsky

ON THE SIMILARITIES OF AMERICAN BLACKS AND WHITES

The history of science teaches us that many ambitious racists attempted to manufacture scientific evidence for their beliefs. Sooner or later, their charlatan style methodology (e.g., the use of skull circumference measurement by Nazi "scientists" during the World War II) and logical inconsistencies resulted in their rejection by the scientific community. A contemporary example of this trend is the work of J. Philippe Rushton. He recently wrote a large number of repetitive articles in which he revived the old-fashioned Nazi method of skull circumference measurement and claimed that Blacks are genetically less intelligent, endowed with smaller brains, oversexed, and more prone to crime and mental disease than Whites. Only some of the numerous methodological flaws in his work are discussed in the present article.

Although Rushton (1988, 1990a, 1991) implied that Blacks are consistently found to have *smaller brains* than Whites, some of the studies listed in his reviews actually show opposite trends: North American Blacks were superior to American Whites in brain weight (see Tobias, 1970, p. 6: 1355 g vs. 1301 g) or were found to have cranial capacities favorably comparable to the average for various samples of Caucasians (see Herskovits, 1930) and number of excess neurons larger than many groups of Caucasoids, for example, the English and the French (see Tobias, 1970, p. 9). In general, skulls from people in countries with poverty and infant malnutrition are smaller regardless of race. This trend is apparent even in Rushton's (1990b) tabularly summary of Herskovits's review: Caucasoids from Cairo had far smaller crania than North American Negroes (see more details in Cernovsky, 1992). In this respect, Rushton (1990a, 1990b, 1990c) also repeatedly misrepresented findings by Beals, Smith, and Dodd (1984) on cranial capacity. Rushton implied that Beals et al. presented large-scale evidence for racial inferiority of the Blacks with respect to cranial size. De facto, extensive statistical analyses by Beals et al. showed that cranial size varies primarily with climatic zones (e.g., distance from the equator), *not* race. According to Beals et al., the correlations of brain size to race are spurious: smaller crania are found in warmer climates, irrespective of race.

From Zack Z. Cernovsky, "On the Similarities of American Blacks and Whites: A Reply to J. P. Rushton," *Journal of Black Studies*, vol. 25, no. 6 (July 1995). Copyright © 1995 by Sage Publications, Inc. Reprinted by permission. Notes and references omitted.

And, although Rushton misleadingly reported Tobias's (1970) and Herskovits's (1930) surveys of cranial data as confirming his theory, their data are more consistent with the model presented by Beals et al. As already mentioned, in their reviews, cranial size and number of excess neurons of North American Blacks compared favorably to those of Caucasoids. It is only by pooling their data with data for Negroids from countries in hot climatic zones (notorious for famine and infant malnutrition) that Rushton obtained an illusory support for his postulates.

Rushton's (1988, Table 1) use of brain and cranial size as indicators of intelligence in humans is statistically absurd: Rushton's (1990a) own data showed that brain size and intelligence, in Homo sapiens, are only weakly related (average Pearson $r = .18$) and the highest correlations reported by Rushton were only .35, implying only 12.3% of shared variance (see critique by Cernovsky, 1991). In the past decades, even some persons with extremely small cerebral cortices were found by Lorber to have IQs in the superior range (> 120) and performed well in academic settings (Lewin, 1980). Rushton's pseudoscientific writings perpetuate lay public's misconceptions and promote racism.

Rushton (1990a, 1990c, 1991) also misrepresents the evidence for racial differences in brain/body size ratio. For example, Herskovits's (1930) data suggest that there is no consistent Black/White difference with respect to stature or crania. And, with respect to Rushton's claim about the relationships of the brain/body size ratio to intelligence, this conceptual framework is suitable for some species of animals but not necessarily for the restricted range of data. The comparison of gender differences on three different brain/body indices by Ho, Roessman, Straumfjord, and Monroe (1980) led to inconsistent results. Further empirical data in this field are necessary: Authoritarian statements "about the reality of racial differences," based on conveniently selected trends in the data, do not qualify as a scientific contribution.

Contrary to Rushton's speculations on *race and crime*, skin color would be a poor predictor of crime rate due to low base rates and very large intragroup variance. His own data (summaries of Interpol statistics, Rushton, 1990c, 1995) can be reinterpreted as showing that relying on race as an indicator of crime leads to 99.8% of false positives (Cernovsky and Litman, 1993a). The average correlations between race and crime are too low and inconsistent to support genetic racial speculations and, in fact, might point to the opposite direction than Rushton postulated (see higher crime rates in Whites than in Blacks in Interpol data analyses, Cernovsky & Litman, 1993b).

To demonstrate that Blacks are *less intelligent* and, perhaps, to allege that this is genetically given, with only minor environmental modifications, Rushton (1988, 1991) refers not only to his own biased review of brain size studies but also to Jensen's work. Yet, it has been shown that the theories favoring hereditarian over environmentalist explanations tend to be based on poor methodology (see Kamin, 1980) and that Jensen's estimates of "hereditability" are based on too many assumptions, which hardly could all be met (Taylor, 1980). Some applications of the heritability estimates were shown to have absurd consequences (Flynn, 1987a). Similarly, Jensen's recent claims about racial differences in reaction time are biased and might lack in scientific integrity (Kamin & Grant-Henry,

1987). There is no solid evidence in favor of heritability over environmental influences with respect to the development of intelligence (see a review in Kamin, 1980, and Flynn, 1987a, 1987b).

In a similar vein, some of Rushton's references to scientific literature with respect to racial differences in *sexual characteristics* turned out to be references to a nonscientific semipornographic book and to an article in the *Penthouse* Forum (see a review in Weizmann, Wiener, Wiesenthal, & Ziegler, 1991). Rushton's claims that *fertility* rates are higher in Blacks disharmonize with well-known high figures for some Caucasoids such as North American Hutterites (a group of Swiss-German ancestry, see a review in Weizmann et al., 1990, 1991). Rushton's claims about racial differences with respect to brain, intelligence, crime, sexuality, and fertility (and also twinning rates; see Lynn, 1989a, 1989b; Weizmann et al., 1991) are based on an extremely biased and inadequate review of literature.

Erroneously relying on data based on hospital admission rates, Rushton (1988) concluded that mental disease is more frequent in Blacks than Whites. Members of the lower socioeconomic class are overrepresented in official hospital admission statistics because the private and more confidential treatment resources are not accessible to them. More adequate epidemiological studies by Robins et al. (1984) based on random sampling show no significant link of lifetime prevalence to race except for simple phobias. There were no significant differences with respect to major psychiatric illness or substance abuse (see a more detailed criticism of Rushton's assumptions in this area in Zuckerman & Brody, 1988).

Rushton (1988, 1991) implies that "racial differences in behavior" are genetic and relatively immutable: He ignores the plasticity of human beings as shown in secular changes and in the intragroup variance (see more detailed criticisms in Weizmann et al., 1990, 1991). The armamentarium of clinical psychologists was shown by a host of empirical investigations to induce desirable behavioral changes in various populations (see, e.g., Turner, Calhoun, & Adams, 1981): Rushton's view of human beings is obsolete.

... If Rushton (1988, 1990a) could heed Jerison's (1973) warning that racial differences in brain size are at most minor and "probably of no significance for intellectual differences," he would not attempt to extend Jerison's findings across species to subgroups within modern mankind. Instead, Rushton (1991) misleadingly refers to Jerison in a manner that implies an expert support from this famous comparative neuropsychologist, without mentioning their disagreement on the most central issue.

Rushton (1991) claimed that racial differences occur "on more than 50 variables," with Blacks being consistently in a less desirable direction. The present article examined the evidence with respect to the key variables only: The examination exemplifies that his claims are fallacious. Furthermore, long lists, such as Rushton's, tend to shrink when appropriate multivariate methods (e.g., the discriminant equation) are used: These techniques eliminate redundancies and remove nonsignificant variables. And, nota bene, if a scientist would search for a suitable "finding" to lower the social prestige of Blacks and examine 50 variables and suppress evidence favorable to Blacks, he or she might, by chance alone, one day, find one or more variables on which a "significant" trend in the desired direction could be located....

Finally, Rushton's most recent "scientific" contribution is the claim that women are likely to be less intelligent than men because his tape measurements of men and women in military settings indicated that males have larger heads (Rushton, 1992). Indeed, the racism is often associated with sexism.

In summary, although Rushton's writings and public speeches instill the vision of Blacks as small-brained, oversexed criminals who multiply at a fast rate and are afflicted with mental disease, his views are neither based on a bona fide scientific review of literature nor on contemporary scientific methodology. His dogma of bioevolutionary inferiority of Negroids is not supported by empirical evidence. Acceptance of similar theories should not be based on *racist prejudice* but on objective standards, that is, conceptual and logical consistency and integrity, quality of methods and data, and an analysis of disconfirmatory trends. Rushton's racial theory does not meet any of these standards.

CHALLENGE QUESTIONS

Is There a Racial Difference in Intelligence?

1. Because scientific knowledge is considered by many to be the ultimate authority, the findings of science can have a large impact on public opinion. Should "dangerous" scientific findings, such as those that would hurt people or cause hatred, be suppressed? What standards should be used, and who should enforce them? Explain.

2. How does the debate over race and intelligence reflect on women's issues? Many of the arguments in this debate are applied to debates over women's intelligence and personality. If you do not believe that there are genetic differences between races, can you justify arguments supporting genetic differences between the genders?

3. Perhaps inherent differences between races could be construed in a positive light. Can you think of reasons why some races might *want* to promote genetic differences between racial groups?

4. If there are indeed racial differences in intelligence, would this finding necessarily change political opinions and government policies? If so, how? If not, why not?

ISSUE 9

Are Memories of Sex Abuse Always Real?

YES: Ellen Bass and Laura Davis, from *The Courage to Heal: A Guide for Women Survivors of Child Sexual Abuse* (Harper & Row, 1988)

NO: Lee Coleman, from "Creating 'Memories' of Sexual Abuse," *Issues in Child Abuse Accusations* (vol. 4, no. 4, 1992)

ISSUE SUMMARY

YES: Ellen Bass and Laura Davis, both counselors of victims of child sexual abuse, assert that even a faint or vague memory of sexual abuse is prime evidence that sexual abuse has occurred.

NO: Psychiatrist Lee Coleman argues that individual memories of sexual abuse are susceptible to manipulation by laypersons and mental health professionals and that "memories" of sexual abuse that never occurred can be created in therapy.

It is hard to imagine a more heinous crime than sexual abuse. Yet, perhaps surprisingly, it is a crime that often goes unpunished. Frequently, sexual abusers are family members and their victims are children who are too young to protest or to know that they are being violated. This is part of the reason why memories have become so significant to the sexual abuse issue. Often it is not until the victims become adults that they realize they were abused.

The problem is that the reliability of memory itself has come into question. Some cognitive psychologists have expressed doubt about the accuracy of memories when people are formally questioned (such as on the witness stand). Another issue is whether or not memory is subject to manipulation. People under hypnosis, for example, tend to be susceptible to the hypnotist's suggestions as to what they "should" remember. Do therapists of alleged victims of sexual abuse make similar suggestions? Could these therapists be unconsciously or consciously "shaping" through therapeutic suggestion the memories of the people they treat?

In the following selections, Ellen Bass and Laura Davis argue that memories of sexual abuse and what they identify as symptoms of sexual abuse are sufficient evidence that a person was abused. They provide a list of experiences that, if remembered, indicate that a person was probably abused. They also describe a number of the symptoms that they contend are commonly experienced by those who have been abused. Bass and Davis emphasize that a lack of explicit memories about sexual abuse does not mean that abuse did not occur.

Lee Coleman refutes the claims of those who place faith in all memories of sexual abuse. He argues that people can be led to believe that they were sexually abused when, in fact, they were not. Coleman presents a case to show that so-called recovered memories of sexual abuse can be created in therapy with the encouragement of mental health professionals. He holds that professionals who consider themselves specialists in sexual abuse recovery tend to accept without question that sexual abuse has occurred if a client says it has, to encourage as many memories as possible, and to accept all allegations of sexual abuse as real. Coleman views these professionals as manipulative and often without awareness.

POINT	COUNTERPOINT
• If someone says that they believe they were sexually abused, they probably were.	• People can be made to believe that they have been sexually abused when, in fact, they have not.
• Memories for traumatic events are likely to be repressed, so they must be "helped" to be recovered.	• "Helping" memories to be recovered can unintentionally create them.
• Mental health professionals do not create people's memories for them.	• Mental health professionals sometimes create false memories for their patients.
• Memory is like a videotape that records things exactly as they occur.	• Evidence shows that memory is not infallible and can be distorted and inaccurate.

YES
Ellen Bass and Laura Davis

THE COURAGE TO HEAL

If you have been sexually abused, you are not alone. One out of three girls, and one out of seven boys, are sexually abused by the time they reach the age of eighteen. Sexual abuse happens to children of every class, culture, race, religion, and gender. Children are abused by fathers, stepfathers, uncles, brothers, grandparents, neighbors, family friends, baby-sitters, teachers, strangers, and sometimes by aunts and mothers.[1] Although women do abuse, the vast majority of abusers are heterosexual men.

All sexual abuse is damaging, and the trauma does not end when the abuse stops. If you were abused as a child, you are probably experiencing long-term effects that interfere with your day-to-day functioning.

However, it is possible to heal. It is even possible to thrive. Thriving means more than just an alleviation of symptoms, more than band-aids, more than functioning adequately. Thriving means enjoying a feeling of wholeness, satisfaction in your life and work, genuine love and trust in your relationships, pleasure in your body.

Until now, much of the literature on child sexual abuse has documented the ravages of abuse, talking extensively about "the tragedy of ruined lives," but little about recovery. This [reading] is about recovery—what it takes, what it feels like, how it can transform your life.

People say "time heals all wounds," and it's true to a certain extent. Time will dull some of the pain, but deep healing doesn't happen unless you consciously choose it. Healing from child sexual abuse takes years of commitment and dedication. But if you are willing to work hard, if you are determined to make lasting changes in your life, if you are able to find good resources and skilled support, you can not only heal but thrive. We believe in miracles and hard work.

HOW CAN I KNOW IF I WAS A VICTIM OF CHILD SEXUAL ABUSE?

When you were a young child or teenager, were you:

• Touched in sexual areas?

Excerpted from Ellen Bass and Laura Davis, *The Courage to Heal: A Guide for Women Survivors of Child Sexual Abuse* (Harper & Row, 1988), pp. 20–22, 70–83. Copyright © 1988 by Ellen Bass and Laura Davis. Reprinted by permission of HarperCollins Publishers, Inc.

- Shown sexual movies or forced to listen to sexual talk?
- Made to pose for seductive or sexual photographs?
- Subjected to unnecessary medical treatments?
- Forced to perform oral sex on an adult or sibling?
- Raped or otherwise penetrated?
- Fondled, kissed, or held in a way that made you uncomfortable?
- Forced to take part in ritualized abuse in which you were physically or sexually tortured?
- Made to watch sexual acts or look at sexual parts?
- Bathed in a way that felt intrusive to you?
- Objectified and ridiculed about your body?
- Encouraged or goaded into sex you didn't really want?
- Told all you were good for was sex?
- Involved in child prostitution or pornography?[2]

If you are unable to remember any specific instances like the ones mentioned above but still have a feeling that something abusive happened to you, it probably did....

Children often cope with abuse by forgetting it ever happened. As a result, you may have no conscious memory of being abused. You may have forgotten large chunks of your childhood. Yet there are things you do remember. When you are touched in a certain way, you feel nauseated. Certain words or facial expressions scare you. You know you never liked your mother to touch you. You slept with your clothes on in junior high school. You were taken to the doctor repeatedly for vaginal infections.

You may think you don't have memories, but often as you begin to talk about what you do remember, there emerges a constellation of feelings, reactions, and recollections that add up to substantial information. To say "I was abused," you don't need the kind of recall that would stand up in a court of law.

Often the knowledge that you were abused starts with a tiny feeling, an intuition. It's important to trust that inner voice and work from there. Assume your feelings are valid. So far, no one we've talked to thought she might have been abused, and then later discovered that she hadn't been. The progression always goes the other way, from suspicion to confirmation. If you think you were abused and your life shows the symptoms, then you were....

* * *

I've looked the memories in the face and smelled their breath. They can't hurt me anymore.

For many survivors, remembering is the first step in healing. To begin with, you may have to remember that you *were* abused at all. Second come specific memories.... The third kind of remembering is the recovery of the feelings you had at the time the abuse took place. Many women have always remembered the physical details of what happened but have forgotten the emotions that went with it. One survivor explained, "I could rattle off the facts of my abuse like a grocery list, but remembering the fear and terror and pain was another matter entirely."

Remembering is different for every survivor. If, as a young woman, you turned your abuser in to the police and testified against him in court, there's not much chance you forgot. Likewise, if you had to raise your abuser's child, or abort it, you've probably always remembered. Or the abuse may have been so present in the daily texture of your life that there was no way to forget.

One woman who'd kept a vivid image of what had happened to her said she sometimes wished she *had* forgotten: "I wish I could have gotten shock treatments like my mother. She had forgotten huge segments of her life, and I used to envy her." On the other hand, this woman said she was glad she'd always known just how bad things were: "At least I knew why I was weird! Knowing what had happened allowed me to work on the damn problem."

You may not have forgotten entirely, but coped by having selective memories.

I always knew that we had an incestuous relationship. I remember the first time I heard the word "incest," when I was seventeen. I hadn't known there was a word for it. I always remembered my father grabbing my breasts and kissing me.

I told my therapist, "I remember every miserable thing that happened to me." It seemed like I remembered so much, how could there be more? I didn't remember anything *but* abuse. But I didn't remember being raped, even though I knew I had been. I categorically told my therapist, "I don't want to remember being raped." We talked about the fact that I didn't want to remember that for months. Yet I knew my father had been my first lover.

There is no right or wrong when it comes to remembering. You may have multiple memories. Or you may just have one. Years of abuse are sometimes telescoped into a single recollection. When you begin to remember, you might have new images every day for weeks on end. Or you may experience your memories in clumps, three or four of them coming in a matter of days, then not again for months. Sometimes survivors remember one abuser, or a specific kind of abuse, only to remember, years later, a second abuser or a different form of abuse.

There are many women who show signs of having been abused without having any memories. You may have only a vague feeling that something happened but be unable to remember what it was. There are reasons for this, and to understand them, we have to first look at the way early memories are stored.

ABOUT MEMORIES

The process of storing memories is complex. We store different experiences in the right and left halves of our brain. The left brain stores sequential, logical, language-oriented experience; the right stores perceptual, spatial experiences. When we try to retrieve right-brain information through left-brain techniques, such as logic and language, we sometimes hit a blank. There are some experiences that we are simply not going to remember in an orderly, precise way.

If you were abused when you were preverbal, or just as you were learning to talk, you had no way of making sense of what was happening to you. Babies don't know the difference between touching someone's penis and touching someone's leg. If a penis is put in their mouth, they will suck it, much as they would a breast or a bottle. Young children are aware of sensations but cannot come up with a name or a concept—like "sexual abuse" —for what is being done to them.

Another thing that makes remembering difficult is the simple fact that you are trying to remember details of something that happened a long time ago. If you ask friends who weren't abused, you will find that most of them also don't remember a great number of details from their childhood. It is even more difficult to remember the times when we were hurt, humiliated, or otherwise violated.

If the abuse happened only once, or if it was an abuse that is hard to name (inappropriate boundaries, lewd looks, subtler forms of abuse), it can be even harder to remember. For others, the constancy of the abuse prevents detailed naming. As one survivor put it, "Do you remember every time you sat down to eat? What you had for dinner the Tuesday you turned six? I remember the flavor. It was a constant, like eating. It was always there."

WHAT REMEMBERING IS LIKE

Recovering occluded memories (those blocked from the surface) is not like remembering with the conscious mind. Often the memories are vague and dreamlike, as if they're being seen from far away.

The actual rape memories for me are like from the end of a tunnel. That's because I literally left my body at the scene. So I remember it from that perspective—there's some physical distance between me and what's going on. Those memories aren't as sharp in focus. It's like they happened in another dimension.

Other times, memories come in bits and pieces.

I'd be driving home from my therapist's office, and I'd start having flashes of things—just segments, like bloody sheets, or taking a bath, or throwing away my nightgown. For a long time, I remembered all the things around being raped, but not the rape itself.

If memories come to you in fragments, you may find it hard to place them in any kind of chronological order. You may not know exactly when the abuse began, how old you were, or when and why it stopped. The process of understanding the fragments is a lot like putting together a jigsaw puzzle or being a detective.

Part of me felt like I was on the trail of a murder mystery, and I was going to solve it. I really enjoyed following all the clues. "Okay, I was looking at the clock. It was mid-afternoon. Why was it mid-afternoon? Where could my mother have been? Oh, I bet she was at..." Tracing down the clues to find out exactly what had happened was actually fun.

Ella is a survivor who remembered in snatches. To make sense of her memories, she began to examine some of her own strange ways of coping. She started to analyze certain compulsive behaviors, like staring at the light fixture whenever she was making love:

I'd be making love and would think, "Why would somebody lay here, when they're supposed to be having a pleasurable experience, and concentrate on a light fixture?" I remember every single lighting fixture in every single house we ever lived in! Why have I always been so obsessed with light under doors, and the interruption of light? That's a crazy thing for an adult woman to be obsessive about —that someone walks past and cracks the light. What's that about?

What it was about was watching to see if her father's footsteps stopped outside her door at night. If they stopped, that meant he'd come in and molest her. Once Ella started to pay attention to these kinds of details, the memories started to fit in place.

Flashbacks

In a flashback, you reexperience the original abuse. Flashbacks may be accompanied by the feelings you felt at the time, or they may be stark and detached, like watching a movie about somebody else's life.

Frequently flashbacks are visual: "I saw this penis coming toward me," or "I couldn't see his face, just the big black belt he always wore." First-time visual memories can be very dramatic:

My husband was beginning to initiate some lovemaking. I had a flash in my mind. The closest way I can describe it is that it was much like viewing slides in a slide show, when the slide goes by too fast, but slow enough to give you some part of the image. It was someone jamming their fingers up my vagina. It was very vivid, and enough of the feelings came sneaking in that I knew it wasn't a fantasy. There was an element of it that made me stop and take notice. I lay there and let it replay a couple of times.

I felt confused. I was aware that it was something that happened to me. I even had a recollection of the pain. I scrambled around in my mind for an explanation. "Was that a rough lover I had?" Immediately I knew that wasn't the case. So I went back into the flash again. Each time I went back, I tried to open it up to see a little more. I didn't see his face, but I could sense an essence of my father.

Sometimes visual memories are more complete. A survivor who's had them both ways explained the difference:

A flashback is like a slide compared to a film. It's the difference between getting one shot or one look into a room and getting the expanded version. A full memory is more like panning over the whole scene, with all the details, sound, feeling, and visuals rolled into one.

But not everyone is visual. One woman was upset that she couldn't get any pictures. Her father had held her at knifepoint in the car, face down in the dark, and raped her. She had never seen anything. But she had heard him. And when she began to write the scene in Spanish, her native language, it all came back to her—his threats, his brutality, his violation.

Regression

Another way to regain memory is through regression. Under the guidance of a trustworthy therapist, it is possible to go back to earlier times. Or you may find yourself going back on such a journey on your own, with only the prompting of your own unconscious.

Most of the regressions I experienced felt almost like going on a ride. They'd last maybe three or four hours at a time. One of the most vivid physical regressions I went through was late one evening, when Barbara and I were talking about her going to visit a friend. All of a sudden, I felt like I was being sucked down a drain. And then I felt like a real baby. I started crying and clinging and saying, "You can't go! You have to stay with me!" And I began to talk in a five-year-old's voice, using words and concepts that a five-year-old might use.

All of a sudden I thought I was just going to throw up. I ran to the bathroom, and then I really started to sob. I saw lots of scenes from my childhood. Times I felt rejected flashed by me, almost in slides.

Barb held me, and kind of coached me through it. "It's okay. You can get through this." Having her just sit there and listen really helped me. I just kept crying, and described to Barbara all these slides that were going by. After about twenty minutes, I fell into the deepest sleep I'd had for months. The next morning when I woke up, I felt a million pounds lighter.

Sense Memory

Often it is a particular touch, smell, or sound that triggers a memory. You might remember when you return to the town, to the house, to the room, where the abuse took place. Or when you smell a certain aftershave the abuser wore.

Thirty-five-year-old Ella says, "It's all real tactile, sensory things that have brought memories back. Textures. Sounds. The smell of my father's house. The smell of vodka on somebody."

Ella had a magic purple quilt when she was a little girl. Her grandmother made it for her. It was supposed to keep her safe—nothing bad could happen to her as long as she was under it. The quilt had been lost for many years, but when Ella finally got it back at twenty-one, it triggered a whole series of memories.

Touch can also reopen memories. Women have had images come up while they were being massaged. You may freeze up and see pictures when you're making love. Your lover breathes in your ear just as your abuser once did, and it all comes spilling back:

Sometimes when we're making love, I feel like my head just starts to float away somewhere. I feel like I literally split off at my shoulders, and I get very lightheaded and dizzy. It's as if someone was blowing a fan down on top of my head. There's a lot of movement down past my hair. It's like rising up out of my head. I get really disoriented.

The other thing I experience is a lot of splitting right at the hips. My legs get very heavy and really solid. They just feel like dead weight, like logs. No energy is passing through them. Then I get real sick to my stomach, just violently ill. I find the minute I get nauseous, whatever it is is very close to me. And if I pay attention to it, I can see it, and move on.

The Body Remembers What the Mind Chooses to Forget

It is also possible to remember only feelings. Memories are stored in our bodies, and it is possible to physically reexperience the terror of the abuse. Your body may clutch tight, or you may feel the screams you could not scream as a child. Or you may feel that you are suffocating and cannot breathe.

I would get body memories that would have no pictures to them at all. I would just start screaming and feel that something was coming out of my body that I had no control over. And I would usually get them right after making love or in the middle of making love, or right in the middle of a fight. When my passion was aroused in some way, I would remember in my body, although I wouldn't have a conscious picture, just this screaming coming out of me.

WAYS TO REMEMBER

Memories come up under many different circumstances. You might remember because you're finally in a relationship that feels safe. Or because you've just been through a divorce and everything in your life is unraveling. Women often remember childhood abuse when they are raped or attacked in adult life.

Memories don't always surface in such dramatic ways. While talking with her friend, one woman suddenly heard herself saying something she didn't realize she knew. "It's as though I always knew it," she explained. "It's just that I hadn't thought about it in twenty or thirty years. Up until that moment, I'd forgotten."

You may remember seemingly out of the blue. Or because you're having persistent nightmares that reach up through sleep to tell you:

> I'd always had a dream about my brother assaulting me. It was a foggy dream, and I had it over and over again. I'd wake up thinking it was really disgusting because I was enjoying it in the dream. I'd think, "You're sick. Why are you having this dream? Is that what you want?" I'd give myself all those kinds of guilt messages, 'cause it was still a dream. It wasn't history yet.
>
> Then, six months ago, I was sitting in a training meeting for working with sexual assault prevention. I don't even remember what the trainer said, but all of a sudden, I realized that it wasn't a dream, and that it had really happened. I can't tell you anything about the rest of the meeting. I was just in shock.

The fact that this woman remembered in the middle of a training session for sexual assault is significant. As the media focus on sexual abuse has increased, more and more women have had their memories triggered.

Media Coverage of Sexual Abuse

Jennierose, who remembered in her mid-forties, was sitting with her lover one night, watching a TV program about sexual offenders in prison. The therapist running the group encouraged the offenders to get very emotional, at which time they'd remember the traumatic events in their own childhoods.

In the middle of the program, Jennierose turned to her lover and said, "I wish there was a therapist like that I could go to, because I know there's something I'm not remembering." As soon as she said that, Jennierose had a vision of the first time her father sodomized her, when she was four and a half and her mother had gone to the hospital to have another baby. "It was a totally detailed vision, to the point of seeing the rose-colored curtains blowing in the window."

Sobbing, Jennierose said to her lover, "I think I'm making something up." Her lover simply said, "Look at yourself! Look at yourself! Tell me you're making it up." And Jennierose couldn't. She knew she was telling the truth.

This kind of memory is common. Often women become very uncomfortable (nauseated, dizzy, unable to concentrate, emotional) when they hear another survivor's story and realize that what's being described happened to them too.

When You Break an Addiction

Many survivors remember their abuse once they get sober, quit drugs, or stop eating compulsively. These and other addictions can effectively block any recollection of the abuse, but once you stop, the memories often surface. Anna Stevens explains:

> At the point I decided to put down drinking, I had to start feeling. The connection to the abuse was almost immediate. And I've watched other people come to AA and do the same thing. They have just enough time to get through the initial shakes, and you watch them start to go through the memories. And you know what's coming, but they don't....

When You Become a Mother

Mothers often remember their own abuse when they see their children's vulnerability, or when their children reach the age they were when their own abuse began. Sometimes they remember because their child is being abused. Dana was court-ordered to go for therapy when her three-year-old daughter, Christy, was molested. Dana first remembered when she unconsciously substituted her own name for her daughter's:

> I was in therapy talking about Christy, and instead of saying "Christy," I said "I." And I didn't even catch it. My therapist did. She had always suspected that I was abused too, but she hadn't said anything to me.
>
> She told me what I had said, and I said, "I did? I said 'I?' I hadn't even heard myself. It was really eerie.
>
> What came out was that I was really dealing with Christy's molestation on a level of my own. The things that I was outraged at and that hurt me the most were things that had happened to me, not things that had happened to Christy. Part of the reason I fell apart and so much came back to me when I found out about Christy was because my husband was doing the same things to her that my father had done with me.

After a Significant Death

Many women are too scared to remember while their abusers are still alive. One woman said, "I couldn't afford to remember until both my parents were dead, until there was nobody left to hurt me." A forty-seven-year-old woman first remembered a year and a half after her mother died: "Then I could no longer hurt my mother by telling her."

FEELING THE FEELINGS

Although some remembering is emotionally detached, when you remember with feeling, the helplessness, terror, and physical pain can be as real as any actual experience. You may feel as if you are being crushed, ripped open, or suffocated. Sexual arousal may also accompany your memories, and this may horrify you, but arousal is a natural response to sexual stimulation. There is no reason to be ashamed.

You might remember feeling close and happy, wrapped in a special kind of love. Disgust and horror are not the only way to feel when you have memories. There is no *right* way to feel, but you must feel, even if it sends you reeling:

> When I first remembered, I shut down emotionally right away. I climbed all the way up into my mind and forgot about the gut level. That's how I protected myself. For a long time it was just an intellectual exercise. "Oh, that's why I have trouble with men and authority. That's why I might not have remembered much about growing up." It took nine months after I first remembered for the feelings to start bubbling up.
>
> I found myself slipping into the feelings I'd had during the abuse, that hadn't been safe to feel at the time. The first was this tremendous isolation. From there, I moved into absolute terror. I got in touch with how frightening the world is. It was the worst of the fear finally coming up. I felt like it was right at the top of my neck all the time, just ready to come out in a scream.
>
> I was right on the edge. I had an encounter with my boss, who said that my performance had been poor. I finally told him what had happened, which was really heavy—telling some male authority figure that you remembered

incest in your family. He is a kind and caring person. The best he could do was back off and leave me alone.

I was then carrying around all this external pressure—my job was in jeopardy, my life was falling apart, and I was having all these feelings I didn't know what to do with. In order to keep myself in control, I started compulsively eating. Finally I decided I didn't want to go through this stuff by myself anymore. I got myself into therapy.

Having to experience the feelings is one of the roughest parts of remembering. "It pisses me off that I have to survive it twice, only this time with feelings," one woman said. "This time it's worse. I'm not so effective at dissociating anymore."

Another woman said, "I started off very butch [tough] about remembering. I kicked into my overachiever thing. I was going to lick this thing. I believed getting the pictures was what was important. I got a ton of memories, all on the intellectual level. It was kind of like I was going to 'do' incest, just like I might take up typing."

It was only after a year of therapy that this woman began to realize that *she* was the one who'd been abused. "I finally realized, I finally *felt*, that this was something that had happened to me, and that it had been damaging. I had to realize that just getting the memories was not going to make it go away. *This was about me!*"

LETTING MEMORIES IN

Few survivors feel they have control over their memories. Most feel the memories have control of them, that they do not choose the time and place a new memory will emerge. You may be able to fight them off for a time, but the price—

headaches, nightmares, exhaustion—is not worth staving off what is inevitable.

Not everyone will know a memory is coming, but many survivors do get warnings, a certain feeling or series of feelings, that clue them in. Your stomach may get tight. You may sleep poorly, have frightening dreams. Or you may be warned in other ways:

I always know when they're coming. I get very tense. I get very scared. I get snappy at things that ordinarily wouldn't make me angry. I get sad. Usually it's anger and anxiety and fear that come first. And I have a choice. It's a real conscious choice. It's either I want it or I don't want it. And I said "I don't want it" a lot. And when I did that, I would just get sicker and sicker. I'd get more depressed. I'd get angry irrationally.

Now I don't say I don't want it. It's not worth it. My body seems to need to release it. The more I heal, the more I see these memories are literally stored in my body, and they've got to get out. Otherwise I'm going to carry them forever.

REMEMBERING OVER TIME

Often when you've resolved one group of memories, another will make its way to the surface.

The more I worked on the abuse, the more I remembered. First I remembered my brother, and then my grandfather. About six months after that I remembered my father. And then about a year later, I remembered my mother. I remembered the "easiest" first and the "hardest" last. Even though it was traumatic for me to realize that everyone in my family abused me, there was something reassuring about it. For a long time I'd felt worse than the initial memories should have made me feel, so remembering the rest of the abuse was actually one of the most grounding things to happen. My life suddenly made sense.

The impact new memories have will shift over time. One woman who has been getting new memories for the past ten years says remembering has become harder over time:

My first flood of memories came when I was twenty-five. The memories I get now are like fine-tuning—more details, more textures. Even though there was more of a feeling of shock and catharsis at first, remembering is harder now. I believe them now. It hurts more. I have the emotions to feel the impact. I can see how it's affected my life.

Laura also says new memories are harder:

Just when I felt that my life was getting back to normal and I could put the incest aside, I had another flashback that was much more violent than the earlier pictures I'd seen. I was furious. I wanted to be finished. I didn't want to be starting in with incest again! And my resistance made the remembering a lot more difficult.

Other survivors say memories have gotten easier to handle:

As I've come to terms with the fact that I was abused, new pictures, new incidents, don't have the same impact. The battle of believing it happened is not one I have to fight each time another piece falls into place. Once I had a framework to fit new memories into, my recovery time got much faster. While my first memories overwhelmed me for weeks, now I might only cry for ten minutes or feel depressed for an hour. It's not that I don't have new memories. It's just that they don't devastate me.

And new memories don't take anything away from the healing you've already done. Paradoxically, *you are already healing from the effects of the things you have yet to remember.*

"BUT I DON'T HAVE ANY MEMORIES"

If you don't remember your abuse, you are not alone. Many women don't have memories, and some never get memories. This doesn't mean they weren't abused.

If you don't have any memory of it, it can be hard to believe the abuse really happened. You may feel insecure about trusting your intuition and want "proof" of your abuse. This is a very natural desire, but it is not always one that can be met. The unconscious has its own way of unfolding that does not always meet your demands or your timetable.

One thirty-eight-year-old survivor described her relationship with her father as "emotionally incestuous." She has never had specific memories of any physical contact between them, and for a long time she was haunted by the fact that she couldn't come up with solid data. Over time, though, she's come to terms with her lack of memories. Her story is a good model if you don't have specific pictures to draw from:

Do I want to know if something physical happened between my father and me? Really, I think you have to be strong enough to know. I think that our minds are wonderful in the way they protect us, and I think that when I'm strong enough to know, I'll know.

I obsessed for about a year on trying to remember, and then I got tired of sitting around talking about what I couldn't remember. I thought, "All right, let's act as if." It's like you come home and your home has been robbed, and everything has been thrown in the middle of the room, and the window is open and the curtain is blowing in the wind, and the cat is gone. You know somebody robbed you, but you're never going to know who. So what are you going to do? Sit there and try to figure it out while your stuff lies around? No, you start to clean it up. You put bars on the windows. You assume somebody was there. Somebody could come along and say, "Now how do you know someone was there?" You don't know.

That's how I acted. I had the symptoms. Every incest group I went to I completely empathized. It rang bells all the time. I felt like there was something I just couldn't get to, that I couldn't remember yet. And my healing was blocked there.

Part of my wanting to get specific memories was guilt that I could be accusing this man of something so heinous, and what if he didn't do it? How horrible for me to accuse him! That's why I wanted the memories. I wanted to be sure. Societally, women have always been accused of crying rape.

But I had to ask myself, "Why would I be feeling all of this? Why would I be feeling all this anxiety if something didn't happen?" If the specifics are not available to you, then go with what you've got.

I'm left with the damage. And that's why I relate to that story of the burglar.

I'm owning the damage. I want to get better. I've been very ill as a result of the damage, and at some point I realized, "I'm thirty-eight years old. What am I going to do—wait twenty more years for a memory?" I'd rather get better.

And then maybe the stronger I am, the more the memories will come back. Maybe I'm putting the cart before the horse. Maybe I've remembered as much as I'm able to remember without breaking down. I don't want to go insane. I want to be out in the world. Maybe I should go with that sense of protection. There is a survivor in here and she's pretty smart. So I'm going with the circumstantial evidence, and I'm working on healing myself. I go to these incest groups, and I tell people, "I don't have any pictures," and then I go on and talk all about my father, and nobody ever says, "You don't belong here."

NOTES

1. For sources on the scope of child sexual abuse, see the "About Sexual Abuse" section of the Resource Guide. A number of these books cite recent studies to which you can refer for more complete statistics.

2. Between 500,000 and 1,000,000 children are involved in prostitution and pornography in this country; a high percentage of them are victims of incest. See *Sex Work: Writings by Women in the Industry*, edited by Frédérique Dellacoste and Priscilla Alexander (Pittsburgh: Cleis Press, 1987).

NO

Lee Coleman

CREATING "MEMORIES" OF
SEXUAL ABUSE

ABSTRACT: An analysis of a case of alleged recovered memories of sexual abuse is presented to illustrate how such mental images can be created in therapy. The memories, although believed by the woman to be of actual events, were the result of suggestions from both lay persons and professionals.

While, just a few years ago, students of child sexual abuse accusations thought they had seen every imaginable brand of irresponsibility on the part of certain mental health professionals, something new and equally terrible has emerged. To the growing number of children trained to say and believe things which never happened is now added a growing number of adults, usually women, being trained to say and believe that they have suddenly "unblocked" memories of childhood sexual abuse.

Just like allegations coming from children, concern about biased and unprofessional methods of eliciting statements from adults should in no way cast doubt on the reality of sexual abuse. There are countless numbers of adults who were molested as children, who did not speak of it, but who now may reveal their experiences as part of our society's belated recognition of such abuse. But to acknowledge the reality of sexual abuse, and the reality of the silence kept by some of the victims, does nothing to mitigate the harm being done by those therapists who are convincing patients that even if sexual abuse is not remembered, it probably happened anyway.

In this article, I will illustrate the process by which a young woman, moderately depressed and unsure of her life goals, but in no way out of touch with reality (psychotic), came to make allegations which were so bizarre that they might easily be thought to be the product of [a] major mental disorder. In such cases, I have repeatedly seen the falsely accused and their closest family and friends make this assumption. This case will show, as have the others I have studied, that the source is not a disorder in the patient, but a "disorder" in the therapist. The problem is the irresponsible adoption by some therapists of a new fad which will be clarified below.

From Lee Coleman, "Creating 'Memories' of Sexual Abuse," *Issues in Child Abuse Accusations*, vol. 4, no. 4 (1992), pp. 169–176. Copyright © 1992 by The Institute for Psychological Therapies. Reprinted by permission of *Issues in Child Abuse Accusations*.

Here, then, is a report I submitted to the Court hearing the civil lawsuit filed by this woman against her cousin. All names and identifying information have been changed.

* * *

Judge John Q. Smith
   Superior Court, All American County
   Anywhere, USA

The following report concerns the suit between Susan Q. Smith and John V. Public. The opinions expressed are based on a study of the Amended List of Documents of the Plaintiff, dated April 6, 1992, Additional Documents (such as police records and Children's Services Records), Examination for Discovery transcripts of Mrs. Smith and Mr. Public, and my examination of Mrs. Smith on May 4, 1992, which lasted somewhat over three hours. I have also studied several videotapes pertinent to the case, enumerated below.

Based upon all this information, as well [as] my prior professional experience, it is my opinion that the alleged "memories" of Mrs. Smith, relating a variety of sexual and abusive acts perpetrated upon her by Mr. Public and others, are not memories at all. They are, instead, mental images which, however sincerely felt by her to be memories of past events, are nonetheless the result of a series of suggestions from both lay persons and professionals.

That Mrs. Smith has succumbed to these influences in no way implies that she suffers from any mental disorder. By her own account, she has had problems of low self-esteem, depression, and bulimia in her past. She has, however, never suffered and does not now suffer a mental disorder which would imply a loss of contact with reality. If the reliability of her claims are to be best evaluated by the Court, it should be understood that there is another way that a person may say things that may not be true, yet be entirely sincere.

Suggestibility is something we all share as part of our being human, with some persons obviously being more suggestible than others. In this case, Mrs. Smith has been involved with individuals and groups, over a period of years, the end result of which has been to promote a process of accepting the false idea that whatever mental image is conjured up, especially if part of "therapy," is necessarily a valid retrieval of past experience, i.e. a "memory."

Let me now document the evidence which has led me to the above conclusions.

1. Mrs. Smith's Suspicions About John Public and His Daughter Alice.

From several sources, such as her deposition, my interview, and investigative interviews, it seems clear that Mrs. Smith suspected for several years that her cousin John Public was engaging in sexual behavior with his daughter Alice. When asked for examples which led to these suspicions, she mentioned alleged comments from him that "a child's hands" felt so good. She also mentioned that no other adults seemed to be concerned about such comments.

Seeing Mr. Public and Alice (approximately eight years old at the time) lying in bed together, in their underwear, reinforced her suspicion, as did the alleged comment from Mr. Public to Mr. Smith (not heard by Mrs. Smith), that his (Smith's) daughter would make him horny. Mrs. Smith also noted that, until age 18 months, her own daughter would cry if Mr. Public attempted to pick her up or get close to her, and Mrs. Smith noted to herself, "She's a smart child." (It should be noted that such behavior in infants of this age is perfectly normal.)

Mrs. Smith told me that she had informed family members on several occasions of her suspicions, but no one else apparently shared her opinions, or felt anything needed to be reported.

The 1986 video of a family Halloween party was the event that convinced Mrs. Smith she should report her suspicions. It is quite important that the Court view this video, in order to judge for itself whether the material could reasonably lead a person to believe something untoward was taking place. My own opinion is there was nothing happening that was unusual or abnormal. It was Alice who first struck a somewhat playful and seductive pose, and such displays are hardly abnormal for a teenage girl. Police investigators likewise saw nothing untoward on this tape.

The question raised, then, is whether Mrs. Smith had for her own personal reasons, upon which I will not attempt to speculate, developed an obsession about Mr. Public and his daughter, one which was leading her (Smith) to overinterpret ordinary behaviors.

It is not surprising, then, that when the report was investigated by Children's Services, no evidence of abuse was uncovered. Mrs. Smith tells me, however, that she was not reassured, and only felt that she had fulfilled an obligation to report something.

2. Early Influences Promoting in Mrs. Smith a Belief That Prior Sexual Abuse Might Have Occurred but Not Be Remembered.

From numerous sources (deposition, my interview, journals, therapy records), it is clear that Mrs. Smith was strongly influenced by a statement she says Dr. Gwen Olson made to her regarding bulimia, a problem Mrs. Smith had suffered from to one degree or another since early adolescence.

Mrs. Smith states that Dr. Olson told her, sometime in early 1987 (the records indicate this was in December 1986), that "one hundred percent of my patients with bulimia have later found out that they were sexual abuse victims." Whether these words were actually spoken by Dr. Olson, or instead interpreted this way by Mrs. Smith, I of course do not know. But in either case, the words Mrs. Smith took away with her are extremely important, because the words "found out" would imply that a person could have been sexually abused, not be aware of it, and later recover such an awareness. I will later on be discussing the lack of evidence for, and major evidence against, any such phenomenon being genuine.

Mrs. Smith told me she was seriously affected by this, experiencing crying and feelings of fear. She began to wonder if she might have been sexually abused. When I asked her if she had ever before that time had such a question, she said that she "had no memories" of any such abuse. She had, in fact, told Children's Services shortly before, during the investigation of Alice, that John Public had "never before abused me... I was relying on my memory."

At this time, Mrs. Smith was being seen in psychotherapy, first by Edna Johnson, and then by Dr. Abraham, for what seems to have been feelings of anxiety and depression. Sexual abuse was apparently not an issue in this therapy. Instead, Mrs. Smith states that her self-esteem was low, and that she was "not functioning" well as a housewife, even though she felt good about her marriage. Both she and Dr. Abraham apparently felt she was "a bored housewife." She decided to start her own business, but this never happened because events leading to the current accusations against John Public interceded.

Mrs. Smith explains that she went to an Entrepreneurs Training Camp in the Fall of 1987, was doing extremely well, but then "sabotaged myself" by performing poorly despite knowing correct answers on an examination. She felt, after the camp, that she needed to work on herself.

In addition, she saw an Oprah Winfrey program on the subject of child abuse. Mrs. Smith told me that she cried as she watched this program, "for me and not for them... I wondered at my feelings and where they were coming from."

Mrs. Smith confirms that it was shortly after seeing this program, with all of the above background in place, that she called the Women's Sexual Assault Center (WSAC) on September 3, 1987.

After a telephone intake, she had a face-to-face contact with Joan Oliver, and told her that "I had concerns, feelings, but no memory of being sexually assaulted.... I thought it would be better to wait (for therapy) until I had a memory. They said OK, and put me on a waiting list."

The records of WSAC generally confirm this account which I received from Mrs. Smith on May 4, 1992. During the first telephone contact, Mrs. Smith related

> ... strong feelings of abuse as a child came up... She can't remember specific things... her GP told her most bulimics have been sexually abused as children...

A second telephone contact, September 16, include[d]

> ... occluded memories. Sister was abused by neighborhood man as a child. Susan gets very retriggered by this and by shows about child abuse. Her doctor told her that close to 100% of bulimics have been sexually abused. This really brought up a lot of feelings and some images but not really a memory.

Yet another important event happened around Christmas 1987, before Mrs. Smith had entered the treatments (with Mary Brown and Veronica Erickson) where the mental images alleged to be "memories" started. This was something I had not discovered from any written materials, and learned about for the first time from Mrs. Smith on May 4, 1992.

Mrs. Smith had a friend, Valerie White, who told her about her treatments for back problems. Biofeedback was used at the pain and stress clinic she attended, and Ms. White told Mrs. Smith that she had started to remember being abused. When I asked Mrs. Smith how she reacted to this, she said, "I felt... that if she was in therapy, remembering, maybe I should start as well. I had no memory, but if she was in therapy..."

To summarize, then, the suggestive influences to this point: Mrs. Smith is still not reassured that Alice is not being abused by John Public; Dr. Olson either says or Mrs. Smith believes she says that in her experience all bulimics are sexual abuse victims; finally, after she decides she shouldn't go into therapy "until she has a memory" of sexual abuse, a friend tells her "the remembering" can wait, and Mrs. Smith concludes she should give it a try.

It is my opinion, based on the above material, that Mrs. Smith was at this point being victimized by lay persons and professionals who were representing to her that sexual abuse might not be remembered, when in truth there is no evidence to support such a claim. While Mrs. Smith may have had her own personal problems and/or motivations for claiming abuse at the hands of Mr. Public (something I will not speculate upon) she was being profoundly influenced by unsound information. It is my opinion that this has persisted to this day.

3. Suggestive and Unprofessional Therapy Creates the "Memories."

In March 1988, Mrs. Smith started seeing Mary Brown for individual psychotherapy, and also had interviews with Veronica Erickson, a student who was writing a thesis on "Recovering Memories of Childhood Sexual Abuse." On March 9, 1988, Ms. Erickson commented that Mrs. Smith had done

> ... a lot of great body work. Worked on her anger, hurt about being sexually abused. Has a few memories about it and wants more.

On March 28, the WSAC records show that the

> "memory recovery process" was getting into high gear:... had lots of memories come to her which she feels good about; 2 "rapes," 9 sodomies, and 2 oral sex (she has remembered both rapes and 1 sodomy and oral sex), 8 sodomies and 1 oral sex to go. Can't wait.

Further WSAC records of Ms. Erickson show just as clearly that she has lost all professional objectivity.... The June 14, 1988 note gives an insight as to the position Ms. Erickson was taking with regard to whether Mrs. Smith's

increasingly severe claims should be automatically assumed to be accurate:

> ... trying to remember a memory that was just beginning to flash... really scared that this memory is made up... I told her I believed her.

If there is any doubt about the stance being adopted by Ms. Erickson, i.e. that whatever Mrs. Smith "recovers" from week to week is a reliable statement about past events, a reading of her Ph.D. thesis makes it abundantly clear that it was simply a given for her and the selected sources she relies on, that the patient's claims must be taken at face value. She writes, for example:

> Validation, feeling believed, was seen as essential for incest survivors struggling to reconcile their memories.

Nowhere in the thesis is mention made of any concern that false claims may arise in therapy specifically aimed at such "uncovering." Next, she speaks of

> ... the ability of counselor... to facilitate the survivor's recall of the abuse... which of course assumes that abuse has taken place.

Just how broadly based is the source of these allegedly reliable "memories," is indicated by her quoting the book, *The Courage to Heal,* which has been influential in promoting the very ideas at the center of this case:

> "Occluded" memories are vague flashbacks, triggered by touches, smells, sounds, body memories, bodily sensations as "warning signs." Some women just intuitively knew that they had been sexually abused and were struggling to trust their intuition.

It is also clear that the proper role for the therapist, according to Ms. Erickson, is not only to accept all images as "memories," but to actively encourage this process. She writes of her method which

> ... serves to continually promote an atmosphere in which the researcher is spontaneously both receptive and actively stimulating the recollection of the participant.... The participants and researcher... create the world within which this study is revealed.

Ms. Erickson says of "Victoria" (pseudonym for Mrs. Smith),

> She thought about who might have abused her and when she said his name, she knew who the offender was but she still had no memories as proof (p. 56 of Erickson thesis).

Let me now turn to her other therapist, Mary Brown. Ms. Brown in her intake notes of March 1, 1988 refers to Mrs. Smith having

> ... flashbacks of childhood sexual abuse experiences, she believes by this same cousin.

Ms. Brown's treatment plan was to "assist Susan express and release the emotions associated with the sexual abuse experience." This is important, because it shows that Ms. Brown, from the beginning, assumed the truth of the allegations.

It wasn't too long after this, the night of March 12/13, that Mrs. Smith's calendar indicates she had a "nightmare," and her "first memories." When I asked Mrs. Smith about this, she said it was

> ... the nightmare which triggered the memory.... In the nightmare, the neighbor had shot her husband in the chest. Her cleaning up his blood, I recalled John blotting up my blood after raping me.

There are, of course, no reputable data which would indicate that a patient or therapist can use dream material to reliably "recover memories" of real events. Ms. Brown, however, seems to have utter confidence in the process, for she wrote to the police on August 3, 1988:

> The treatment methods I use enable clients to express and release the very deepest feelings that may have been stifled.... It is precisely because the emotional intensity of sexual abuse in childhood is greater than what most children can integrate that these experiences are quickly lost to memory. The ensuing, forgetting and denial are the mind's way of protecting the individual from total disruption of their cognitive functioning. This was particularly true of survivors of sexual abuse whose experiences occurred more than ten years ago. The reason for this is that there was not the social awareness nor the professional expertise for dealing with these problems at that time. Children instinctively know when the adults around them are going to be able to help them. When they find themselves in situations where they may either be disbelieved... this forgetting and denial comes into play even more strongly....

> Memories tend to return in fragments and to be unclear or non-specific in the beginning... the blocks in the way of memory are gradually removed.... This is precisely what occurred... with Susan Smith. It is my clinical judgment that Susan had reached a point in her healing process when the memories that were returning were completely reliable.... She was unprepared to report until she herself was certain and until she received validation from me that I was in agreement that the memories could be trusted...

That Ms. Brown was not only accepting all statements as real events, but actively encouraging them, is seen by the following passage from the same letter:

> Susan herself questioned any inconsistency.... It took some education on my part for her to... understand the whole process of how it is that the recall process works...

Ms. Brown was even willing to assure the police that the other persons that Mrs. Smith was gradually naming as victims during that Spring and Summer of 1988 would also need "help" in remembering.

> ... It is highly likely that most or all of the children that Susan remembers... will be unable to remember these experiences. This does not mean they did not occur any more than Susan's former amnesia means that these events had not happened to her. One of these (youngsters) may be precipitated to remember and recapture the experiences through a process similar to what occurred for Susan.

There is, of course, absolutely no evidence that this whole process has anything to do with memory, or a recall of past events. The only professionals who advocate these ideas are those making up a small, fringe group who hold themselves out as "specialists in treating sexual abuse," but who (as this case shows) seem to assume that it is permissible to pass off wild theories, like the ones above, to both patients, families, and investigative agencies.

Most important, however, is that outsiders evaluate the possible impact of such ideas on persons like Mrs. Smith. The evidence is clear that she has raised doubts from time to time, but each time, these "specialists" have told her that her mental images must represent real events. In this sense, I believe the professionals (Brown, Erickson, and others to be mentioned) are most responsible for creating the unreliable information in this case.

Not only do the ideas promoted by Brown and Erickson hold great potential to contaminate information coming from such counseling, but the techniques used with Mrs. Smith would likely heighten this possibility. Mrs. Smith described pounding pillows and being encouraged to express her anger in sessions with Ms. Erickson, and in individual and group sessions with Ms. Brown, she described exercises in which she was using hyperventilation or bending from the waist. The many group sessions she has attended, focusing on "recovery from sexual abuse," have a potentially profound influence on the participants.

In addition, Ms. Brown had a technique, which she called the "denial game," that was used when Mrs. Smith expressed caution about whether her mental images were reliable. This process had the intended effect of causing Mrs. Smith to once more *assume that whatever she could think of had actually happened.*

The police investigation was dropped for lack of evidence, for lack of corroboration from any of the many alleged victims named by Mrs. Smith, and because an outside consultant told the police that the impact of the therapy might be contaminating the information....

Mrs. Smith's statements to police include "trying to see" alleged events, having

> a flash... (a) visual memory of a spirit part of me coming out of me via my mouth and sitting on a head board. I now understand this to be dissociation....

The police, quite understandably, wondered whether this might be a sign of major mental disorder, like a psychosis. Instead, such statements reflect not that Mrs. Smith was suffering a major mental disorder, but simply that she was absorbing unsupported ideas from her therapists. I have studied the process by which some mental health professionals are passing these ideas to patients, via articles, speeches, and in therapy sessions. Many, if not most, patients, will accept these ideas as accepted scientific information, coming as they do from a professional therapist.

Just how much Mrs. Smith had come to believe in this process, already by April, 1988, is seen by her telling the police on April 20, 1988 that

> These are not complete memories at this point but there are bits and pieces of which I would like to tell you now and when I have the complete memory back I will talk to you again.... I would like to add that I expect to have further recall of incidents as I have just begun to have recall in the last five weeks or so....

4. The Growth of the Allegations.

The process described above will often lead to a virtual flood of allegations which grow and grow. Particularly if there are emotional rewards for producing more claims, the sky is the limit. In this case, it ultimately led to claims of ritual abuse, animal killings, gang rape, multiple personalities, etc. which Mrs. Smith now seems to disavow but which she at the time was claiming as legitimate memory. A brief review of these developments offers important perspective on the unreliable nature of this entire process.

Dr. Wagner saw Mrs. Smith from May 20, 1988 to January 27, 1989. He used a method Mrs. Smith describes as "regression," and which she now does not trust. She feels that some of the things she said as a result of these methods may not have happened.

For example, Dr. Wagner's notes of November 24, 1988 speak of "...memory of John and 'Joe.' Tying her up—raping her. Two others came in, Evan and [unreadable]." Mrs. Smith says she doesn't recall saying this to Dr. Wagner, doesn't believe she said it to him, believes his records are incorrect, and believes she talked about "Sam."

Dr. Wagner, while nowhere in his records expressing any doubt about the reality of these statements, did mention at the outset (June 3, 1988) that he thought Mrs. Smith was: "I suspect getting a lot of mileage out of sexual abuse. Attention and support from home she never got from mom and dad?"

When I questioned Mrs. Smith about other examples of statements drawn from the notes of the many therapists she saw in the coming months, I noted an interesting pattern. Whenever a statement in therapy records referred to events which she now says may not have happened, like seeing a boy with slits for eyes and no face, she says that she cannot recall saying any of this. She repeatedly said it was only her study of the therapy records which allows her to remember what she might have said in therapy.

However, when I asked her about a note from Morton Hunt's evaluation of January 15, 1991, she was quite clear that she did not say the following "... Then had nightmare. Chose John. Just knew it was him (reviewed possible men)."

Such selective "memory" merely reinforces my opinion that these multiple therapy contacts, of the nature described, make a mockery of the idea that claims growing out of the sessions, or growing out of the mental images of a patient between such sessions, are reliable.

The fact that Mrs. Smith was in much more therapy than I have yet summarized, only deepens the dilemmas. She was in group therapy with Ms. Summers, for 32 sessions, from March 21, 1989 to December 1, 1989, and Ms. Summers, who is another of those who specialize in "working mainly with women recovering from childhood sexual abuse," wrote in her records that "Susan's abuse was the most cruel and degrading I have encountered."

Once again, unquestioning acceptance seems to be the *sine qua non* of many of the therapists in this case. Sadly, such an attitude may be quite destructive to patients. A review of her journals, which I will highlight, shows that (as Dr. Wagner had indicated) Mrs. Smith was getting a lot of positive feedback from more and more "memories." A patient might feel good at the time of such feedback, but the encouragement of this process does not bode well for the long-term welfare of such patients.

May 24, 1988—"Another memory came back—arms tied,.... I know there are things I can't even imagine yet that they did to me. I know I still have a lot of memories to go... I know I'll have the strength to handle them... I'm on my way to a happy successful life... I love my strength.

May 26, 1988—This morning at the Mom's Group... another memory came back.... I called WSAC. The more I discover about what I've been through the more I wonder how I ever survived.... You're so strong Susan, so wonderful. You're capable of whatever you believe in. You're OK, Susan Smith. You're

strong, you're a survivor, and a winner, you're going straight to the top, head of the class. You're OK, you're a winner. I'm really truly beginning to like myself and I really like that—all these years I hated myself.

May 27—I begin my workshop with my therapist. (Mary Brown)

May 28—... we did rapid breathing... I went to my sexual abuse... my body was twitching and squirming just as if it were tied up by the hands... I started getting these vague recollections of this blond male being Warren and some occurrence happening.... I wasn't ready to look at it until I could intellectually figure out how this could be...

May 31—Describes Dave* meeting with Smith—He explained to him that these memories had been undisturbed for twenty years and had not been distorted... and that I was not making it up... I knew Dave was not ready to look at his abuse... at WSAC I went into denial mode... Veronica played the denial game with me just to show me that I was crazy to believe I was making this up.

June 14, 1988—Saw Veronica, talked about Yellowstone incident with Gretchen involved, how I was blocking everything because I had no proof John was in Yellowstone and the fact that Gretchen must have repressed and that she would probably deny remembering such an incident... so she had me "hang" and it took a much longer time for the feelings to come, but they did, I cried, pound pillows, yelled, and got back more memories... so much doesn't make sense. Where is everyone else?

Nov. 9, 1988—What I learned in therapy today: When I was abused it happened to my body. It happened to a part of me that I dissociated from. I have separated from and disowned the part of

---

*A cousin of Mrs. Smith, and one of the other alleged victims, none of whom had any memories of abuse.

me that it happened to.... I am ashamed of my body... so I abuse it.

April 18, 1989—I love myself and that's something I couldn't have said a year ago. I've come a long way.... Signed Terrific Susan.

May ?, 1989—... I let my little girls talk... etc.

June 8, 1989—attended Conference on Child Sexual Abuse... I learned a lot... talked to Gretchen two weeks ago. More about her "other personalities."... Memories, memories. Where are they. I want to remember all the mean sadistic things John did to me.

July 5, 1989—I know I am going to go on and achieve great things in my life... speak out against abuse of children, especially sexual abuse. 1 know I'm strong, a survivor, and a successeder. (sic)

Oct. 16, 1989—I got back memories of what happened after John gave my body to the two "tough men" in exchange for drugs.

October 29, 1989—I don't think this can happily, successfully end for me unless I have power over him.

Nov. 29, 1989—Cousin Joe called and told me Warren had memories of being sexually assaulted by John. The memories are just beginning... I told Warren... I was really proud of him.

Nov. 27, 1990—... I don't want any more memories!!! ... I called WSAC this afternoon and bits of memories came up. One was John beside me, and about 5 men, in black robes, or gowns—full length with hoods on their heads.... These men had swordlike daggers in their hands... a memory of John slitting the throat of a cat with a knife... telling us that this is what would happen to us if we ever told about him.

Dec. 16, 1990—I think I might have multiple personalities. It is something I've wondered about before, but believed you only developed multiples if you were severely abused before age 8.... My first day with Veronica there was this other part of me talking. She named herself Julie... it was really weird cause I knew what was happening... I'm going to get to the other side of this—new and improved. But in the mean time, I'm a nuttsy basketcase.

Dec. 25, 1990—I started back in therapy mid-December, I could no longer contain the memories within me.... I want to write about and keep track of my memories. I've had a feeling for several months now that there might have been ritual abuse. When I started having flashes of white candles, lots of them, burning, I thought well, this is probably just an image I've seen on TV.... My 2nd day in therapy (3rd time I'd seen June) I had this memory—a faceless boy,... he had no nose and only slits for eyes.... They told us if we didn't behave, or if we ever told they would burn our faces with an iron.... They told the girls they use their genitals as eyes, then when they grow older they'd have furry, hairy eyes and everyone would laugh.

Toward the end of our meeting, I asked Mrs. Smith how she distinguished between the many allegations which she insists took place, and the many allegations which she made but now says she cannot remember saying and isn't sure they are real. The gist of her answer (the tape is of course available) was that "memories" which were like a "videotape," where a picture is complete, from start to finish, and which occurred to her sometimes in therapy but often by herself, are reliable. Brief images, or "flashes," which are incomplete, and which were often in response to therapeutic techniques she now is critical of, like those of June Schreiber and others, she distrusts.

I find this distinction, which I must assume to be sincere on Mrs. Smith's part, to be utterly unreliable. First, the therapy from the beginning has been manipulative, even though I have no doubt that all the therapists were sincere in wanting to help. They all, nonetheless, adopted the position that "the more memory the better."

While this might be interpreted to mean that this is standard practice in the therapeutic community, since so many therapists in this case acted in this manner, it is instead an artifact which resulted when Mrs. Smith sought out or was referred to a selected group of therapists who "specialize in recovery from sexual abuse." Amongst this group, whose work and education I have studied intensively, it is common practice to assume abuse occurs if anyone claims it has, common practice to encourage as many "memories" as possible, common practice to encourage anger and "empowerment," and common practice to accept all allegations, however unlikely, as being real.

All this is terribly unscientific, without general agreement from the mental health community, and in my view highly destructive to many patients. Perhaps most important here, in the context of litigation, is the fact that these techniques absolutely fly in the face of reliable fact-finding.

I cannot emphasize strongly enough how important it is for the Court, in studying this case and deciding what is reliable and what is not, to understand that if commonsense leads to one conclusion about where the truth lies, the use of psychiatric labels and esoteric explanations should not cause the Court to abandon what the facts otherwise seem to show.

* * *

As of this writing, the Court has yet to render a verdict. But whatever is decided in this case, it should be clear that our society is about to experience yet another wave of unreliable sexual abuse allegations. Once again, it is the promulgation of faulty ideas by a small segment of the mental health community (see for example Bass & Davis, 1988; Blume, 1990; Briere & Conte, in press; Cozolino, 1989; Maltz, 1990; Herman & Schatzow, 1987; Summit, 1987; Young, Sachs, Braun, & Watkins, 1991), coupled with the apathy of the bulk of the mental health community, which promises to create a new form of abuse of patients, families, and the falsely accused. The moral and economic costs are incalculable, and the promotion of pseudoscientific ideas which confuse memory with mental imagery is already confusing the scientific literature.

Fortunately, clearer heads are also in evidence (see Ganaway, 1991; Lanning, 1989 and 1992; Mulhern, 1991a, 1991b, 1991c; Nathan, 1989, 1990, 1991; Passantino, Passantino, & Trott, 1989; Price, 1992; Putnam, 1991; Wakefield & Underwager, 1992 and undated). Given our society's tendency to become infatuated with all manner of fads, it should be obvious that this latest development in the child sexual abuse circus is not going to go away quickly or easily. It will take insight and perseverance to counteract the tendency of the media and most lay persons to uncritically accept the "blocked memory" claims now emerging with increasing regularity. If our society is serious about responding to the reality of childhood sexual abuse, a critical ingredient is the avoidance of irresponsible empire-building by some mental health professionals who have abandoned both science and reason.

REFERENCES

Bass, E., & Davis, L. (1988). *The courage to heal.* New York, Harper & Row.

Blume, E. (1990). *Secret survivors: Uncovering incest and its aftereffects in women.* New York: J. Wiley & Sons.

Briere, J., & Conte, J. (in press). Self reported amnesia for abuse in adults molested as children. *Journal of Traumatic Stress.*

Cozolino, L. (1989). The ritual abuse of children: Implications for clinical practice and research, *The Journal of Sex Research, 26(1),* 131–138.

Ganaway, G. K. (1991, August 19). *Alternate hypotheses regarding satanic ritual abuse memories.* Presented at the 99th Annual Convention of the American Psychological Association, San Francisco.

Herman, J. L., & Schatzow, E. (1987). Recovery and verification of memories of childhood sexual trauma. *Psychoanalytic Psychology, 4(1),* 1–14.

Lanning, K. V. (1989, October). *Satanic, occult, ritualistic crime: A law enforcement perspective.* National Center for the Analysis of Violent Crime, FBI Academy, Quantico, VA.

Lanning, K. V. (1992). *Investigator's guide to allegations of "ritual" child abuse.* National Center for the Analysis of Violent Crime: Quantico, VA.

Maltz, W. (1990, December). Adult survivors of incest: How to help them overcome the trauma. *Medical Aspects of Human Sexuality,* 42–47.

Mulhern, S. (1991a). *Ritual abuse: Defining a syndrome v. defending a belief.* Unpublished manuscript.

Mulhern, S. (1991b). [Letter to the Editor]. *Child Abuse & Neglect, 15,* 609–610.

Mulhern, S. (1991c). Satanism and psychotherapy: A rumor in search of an inquisition. In J. T. Richardson, J. Best, & D. G. Bromley (Eds.), *The Satanism scare* (pp. 145–172). New York: Aldine de Gruyter.

Nathan, D. (1989, June 21). The Devil and Mr. Mattox, *Texas Observer,* pp. 10–13.

Nathan, D. (1991). Satanism and child molestation: Constructing the ritual abuse scare. In J. T. Richardson, J. Best, & D. G. Bromley (Eds.), *The Satanism scare* (pp. 75–94). New York: Aldine de Gruyter.

Nathan, D. (1990, June 20). The ritual sex abuse hoax, *Village Voice,* pp. 36–44.

Passantino, G., Passantino, B., & Trott, J. (1989). Satan's sideshow. *Cornerstone, 18(90),* 23–28.

Price, L. (1992, April 20). Presentation at the Midwest Regional False Memory Syndrome Foundation Meeting. Benton Harbor, Michigan.

Putnam, F. (1991). The satanic ritual abuse controversy. *Child Abuse & Neglect, 15,* 175–179.

Summit, R. (1987, July). Declaration of Roland Summit, MD, Regarding *People v. Dill.*

Wakefield, H., & Underwager, R. (1992, June 20). *Recovered memories of alleged sexual abuse: Lawsuits against parents.* Presentation at 4th Annual Convention of the American Psychological Society, San Diego, CA. (Also, *Behavioral Sciences and the Law,* in press.)

Wakefield, H., & Underwager, R. (undated). Magic, mischief, and memories: Remembering repressed abuse. Unpublished manuscript. (Also see *Issues in Child Abuse Accusations,* 1991, Vol. 3, No. 3.)

Young, W. C., Sachs, R. G., Braun, B. G., & Watkins, R. (1991). Patients reporting ritual abuse in childhood: A clinical syndrome of 37 cases. *Child Abuse & Neglect, 15,* 181–189.

CHALLENGE QUESTIONS

Are Memories of Sex Abuse Always Real?

1. Can a psychologist or other mental health professional lead a patient to believe something that is not true? If so, how can this happen?

2. Can you think of any explanations for the "instances" described by Bass and Davis other than prior sexual abuse?

3. How would you go about proving that someone had been sexually abused? What evidence would you need?

4. What are your beliefs about how memories are stored and retrieved?

On the Internet . . .

http://www.dushkin.com

Health Information Resources

Here is a long list of toll-free numbers for organizations that provide health-related information. The numbers do not offer diagnosis or treatment, but some do offer recorded information. Others provide personalized counseling, referrals, and/or written materials.
http://nhic-nt.health.org/Scripts/Tollfree.cfm

Mental Health Infosource: Disorders

This no-nonsense page lists hotlinks to pages dealing with psychological disorders, including anxiety, panic, phobic disorders, schizophrenia, and violent/self-destructive behaviors.
http://www.mhsource.com/disorders/

Mental Health Net

This comprehensive online guide to mental health features more than 7,000 individual resources, including resources on mental disorders; professional resources in psychology, psychiatry, and social work; and journals and self-help magazines. *http://www.cmhc.com/*

Suicide Awareness: Voices of Education

This is the most popular suicide site on the Internet. A very thorough site, it includes information on dealing with suicide (both before and after) and material from the organization's many education sessions.
http://www.save.org/

PART 5

Mental Health

A mental disorder is often defined as a pattern of thinking or behaving that is either disruptive to others or uncomfortable for the person with the disorder. This definition seems straightforward; however, is it universally applicable? Certain patterns of social behavior fit this definition, but does this make them "diseases" in the medical sense? Some researchers have recently argued that physician-assisted suicide, or euthanasia, is an acceptable way for terminally ill patients to end their suffering. Others maintain that patients who wish to die are suffering from mental disorders that can and should be treated. Which interpretation will likely result in the best care for patients?

■ Is Schizophrenia a Biological Disorder?

■ Are There Valid Psychological Reasons for Physician-Assisted Suicide?

ISSUE 10

Is Schizophrenia a Biological Disorder?

YES: Nancy C. Andreasen, from "Linking Mind and Brain in the Study of Mental Illnesses: A Project for Scientific Psychopathology," *Science* (March 14, 1997)

NO: Victor D. Sanua, from "The Myth of the Organicity of Mental Disorders," *The Humanistic Psychologist* (Spring 1996)

ISSUE SUMMARY

YES: Clinical psychiatrist Nancy C. Andreasen asserts that a variety of modern technologies, including neuroimaging and animal modeling, show that although schizophrenia is a disease that manifests itself in the mind, it arises from the brain.

NO: Clinical psychologist Victor D. Sanua contends that the assumption that schizophrenia is a biological disorder is not supported by research but is, instead, maintained by many scientists who have a misguided faith in an elusive future technology that will supposedly show the connection between mind and brain.

For centuries philosophers have considered the issue of how the mind and the body are connected. The man viewed by many as the father of modern philosophy, René Descartes (1596–1650), suggested that the mind and the body are linked in the pineal gland of the brain. Although this notion was later discarded, philosophers and, more recently, psychologists have continued to search for a link between the mind and the body.

Today most psychologists assume that the mind and the body are connected in some way. Furthermore, many assume that what we call the mind is not only connected to the body but arises from the body in the brain. Some researchers believe that modern technology has made it possible to show this mind/brain connection. They assume that a more sophisticated future technology will prove that all mental activity results from brain activity. Other researchers, however, consider this too optimistic—a product of philosophical bias rather than scientific data.

In the following selections, Nancy C. Andreasen notes that although there are currently no biological markers for mental illness, scientific psychopathologists maintain that mental disorders are rooted in the brain and result from a brain dysfunction of some sort. This hypothesis has been tested in numerous ways by researchers from a variety of disciplines. Andreasen contends that this multidisciplinary approach has provided considerable insight into the activities of the brain that are responsible for mental disorders. She uses the example of schizophrenia to illustrate how research that stems from several different perspectives converges on one finding—that the mind and the brain are linked.

In stark contrast, Victor D. Sanua argues that although studies looking at how the brain might cause mental disorders have been conducted for nearly a century, the results of these studies have failed to evidence a mind/brain connection. Nevertheless, researchers such as Andreasen maintain the hope that improved technology and better research methods will eventually prove the connection. Sanua finds this hope to be unfounded because the research to date has provided so few genuine results. In conclusion, Sanua suggests that researchers might be looking in the wrong places for answers about mental illness.

POINT	COUNTERPOINT
• Clinicians should focus on the biological aspects of the human mind to understand mental disorders.	• Clinicians should focus on the social and psychological aspects of the human mind to understand mental disorders.
• Recent advances in brain research support the hypothesis that mental disorders derive from the brain.	• Research conducted over the last 100 years has failed to produce substantial proof that mental disorders derive from the brain.
• Schizophrenia can be used as an example to show the link between the mind and the brain.	• Investigations of schizophrenia have failed to show any link between the mind and the brain.
• With increased sophistication and technology, biological markers for mental disease will be discovered.	• More sophisticated technology will not show any link between the mind and the body.
• Multiple biopsychological disciplines should continue to investigate the biological causes of mental disorders.	• Psychologists should explore potential origins of mental disorders besides biology.

YES

Nancy C. Andreasen

LINKING MIND AND BRAIN IN THE STUDY OF MENTAL ILLNESSES

FUNDAMENTAL CONCEPTUAL ISSUES

The relationship between mind and brain.   Mental illnesses have historically been distinguished from other medical illnesses because they affect the higher cognitive processes that are referred to as "mind." The relationship between mind and brain has been extensively discussed in contemporary philosophy and psychology, without any decisive resolution. One heuristic solution, therefore, is to adopt the position that the mind is the expression of the activity of the brain and that these two are separable for purposes of analysis and discussion but inseparable in actuality. That is, mental phenomena arise from the brain, but mental experience also affects the brain, as is demonstrated by the many examples of environmental influences on brain plasticity. The aberrations of mental illnesses reflect abnormalities in the brain/mind's interaction with its surrounding world; they are diseases of a psyche (or mind) that resides in that region of the soma (or body) that is the brain.

Mind and brain can be studied as if they are separate entities, however, and this is reflected in the multiple and separate disciplines that examine them. Each uses a different language and methodology to study the same quiddity. The challenge in developing a scientific psychopathology in the 1990s is to use the power of multiple disciplines. The study of mind has been the province of cognitive psychology, which has divided mind into component domains of investigation (such as memory, language, and attention), created theoretical systems to explain the workings of those domains (constructs such as memory encoding versus retrieval), and designed experimental paradigms to test the hypotheses in human beings and animals. The study of brain has been the province of several disciplines. Neuropsychology has used the lesion method to determine localization by observing absence of function after injury, whereas neuroanatomy and neurobiology have mapped neural development and connectivity and studied functionality in animal models. The boundaries between all these disciplines have become increasingly less distinct, however, creating the broad discipline of cognitive neuroscience. The term "cognitive" has definitions that range from broad to narrow; its usage here is broad and refers to all activities of mind, including emotion, perception, and regulation of behavior.

Contemporary psychiatry studies mental illnesses as diseases that manifest as mind and arise from brain. It is the discipline within cognitive neuroscience that integrates information from all these related disciplines in order to develop models that explain the cognitive dysfunctions of psychiatric patients based on knowledge of normal brain/mind function.

Using the phenomenotype to find the biotype. There are at present no known biological diagnostic markers for any mental illnesses except dementias such as Alzheimer's disease. The to-be-discovered lesions that define the remainder of mental illnesses are likely to be occurring at complex or small-scale levels that are difficult to visualize and measure, such as the connectivity of neural circuits, neuronal signaling and signal transduction, and abnormalities in genes or gene expression. Despite their lack of a defining objective index such as glucosuria is for diabetes, however, these illnesses are very real. Not only do they produce substantial morbidity and mortality, but advances in psychiatric nosology have produced objective, criterion-based, assessment techniques that produce reliable and precise diagnoses. In the absence of a pathological marker, the current definitions of mental illnesses are syndromal and are based on a convergence of signs, symptoms, outcome, and patterns of familial aggregation.

Finding the neural mechanisms of mental illnesses must be an iterative process; syndromal clinical definitions (or the phenomenotype) are progressively tested, refined, and redefined through the measurement of neurobiological aspects (or the biotype). This process is not fundamentally different from that used to study other diseases. The diagnosis of diabetes, for example, has evolved from the observation of glucosuria to multiple subdivisions based on age of onset, severity of symptoms and complications, degree of islet cell involvement, and genetic factors. For most mental illnesses, the task is simply made more challenging by the absence of an objective criterion that can provide an initial clue to assist in finding mechanisms, as neuritic plaques have done for Alzheimer's disease....

LINKING MIND AND BRAIN: THE EXAMPLE... OF SCHIZOPHRENIA...

Advances that have been made in the study of schizophrenia... illustrate the power of developing cognitive models that derive from different perspectives and apply techniques from multiple domains.

Finding the common thread in schizophrenia. The name "schizophrenia" ("fragmented mind") was coined by Eugen Bleuler, who wished to emphasize that it was a cognitive disorder in which the "fabric of thought and emotion" was torn or fragmented, and normal connections or associations were no longer present. Schizophrenia poses special challenges to the development of cognitive models because of the breadth and diversity of its symptoms. The symptoms include nearly all domains of function: perception (hallucinations), inferential thinking (delusions), fluency of thought and speech (alogia), clarity and organization of thought and speech ("formal thought disorder"), motor activity (catatonia), emotional expression (affective blunting), ability to initiate and complete goal-directed behavior (avolition), and ability to seek out and experience emotional gratification (anhedonia). Not all these symptoms are present in any given patient, however, and none is pathognomonic of the illness. An initial survey of the diversity of symptoms might suggest that multiple brain regions are involved, in a spotty pattern much as once occurred in neurosyphilis. In the absence of visible lesions and known pathogens, however, investigators have turned to the exploration of models that could explain the diversity of symptoms by a single cognitive mechanism. Exemplifying this strategy are four different models that illustrate the melding of cognitive neuroscience and psychiatry, beginning at four different points of departure. The convergent conclusions of these different models are striking.

Cognitive psychology. Approaching schizophrenia from the background of cognitive psychology, C. D. Frith has divided the symptoms of schizophrenia into three broad groups or dimensions: disorders of willed action (which lead to symptoms such as alogia and avolition), disorders of self-monitoring (which lead to symptoms such as auditory hallucinations and delusions of alien control), and disorders in monitoring the intentions of others ("mentalizing") (which lead to symptoms such as "formal thought disorder" and delusions of persecution). Frith believes that all these are special cases of a more general underlying mechanism: a disorder of consciousness or self-awareness that impairs the ability to think with "metarepresentations" (higher order abstract concepts that are representations of mental states). Frith and his collaborators are currently testing this conceptual framework using positron emission tomography (PET)....

Neurobiology. Approaching schizophrenia from a background that blends lesion studies and single-cell recordings in nonhuman primates for the study of cognition, P. Goldman-Rakic has proposed a model suggesting that the fundamental impairment in schizophrenia is an inability to guide behavior by representation, often referred to as a defect in working memory. Working memory, or the ability to hold a representation "online" and perform cognitive operations using it, permits individuals to respond in a flexible manner, to formulate and modify plans, and to base behavior on internally held ideas and thoughts rather than being driven by external stimuli. A defect in this ability can explain a variety of symptoms of schizophrenia. For example, the inability to hold a discourse plan in mind and monitor speech output leads to disorganized speech and thought disorder; the inability to maintain a plan for behavioral activities could lead to negative symptoms such as avolition or alogia; and the inability to reference a specific external or internal experience against associative memories (mediated by cortical and subcortical circuitry involving frontal/parietal/temporal regions and the thalamus) could lead to an altered consciousness of sensory experience and would be expressed as delusions or hallucinations. The model... is consistent with the compromised blood flow to the prefrontal cortex seen in these patients....

Psychobiology and neurophysiology. Using techniques originally derived from neurophysiology, D. L. Braff and colleagues have developed another complementary model. This model begins from the perspective of techniques used to measure brain electrical activity, particularly various types of evoked potentials, and hypothesizes that the core underlying deficit in schizophrenia involves information processing and attention. This model derives from the empirical clinical observation that patients with schizophrenia frequently complain that they are bombarded with more stimuli than they can interpret. Consequently, they misinterpret (that is, have delusions), confuse internal with external stimuli (hallucinations), or retreat to safety ("negative symptoms" such as alogia, anhedonia, or avolition). Early interpretations of this observation... postulated that patients had problems with early stages in serial order processing that led to downstream effects such as psychotic or negative symptoms. As serial models have been supplanted by distributed models, the deficit may be better conceptualized in terms of resource allocation: Patients cannot mobilize attentional resources and allocate them to relevant tasks....

Clinical psychiatry. Our group has used the clinical presentation of schizophrenia as a point of departure, initially attempting to localize the various symptoms in brain regions through the use of structural and functional neuroimaging techniques. This strategy has led to a search for abnormalities in specific brain regions and theories about symptom-region relationships (such as negative symptoms in the frontal cortex or hallucinations in the superior temporal gyrus), which have been examined by a variety of investigators. This approach is oversimplified, however, and we are currently testing an integrated model that explains clinical symptoms as a consequence of disruptions in anatomically identified circuits that mediate a fundamental cognitive process....

The common thread. The common thread in all these observations, spun from four different starting points, is that schizophrenia reflects a disruption in a fundamental cognitive process that affects specific circuitry in the brain and that may be improved through medications that affect that circuitry. The various teams use differing terminology and somewhat different concepts—metarepresentations, representationally guided behavior, information processing/attention, cognitive dysmetria—but they convey a common theme. The cognitive dysfunction in schizophrenia is an inefficient temporal and spatial referencing of information and experience as the person attempts to determine boundaries between self and not-self and to formulate effective decisions or plans that will guide him or her through the small-scale (speaking a sentence) or large-scale (finding a job) maneuvers of daily living. This capacity is sometimes referred to as consciousness.

Using diverse technologies and techniques—PET scanning, animal models, lesion methods, single-cell recordings, evoked potentials—the investigators also converge on similar conclusions about the neuroanatomic substrates of the cognitive dysfunction. All concur that it must involve distributed circuits rather than a single specific "localization," and all suggest a key role for interrelationships among the prefrontal cortex, other interconnected cortical regions, and subcortical regions, particularly the thalamus and striatum. Animal and molecular models are being developed that are based on knowledge of this circuitry and the fundamental cognitive process, which can be applied to understanding the mechanism of drug actions and developing new medications. . . .

SUMMARY AND CONCLUSION

Examples of work applying diverse techniques of cognitive neuroscience to the study of . . . schizophrenia indicate that increasingly sophisticated strategies and conceptualizations are emerging as powerful new technologies are being applied. Focal regions have been replaced by circuits and static changes by plasticity and molecular mechanisms. The power of models is enhanced by efforts to design experiments that can be used in nonhuman species, in order to obtain in vivo measures that will illuminate mechanisms. The power of neuroimaging is also permitting in vivo measures of circuits and mechanisms in the human brain. These advances have created an era in which a scientific psychopathology that links mind and brain has become a reality.

NO

Victor D. Sanua

THE MYTH OF THE ORGANICITY OF MENTAL DISORDERS

In 1994, I attended a conference on schizophrenia arranged by the Columbia University College of Physicians and Surgeons (9th Annual Schizophrenia Conference) and the Alliance for the Mentally Ill. Herbert Pardes, Chairman of the Department of Psychiatry and Dean of the Faculty of Medicine, stated in his introductory remarks that Columbia was installing the largest Magnetic Resonance Imaging (MRI) machine in the world, which would enable scientists to see the workings of the brain. His remarks were sprinkled with optimistic adjectives like, "tremendous excitement," "new hope," and so on. The rest of the day was mostly presentations by the Columbia Faculty on the various theories about the causation of schizophrenia and the research on new antipsychotic drugs. The following are some of the areas of research on causation: genetics, immunological systems, nutritional deficiencies, exposure to influenza, obstetrical complications, structural brain changes, season of birth, neurotropic factors, loss of brain tissue, virus infecting the fetal brain, and others. Basically, schizophrenia was seen as a biological disorder whose mystery would be unveiled only by laboratory work. It should be noted that during the conference, there were no formal discussions about the relationship between neurotransmitters and schizophrenia. The hypotheses of the dysfuctions of the neurotransmitters like serotonin, endorphin and dopamine, which have been quite popular in the past, do not seem to be viable at this time.

There was a general enthusiasm that there would soon be a breakthrough with the kind of scientific research being carried out in modern laboratory facilities. However, such optimism does not seem warranted. A well-known German psychiatrist, Hafner stated, "Our knowledge of the etiology of the disease called schizophrenia has not yet made much progress from [Emil] Kraepelin's days" (1987, p. 366). The fact that there are still so many areas of research awaiting investigation at the Columbia University Conference corroborates Hafner's point. In a workshop in the afternoon, devoted to genetics, evidence for the genetic causation was the much higher concordance of schizophrenia among monozygotic twins than among dizygotic twins.

From Victor D. Sanua, "The Myth of the Organicity of Mental Disorders," *The Humanistic Psychologist*, vol. 24 (Spring 1996). Copyright © 1996 by The American Psychological Association. Reprinted by permission. References omitted.

When I suggested to the speaker that this could also be attributed to a similar environment for the monozygotic twins, the response of the presenter was that the evidence is further provided by the adoption studies of Heston (1966), Kety, Rosenthal, Wender and Schulsinger, and Jacobsen, (1975)....

A year later, in a similar conference by Columbia University, Malespina, a biopsychiatrist, stated that it is humbling to the profession to realize that Kraepelin had predicted that it must be left to the future to see how far his theories about schizophrenia are confirmed. According to Malespina, it seems that the future is now because of the new scientific technologies.

Thus psychiatry, at the Columbia University Conference maintained the disease model in its purest form, I never heard in the course of the day any reference to poverty, social class, child abuse, family stress, rejection, ethnicity, aggression, divorce, social conflicts, social disintegration, and [so] on which are so much part of life and which could have a major effect on abnormal behavior. The individual was presented as if it were a machine with some "broken" (Andreasen, 1984) parts, mostly in the brain, which needed to be fixed.

In 1987, Van Kammen, the editor of *Biological Psychiatry*, wrote an editorial, "5 HT, a neurotransmitter for all seasons?" about the constant appearance of studies showing how serotonin has been found to be responsible for numerous aberrations. He stated:

> As clinical researchers, we may look for low CSF 5–HIAA, decreased imipramine binding, decreased alpha receptor activity and positive DST (not again!) in patients with borderline personality disorder, alcoholism, in cocaine or marijuana

abusers, cigarette smokers, compulsive gamblers, sadists, flashers and nail biters, rapists, aggressive lesbians, shoplifters, and spouse beaters. (1987, p. 1)

A cover story entitled "The Genetic Revolution" in a major periodical reported on the various ailments which result from faulty genes. Since the article did not include any references on the genetic causation of mental disorders often found in the psychiatric and popular media, I wrote a letter to the editor inquiring about the fact that there is no mention of the genetic causation of mental disorders in this otherwise well-documented article on genetic diseases. His response follows:

Dear Mr. Sanua,

Thank you for writing in response to the cover story "The Genetic Revolution." We certainly appreciate your interest in learning more about genetic indicators for medical disorders. It seems logical that there would be particular genes responsible for conditions of schizophrenia, and researchers have indeed been working to identify them. Despite ongoing study, however, *most finds to date require substantial further study, and some have been retracted because of problems with methodology* [italics added]. We hope to be able to report soon on encouraging news about genetic advances for mental disorders, of course, and we are pleased that you took the time to register your thoughts on this matter...

In the February 21, 1994 issue of *Time*, Overbye, an essayist for the publication entitled his essay "Born to raise hell?" in which he referred to a study which attributed aggression to genetic causation. To demonstrate, in a ludicrous way, how this ideology of genetic factors is connected to a large number of aberrations, Overbye wrote:

> Some of us, it seems were born to be bad. Scientists say they are on the verge of pinning down genetic and biochemical abnormalities that predispose their bearers to violence. An article in the journal *Science* last summer carried the headline "Evidence found for a possible 'aggression gene.'" Waiting in the wings are child-testing programs, drug manufacturers, insurance companies, civil right advocates, defense attorneys, and anxious citizens for whom the violent criminal has replaced the beady-eyed communist as the bogeyman. Crime thus joins homosexuality, smoking, divorce, schizophrenia, alcoholism, shyness, political liberalism, intelligence, religiosity, cancer and blue eyes among the many aspects of human life for which it is claimed that biology is destiny. Physicists have been pilloried for years for this kind of reductionism, but in biology it makes everybody happy: the scientists and pharmaceutical companies expand their domain; politicians have "progress" to point to; the smoker, divorces and serial killers get to blame their problems on biology, and we get the satisfaction of knowing they are sick—not like us at all. (p. 76)

Weinberger (1991), a well-known investigator on the biology of schizophrenia urged his colleagues to have a more cautious attitude about the usual claims we regularly read. He wrote:

> It would be naive to conclude that current research with its neurobiologic emphasis is totally immune to the pitfalls of prior scientific research. Many of the findings that appear rock solid today will likely turn out to be epiphenomena and trivial. This has been the case throughout this century with schizophrenia, a disorder that is still researched largely at the phenomenological level. (p. 3)

However Weinberger seems rather optimistic and belies his cautiousness when he states, on the same page, that neuroanatomical, neurochemical, and neurophysiologic correlates of schizophrenia have accumulated at a seemingly *geometric rate*. [italics added] (p. 3).

A heavy dosage of headlines on the organicity of mental disorders has had some serious influence on a small but very powerful group of clinical psychologists connected with APA [American Psychological Association] who have adopted the medical model as an ideology for the purpose of espousing "prescription privileges" for the profession. I have documented (Sanua, 1993, 1994a) the pronouncement of these psychologists who have not provided in their articles the rationale and the scientific source for their inspiration. In one case, Fox (1988) supports the need for prescription privileges for psychologists (p. 503) based on an article by Adams (1986) which appeared in the *Georgia Psychologist*. Why do biopsychiatrists continue to attribute mental disorders to organic factors, while ignoring completely social factors which offer a more parsimonious explanation for the development of mental disorders? Kovacs (1987) voiced the possibility that if organic causation is deemphasized, in time biopsychiatrists will have no reason to exist. Szasz (1987) made a very pertinent observation to the effect that books on pathology do not mention anything about schizophrenia or manic-depressive psychosis. It is felt that pathologists ought to know more than anybody else about bodily pathological dysfunctions that explain mental disorders. Thus while psychiatrists have not been able to convince pathologists, they seem to be deluding themselves that mental disorders are organic and, worse, seem to be successful in convincing the general public of their pseudo-scientific findings.

The psychiatric journals are replete with presumably sophisticated articles which basically discuss structural and functional dysfunctions of the brain, genetic inheritance, and the chemistry of the urine and blood. These are being analyzed in order to discover some aberration which could be related to the mental disorders. This is being done without ever dealing with the human aspects of the patients, his feelings, his intellect, his expectations and his anxieties about his condition. Modrow (1992) provides a good example of the organic emphasis in mental disorder. If he puts forth the whimsical theory that schizophrenia is a brain disease caused by an allergy to cats, while there are schizophrenics that have never been near a cat, it can always be said that some form of schizophrenia has been caused by an allergy to cats and some forms are not, and thus the theory cannot be falsified. To me this is not a far-fetched or whimisical theory. In the course of my attendance at the Conference on Schizophrenia at Columbia University, I made the acquaintance of a psychiatrist who told me that he knew what causes schizophrenia and he would mail me an article. The two-page article revealed that schizophrenia results from mosquito bites.

... What is hoped for is that with further development of laboratory equipment, like the imaging techniques, the "truth" about the causation of schizophrenia will soon be revealed because "it is around the corner." The "truth" around the corner has been around for almost 100 years. All I can say in reading [the] extensive literature [provided by the National Institute of Mental Health] is that there has never been so much written material that has been published with such few results.

... My analysis of the tremendous efforts spent on biological research reminds me of a story which when applied to the problem of schizophrenia reflects a tragic analogy. This is the story of a drunken man who was looking for something around the lamp post in the evening. When he was asked what he was looking for, he said that he had lost his keys. When he was asked further whether he had lost them around the lamp post, he stated that he was not sure, but that this was the only place with light and, therefore, he was going to look for his keys there.

CHALLENGE QUESTIONS

Is Schizophrenia a Biological Disorder?

1. Sanua suggests that biopsychological researchers might be looking in the wrong place for the causes of mental disorders. Where else does he imply that psychologists should look to understand the causes of mental disorders? What evidence can you find for this alternative?

2. Andreasen contends that the evidence gained from a variety of methods supports the thesis that the mind and the brain are connected. What are the advantages of multidisciplinary approaches to scientific study? What are the disadvantages?

3. Sanua concludes that the search for biological causes of mental disorders has failed. If this were true, why would scientists continue to work on this project? Are there factors that are unrelated to data that could be involved in conducting this research?

4. Both Andreasen and Sanua focus their remarks on schizophrenia. Investigate another mental disorder and report on the extent to which this disorder is biologically determined.

5. Andreasen seems to express faith in the ability of future technology to uncover the specific activities of the brain that are responsible for mental disorders. To what extent is this "faith" consistent with the scientific notion that only things that have been empirically demonstrated should be accepted as true?

ISSUE 11

Are There Valid Psychological Reasons for Physician-Assisted Suicide?

YES: H. S. Cohen, from "Euthanasia as a Way of Life," in A. O. Smook and B. De Vos-Schippers, eds., *Right to Self-Determination: Proceedings of the Eighth World Congress of Right-to-Die Societies* (VU University Press, 1993)

NO: Herbert Hendin and Gerald Klerman, from "Physician-Assisted Suicide: The Dangers of Legalization," *American Journal of Psychiatry* (January 1993)

ISSUE SUMMARY

YES: Dutch physician H. S. Cohen argues that control over one's death allows for a healthier outlook on one's life, particularly when one has a terminal illness.

NO: Psychiatrists Herbert Hendin and Gerald Klerman assert that those who wish to die are probably suffering from a variety of treatable mental illnesses.

The rationality of suicide has long been a controversial subject. Could people have valid, clearly thought-out reasons for taking their own lives? Although this is certainly conceivable, it is probably safe to say that most psychologists would consider this possibility to be more the exception than the rule. Too many suicides are committed impulsively—without thinking clearly—and too many are committed when patients are in the throes of mental disorders of which they are unaware.

However, a new factor has recently entered this controversy—the medical professional who "assists" with the suicide. This new factor minimizes the impulsivity of the act and reduces the chance of its being the product of a mental disorder. With physician-assisted suicides, patients are forced to take time to carefully consider their decision. No impulsive acts are permitted. The physician also serves as a safeguard in that she or he is able to diagnose any mental disorder that could hamper the decision-making process. Therefore, the issue of suicide arises in a new context: Are there valid psychological reasons—particularly when assisted by a professional—to commit suicide?

In the following selection, which is based on an address to a Dutch conference on the "right to die," H. S. Cohen answers this question affirmatively. Indeed, he contends that the option of euthanasia—of assisted suicide—is part of any good medical and spiritual care. Cohen admits that enhancing one's life through control of one's death might seem paradoxical. However, he believes that the option of assisted suicide can actually prolong one's life because it offers a sane and humane way of dying while allaying any fears of protracted suffering or loss of control. Squarely confronting the possibility of death, says Cohen, also allows one to cut through polite conversation to more meaningful dialogue with loved ones and professionals.

Herbert Hendin and Gerald Klerman, in the second selection, cite several reasons why they are against physician-assisted suicide. They consider the movement to assist with suicide a "drastic departure from established social policy and medical tradition." They also contend that 95 percent of those who commit suicide have diagnosable psychiatric illnesses, the vast majority of which are treatable. Even people who seem rational about a terminal illness are usually suffering from treatable depression. Furthermore, many who commit suicide have important, nonrational elements in their wish to die. The average physician is not trained to assess these nonrational elements or detect these mental illnesses. According to Hendin and Klerman, this lack of training can lead to the abuse of patients who are vulnerable to exploitation or frightened by illness.

POINT	COUNTERPOINT
• Allowing patients the option of assisted suicide can be life-affirming and comforting.	• Few contemplate suicide from any sort of healthy perspective.
• Providing patients with some control over their suffering is humane.	• The possibility for abuse of vulnerable or depressed patients is too great.
• People should not be able to dictate to others their own beliefs about whether or not assisted suicide is wrong.	• To allow people to choose suicide is to change long-standing traditions of society and medicine.
• Patients who are allowed the option of assisted suicide confront death more realistically.	• People who wish to die are probably suffering from some treatable mental illness.
• Patients who face death through the option of assisted suicide can communicate with family and friends more meaningfully.	• Those who wish to die may be easily treated so that they can affirm life again.

YES

H. S. Cohen

EUTHANASIA AS A WAY OF LIFE

In this contribution I shall concentrate on a not so straightforward, but fascinating question: What is the effect of the option of euthanasia before it is performed? More specifically on the life of patients, relatives, doctors, nurses, volunteers and on society as a whole. That such an influence exists and is profound indeed, I hope to demonstrate.

Let me first concentrate on individuals who have a considerable stretch of life and suffering waiting for them, e.g., patients with AIDS and those severely handicapped by multiple sclerosis. (The use of the word "patient" does not suggest a kind of inferior race. It just means you and me somewhere in the future when we shall be not as healthy as we are now.) Anybody with bedside experience must have noted the change that comes over these patients when a request for euthanasia is being seriously negotiated and the end of life is no longer a conversational topic to be hushed up. After becoming aware of it, this effect can be observed more often and more clearly. I cannot offer any proper scientific evidence in this field, just observations and speculations. To describe this change in the sick person, which of course is different for every individual, I would use words ranging from "acceptance," and "tranquility" up to "radiating peace" and "happiness." In careful euthanasia the decision-making process usually takes weeks or even months. In my memory it is the patient himself or herself who grows and matures in this period and gradually provides relatives with support and consolation. Euthanasia takes away the fear of unknown suffering in unknown intensity for an unknown period.

But I want to stress a second point, i.e., that euthanasia forces us to communicate about life and death in a very direct way, without the usual social chitchat and niceties. A tendency towards non-verbal communication comes quite naturally. Hugging and kissing are not inappropriate. Doctors should not discuss euthanasia, standing at the foot of the bed, in a white coat, mumbling Latin incantations. The least is to sit down, hold hands, and speak only if silence does not speak for itself. This kind of attitude is bound to be catching in the family and will improve the closeness and warmth and understanding between relatives and friends. I'm convinced that in fact a substantial part

From H. S. Cohen, "Euthanasia as a Way of Life," in A. O. Smook and B. De Vos-Schippers, eds., *Right to Self-Determination: Proceedings of the Eighth World Congress of Right-to-Die Societies* (VU University Press, 1993). Copyright © 1993 by VU University Press. Reprinted by permission.

of the bereavement is experienced before the patient passes away. Of course there is grief afterwards as well. But, in my experience grief of a "healthy" kind, often mixed with sincere relief and cheerfulness. Dr. Admiraal has often stated that the performance of euthanasia is part of good medical care. In this line the option of euthanasia might well be considered part of spiritual care.

The paradox that euthanasia is good for life goes further. Can it even prolong life, that is, an acceptable form of life? Let's consider an AIDS patient who is determined to commit suicide before the going gets too rough. He'll have to execute his plans while he still has the strength to do so himself. In this situation the promise of assisted suicide or euthanasia takes away the urgency of executing his intention. Euthanasia can indeed prolong life by offering a humane way of dying.

In a well-known experiment, published [recently] in the *Lancet*, Dr. Spiegel of Stanford University offered psycho-social group therapy to women with breast cancer. He found that these patients lived for an average [of] 36 months. The matched control group lived for 19 months only. The gained life-span of 17 months is attributed to the psycho-social treatment. Other research also suggests that social interventions (and why not euthanasia?) in fact may prolong not only the quality, but the quantity of life as well.

In postgraduate courses for nurses or doctors quite often the question pops up whether it is appropriate for a doctor or nurse to take the initiative in bringing up the subject of euthanasia. This is a tricky dilemma of course. It could be misunderstood as a sign of impatience on the part of the doctor. Still I want to answer that question in the affirmative.

In terminal care time runs faster and the future is nearer than one might hope. To have plenty of time to discuss the subject leisurely, without being pressed by the progress of disease, creates circumstances for careful preparation and, as I have mentioned, contributes to the quality of life.

Does euthanasia affect the life of healthy people, like you and me, the patients of the future? Does it affect those who have witnessed the process, in the first place the volunteers of the Dutch Members Aid Service, but also relatives, doctors and nurses? Speaking for myself it has indeed. The subjects of death and illness and ageing have lost much of their terror. The fountain of youth does not exist and I don't mind anymore. We rather avoid thinking of ourselves as mortals. That seems to be one reason for the shortage of organ-donors for transplantation. It could also explain the small membership of euthanasia societies in contrast to the majorities in favor in opinion polls. It has taught me to approach patients with a warm heart and a clear head. After those moments of closeness and sharing one realizes how much time is lost in polite conversations and good manners. On the other hand it is most important not to be carried away by emotions, but to remain firmly in charge of oneself and the situation. Our efforts in this field are properly rewarded with personal growth and maturing.

So much for individuals, now about society: Let me quote Joseph Fletcher in a milestone article on 'The courts and euthanasia': "Poll after poll of public opinion shows a clear and growing majority in favor of the right to choose to die, and to have medical help in doing so. The taboo is simply dying away, as most taboos do sooner or later. The hurdle in the way is a psychological or visceral one, not logical or ethical, as we break through the conventional wisdom." The polls result indeed in astonishing numbers: Sometimes over 80% of the population and 50% of the doctors [are] in favor. The last bulletin of the Belgian Euthanasia Society written by professor Kenis presents a clear review. But taboos are still with us. Even in Holland, which to many of you must appear to be Utopia. The foremost one is still the fear of death and dying. And indeed our real adversaries are not the pope or the archbishop of Canterbury but the makers of television commercials, brainwashing us with the notion that only youth makes life worthwhile.

Euthanasia forces society to reconsider the limits of tolerance: Will those opposed allow the other side to practice euthanasia? Will those in favor respect the freedom of conscientious objectors to not be involved? In respect of the latter, the qualification "voluntary" goes not only for the patient's request but for the cooperation of doctors and nurses as well. The usual arguments in the debate clearly demonstrate that tolerance is still a sapling in need of a lot of care and nursing.

There is the rather easy mud [s]linging and character defamation: people in favor of euthanasia must be cruel, lazy, atheist doctors. Or greedy, careless relatives. Let anybody prove such an allegation! As an experienced colleague of mine remarked: "If you want the best care and the most attention from your doctor, just ask for euthanasia."

The second class of objections is of [a] religious or philosophical nature: "We are the stewards of life, not the owners." "Thou shalt not kill," or in the new English translation "You must not commit murder." The Bible seems to offer great support to any opinion whether it be in favor or against. These considerations must carry much weight for believers and may in fact wholly determine their conduct. But they do not regard those of differing convictions. Legislation or the attitude of society in general are political subjects! Most of our societies are permissive enough to let citizens [be] free to indulge in drinking, to have twenty children, to take part in motor-races. All rather unhealthy activities, but tolerated. Euthanasia is more unobtrusive than any of those.

What does affect us are the slippery slope type arguments: the idea that use will be followed by abuse. The fear that safeguards will shrink to a shoddy routine. It is a very human reaction to resist any change and to feel secure in the trusted routines. All parents observe that in their children. I do take this argument as an incentive to keep my eyes open. Those involved in euthanasia themselves should be the guardians of this slippery slope and watch closely for strict observance of all safeguards. And it works in [my] country. In the hundreds of cases that have been examined by judicial authorities no trend of laxity has been detected. On the contrary. I do not advocate to transplant the Dutch system of guidelines to every country in the world. We are fortunate to have a health care system that is available for every citizen. So euthanasia does not have to be a substitute for lack of medical care. And secondly our medical establishment is not commercially inclined. I can easily imagine the necessity of stricter safeguards and checks in many other communities.

I'm consulted two to four times a week on euthanasia. These consultations of today differ markedly from those five years ago. There is much improvement in the knowledge of principles and procedures involved. Panic situations have become exceptional. Effective medical interventions are rarely overlooked. And to my great satisfaction, growing skills in terminal and palliative care are evident.

Still a lot of work is to be done, even in Holland. Quite separate from the matter of legislation, euthanasia is still not fully integrated in our culture. It does not have a firm place in the curriculum of all medical and nursing schools. It is not discussed in high schools as is contraception or voting rights. It deserves such a place because euthanasia, by its sheer existence as an option stimulates terminal care, makes patients aware of their rights. And generally speaking it has a very healthy influence on the attitude of doctors.

NO

Herbert Hendin and Gerald Klerman

PHYSICIAN-ASSISTED SUICIDE: THE DANGERS OF LEGALIZATION

There are situations when helping a terminally ill patient end his or her life seems appropriate. For centuries physicians have helped such patients die. Why should we not protect them and at the same time make it easier for the terminally ill to end their lives by legalizing physician-assisted suicide? The movement to do so represents such a drastic departure from established social policy and medical tradition that it needs to be evaluated in the light of what we now know about suicide and terminal illness.

We know that 95% of those who kill themselves have been shown to have a diagnosable psychiatric illness in the months preceding suicide. The majority suffer from depression, which can be treated. This is particularly true of the elderly, who are more prone than younger victims to take their lives during the type of acute depressive episode that responds most effectively to modern available treatments. Other diagnoses among the suicides include alcoholism, substance abuse, schizophrenia, and panic disorder; treatments are available for all of these illnesses.

Advocates of physician-assisted suicide try to convey the impression that in terminally ill patients the wish to die is totally different from suicidal intent in those without terminal illness. However, like other suicidal individuals, patients who desire an early death during a terminal illness are usually suffering from a treatable mental illness, most commonly a depressive condition. Strikingly, the overwhelming majority of the terminally ill fight for life to the end. Some may voice suicidal thoughts in response to transient depression or severe pain, but these patients usually respond well to treatment for depressive illness and pain medication and are grateful to be alive.

Studies of those who have died by suicide have pointed out the nonrational elements of the wish to die in reaction to serious illness. More individuals, particularly elderly individuals, killed themselves because they feared or *mistakenly* believed they had cancer than killed themselves and actually had cancer. In the same vein, preoccupation with suicide is greater in those await-

From Herbert Hendin and Gerald Klerman, "Physician-Assisted Suicide: The Dangers of Legalization," *American Journal of Psychiatry*, vol. 150, no. 1 (January 1993), pp. 143–145. Copyright © 1993 by The American Psychiatric Association. Reprinted by permission. References omitted.

ing the results of tests for HIV antibodies than in those who know that they are HIV positive.

Given the advances in our medical knowledge and treatment ability, a thorough psychiatric evaluation for the presence of a treatable disorder may literally make the difference between choosing life or choosing death for patients who express the wish to die or to have assisted suicide. This is not an evaluation that can be made by the average physician unless he or she has had extensive experience with depression and suicide.

Even the highly publicized cases that have been put forward by the advocates of legalizing assisted suicide dramatize the dangers and abuses we would face when those who are not qualified to do so evaluate such patients or when we accept at face value a patient's assertion that he or she prefers death. Perhaps the first such case was featured in a front-page story more than a decade ago. It concerned a woman who, after being diagnosed as having breast cancer, brought together her friends and her husband (who was a psychologist), filmed her farewells, and took a lethal overdose. For years the woman had been an advocate of the "right to suicide." Her film became a television documentary, and media stories portrayed her as something of a pioneer. A pioneer for what? Does her story contain a message we wish to send to the thousands of women facing possible breast surgery? The woman was not terminally ill; her cancer was operable. Although her psychologist husband supported her decision and felt it was appropriate, surely he was not the person to evaluate her. Was her choice as rational as everyone claimed?

Suicidal individuals are prone, just as this woman was, to make conditions on life: "I won't live if I lose my breast," "if this person doesn't care for me," "if I don't get this job" or "if I lose my looks, power, prestige, or health." Depression, often precipitated by discovering a cancer, exaggerates the tendency toward rigid thinking, toward seeing problems in black-and-white terms.

More recent cases are equally troubling. In the *New England Journal of Medicine,* a physician published the case of a woman whom he helped to commit suicide. The woman had a past history of both alcoholism and depression and had recently been diagnosed as having acute leukemia. Her chances of surviving painful chemotherapy and radiation were assessed as one in four. She told her doctor that "she talked to a psychologist she had seen in the past" and implied that the psychologist supported her decision to commit suicide. The physician helped her to implement her decision to end her life. He then published an account of what transpired in an attempt to persuade the medical community of the need for legal sanction for his actions.

The fact that this or any patient may find relief in the prospect of death is not necessarily a sign that the decision is appropriate. Many who are depressed and suicidal appear less depressed after deciding to end their lives. It is coping with the uncertainties of life and death that agitate and depress them. One would need a far more extended examination by someone knowledgeable about suicide to evaluate this woman.

Depression, which is often covert and can coexist with physical illness, is, together with anxiety and the wish to die, often the first reaction to the knowledge of serious illness and possible death. This demoralizing triad can usually be treated by a combination of empathy, psychotherapy, and medication. The decision whether or not to live with illness is likely to be different with such treatment.

The publications of groups like the Hemlock Society, who advocate a more general "right to suicide," make clear that physician-assisted suicide for patients who have less than 6 months to live (as in the recently defeated California and State of Washington proposals) is but a first step in their campaign. Only a small percentage of the people they are trying to reach are terminally ill. The terminally ill, in fact, constitute only a small portion (less than 3%) of the total number of suicides. Right-to-suicide groups have been joined in their efforts by well-meaning physicians concerned with the plight of the terminally ill.

Discussions of the right to suicide or the rationality of suicide in particular cases have tended to ignore the potential for abuse were physician-assisted suicide to be legalized. Particularly vulnerable potential victims would be the elderly, those frightened by illness, and the depressed of all ages.

The elderly are often made to feel that their families would prefer that they were gone. Societal sanction for physician-assisted suicide for the terminally ill is likely to encourage family members so inclined to pressure the infirm and the elderly and to collude with uninformed or unscrupulous physicians to provide such deaths. Some advocates of changing social and medical policy toward suicide concede that such abuses are likely to occur but feel that this is a price we should be willing to pay.

Those whose terror of illness persuades them that quick death is the best solution may be willing victims of physicians who advocate assisted suicide. A woman in the early stages of Alzheimer's who was fearful of the progress of the disease was seen briefly by Dr. Jack Kevorkian, a retired pathologist in Michigan with a passionate commitment to promoting assisted suicide and the use of his "suicide machine." After a brief contact he decided she was a suitable candidate. He used the machine to help her kill herself. Is he the person who should be making such a determination? No Michigan law prohibits assisted suicide (19 states do not have such laws), but Dr. Kevorkian was admonished by the court not to engage in the practice again. Disregarding the admonition, he subsequently provided machines to two more women who were seriously but not terminally ill. They used the machines to kill themselves. Dr. Kevorkian's license to practice medicine has since been "summarily suspended," but a Michigan judge ruled that he could not be prosecuted for murder in the absence of a state law prohibiting assisting a suicide.

Societal sanction for physician-assisted suicide is likely to encourage assisted suicide by nonphysicians, rendering those who are depressed, with or without physical illness, vulnerable to exploitation. Such abuse already exists. For example, a young man gave a depressed young woman he knew a lethal quantity of sleeping pills. He sat with her and fed them to her as she ate ice cream. While she was doing so, he persuaded her that, since she was going to die, she should write out a will leaving him her possessions. He went home and told his roommate what he had done; the roommate called the police and the young woman was saved. The young man went unpunished because he did what he did in a state with no law prohibiting assisted suicide. . . .

Surely there is a price to be paid for current policy where physicians, patients, and family members must act secretly or may be unwilling to act even in situations where it seems appropriate. The protection of the honorable physician does not now warrant legalizing physician-assisted suicide in a society where the public is relatively uninformed of present abuses involving assisted suicide and the potential for much greater abuses if legalization occurs. It took us several decades to become knowledgeable about when it may be appropriate to withdraw life support systems. We are not close to that point with physician-assisted suicide.

Nor by itself can evaluation of the patient by psychiatrists knowledgeable about suicide, depression, and terminal illness provide us with a simple solution to a complex social problem. Certainly, the individual physician confronted with someone requesting assisted suicide should seek such consultation. There is still too much we do not know about such patients, too much study yet to be done before we could mandate psychiatric evaluation for such patients and define conditions under which assisted suicide would be legal. We are likely to find that those who seek to die in the last days of terminal illness are a quite different population from those whose first response to the knowledge of serious illness is to turn to suicide.

Not all problems are best resolved by a statute. We do not convict or prosecute every case in which someone assists in a suicide, even in states where it is illegal. Given the potential for abuse, however, to give assisted suicide legal sanction is to give a dangerous license.

In some cultures (the Alorese are perhaps the most famous example), when people became seriously ill, they took to their beds, stopped eating, and waited to die. How we deal with illness, age, and decline says a great deal about who and what we are, both as individuals and as a society. The growing number of people living to old age and the increasing incidence of depression in people of all ages present us with a medical challenge. Our efforts should concentrate on providing treatment, relieving pain for the intractably ill, and, in the case of terminal illness, helping the individual come to terms with death.

If those advocating legalization of assisted suicide prevail, it will be a reflection that as a culture we are turning away from efforts to improve our care of the mentally ill, the infirm, and the elderly. Instead, we would be licensing the right to abuse and exploit the fears of the ill and depressed. We would be accepting the view of those who are depressed and suicidal that death is the preferred solution to the problems of illness, age, and depression.

CHALLENGE QUESTIONS

Are There Valid Psychological Reasons for Physician-Assisted Suicide?

1. What do existential psychologists say about the importance of death for cherishing life? Relate this to Cohen's position.

2. If you were told that you were going to die of a debilitating illness that included considerable suffering during the last few months of your life, would you consider physician-assisted suicide? Why, or why not?

3. What are the statistics regarding suicide in the United States? Why do so many young people commit suicide?

4. If you had a debilitating illness that would involve considerable suffering before you died, would the option of a physician's assistance make you more or less likely to consider suicide?

On the Internet . . .

JungWeb
Dedicated to the work of Carl Jung, this site is a comprehensive resource for Jungian psychology. Links to Jungian psychology, reference materials, graduate programs, dream psychology, multilingual sites, and related Jungian themes are available.
http://www.onlinepsych.com/jungweb/

Knowledge Exchange Network (KEN)
The Center for Mental Health Services (CMHS) National Mental Health Services Knowledge Exchange Network (KEN) provides information about mental health via toll-free telephone services, an electronic bulletin board, and publications. It is a one-stop source for information and resources on prevention, treatment, and rehabilitation services for mental illness, and it also has many links to related sources.
http://www.mentalhealth.org/about/index.htm

Sigmund Freud and the Freud Archives
Internet resources related to Sigmund Freud can be accessed through this site. A collection of libraries, museums, and biographical materials, as well as the Brill Library archives, can be found here.
http://plaza.interport.net/nypsan/freudarc.html

PART 6

Psychological Treatment

Psychotherapists have always been concerned about the safety and effectiveness of their treatments. But not all therapists are in agreement about which treatments are the safest and most effective. Some treatments can be emotionally harmful or simply a waste of time. For example, is the treatment of depression with drug therapy effective? Looking at the bigger picture, should psychologists even be given the power to prescribe drugs?

We usually think of diagnosis as an important prerequisite to treatment. But when we apply it to behavior we run the risk of prejudicing the way we think about that behavior. How great is that risk for competent treatment?

■ Should Psychologists Be Allowed to Prescribe Drugs?

■ Have Antidepressant Drugs Proven to Be Effective?

■ Classic Dialogue: Do Diagnostic Labels Hinder Treatment?

ISSUE 12

Should Psychologists Be Allowed to Prescribe Drugs?

YES: Patrick H. DeLeon and Jack G. Wiggins, Jr., from "Prescription Privileges for Psychologists," *American Psychologist* (March 1996)

NO: Steven C. Hayes and Elaine Heiby, from "Psychology's Drug Problem: Do We Need a Fix or Should We Just Say No?" *American Psychologist* (March 1996)

ISSUE SUMMARY

YES: Psychologist and lawyer Patrick H. DeLeon and Jack G. Wiggins, Jr., former president of the American Psychological Association, argue that giving prescription privileges to psychologists will allow them to address society's pressing needs.

NO: Psychologists Steven C. Hayes and Elaine Heiby maintain that prescription privileges will cost the discipline of psychology its unique professional identity and compromise public safety.

Psychology, like most disciplines, is continually modifying and expanding its caregiving role. A recent and highly controversial expansion of this role entails prescription privileges. That is, many psychologists are now seeking the legal privilege to prescribe drugs. Drugs have been increasingly recognized as contributing to the effective treatment of mental disorders. Because such treatment has traditionally been the province of psychology, many psychologists have advocated that they should be allowed to use all the effective treatments available, including prescription medications.

The most controversial aspect of this proposal, however, is that only psychiatrists (and a few other allied professionals) are currently permitted to prescribe drugs in the mental health field. Thus, if given prescription privileges, the psychologist would be moving into the professional and economic territory of the psychiatrist. Psychiatrists are medical doctors whose primary training is in the anatomy and physiology of the human body. Psychologists, on the other hand, are experts in human relations. Although some psychologists receive considerable education in pharmacology (the study of medications), few currently have the training necessary to competently prescribe drugs. The question then arises, What if an appropriate level of training were obtained? Couldn't psychologists then prescribe drugs to their patients?

Patrick H. DeLeon and Jack G. Wiggins, Jr., in the first selection, answer this question affirmatively. They claim that current technology would allow psychologists to safely prescribe psychoactive drugs without the medical knowledge required of a physician. The authors also describe several psychologists who have been functionally prescribing drugs with little or no training and who have experienced no problems. DeLeon and Wiggins see prescription privileges as a natural outgrowth of psychology's development as a discipline.

By contrast, Steven C. Hayes and Elaine Heiby see prescription privileges as radically changing psychology—ultimately into a field of medicine. This change would undermine the mental health professional's appreciation for psychology as a unique science. The granting of prescription privileges, Hayes and Heiby argue, undervalues the psychological side of people in favor of an exclusively biological emphasis. Rather than a fulfillment of psychology's disciplinary development, Hayes and Heiby see prescription privileges as a compromise of psychology's main objective—to better understand the nature of psychological phenomena.

POINT	COUNTERPOINT
• Current technology would allow psychologists to prescribe drugs with little medical training.	• To prescribe any drug, it is essential to have medical training to understand how the drug affects all of the body's systems.
• Psychologists with prescription privileges could help prevent abuse of psychoactive drugs because they would have a fuller understanding of patients' psychological needs.	• Psychologists would not understand patients' biological changes enough to ensure responsible use of medication.
• The desire to treat patients more effectively with medications is widespread throughout the field.	• Most psychologists believe that the more important treatment is helping patients to understand the psychological aspects of their problems.
• Obtaining access to a particular type of treatment will not cause psychology to forget its roots.	• Prescription privileges will change psychology into a medical field and cause psychological assessment to become undervalued.

YES

Patrick H. DeLeon and
Jack G. Wiggins, Jr.

PRESCRIPTION PRIVILEGES
FOR PSYCHOLOGISTS

From our vantage point, the issue of psychologists obtaining prescription privileges is a rather straight-forward one and one that is an outgrowth of the gradual maturation of the profession. In 1950, there were only 7,273 members of the American Psychological Association (APA); today, there are in excess of 110,000. In 1945, the Connecticut legislature provided psychology with its first state "scope of practice" (licensing–certification) act; by the year 1977, psychology had obtained statutory recognition in all 50 states as a fully autonomous profession (i.e., licensed–certified to independently "diagnose and treat"). Furthermore, we have no doubt that, for psychologists, obtaining the particular clinical responsibility of prescription authority ultimately represents both good public policy and good clinical policy. . . .

TRAINING MODULES

In many ways, one can readily conceptualize the prescription privilege agenda as being primarily an educational one; that is, to what extent have our nation's health-professional training programs developed credible (and objectively measurable) training modules that ensure that their practitioners possess both a conceptual basis for making medication decisions (i.e., didactic training) and sufficient clinical experience to evaluate the consequences of those decisions (i.e., "hands-on" supervision)? . . .

In our judgment, the decision of whether or not to use specific psychotropic medications and at what dosage—once the correct diagnosis has been made by a licensed–certified mental health professional—represents little more than a probability algorithm, where various observable behavioral factors are computed such as symptomatology, patient age and body size, and drug-dosage response. These relatively few algorithms could easily be learned by psychologists. Furthermore, in today's practices, one should expect to use up-to-date desktop computer technology in making this determination. An analogy would be that one only needs to know how to use the most up-to-date com-

From Patrick H. DeLeon and Jack G. Wiggins, Jr., "Prescription Privileges for Psychologists," *American Psychologist*, vol. 51, no. 3 (1996). Copyright © 1996 by The American Psychological Association. Reprinted by permission. References omitted.

puter software, not how to design one's own software or computer. This latter skill should be learned perhaps by true psychopharmacological specialists, but it absolutely should not be viewed as a requirement for doctoral-level psychologists to competently and safely serve their clients, notwithstanding organized psychiatry's alleged concerns.

DEMONSTRATION PROJECTS

Historically, state governments have a long and impressive track record of exploring alternative health care delivery systems, including the development of innovative health professional training programs. For example, in 1965 the state of Colorado pioneered the establishment of pediatric nurse practitioners—a specialty that today, by federal mandate, must be reimbursed under every state's Medicaid plan, "whether or not (the practitioner) is under the supervision of, or associated with, a physician or other health care provider."

In 1982, the state of California released its landmark prescription report titled "Prescribing and Dispensing Pilot Projects." ... Under the California program, over one million patients were seen by nonphysician prescribing and dispensing trainees during a three-year period. The results clearly indicated that both the patients and supervising physicians were comfortable with the clinical performance of the trainees. Most important, there were no reported "quality of care" problems. Given the substantial potential cost savings involved, the state authorities ultimately recommended that clear statutory authority be enacted so that these nonphysicians would be able to prescribe and dispense drugs. Of particular interest to psychologists should be

that 56% of these graduates possessed a bachelors degree or higher; that is, 44% did not! Furthermore, the principal teaching methods used were lectures and seminars, which varied from 16 hours to 95 hours in length—hardly comparable to a medical school curriculum.

The authors have admittedly become the focal point of much of the prescription debate in psychology, and, as a direct consequence, we have learned (among other things) that a very significant number of our professional colleagues have been "functionally prescribing" for years, often without any documented training, having learned, for example, of the psychoactive effects of medications their patients have received for cardiac, diabetic, thyroid, or other health conditions. And we have come to appreciate that, not surprisingly, they have not had any "quality of care" problems. This is particularly true in rural America and in the federal system (e.g., in the Veterans Administration and the military [Barclay, 1989]). There are many forms that this functional prescriptive practice takes, ranging from possessing pre-signed scrips (which would be legal in state and federal systems), to having developed close and long-standing relationships with physician colleagues where medication consultations are readily available. We have learned that a number of our colleagues are on the faculty of nursing, dental, and medical schools where they train the students in these professions to prescribe, particularly in narrowly defined specialties such as pediatrics....

Although some have suggested that only a vocal minority of psychologists are seriously interested in the prescription agenda, it has been our experience that the interest in obtaining relevant and targeted psychopharmacological training expressed by our child-oriented colleagues is becoming increasingly widespread throughout the field, thus enhancing the probability that in the foreseeable future, our (or perhaps nursing's) professional schools will make this experience readily available. Questions on prescription authority are becoming increasingly common in university doctoral comprehensive examinations and dissertation committees. At least two doctoral research projects (Evans, 1995; Smith, 1992) recently explored either attitudes of graduate students toward prescribing or the interest of directors of clinical programs in offering training in psychopharmacology. A survey of 40 APA-approved graduate schools across the nation found that second- and third-year students responded with strong support for these privileges, with 61% endorsing privileges for the field and 47% reporting they desired privileges for themselves (Smith, 1992). There were no significant differences in responses on the basis of program type, theoretical orientation, gender, age, undergraduate major, or the student's choice of future client population. It was felt that the two strongest supportive arguments for obtaining this privilege were (a) the ability to provide services to underserved groups and (b) the collection of third party reimbursement. The two strongest arguments opposing obtaining this authority were (a) damage to credibility and distinctiveness of psychology and (b) the possible impediment of collaboration with psychiatrists (Smith, 1992).

Another 1990 survey of the general APA membership similarly reported that, "There is very strong support for prescription privileges for psychologists (and that) the proposition that psychologists could do a better job of prescribing than the general practitioners who now prescribe most psychoactive drugs in the most effective argument in support of prescription privileges... There is overwhelming support for a demonstration project on prescription privileges (Frederick/Schneiders, 1990). Even among opponents of the general proposal, a majority support the demonstration project" (pp. 3–4).

Currently, we are aware of at least 25 state or country psychological associations that have formally established task forces on the issue and a number of educational institutions that are exploring how to best provide the type of didactic and hands-on training experiences that the field desires. Interestingly, within the educational leadership of professional nursing, a concerted effort is currently underway to identify commonalities and differences in their prescription training programs, not to mention developing appropriate programs targeted toward addressing the needs of their experienced clinicians (e.g., the establishment of special executive tracks or intensive summer workshops). With these developments in mind, the ongoing Department of Defense two- to three-year full-time training program clearly seems excessive.

QUALITY OF CARE ISSUES

It is of considerable interest to us that the prime argument those who are external to psychology consistently use to oppose our profession's obtaining prescription authority is the public health hazard allegation. Yet, none of the available objective evidence supports their emotional rhetoric. The nursing literature, for example, demonstrates that the medication decisions of nurse practitioners are very similar to those of their medical colleagues, and some researchers have found that they actually use medication less frequently than their physician counterparts. At the public policy level, we find it simply fascinating, to put it mildly, that no one seems to find it objectionable that in the mental health arena, of the 135.8 million psychotherapeutic scripts written in 1991, only 17.3% were by psychiatrists per se. That year, both internists and family practitioners prescribed more mental health medications than their mental health specialist colleagues. Stated slightly differently, of the psychotherapeutic medications prescribed that year by physicians, more than 82% were by practitioners who simply did not possess significant training in the mental health field. Given these data, for psychiatry to proclaim that doctoral-trained licensed psychologists cannot learn to safely use this particular clinical modality seems an incredible, if not downright arrogant, indictment of our educational system.

If one looks closely at the manner in which psychotropic medications are currently used, there are a number of troubling statistics. Study after study used indicated that even today certain populations are dramatically over medicated or inappropriately medicated—this is particularly true with minority, aging, and female clients—and there is even growing evidence that psychotherapy per se (and not medication) is crucial to resolving depression. More than 40% of nursing home patients receive psychotropic medications, despite the fact that most of them do not have mental health diagnoses. Why, we would rhetorically ask, did the Health Care Financing Administration (HCFA) recently feel it was necessary to promulgate federal regulations addressing the conditions under which certain medications could be used in nursing homes? Were not all issued medications being ordered by licensed physicians? Of course they were. In our judgment, one of the major clinical advances that will come with psychology obtaining prescription privileges will be the authority of behavioral scientists to determine with proper legal standing when and whether certain medications are necessary and appropriate; that is, the essence of the power to prescribe is the power not to prescribe. And this, we suggest, will ultimately revolutionize the delivery of mental health care in our nation.

CONCLUSION

In our judgment, there is no question that doctoral-trained psychologists can readily be trained to use psychotropic medications in a safe, cost-effective, and competent manner. This is psychology's next frontier, and we are confident that society will be well served by this evolution. We are not at all concerned that, by obtaining this particular clinical modality, psychology will lose its therapeutic expertise or forget its roots—our becoming intimately involved in the judicial system increased society's access to psychological care and did not negatively harm the field. In all candor, we have very little respect for the validity of the public health hazard allegations that have been made by those external to psychology and would merely suggest that those opposed should carefully review the available literature.

NO   Steven C. Hayes and Elaine Heiby

PSYCHOLOGY'S DRUG PROBLEM

Prescription privileges for psychologists have only been considered seriously by most psychologists for the past few years. Just eight years have passed since American Psychological Association (APA) governance recommended "moving to the highest APA priority" the creation of "psychologically managed psychopharmacological intervention" (DeLeon et al., 1991, p. 391). Much has happened in those eight years. Slowly at first, but then with increased speed, continuing education curricula have been written, pilot projects have been launched, and legislatures have been lobbied. The prescription train gives many indications it is about to leave the station, whether or not all—or even most—of psychology is on board....

PRESCRIPTION PRIVILEGE ALTERNATIVE

Driven by ... professional pressures, intellectual changes, and market forces, the leadership of the practice community has for several years been working systematically to prepare the way for psychologists' use of chemical interventions. Prescription privileges, they purport, solve many of the problems facing the professional practice of psychology today. It solves the over-reliance on psychotherapy. Practitioners will be paid as much or more for medication visits, and only psychiatrists, other physicians, and psychologists will be eligible. It solves the problem of oversupply. For a time, master's-level providers will be held at bay. It solves the problem of managed care, or at least gives psychologists some way of differentiating their services from other mental health professionals in such a way that managed care organizations might be more interested in hiring doctoral-level psychologists....

What This Issue Is Not About
It is sometimes difficult to remain focused on the real issues in this debate. Like combatants in a political campaign, both sides speak around each other for tactical reasons. We want to put aside two issues so as to avoid fruitless interactions.

Excerpted from Steven C. Hayes and Elaine Heiby, "Psychology's Drug Problem: Do We Need a Fix or Should We Just Say No?" *American Psychologist*, vol. 51, no. 3 (1996), pp. 198, 201–203, 205. Copyright © 1996 by The American Psychological Association. Reprinted by permission. Notes and references omitted. This article has been reduced from its original appearance in *American Psychologist*.

False issue 1: Psychologists cannot be trained to prescribe

Psychologists are generally quite bright people. With the right kind of curriculum they can surely be trained to prescribe. It also seems unlikely that it would take seven or eight years to do so, which is the time it takes to complete medical school and a psychiatric residency.

This does not mean that training psychologists to prescribe psychotropic medication will be easy. Many psychologists do not have the right kind of science background to make physiologically-oriented training readily accessible....

False issue 2: Medications do not work and biology is not involved in behavior

Pro-prescription psychologists often e-quate opposition to prescription authority for psychologists with opposition to psychoactive medication per se or a failure to acknowledge that clients are also biological organisms (Brentar & McNamara, 1991; Fox, 1988). Some proponents accuse those who resist prescription authority of ascribing to a discredited mind–body dualism (Brentar & McNamara, 1991; Fox, 1988).

When the debate consists of exchanges about false issues, little productive discussion is likely. Some psychologists are indeed opposed to psychoactive medication, but most are not. Despite the substantial methodological difficulties in the pharmacotherapy literature (e.g., Fisher & Greenberg, 1993) most scientifically-oriented psychologists agree that at least under some circumstances, pharmacotherapy is helpful in the treatment of traditional psychological disorders. Thus, when the utility of medication is cast as a simple or absolute issue, pro-prescription advocates are on fairly firm ground. For example, Patrick DeLeon, a

leading advocate of prescription authority for psychologists, recently responded to our own opposition against prescription authority as follows: "Dr. Hayes is talking about something he really does not understand... The data is clear that some individuals will benefit from appropriate medications" (Saeman, 1995, p. 10). Although DeLeon apparently meant it as a point of departure, we actually agree with the second sentence. But this issue is not about whether medications ever work. It is about whether psychologists should be the ones prescribing them....

NEGATIVE IMPACT OF DRUG PRESCRIPTION AUTHORITY: DO WE REALLY WANT TO REDEFINE PSYCHOLOGY?

There are three dominant areas in which prescription authority seems likely to lead to major negative impacts for psychology. Although these arguments are rapidly becoming well-worn, they deserve repeating. First, this authority seems likely to undermine an appreciation for the psychological level of analysis. Second, it could have a negative impact on clients. Third, if this negative impact on clients is avoided, prescriptive authority seems likely to have a major and negative impact on psychological training.

Level of Analysis: Psychology Is a Science in Its Own Right

... Some advocates have argued that prescription privileges would render no change in the definition of the discipline [of psychology] and would simply add biological assessment and treatment devices [of] the profession (Burns, DeLeon, Chemtob, Welch, & Samuels, 1988). This *additive effect* is not the only possible outcome, however (e.g., Butz, 1994). It assumes that the effects of prescription authority on the behavior of psychologists are linear and that the training involved to prescribe would be supplemental. It seems equally if not more likely that the medication of psychology would have a nonlinear dynamical effect—an irreversible qualitative shift in the discipline (Butz, 1994).

Psychologists who have also trained as psychiatrists generally take the latter view. For example, Kingsbury's (1992) experiences as a psychologist and a psychiatrist have convinced him that "the definition of psychology would have to be transformed if prescription privileges were granted" (p. 5). The limited experience with supplemental training for psychologists... tends toward the same conclusion. Indeed, some advocates of prescription privileges seem to agree with the dynamic view that psychology would be redefined (DeLeon, Fox, & Graham, 1991; Lorion, 1996). To prescription opponents, this redefinition "represents the ultimate denial or betrayal of our own, scientifically grounded knowledge-base and professional competency in favor of an alien, biomedical model, for no logical or conceptually defensible purpose" (McColskey, 1993, p. 57)....

Implications of science-based practice for this issue. Most APA-approved applied training programs in psychology claim that their training is based on the scientific discipline of psychology. If that is a central value, the issue of prescription privileges can be recast as follows: If the knowledge needed to prescribe drugs safely is part of psychology's technical, scientific knowledge base—if it is indeed part of the discipline of psychology—then drug prescriptions should be part of the practice of psychology. In order to make this argument, pro-prescription advocates need to be clear about what their view is of psychology as a discipline.

Pro-prescription advocates have generally argued vaguely that because medications can influence behavior, prescribing medications should be part of the discipline of psychology (e.g., Burns et al., 1988). This view (behavior = psychology) fails to draw reasonable distinctions among different parts of the discipline. By the same logic, brain surgery and electroconvulsive therapy are also part of psychology. Similarly, nonpsychiatric medicine, sociology, biochemistry, anthropology, political science, economics, law, and many other disciplines are part of psychology. Psychology overlaps with all of these fields and more, and some psychologists will fruitfully conduct research within each area of overlap. But that does not mean that psychology is the same as these other fields. The establishment of professional "boundaries is in no way an endorsement of an artificial mind-body dualism. The time has long passed when there was only one variety of health care provider who did everything for everybody" (DeNelsky, 1991, p. 191).

Drug–behavior relations are not enough. There are clear reasons to distinguish between the disciplines of medicine and psychology. Responsibly prescribing the consumption of powerful chemicals requires the study of organ systems and their mutual interdependence, not just the study of the behavioral impact of these chemicals. For example, prescribing psychologists should know such things as how drugs affect the kidneys, now aging alters the functioning of the digestive system so that drugs are absorbed differently over time, how a diseased liver can make a specific drug combination more risky, or how exercise changes the excretion of particular drugs compared to others. These are inherently biological/medical topics because they deal with the physical relationship among organ systems per se. This kind of knowledge has never been the focus of psychology as a discipline. . . .

To fail to make meaningful distinctions between disciplines—even when they overlap and interact—runs the risk of treating psychology as a branch of medicine and not as a science in its own right. If the role of prescribing psychologists is indeed the same as psychiatrists . . . it is not because psychiatry has become more like psychology. . . .

Risks to patients and prescribers. Older adults often face many chronic ailments—each of which may be treated by a different provider, often through the use of drugs. They may have decreased abilities to tolerate chemical interventions. They may be unable to report to each provider how many medications are being taken and of what kind. Psychoactive medications are among the most harmful to this population. Some geropsychologists have estimated that the majority of behavioral disorders in older people are due to medical overprescribing or to drug interactions (Hayden & Safford, 1992). The third largest category of drugs used by older persons are the psychopharmacological agents such as antidepressants and antipsychotics (Wolfe, Fugate, Hulstrand, & Kamimoto, 1988). Adverse effects being very common, one recent review concluded that the excessive use of psychoactive medication with older people amounts to "a major public health problem" (Hayden & Saf-

ford, 1992, p. 42). Pro-prescription advocates argue that these problems support prescription privileges for psychologists (DeLeon, 1993; DeLeon, Fox, & Graham, 1991) because they believe that somehow psychologists would do a better job. Psychologists may better understand some of the developmental psychological processes involved with older adults, but it seems incredible that they would better understand development physiology —and ignoring that very knowledge base is at the core of prescription problems for older persons. . . .

The same thing occurs at the other end of the age spectrum. Despite the fact that "there is a relative lack of empirical support for pediatric psychotropic safety and efficacy" (Kubiszyn, 1994), psychoactive medications are very widely prescribed to children. Highly variable responses due to children's developing physiological system can occur (American Medical Association, 1991).

Those who prescribe psychoactive medication are responsible for the general health status of the individual, as well as for adverse organic and behavioral side effects. The toxic nature of commonly prescribed psychoactive medications has been well established (Bezchlibnyk-Butler, 1990).

Historically, psychologists have studied how individual organisms interact over time with their social and nonsocial world. The structure of the organism is part of that interaction; as is the structure of the environment; as is the history of previous psychological interactions. Psychologists study these things to help elucidate the nature of the psychological interaction between an organism and its world. Psychologists, for example, study how the brain is part of a psychological interaction or how culture alters such interactions. But psychologists are not thereby biologists nor physicians, and they are neither anthropologists nor sociologists....

Does the public need more prescribers? Psychology is a science in its own right, with a science-based practice that has a unique identity and that serves legitimate societal needs. There is no convincing evidence that mental health consumers are clamoring for medications to solve life's problems or that said consumers are dissatisfied with psychological knowledge. A survey recently prepared for the American Psychological Association's Practice Directorate (American Psychological Association, 1992) reported that 63% of psychologists who responded indicated that "helping a person understand" was the most important treatment for alleviating a mental health problem, whereas 15% indicated medication was most important. Generally, consumer surveys have indicated that psychological services are preferred over psychiatric services (Sanua, 1993).

Why then do pro-prescription psychologists so often emphasize the need for medications? Could it be that the loss of a clear focus on the psychological level of analysis is already occurring....

CONCLUSION

If a psychologist wants to prescribe medications, there are means to do so now in the form of MD/PhD, or physician's assistant programs. If psychiatry or pharmacotherapy require new models (e.g., more limited or more focused forms of medical training), these could be pursued more generally rather than by linking such changes to any specific nonmedical field. Prescription authority may permit psychologists to compete financially, but only by grafting some other profession onto the discipline.

A better and more honorable alternative is to build on psychology's traditional core through scientifically based standards of care, program development, and treatment manualization linked to these standards, training, supervision, and program evaluation (Hayes, Follette, Dawes, & Grady, 1995). Managed care companies need these services, and psychological scientist–practitioners are best positioned to deliver them. Direct delivery of services by doctoral psychologists paid by third parties may ultimately be focused on more complex cases not touched by manualized and validated therapy, and on areas in which doctoral providers have been shown to be more effective.

The title of this article asks if psychology needs a fix. The word *fix* means both to repair something that is broken and to hold something in place. Pro-prescription psychologists, who find it difficult to hold the independent practice of psychology in place, essentially argue that the practice of psychology is broken. It has a missing psychopharmacological piece. To the contrary, we argue that the independent practice of psychology needs to change rather than be held in place, and it needs to change in a way that fits with the best historical and scientific traditions of the discipline.

CHALLENGE QUESTIONS

Should Psychologists Be Allowed to Prescribe Drugs?

1. If psychologists were to obtain the privilege to prescribe medications, how would they be different from psychiatrists? How might your answer affect psychology's future?

2. Underlying this issue is what some theorists call reductionism. Reductionism is the notion that all psychological entities (e.g., mind, feelings, unconscious) can ultimately be reduced to biological entities. How might this theoretical notion be affecting the current controversy? How might one's stance on reductionism affect one's stance on this issue?

3. How does a profession like psychology balance the sometimes competing interests of its "marketability" with the good of the public?

4. Hayes and Heiby assert that most psychologists see their job as helping clients to understand their problems. How would psychologists who prescribe medications help their clients to understand their problems? Would you want a psychologist to prescribe medication for you if you were struggling with life issues? Support your answer.

5. DeLeon and Wiggins disagree with Hayes and Heiby about the medical knowledge required for psychologists to prescribe drugs safely. How much medical training would you require a mental health professional to have before you would feel comfortable accepting a prescription? Support your answer.

ISSUE 13

Have Antidepressant Drugs Proven to Be Effective?

YES: Peter D. Kramer, from *Listening to Prozac: A Psychiatrist Explores Antidepressant Drugs and the Remaking of the Self* (Viking Penguin, 1993)

NO: Seymour Fisher and Roger P. Greenberg, from "Prescriptions for Happiness?" *Psychology Today* (September/October 1995)

ISSUE SUMMARY

YES: Psychiatrist Peter D. Kramer argues that antidepressant drugs such as Prozac can transform depressed patients into happy people with almost no side effects.

NO: Professors of psychology Seymour Fisher and Roger P. Greenberg claim that the studies that demonstrate the effectiveness of antidepressants are seriously flawed.

Antidepressants are drugs that are "anti-" or "against" depression. The use of antidepressants has recently risen dramatically. However, the relatively high number of people who report serious depression (10 percent of the population) does not account for this increase. The increasing use of antidepressants is due to the fact that more and more physicians and psychiatrists are prescribing them for psychological problems other than clinical depression. Antidepressants are now prescribed for people with "the blues," stress, obsessions, compulsions, and a host of other personal and social difficulties.

A major reason for this widespread use is that antidepressant drugs, especially Prozac, seem to work well with few side effects. Popular news magazines, such as *Newsweek* and *Time*, have heralded the supposed "miracle" power of these drugs: Not only do such drugs help cure what psychologically ails you (e.g., depression), but they are also able to "transform" your personality to a new and better you! In the past, the promise of such benefits was always balanced by the potential side effects of the drugs. People who take traditional antidepressants can experience a variety of symptoms, including dry mouth, a lack of energy, and weight gain. However, with the new types of antidepressants, such as Prozac, there appear to be very few side effects. Why not take antidepressants if they will make us better, happier people without the worry of side effects?

This is the sentiment of Peter D. Kramer, who wrote his best-selling book *Listening to Prozac* after successfully prescribing antidepressant medications to his patients. In the following selection, Kramer tells of one of his patient's experiences with Prozac: the drug not only ameliorated her depressive symptoms, but it also "reshaped [her] identity." Kramer wrestles with the implications of this success. Should such medications be prescribed more widely and more often? Is it acceptable for certain people to be on Prozac for life? These issues need to be addressed, according to Kramer, by "listening" to what drugs like Prozac have to teach us.

Seymour Fisher and Roger P. Greenberg contend that none of the issues that Kramer struggles with are relevant if antidepressants such as Prozac are not effective to begin with. After carefully reviewing the research, Fisher and Greenberg found that fully two-thirds of all the cases did as well with placebos (inert or nonactive pills) as they did with antidepressants. The authors also maintain that studies that do show some benefits of antidepressant medications have "crucial problems" in the methods used to evaluate such drugs.

POINT	COUNTERPOINT
• Antidepressant medications are amazingly effective.	• The effectiveness of antidepressant medications is mixed at best.
• The newer antidepressants, such as Prozac, are more effective than the older antidepressants.	• Many drug researchers and manufacturers are biased in favor of new drug development.
• Some patients who take antidepressant drugs report improvement not only in their depression but in their personalities as well.	• Such testimonials are not as reliable a measure of a drug's effectiveness as controlled studies.
• Research and experience have overwhelmingly indicated the effectiveness and safety of antidepressants.	• Much research is tainted by procedural and researcher biases.
• Many patients do not feel as well when they are off the medication as when they are on it.	• Research has shown that this may actually be a placebo effect.

YES

Peter D. Kramer

MAKEOVER

My first experience with Prozac involved a woman I worked with only around issues of medication....

Tess was the eldest of ten children born to a passive mother and an alcoholic father in the poorest public-housing project in our city. She was abused in childhood in the concrete physical and sexual senses which everyone understands as abuse. When Tess was twelve, her father died, and her mother entered a clinical depression from which she had never recovered. Tess—one of those inexplicably resilient children who flourish without any apparent source of sustenance—took over the family. She managed to remain in school herself and in time to steer all nine siblings into stable jobs and marriages....

Meanwhile, Tess had made a business career out of her skills at driving, inspiring, and nurturing others....

That her personal life was unhappy should not have been surprising. Tess stumbled from one prolonged affair with an abusive married man to another. As these degrading relationships ended, she would suffer severe demoralization. The current episode had lasted months, and, despite a psychotherapy in which Tess willingly faced the difficult aspects of her life, she was now becoming progressively less energetic and more unhappy. It was this condition I hoped to treat, in order to spare Tess the chronic and unremitting depression that had taken hold in her mother when she was Tess's age....

* * *

What I found unusual on meeting Tess was that the scars were so well hidden. Patients who have struggled, even successfully, through neglect and abuse can have an angry edge or a tone of aggressive sweetness. They may be seductive or provocative, rigid or overly compliant. A veneer of independence may belie a swamp of neediness. Not so with Tess.

She was a pleasure to be with, even depressed. I ran down the list of signs and symptoms, and she had them all: tears and sadness, absence of hope, inability to experience pleasure, feelings of worthlessness, loss of sleep and appetite, guilty ruminations, poor memory and concentration. Were it not for her many obligations, she would have preferred to end her life. And yet I felt comfortable in her presence....

Tess had ... done poorly in her personal life. She considered herself unattractive to men and perhaps not even as interesting to women as she would have liked. For the past four years, her principal social contact had been with a married man —Jim—who came and went as he pleased and finally rejected Tess in favor of his wife. Tess had stuck with Jim in part, she told me, because no other men approached her. She believed she lacked whatever spark excited men; worse, she gave off signals that kept men at a distance.

Had I been working with Tess in psychotherapy, we might have begun to explore hypotheses regarding the source of her social failure: masochism grounded in low self-worth, the compulsion of those abused early in life to seek out further abuse.... For the moment, my function was to treat my patient's depression with medication.

* * *

I began with imipramine, the oldest of the available antidepressants and still the standard by which others are judged. Imipramine takes about a month to work, and at the end of a month Tess said she was substantially more comfortable. She was sleeping and eating normally—in fact, she was gaining weight, probably as a side effect of the drug. "I am better," she told me. "I am myself again."

She did look less weary. And as we continued to meet, generally for fifteen minutes every month or two, all her overt symptoms remitted. Her memory and concentration improved. She regained the vital force and the willpower to go on with life. In short, Tess no longer

met a doctor's criteria for depression. She even spread the good word to one of her brothers, also depressed, and the brother began taking imipramine.

But I was not satisfied.

* * *

It was the mother's illness that drove me forward. Tess had struggled too long for me to allow her, through any laxness of my own, to slide into the chronic depression that had engulfed her mother.

Depression is a relapsing and recurring illness. The key to treatment is thoroughness. If a patient can put together a substantial period of doing perfectly well— five months, some experts say; six or even twelve, say others—the odds are good for sustained remission. But to limp along just somewhat improved, "better but not well," is dangerous. The partly recovered patient will likely relapse as soon as you stop the therapy, as soon as you taper the drug. And the longer someone remains depressed, the more likely it is that depression will continue or return.

Tess said she was well, and she was free of the signs and symptoms of depression. But doctors are trained to doubt the report of the too-stoical patient, the patient so willing to bear pain she may unwittingly conceal illness. And, beyond signs and symptoms, the recognized abnormalities associated with a given syndrome, doctors occasionally consider what the neurologists call "soft signs," normal findings that, in the right context, make the clinical nose twitch.

I thought Tess might have a soft sign or two of depression.

She had begun to experience trouble at work—not major trouble, but something to pay attention to. The conglomerate she worked for had asked Tess to take over a company beset with labor problems. Tess always had some difficulty in situations that required meeting firmness with firmness, but she reported being more upset by negotiations with this union than by any in the past. She felt the union leaders were unreasonable, and she had begun to take their attacks on her personally. She understood conflict was inevitable; past mistakes had left labor-management relations too strained for either side to trust the other, and the coaxing and cajoling that characterized Tess's management style would need some time to work their magic. But, despite her understanding, Tess was rattled.

As a psychotherapist, I might have wondered whether Tess's difficulties had a symbolic meaning. Perhaps the hectoring union chief and his foot-dragging members resembled parents—the aggressive father, the passive mother—too much for Tess to be effective with them. In simpler terms, a new job, and this sort especially, constitutes a stressor. These viewpoints may be correct. But what level of stress was it appropriate for Tess to experience? To be rattled even by tough negotiations was unlike her.

And I found Tess vulnerable on another front. Toward the end of one of our fifteen-minute reviews of Tess's sleep, appetite, and energy level, I asked about Jim, and she burst into uncontrollable sobs. Thereafter, our meetings took on a predictable form. Tess would report that she was substantially better. Then I would ask her about Jim, and her eyes would brim over with tears, her shoulders shake. People do cry about failed romances, but sobbing seemed out of character for Tess.

These are weak reeds on which to support a therapy. Here was a highly competent, fully functional woman who no longer considered herself depressed and who had none of the standard overt indicators of depression. Had I found her less remarkable, considered her less capable as a businesswoman, been less surprised by her fragility in the face of romantic disappointment, I might have declared Tess cured. My conclusion that we should try for a better medication response may seem to be based on highly subjective data—and I think this perception is correct. Pharmacotherapy, when looked at closely, will appear to be as arbitrary—as much an art, not least in the derogatory sense of being impressionistic where ideally it should be objective—as psychotherapy. Like any other serious assessment of human emotional life, pharmacotherapy properly rests on fallible attempts at intimate understanding of another person.

* * *

When I laid out my reasoning, Tess agreed to press ahead. I tried raising the dose of imipramine; but Tess began to experience side effects—dry mouth, daytime tiredness, further weight gain—so we switched to similar medications in hopes of finding one that would allow her to tolerate a higher dose. Tess changed little.

And then Prozac was released by the Food and Drug Administration. I prescribed it for Tess, for entirely conventional reasons—to terminate her depression more thoroughly, to return her to her "premorbid self." My goal was not to transform Tess but to restore her.

* * *

But medications do not always behave as we expect them to.

Two weeks after starting Prozac, Tess appeared at the office to say she was no longer feeling weary. In retrospect, she said, she had been depleted of energy for as long as she could remember, had almost not known what it was to feel rested and hopeful. She had been depressed, it now seemed to her, her whole life. She was astonished at the sensation of being free of depression.

She looked different, at once more relaxed and energetic—more available—than I had seen her, as if the person hinted at in her eyes had taken over. She laughed more frequently, and the quality of her laughter was different, no longer measured but lively, even teasing.

With this new demeanor came a new social life, one that did not unfold slowly, as a result of a struggle to integrate disparate parts of the self, but seemed, rather, to appear instantly and full-blown.

"Three dates a weekend," Tess told me. "I must be wearing a sign on my forehead!"

Within weeks of starting Prozac, Tess settled into a satisfying dating routine with men. She had missed out on dating in her teens and twenties. Now she reveled in the attention she received. She seemed even to enjoy the trial-and-error process of learning contemporary courtship rituals, gauging norms for sexual involvement, weighing the import of men's professed infatuation with her.

I had never seen a patient's social life reshaped so rapidly and dramatically. Low self-worth, competitiveness, jealousy, poor interpersonal skills, shyness, fear of intimacy—the usual causes of social awkwardness—are so deeply ingrained and so difficult to influence that ordinarily change comes gradually if at all. But Tess blossomed all at once.

"People on the sidewalk ask me for directions!" she said. They never had before.

The circle of Tess's women friends changed. Some friends left, she said, because they had been able to relate to her only through her depression. Besides, she now had less tolerance for them. "Have you ever been to a party where other people are drunk or high and you are stone-sober? Their behavior annoys you, you can't understand it. It seems juvenile and self-centered. That's how I feel around some of my old friends. It is as if they are under the influence of a harmful chemical and I am all right—as if I had been in a drugged state all those years and now I am clearheaded."

The change went further: "I can no longer understand how they tolerate the men they are with." She could scarcely acknowledge that she had once thrown herself into the same sorts of self-destructive relationships. "I never think about Jim," she said. And in the consulting room his name no longer had the power to elicit tears.

This last change struck me as most remarkable of all. When a patient displays any sign of masochism, and I think it is fair to call Tess's relationship with Jim masochistic, psychiatrists anticipate a protracted psychotherapy. It is rarely easy to help a socially self-destructive patient abandon humiliating relationships and take on new ones that accord with a healthy sense of self-worth. But once Tess felt better, once the weariness lifted and optimism became possible, the masochism just withered away, and she seemed to have every social skill she needed....

* * *

There is no unhappy ending to this story. It is like one of those Elizabethan dramas —Marlowe's *Tamburlaine*—so foreign to modern audiences because the Wheel of Fortune takes only half a turn: the patient recovers and pays no price for the recovery. Tess did go off medication, after about nine months, and she continued to do well. She was, she reported, not quite so sharp of thought, so energetic, so free of care as she had been on the medication, but neither was she driven by guilt and obligation. She was altogether cooler, better controlled, less sensible of the weight of the world than she had been.

After about eight months off medication, Tess told me she was slipping. "I'm not myself," she said. New union negotiations were under way, and she felt she could use the sense of stability, the invulnerability to attack, that Prozac gave her. Here was a dilemma for me. Ought I to provide medication to someone who was not depressed? I could give myself reason enough—construe it that Tess was sliding into relapse, which perhaps she was. In truth, I assumed I would be medicating Tess's chronic condition, call it what you will: heightened awareness of the needs of others, sensitivity to conflict, residual damage to self-esteem—all odd indications for medication. I discussed the dilemma with her, but then I did not hesitate to write the prescription. Who was I to withhold from her the bounties of science? Tess responded again as she had hoped she would, with renewed confidence, self-assurance, and social comfort.

* * *

I believe Tess's story contains an unchronicled reason for Prozac's enormous popularity: its ability to alter personality. Here was a patient whose usual method of functioning changed dramatically. She became socially capable, no longer a wallflower but a social butterfly. Where once she had focused on obligations to others, now she was vivacious and fun-loving. Before, she had pined after men; now she dated them, enjoyed them, weighed their faults and virtues. Newly confident, Tess had no need to romanticize or indulge men's shortcomings.

Not all patients on Prozac respond this way. Some are unaffected by the medicine; some merely recover from depression, as they might on any antidepressant. But a few, a substantial minority, are transformed. Like Garrison Keillor's marvelous Powdermilk biscuits, Prozac gives these patients the courage to do what needs to be done.

What I saw in Tess—a quick alteration in ordinarily intractable problems of personality and social functioning— other psychiatrists saw in their patients as well. Moreover, Prozac had few immediate side effects. Patients on Prozac do not feel drugged up or medicated. Here is one place where the favorable side-effect profile of Prozac makes a difference: if a doctor thinks there is even a modest chance of quickly liberating a chronically stymied patient, and if the risk to the patient is slight, then the doctor will take the gamble repeatedly.

And of course Prozac had phenomenal word of mouth, as "good responders" like Tess told their friends about it. I saw this effect in the second patient I put on Prozac. She was a habitually withdrawn, reticent woman whose cautious behavior had handicapped her at work and in courtship. After a long interval between sessions, I ran into her at a local bookstore. I tend to hang back when I see a patient in a public place, out of uncertainty as to how the patient may want to be greeted, and I believe that, while her chronic depression persisted, this woman would have chosen to avoid me. Now she strode forward and gave me a bold "Hello." I responded, and she said, "I've changed my name, you know."

I did not know. Had she switched from depression to mania and then married impulsively? I wondered whether I should have met with her more frequently. She had, I saw, the bright and open manner that had brought Tess so much social success.

"Yes," she continued, "I call myself Ms. Prozac."

There is no Ms. Asendin, no Ms. Pamelor. Those medicines are quite wonderful—they free patients from the bondage of depression. But they have not inspired the sort of enthusiasm and loyalty patients have shown for Prozac.

* * *

No doubt doctors should be unreservedly pleased when their patients get better quickly. But I confess I was unsettled by Ms. Prozac's enthusiasm, and by Tess's as well. I was suspicious of Prozac, as if I had just taken on a cotherapist whose charismatic style left me wondering whether her magic was wholly trustworthy.

The more rational component to my discomfort had to do with Tess. It makes a psychiatrist uneasy to watch a medicated patient change her circle of friends, her demeanor at work, her relationship to her family. All psychiatrists have seen depressed patients turn manic and make decisions they later regret. But Tess never showed signs of mania. She did not manifest rapid speech or thought, her judgment remained sound, and, though

she enjoyed life more than she had before, she was never euphoric or Pollyannaish. In mood and level of energy, she was "normal," but her place on the normal spectrum had changed, and that change, from "serious," as she put it, to vivacious, had profound consequences for her relationships to those around her.

As the stability of Tess's improvement became clear, my concern diminished, but it did not disappear. Just what did not sit right was hard to say. Might a severe critic find the new Tess a bit blander than the old? Perhaps her tortured intensity implied a complexity of personality that was now harder to locate. I wondered whether the medication had not ironed out too many character-giving wrinkles, like overly aggressive plastic surgery. I even asked myself whether Tess would now give up her work in the projects, as if I had administered her a pill to cure warmheartedness and progressive social beliefs. But in entertaining this thought I wondered whether I was clinging to an arbitrary valuation of temperament, as if the melancholy or saturnine humor were in some way morally superior to the sanguine. In the event, Tess did not forsake the projects, though she did make more time for herself.

Tess, too, found her transformation, marvelous though it was, somewhat unsettling. What was she to make of herself? Her past devotion to Jim, for instance—had it been a matter of biology, an addiction to which she was prone as her father had been to alcoholism? Was she, who defined herself in contrast to her father's fecklessness, in some uncomfortable way like him? What responsibility had she for those years of thralldom to degrading love? After a prolonged struggle to understand the self, to find the Gordian knot dissolved by medication is a mixed pleasure: we want some internal responsibility for our lives, want to find meaning in our errors. Tess was happy, but she talked of a mild, persistent sense of wonder and dislocation....

* * *

I wondered what I would have made of Tess had she been referred to me just before Jim broke up with her, before she had experienced acute depression. I might have recognized her as a woman with skills in many areas, one who had managed to make friends and sustain a career, and who had never suffered a mental illness; I might have seen her as a person who had examined her life with some thoroughness and made progress on many fronts but who remained frustrated socially. She and I might suspect the trouble stemmed from "who she is"—temperamentally serious or timid or cautious or pessimistic or emotionally unexpressive. If only she were a little livelier, a bit more carefree, we might conclude, everything else would fall into place.

Tess's family history—the depressed mother and alcoholic father—constitutes what psychiatrists call "affective loading." (Alcoholism in men seems genetically related to depression in women; or, put more cautiously, a family history of alcoholism is moderately predictive of depression in near relatives.) I might suspect that, in a socially stymied woman with a familial predisposition to depression, Prozac could prove peculiarly liberating. There I would sit, knowing I had in hand a drug that might give Tess just the disposition she needed to break out of her social paralysis.

Confronted with a patient who had never met criteria for any illness, what would I be free to do? If I did prescribe medication, how would we characterize this act?

For years, psychoanalysts were criticized for treating the "worried well," or for "enhancing growth" rather than curing illness. Who is not neurotic? Who is not a fit candidate for psychotherapy? This issue has been answered through an uneasy social consensus. We tolerate breadth in the scope of psychoanalysis, and of psychotherapy in general; few people today would remark on a patient's consulting a therapist over persistent problems with personality or social interactions, though some might object to seeing such treatments covered by insurance under the rubric of illness.

But I wondered whether we were ready for "cosmetic psycho-pharmacology." It was my musings about whether it would be kosher to medicate a patient like Tess in the absence of depression that led me to coin the phrase. Some people might prefer pharmacologic to psychologic self-actualization. Psychic steroids for mental gymnastics, medicinal attacks on the humors, antiwallflower compound —these might be hard to resist. Since you only live once, why not do it as a blonde? Why not as a peppy blonde? Now that questions of personality and social stance have entered the arena of medication, we as a society will have to decide how comfortable we are with using chemicals to modify personality in useful, attractive ways. We may mask the issue by defining less and less severe mood states as pathology, in effect saying, "If it responds to an antidepressant, it's depression." Already, it seems to me, psychiatric diagnosis had been subject to a sort of "diagnostic bracket creep"— the expansion of categories to match the scope of relevant medications.

How large a sphere of human problems we choose to define as medical is an important social decision. But words like "choose" and "decision" perhaps misstate the process. It is easy to imagine that our role will be passive, that as a society we will in effect permit the material technology, medications, to define what is health and what is illness....

*   *   *

An indication of the power of medication to reshape a person's identity is contained in the sentence Tess used when, eight months after first stopping Prozac, she telephoned me to ask whether she might resume the medication. She said, "I am not myself."

I found this statement remarkable. After all, Tess had existed in one mental state for twenty or thirty years; she then briefly felt different on medication. Now that the old mental state was threatening to re-emerge—the one she had experienced almost all her adult life —her response was "I am not myself." But who had she been all those years if not herself? Had medication somehow removed a false self and replaced it with a true one? Might Tess, absent the invention of the modern antidepressant, have lived her whole life—a successful life, perhaps, by external standards—and never been herself?

When I asked her to expand on what she meant, Tess said she no longer felt like herself when certain aspects of her ailment—lack of confidence, feelings of vulnerability—returned, even to a small degree. Ordinarily, if we ask a person why she holds back socially, she may say, "That's just who I am," meaning shy or hesitant or melancholy or overly cautious. These characteristics often per-

sist throughout life, and they have a strong influence on career, friendships, marriage, self-image.

Suddenly those intimate and consistent traits are not-me, they are alien, they are defect, they are illness—so that a certain habit of mind and body that links a person to his relatives and ancestors from generation to generation is now "other." Tess had come to understand herself—the person she had been for so many years —to be mildly ill. She understood this newfound illness, as it were, in her marrow. She did not feel herself when the medicine wore off and she was rechallenged by an external stress.

On imipramine, no longer depressed but still inhibited and subdued, Tess felt "myself again." But while on Prozac, she underwent a redefinition of self. Off Prozac, when she again became inhibited and subdued—perhaps the identical sensations she had experienced while on imipramine—she now felt "not myself." Prozac redefined Tess's understanding of what was essential to her and what was intrusive and pathological.

This recasting of self left Tess in an unusual relationship to medication. Off medication, she was aware that, if she returned to the old inhibited state, she might need Prozac in order to "feel herself." In this sense, she might have a lifelong relationship to medication, whether or not she was currently taking it. Patients who undergo the sort of deep change Tess experienced generally say they never want to feel the old way again and would take quite substantial risks— in terms, for instance, of medication side effects—in order not to regress. This is not a question of addiction or hedonism, at least not in the ordinary sense of those words, but of having located a self that feels true, normal, and whole, and of understanding medication to be an occasionally necessary adjunct to the maintenance of that self.

Beyond the effect on individual patients, Tess's redefinition of self led me to fantasize about a culture in which this biologically driven sort of self-understanding becomes widespread. Certain dispositions now considered awkward or endearing, depending on taste, might be seen as ailments to be pitied and, where possible, corrected. Tastes and judgments regarding personality styles do change. The romantic, decadent stance of Goethe's young Werther and Chateaubriand's René we now see as merely immature, overly depressive, perhaps in need of treatment. Might we not, in a culture where over-seriousness is a medically correctable flaw, lose our taste for the melancholic or brooding artists—Schubert, or even Mozart in many of his moods?

These were my concerns on witnessing Tess's recovery. I was torn simultaneously by a sense that the medication was too far-reaching in its effects and a sense that my discomfort was arbitrary and aesthetic rather than doctorly. I wondered how the drug might influence my profession's definition of illness and its understanding of ordinary suffering. I wondered how Prozac's success would interact with certain unfortunate tendencies of the broader culture. And I asked just how far we—doctors, patients, the society at large—were likely to go in the direction of permitting drug responses to shape our understanding of the authentic self.

My concerns were imprecisely formulated. But it was not only the concerns that were vague: I had as yet only a sketchy impression of the drug whose effects were so troubling. To whom were my patients and I listening? On that question depended the answers to the list of social and ethical concerns; and the exploration of that question would entail attending to accounts of other patients who responded to Prozac.

* * *

My first meeting with Prozac had been heightened for me by the uncommon qualities of the patient who responded to the drug. I found it astonishing that a pill could do in a matter of days what psychiatrists hope, and often fail, to accomplish by other means over a course of years: to restore to a person robbed of it in childhood the capacity to play. Yes, there remained a disquieting element to this restoration. Were I scripting the story, I might have made Tess's metamorphosis more gradual, more humanly comprehensible, more in sync with the ordinary rhythm of growth. I might even have preferred if her play as an adult had been, for continuity's sake, more suffused with the memory of melancholy. But medicines do not work just as we wish. The way neurochemicals tell stories is not the way psychotherapy tells them. If Tess's fairy tale does not have the plot we expect, its ending is nonetheless happy.

By the time Tess's story had played itself out, I had seen perhaps a dozen people respond with comparable success to Prozac. Hers was not an isolated case, and the issues it raised would not go away. Charisma, courage, character, social competency—Prozac seemed to say that these and other concepts would need to be re-examined, that our sense of what is constant in the self and what is mutable, what is necessary and what contingent, would need, like our sense of the fable of transformation, to be revised.

NO

Seymour Fisher and
Roger P. Greenberg

PRESCRIPTIONS FOR HAPPINESS?

The air is filled with declarations and advertisements of the power of biological psychiatry to relieve people of their psychological distress. Some biological psychiatrists are so convinced of the superiority of their position that they are recommending young psychiatrists no longer be taught the essentials of doing psychotherapy. Feature stories in such magazines as *Newsweek* and *Time* have portrayed drugs like Prozac as possessing almost a mystical potency. The best-selling book *Listening to Prozac* by psychiatrist Peter Kramer, M.D., projects the idyllic possibility that psychotropic drugs may eventually be capable of correcting a spectrum of personality quirks and lacks.

As longtime faculty members of a number of psychiatry departments, we have personally witnessed the gradual but steadily accelerated dedication to the idea that "mental illness" can be mastered with biologically based substances. Yet a careful sifting of the pertinent literature indicates that modesty and skepticism would be more appropriate responses to the research accumulated thus far. In 1989, we first raised radical questions about such biological claims in a book, *The Limits of Biological Treatments for Psychological Distress: Comparisons with Psychotherapy and Placebo* (Lawrence Erlbaum). Our approach has been to filter the studies that presumably anchor them through a series of logical and quantitative (meta-analytic) appraisals.

HOW EFFECTIVE ARE ANTIDEPRESSANT DRUGS?

Antidepressants, one of the major weapons in the biological therapeutic arsenal, illustrate well the largely unacknowledged uncertainty that exists in the biological approach to psychopathology. We suggest that, at present, no one actually knows how effective antidepressants are. Confident declarations about their potency go well beyond the existing evidence.

To get an understanding of the scientific status of antidepressants, we analyzed how much more effective the antidepressants are than inert pills called "placebos." That is, if antidepressants are given to one depressed group and a placebo to another group, how much greater is the recovery of those taking

From Seymour Fisher and Roger P. Greenberg, "Prescriptions for Happiness?" *Psychology Today* (September/October 1995). Copyright © 1995 by Seymour Fisher. Reprinted by permission.

the active drug as compared to those taking the inactive placebo? Generous claims that antidepressants usually produce improvement in about 60 to 70 percent of patients are not infrequent, whereas placebos are said to benefit 25 to 30 percent. If antidepressants were, indeed, so superior to placebos, this would be a persuasive advertisement for the biological approach.

We found 15 major reviews of the antidepressant literature. Surprisingly, even the most positive reviews indicate that 30 to 40 percent of studies show no significant difference in response to drug versus placebo! The reviews indicate overall that one-third of patients do not improve with antidepressant treatment, one-third improve with placebos, and an additional third show a response to medication they would not have attained with placebos. In the most optimistic view of such findings, two-thirds of the cases (placebo responders and those who do not respond to anything) do as well with placebo as with active medication.

We also found two large-scale quantitative evaluations (meta-analyses) integrating the outcomes of multiple studies of antidepressants. They clearly indicated, on the average, quite modest therapeutic power.

We were particularly impressed by the large variation in outcomes of studies conducted at multiple clinical sites or centers. Consider a study that compared the effectiveness of an antidepressant among patients at five different research centers. Although the pooled results demonstrate that the drug was generally more effective than placebo, the results from individual centers reveal much variation. After six weeks of treatment, every one of the six measures of effectiveness showed the antidepressant (imipramine) to be merely equivalent to placebo in two or more of the centers. In two of the settings, a difference favoring the medication was detected on only one of 12 outcome comparisons.

In other words, the pooled, apparently favorable, outcome data conceal that dramatically different results could be obtained as a function of who conducted the study and the specific conditions at each locale. We can only conclude that a good deal of fragility characterized the apparent superiority of drug over placebo. The scientific literature is replete with analogous examples.

Incidentally, we also looked at whether modern studies, which are presumably better protected against bias, use higher doses, and often involve longer treatment periods, show a greater superiority of the antidepressant than did earlier studies. The literature frequently asserts that failures to demonstrate antidepressant superiority are due to such methodological failures as not using high enough doses, and so forth.

We examined this issue in a pool of 16 studies assembled by psychiatrists John Kane and Jeffrey Lieberman in 1984. These studies all compare a standard drug, such as imipramine or amitriptyline, to a newer drug and a placebo. They use clearer diagnostic definitions of depression than did the older studies and also adopt currently accepted standards for dosage levels and treatment duration. When we examined the data, we discovered that the advantage of drug over placebo was modest. Twenty-one percent more of the patients receiving a drug improved as compared to those on placebo. Actually, most of the studies showed no difference in the percentage of patients significantly improved by drugs. There was no indication that these studies, using more careful methodology, achieved better outcomes than older studies.

Finally, it is crucial to recognize that several studies have established that there is a high rate of relapse among those who have responded positively to an antidepressant but then are taken off treatment. The relapse rate may be 60 percent or more during the first year after treatment cessation. Many studies also show that any benefits of antidepressants wane in a few months, even while the drugs are still being taken. This highlights the complexity of evaluating antidepressants. They may be effective initially, but lose all value over a longer period.

ARE DRUG TRIALS BIASED?

As we burrowed deeper into the antidepressant literature, we learned that there are also crucial problems in the methodology used to evaluate psychotropic drugs. Most central is the question of whether this methodology properly shields drug trials from bias. Studies have shown that the more open to bias a drug trial is, the greater the apparent superiority of the drug over placebo. So questions about the trustworthiness of a given drug-testing procedure invite skepticism about the results.

The question of potential bias first came to our attention in studies comparing inactive placebos to active drugs. In the classic double-blind design, neither patient nor researcher knows who is receiving drug or placebo. We were struck by the fact that the presumed protection provided by the double-blind design was undermined by the use of placebos that simply do not arouse as many body sensations as do active drugs. Research shows that patients learn to discriminate between drug and placebo largely from body sensations and symptoms.

A substance like imipramine, one of the most frequently studied antidepressants, usually causes clearly defined sensations, such as dry mouth, tremor, sweating, constipation. Inactive placebos used in studies of antidepressants also apparently initiate some body sensations, but they are fewer, more inconsistent, and less intense as indicated by the fact that they are less often cited by patients as a source of discomfort causing them to drop out of treatment.

Vivid differences between the body sensations of drug and placebo groups could signal to patients as to whether they are receiving an active or inactive agent. Further, they could supply discriminating cues to those responsible for the patients' day-to-day treatment. Nurses, for example, might adopt different attitudes toward patients they identify as being "on" versus "off" active treatment—and consequently communicate contrasting expectations.

THE BODY OF EVIDENCE

This is more than theoretical. Researchers have reported that in a double-blind study of imipramine, it was possible by means of side effects to identify a significant number of the patients taking the active drug. Those patients receiving a placebo have fewer signals (from self and others) indicating they are being actively treated and should be improving. By the same token, patients taking an active drug receive multiple signals that may well amplify potential placebo effects linked to the therapeutic context. Indeed, a doctor's strong belief in the power of the active drug enhances the apparent therapeutic power of the drug or placebo.

Is it possible that a large proportion of the difference in effectiveness often reported between antidepressants and placebos can be explained as a function of body sensation discrepancies? It is conceivable, and fortunately there are research findings that shed light on the matter.

Consider an analysis by New Zealand psychologist Richard Thomson. He reviewed double-blind, placebo-controlled studies of antidepressants completed between 1958 and 1972. Sixty-eight had employed an inert placebo and seven an active one (atropine) that produced a variety of body sensations. The antidepressant had a superior therapeutic effect in 59 percent of the studies using inert placebo—but in only one study (14 percent) using the active placebo. The active placebo eliminated any therapeutic advantage for the antidepressants, apparently because it convinced patients they were getting real medication.

HOW BLIND IS DOUBLE-BLIND?

Our concerns about the effects of inactive placebos on the double-blind design led us to ask just how blind the double-blind really is. By the 1950s reports were already surfacing that for psychoactive drugs, the double-blind design is not as scientifically objective as originally assumed. In 1993 we searched the world literature and found 31 reports in which patients and researchers involved in studies were asked to guess who was receiving the active psychotropic drug and who the placebo. In 28 instances the guesses were significantly better than chance—and at times they were surprisingly accurate. In one double-blind study that called for administering either imipramine, phenelzine, or placebo to depressed patients, 78 percent of patients and 87 percent of psychiatrists correctly distinguished drug from placebo.

One particularly systematic report in the literature involved the administration of alprazolam, imipramine, and placebo over an eight-week period to groups of patients who experience panic attacks. Halfway through the treatment and also at the end, the physicians and the patients were asked to judge independently whether each patient was receiving an active drug or a placebo. If they thought an active drug was being administered, they had to decide whether it was alprazolam or imipramine. Both physicians (with an 88 percent success rate) and patients (83 percent) substantially exceeded chance in the correctness of their judgments. Furthermore, the physicians could distinguish alprazolam from imipramine significantly better than chance. The researchers concluded that "double-blind studies of these pharmacological treatments for panic disorder was not really 'blind.'"

Yet the vast majority of psychiatric drug efficacy studies have simply *assumed* that the double-blind design is effective; they did not test the blindness by determining whether patients and researchers were able to differentiate drug from placebo.

We take the somewhat radical view that this means most past studies of the efficacy of psychotropic drugs are, to unknown degrees, scientifically untrustworthy. At the least, we can no longer speak with confidence about the true differences in therapeutic power between active psychotropic drugs and placebos. We must suspend judgment until future studies are completed with more adequate controls for the defects of the double-blind paradigm.

Other bothersome questions arose as we scanned the cascade of studies focused on antidepressants. Of particular concern is how unrepresentative the patients are who end up in the clinical trials. There are the usual sampling problems having to do with which persons seek treatment for their discomfort, and, in addition, volunteer as subjects for a study. But there are others. Most prominent is the relatively high proportion of patients who "drop out" before the completion of their treatment programs.

Numerous dropouts occur in response to unpleasant side effects. In many published studies, 35 percent or more of patients fail to complete the research protocol. Various procedures have been developed to deal fairly with the question of how to classify the therapeutic outcomes of dropouts, but none can vitiate the simple fact that the final sample of fully treated patients has often been drastically reduced.

There are still other filters that increase sample selectivity. For example, studies often lose sizable segments of their samples by not including patients who are too depressed to speak, much less participate in a research protocol, or who are too disorganized to participate in formal psychological testing. We also found decisions not to permit particular racial or age groups to be represented in samples or to avoid using persons below a certain educational level. Additionally, researchers typically recruit patients whose depression is not accompanied by any other type of physical or mental disorder, a situation that does not hold for the depressed in the general population.

So we end up wondering about the final survivors in the average drug trial. To what degree do they typify the average individual in real life who seeks treatment? How much can be generalized from a sample made up of the "leftovers" from multiple depleting processes? Are we left with a relatively narrow band of those most willing to conform to the rather rigid demands of the research establishment? Are the survivors those most accepting of a dependent role?

The truth is that there are probably multiple kinds of survivors, depending upon the specific local conditions prevailing where the study was carried out. We would guess that some of the striking differences in results that appear in multicenter drug studies could be traced to specific forms of sampling bias. We do not know how psychologically unique the persons are who get recruited into, and stick with, drug research enterprises. We are not the first to raise this question, but we are relatively more alarmed about the potential implications.

RESEARCHER MOTIVATION AND OUTCOME

We recently conducted an analysis that further demonstrates how drug effectiveness diminishes as the opportunity for bias in research design wanes. This analysis seized on studies in which a new antidepressant is compared (under double-blind conditions) with an older, standard antidepressant and a placebo. In such a context the efficacy of the newer drug (which the drug company hopes to introduce) is of central interest to the researcher, and the effectiveness of the older drug of peripheral import. Therefore, if the double-blind is breached (as is likely), there would presumably be less bias to enhance the efficacy of the older drug than occurred in the original trials of that drug.

We predicted that the old drug would appear significantly less powerful in the newer studies than it had in earlier designs, where it was of central interest of the researcher. To test this hypothesis, we located 22 double-blind studies in which newer antidepressants were compared with an older antidepressant drug (usually imipramine) and a placebo. Our meta-analysis revealed, as predicted, that the efficacy rates, based on clinicians's judgments of outcome, were quite modest for the older antidepressants. In fact, they were approximately one-half to one-quarter the average size of the effects reported in earlier studies when the older drug was the only agent appraised.

Let us be very clear as to what this signifies: When researchers were evaluating the antidepressant in a context where they were no longer interested in proving its therapeutic power, there was a dramatic decrease in that apparent power, as compared to an earlier context when they were enthusiastically interested in demonstrating the drug's potency. A change in researcher motivation was enough to change outcome. Obviously this means too that the present double-blind design for testing drug efficacy is exquisitely vulnerable to bias.

Another matter of pertinence to the presumed biological rationale for the efficacy of antidepressants is that no consistent links have been demonstrated between the concentration of drug in blood and its efficacy. Studies have found significant correlations for some drugs, but of low magnitude. Efforts to link plasma levels to therapeutic outcome have been disappointing.

Similarly, few data show a relationship between antidepressant dosage levels and their therapeutic efficacy. That is, large doses of the drug do not necessarily have greater effects than low doses. These inconsistencies are a bit jarring against the context of biological explanatory framework.

We have led you through a detailed critique of the difficulties and problems that prevail in the body of research testing the power of the antidepressants. We conclude that it would be wise to be relatively modest in claims about their efficacy. Uncertainty and doubt are inescapable.

While we have chosen the research on the antidepressants to illustrate the uncertainties attached to biological treatments of psychological distress, reviews of other classes of psychotropic drugs yield similar findings. After a survey of anti-anxiety drugs, psychologist Ronald Lipman concluded there is little consistent evidence that they help patients with anxiety disorders: "Although it seems natural to assume that the anxiolytic medications would be the most effective psychotropic medications for the treatment of anxiety disorders, the evidence does not support this assumption."

BIOLOGICAL VERSUS PSYCHOLOGICAL?

The faith in the biological approach has been fueled by a great burst of research. Thousands of papers have appeared probing the efficacy of psychotropic drugs. A good deal of basic research has attacked fundamental issues related to the nature of brain functioning in those who display psychopathology. Researchers in these areas are dedicated and often do excellent work. However, in their zeal, in their commitment to the so-called biological, they are at times overcome by their expectations. Their hopes become rigidifying boundaries. Their vocabulary too easily becomes a jargon that camouflages over-simplified assumptions.

A good example of such oversimplification is the way in which the term "biological" is conceptualized. It is too often viewed as a realm distinctly different from the psychological. Those invested in the biological approach all too often practice the ancient Cartesian distinction between somatic-stuff and soul-stuff. In so doing they depreciate the scientific significance of the phenomena they exile to the soul-stuff category.

But paradoxically, they put a lot of interesting phenomena out of bounds to their prime methodology and restrict themselves to a narrowed domain. For example, if talk therapy is labeled as a "psychological" thing—not biological—this implies that biological research can only hover at the periphery of what psychotherapists do. A sizable block of behavior becomes off limits to the biologically dedicated.

In fact, if we adopt the view that the biological and psychological are equivalent (biological monism), there is no convincing real-versus-unreal differentiation between the so-called psychological and biological. It *all* occurs in tissue and one is not more "real" than the other. A patient's attitude toward the therapist is just as biological in nature as a patient's response to an antidepressant. A response to a placebo is just as biological as a response to an antipsychotic drug. This may be an obvious point, but it has not yet been incorporated into the world views of either the biologically or psychologically oriented.

Take a look at a few examples in the research literature that highlight the overlap or identity of what is so often split apart. In 1992, psychiatrist Lewis Baxter and colleagues showed that successful psychotherapy of obsessive-compulsive patients results in brain imagery changes equivalent to those produced by successful drug treatment. The brain apparently responds in equivalent ways to both the talk and drug approaches. Even more dramatic is a finding that instilling in the elderly the illusion of being in control of one's surroundings (by putting them in charge of some plants) significantly increased their life span compared to a control group. What could be a clearer demonstration of the biological nature of what is labeled as a psychological expectation than the postponement of death?

Why are we focusing on this historic Cartesian confusion? Because so many who pursue the so-called biological approach are by virtue of their tunnel vision motivated to overlook the psychosocial variable that mediate the administration of such agents as psychotropic drugs and electroconvulsive therapy. They do not permit themselves to seriously grasp that psychosocial variables are just as biological as a capsule containing an antidepressant. It is the failure to understand this that results in treating placebo effects as if they were extraneous or less of a biological reality than a chemical agent.

PLACEBO EFFECTS

Indeed, placebos have been shown to initiate certain effects usually thought to be reserved for active drugs. For example, placebos clearly show dose-level effects. A larger dose of a placebo will have a greater impact than a lower dose. Placebos can also create addictions.

Patients will poignantly declare that they cannot stop taking a particular placebo substance (which they assume is an active drug) because to do so causes them too much distress and discomfort.

Placebos can produce toxic effects such as rashes, apparent memory loss, fever, headaches, and more. These "toxic" effects may be painful and even overwhelming in their intensity. The placebo literature is clear: Placebos are powerful body-altering substances, especially considering the wide range of body systems they can influence.

Actually, the power of the placebo complicates all efforts to test the therapeutic efficacy of psychotropic drugs. When placebos alone can produce positive curative effects in the 40 to 50 percent range (occasionally even up to 70–80 percent), the active drug being tested is hard-pressed to demonstrate its superiority. Even if the active drug exceeds the placebo in potency, the question remains whether the advantage is at least partially due to the superior potential of the active drug itself to mobilize placebo effects because it is an active substance that stirs vivid body sensations. Because it is almost always an inactive substance (sugar pill) that arouses fewer genuine body sensations, the placebo is less convincingly perceived as having therapeutic prowess.

Drug researchers have tried, in vain, to rid themselves of placebo effects, but these effects are forever present and frustrate efforts to demonstrate that psychoactive drugs have an independent "pure" biological impact. This state of affairs dramatically testifies that the labels "psychological" and "biological" refer largely to different perspectives on events that all occur in tissue. At present, it is somewhat illusory to separate the so-called biological and psychological effects of drugs used to treat emotional distress.

The literature is surprisingly full of instances of how social and attitudinal factors modify the effects of active drugs. Antipsychotic medications are more effective if the patient likes rather than dislikes the physician administering them. An antipsychotic drug is less effective if patients are led to believe they are only taking an inactive placebo. Perhaps even more impressive, if a stimulant drug is administered with the deceptive instruction that it is a sedative, it can initiate a pattern of physiological response, such as decreased heart rate, that it is sedative rather than arousing in nature. Such findings reaffirm how fine the line is between social and somatic domains.

What are the practical implications for distressed individuals and their physicians? Administering a drug is not simply a medical (biological) act. It is, in addition, a complex social act whose effectiveness will be mediated by such factors as the patient's expectations of the drug and reactions to the body sensations created by that drug, and the physician's friendliness and degree of personal confidence in the drug's power. Practitioners who dispense psychotropic medications should become thoroughly acquainted with the psychological variables modifying the therapeutic impact of such drugs and tailor their own behavior accordingly. By the same token, distressed people seeking drug treatment should keep in mind that their probability of benefiting may depend in part on whether they choose a practitioner they truly like and respect. And remember this: You are the ultimate arbiter of a drug's efficacy.

How to go about mastering unhappiness, which ranges from "feeling blue" to despairing depression, puzzles everyone. Such popular quick fixes as alcohol, conversion to a new faith, and other splendid distractions have proven only partially helpful. When antidepressant drugs hit the shelves with their seeming scientific aura, they were easily seized upon. Apparently serious unhappiness (depression) could now be chemically neutralized in the way one banishes a toothache.

But the more we learn about the various states of unhappiness, the more we recognize that they are not simply "symptoms" awaiting removal. Depressed feelings have complex origins and functions. In numerous contexts —for example, chronic conflict with a spouse—depression may indicate a realistic appraisal of a troubling problem and motivate a serious effort to devise a solution.

While it is true that deep despair may interfere with sensible problem-solving, the fact is that, more and more, individuals are being instructed to take antidepressants at the earliest signs of depressive distress and this could interfere with the potentially constructive signaling value of such distress. Emotions are feelings full of information. Unhappiness is an emotion, and despite its negativity, should not be classified single-mindedly as a thing to tune out. This in no way implies that one should submit passively to the discomfort of feeling unhappy. Actually, we all learn to experiment with a variety of strategies for making ourselves feel better, but the ultimate aim is long-term effective action rather than a depersonalized "I feel fine."

CHALLENGE QUESTIONS

Have Antidepressant Drugs Proven to Be Effective?

1. Assume that "mood brighteners" such as Prozac are as effective as Kramer says they are for Tess and that they are also perfectly safe. What would be some of the problems and prospects of this "brightened" world?

2. Fisher and Greenberg say that "depressed feelings have complex origins and functions." What function could such feelings have? How would their removal by antidepressants be problematic?

3. How would you account for what Fisher and Greenberg term "the power of the placebo"? How could this be used in psychotherapy?

4. Draw up a list of recommendations for improving drug evaluation research.

5. How do you account for the seemingly phenomenal success of Prozac as seen by psychiatrists such as Kramer?

ISSUE 14

Classic Dialogue: Do Diagnostic Labels Hinder Treatment?

YES: D. L. Rosenhan, from "On Being Sane in Insane Places," *Science* (January 13, 1973)

NO: Robert L. Spitzer, from "On Pseudoscience in Science, Logic in Remission and Psychiatric Diagnosis: A Critique of 'On Being Sane in Insane Places,'" *Journal of Abnormal Psychology* (vol. 84, 1975)

ISSUE SUMMARY

YES: Psychologist D. L. Rosenhan describes an experiment that he contends demonstrates that once a patient is labeled as schizophrenic, his behavior is seen as such by mental health workers regardless of the true state of the patient's mental health.

NO: Psychiatrist Robert L. Spitzer argues that diagnostic labels are necessary and valuable and that Rosenhan's experiment has many flaws.

Traditionally, the first step in treating a disorder is to diagnose it. When a disorder is diagnosed, presumably the most effective treatment can then be applied. But diagnosis often involves classifying the person and attaching a label. Could such a label do more harm than good?

How would you think and behave if you were introduced to someone described as a high school dropout? A heroin addict? A schizophrenic? What would you think and how would you behave if, having recently taken a series of personality tests, you were told by an expert that you were schizophrenic?

Some people believe that diagnostic labels may actually serve as self-fulfilling prophecies. Labels seem to have a way of putting blinders on the way a problem is seen. Those who are labeled may behave differently toward others or develop self-concepts consistent with the diagnosis—and thereby exaggerate, or even create anew, behavior considered to be "abnormal."

In the following selections, D. L. Rosenhan asks the question, "If sanity and insanity exist, how shall we know them?" He then describes an experiment that he conducted to help answer this question. Rosenhan interprets the results of his investigation as demonstrating that "the normal are not detectably sane" by a mental hospital staff because "having once been labeled schizophrenic, there is nothing the [patient] can do to overcome this tag." He believes that mental institutions impose a specific environment in which the meaning of even normal behaviors can be construed as abnormal. If this is so, Rosenhan wonders, "How many people are sane ... but not recognized as such in our psychiatric institutions?"

Robert L. Spitzer criticizes Rosenhan's experiment on many grounds and, in fact, contends that "a correct interpretation of his own [Rosenhan's] data contradicts his conclusions." Rosenhan's data, Spitzer contends, show that in "a psychiatric hospital, psychiatrists are remarkably able to distinguish the 'sane' from the 'insane.'" Although Spitzer recognizes some of the dangers of diagnostic classification, he believes that Rosenhan has not presented fairly the purpose and necessity of diagnoses. The misuse of diagnoses, he maintains, "is not a sufficient reason to abandon their use because they have been shown to be of value when properly used." They "enable mental health professionals to communicate with each other ..., comprehend the pathological processes involved ..., and control psychiatric disorders," says Spitzer.

POINT

- Psychiatric diagnoses are in the minds of the observers and do not reflect the behavior of the patients.

- A diagnosis can become a self-fulfilling prophecy for the doctor or the patient.

- In the setting of a mental institution, almost any behavior could be considered abnormal.

- Diagnostic labels serve no useful purpose, especially in view of the harm they do.

COUNTERPOINT

- A diagnosis based on real or false symptoms *is* based on a patient's behavior.

- Competent diagnoses derive from a necessary classification of the symptoms of a disorder.

- Mental patients *do* eventually get discharged when they continue to show no symptoms of behavioral pathology.

- Diagnoses enable psychiatrists to communicate, comprehend, and control disorders.

YES   D. L. Rosenhan

ON BEING SANE IN INSANE PLACES

If sanity and insanity exist, how shall we know them?

The question is neither capricious nor itself insane. However much we may be personally convinced that we can tell the normal from the abnormal, the evidence is simply not compelling. It is commonplace, for example, to read about murder trials wherein eminent psychiatrists for the defense are contradicted by equally eminent psychiatrists for the prosecution on the matter of the defendant's sanity. More generally, there are a great deal of conflicting data on the reliability, utility, and meaning of such terms as "sanity," "insanity," "mental illness," and "schizophrenia." Finally, as early as 1934, Benedict suggested that normality and abnormality are not universal. What is viewed as normal in one culture may be seen as quite aberrant in another. Thus, notions of normality and abnormality may not be quite as accurate as people believe they are.

To raise questions regarding normality and abnormality is in no way to question the fact that some behaviors are deviant or odd. Murder is deviant. So, too, are hallucinations. Nor does raising such questions deny the existence of the personal anguish that is often associated with "mental illness." Anxiety and depression exist. Psychological suffering exists. But normality and abnormality, sanity and insanity, and the diagnoses that flow from them may be less substantive than many believe them to be.

At its heart, the question of whether the sane can be distinguished from the insane (and whether degrees of insanity can be distinguished from each other) is a simple matter: do the salient characteristics that lead to diagnoses reside in the patients themselves or in the environments and contexts in which observers find them? From Bleuler, through Kretchmer, through the formulators of the recently revised *Diagnostic and Statistical Manual* of the American Psychiatric Association, the belief has been strong that patients present symptoms, that those symptoms can be categorized, and, implicitly, that the sane are distinguishable from the insane. More recently, however, this belief has been questioned. Based in part on theoretical and anthropological considerations, but also on philosophical, legal, and therapeutic ones, the view has grown that psychological categorization of mental illness is useless at best and downright harmful, misleading, and pejorative at worst. Psychiatric diagnoses, in this view, are in the minds of the observers and are not valid summaries of characteristics displayed by the observed.

Gains can be made in deciding which of these is more nearly accurate by getting normal people (that is, people who do not have, and have never suffered, symptoms of serious psychiatric disorders) admitted to psychiatric hospitals and then determining whether they were discovered to be sane and, if so, how. If the sanity of such pseudopatients were always detected, there would be prima facie evidence that a sane individual can be distinguished from the insane context in which he is found. Normality (and presumably abnormality) is distinct enough that it can be recognized wherever it occurs, for it is carried within the person. If, on the other hand, the sanity of the pseudopatients were never discovered, serious difficulties would arise for those who support traditional modes of psychiatric diagnosis. Given that the hospital staff was not incompetent, that the pseudopatient had been behaving as sanely as he had been outside of the hospital, and that it had never been previously suggested that he belonged in a psychiatric hospital, such an unlikely outcome would support the view that psychiatric diagnosis betrays little about the patient but much about the environment in which an observer finds him.

This article describes such an experiment. Eight sane people gained secret admission to 12 different hospitals. Their diagnostic experiences constitute the data of the first part of this article; the remainder is devoted to a description of their experiences in psychiatric institutions. Too few psychiatrists and psychologists, even

those who have worked in such hospitals, know what the experience is like. They rarely talk about it with former patients, perhaps because they distrust information coming from the previously insane. Those who have worked in psychiatric hospitals are likely to have adapted so thoroughly to the settings that they are insensitive to the impact of the experience. And while there have been occasional reports of researchers who submitted themselves to psychiatric hospitalization, these researchers have commonly remained in the hospitals for short periods of time, often with the knowledge of the hospital staff. It is difficult to know the extent to which they were treated like patients or like research colleagues. Nevertheless, their reports about the inside of the psychiatric hospital have been valuable. This article extends those efforts.

PSEUDOPATIENTS AND THEIR SETTINGS

The eight pseudopatients were a varied group. One was a psychology graduate student in his 20s. The remaining seven were older and "established." Among them were three psychologists, a pediatrician, a psychiatrist, a painter, and a housewife. Three pseudopatients were women, five were men. All of them employed pseudonyms, lest their alleged diagnoses embarrass them later. Those who were in mental health professions alleged another occupation in order to avoid the special attentions that might be accorded by staff, as a matter of courtesy or caution, to ailing colleagues. With the exception of myself (I was the first pseudopatient and my presence was known to the hospital administrator and chief psychologist and, so far as I can tell, to them alone), the presence of pseudopatients and the nature of the research program was not known to the hospital staffs.

The settings were similarly varied. In order to generalize the findings, admission into a variety of hospitals was sought. The 12 hospitals in the sample are located in five different states on the East and West coasts. Some were old and shabby, some were quite new. Some were research-oriented, others not. Some had good staff-patient ratios, others were quite understaffed. Only one was a strictly private hospital. All the others were supported by state or federal funds or, in one instance, by university funds.

After calling the hospital for an appointment, the pseudopatient arrived at the admissions office complaining that he had been hearing voices. Asked what the voices said, he replied that they were often unclear, but as far as he could tell they said "empty," "hollow," and "thud." The voices were unfamiliar and were of the same sex as the pseudopatient. The choice of these symptoms was occasioned by their apparent similarity to existential symptoms. Such symptoms were alleged to arise from painful concerns about the perceived meaninglessness of one's life. It is as if the hallucinating person were saying, "My life is empty and hollow." The choice of these symptoms was also determined by the *absence* of a single report of existential psychoses in the literature.

Beyond alleging the symptoms and falsifying name, vocation, and employment, no further alterations of person, history, or circumstances were made. The significant events of the pseudopatient's life history were presented as they had actually occurred. Relationships with parents and siblings, with spouse and children, with people at work and in school, consistent with the aforementioned exceptions, were described as they were or had

been. Frustrations and upsets were described along with joys and satisfactions. These facts are important to remember. If anything, they strongly biased the subsequent results in favor of detecting sanity, since none of their histories or current behaviors were seriously pathological in any way.

Immediately upon admission to the psychiatric ward, the pseudopatient ceased simulating *any* symptoms of abnormality. In some cases, there was a brief period of mild nervousness and anxiety, since none of the pseudopatients really believed that they would be admitted so easily. Indeed their shared fear was that they would be immediately exposed as frauds and greatly embarrassed. Moreover, many of them had never visited a psychiatric ward; even those who had, nevertheless had some genuine fears about what might happen to them. Their nervousness, then, was quite appropriate to the novelty of the hospital setting, and it abated rapidly.

Apart from that short-lived nervousness, the pseudopatient behaved on the ward as he "normally" behaved. The pseudopatient spoke to patients and staff as he might ordinarily. Because there is uncommonly little to do on a psychiatric ward, he attempted to engage others in conversation. When asked by staff how he was feeling, he indicated that he was fine, that he no longer experienced symptoms. He responded to instructions from attendants, to calls for medication (which was not swallowed), and to dining-hall instructions. Beyond such activities as were available to him on the admissions ward, he spent his time writing down his observations about the ward, its patients, and the staff. Initially these notes were written "secretly," but as it soon became clear that no one much cared, they were subsequently written on standard tablets of paper in such public places as the dayroom. No secret was made of these activities.

The pseudopatient, very much as a true psychiatric patient, entered a hospital with no foreknowledge of when he would be discharged. Each was told that he would have to get out by his own devices, essentially by convincing the staff that he was sane. The psychological stresses associated with hospitalization were considerable, and all but one of the pseudopatients desired to be discharged almost immediately after being admitted. They were, therefore, motivated not only to behave sanely, but to be paragons of cooperation. That their behavior was in no way disruptive is confirmed by nursing reports, which have been obtained on most of the patients. These reports uniformly indicate that the patients were "friendly," "cooperative," and "exhibited no abnormal indications."

THE NORMAL ARE NOT DETECTABLY SANE

Despite their public "show" of sanity, the pseudopatients were never detected. Admitted, except in one case, with a diagnosis of schizophrenia each was discharged with a diagnosis of schizophrenia "in remission." The label "in remission" should in no way be dismissed as a formality, for at no time during any hospitalization had any question been raised about any pseudopatient's simulation. Nor are there any indications in the hospital records that the pseudopatient's status was suspect. Rather, the evidence is strong that, once labeled schizophrenic, the pseudopatient was stuck with that label. If the pseudopatient was to be discharged, he must naturally be "in remission"; but he was

not sane, nor, in the institution's view, had he ever been sane.

The uniform failure to recognize sanity cannot be attributed to the quality of the hospitals, for, although there were considerable variations among them, several are considered excellent. Nor can it be alleged that there was simply not enough time to observe the pseudopatients. Length of hospitalization ranged from 7 to 52 days, with an average of 19 days. The pseudopatients were not, in fact, carefully observed, but this failure clearly speaks more to traditions within psychiatric hospitals than to lack of opportunity.

Finally, it cannot be said that the failure to recognize the pseudopatients' sanity was due to the fact that they were not behaving sanely. While there was clearly some tension present in all of them, their daily visitors could detect no serious behavioral consequences— nor, indeed, could other patients. It was quite common for the patients to "detect" the pseudopatients' sanity. During the first three hospitalizations, when accurate counts were kept, 35 of a total of 118 patients on the admissions ward voiced their suspicions, some vigorously. "You're not crazy. You're a journalist, or a professor [referring to the continual note-taking]. You're checking up on the hospital." While most of the patients were reassured by the pseudopatient's insistence that he had been sick before he came in but was fine now, some continued to believe that the pseudopatient was sane throughout his hospitalization. The fact that the patients often recognized normality when staff did not raises important questions.

Failure to detect sanity during the course of hospitalization may be due to the fact that physicians operate with a strong bias toward what statisticians call the type 2 error. This is to say that physicians are more inclined to call a healthy person sick (a false positive, type 2) than a sick person healthy (a false negative, type 1). The reasons for this are not hard to find: it is clearly more dangerous to mis-diagnose illness than health. Better to err on the side of caution, to suspect illness even among the healthy.

But what holds for medicine does not hold equally well for psychiatry. Medical illnesses, while unfortunate, are not commonly pejorative. Psychiatric diagnoses, on the contrary, carry with them personal, legal, and social stigmas. It was therefore important to see whether the tendency toward diagnosing the sane insane could be reversed. The following experiment was arranged at a research and teaching hospital whose staff had heard these findings but doubted that such an error could occur in their hospital. The staff was informed that at some time during the following 3 months, one or more pseudopatients would attempt to be admitted into the psychiatric hospital. Each staff member was asked to rate each patient who presented himself at admissions or on the ward according to the likelihood that the patient was a pseudopatient. A 10-point scale was used, with a 1 and 2 reflecting high confidence that the patient was a pseudopatient.

Judgments were obtained on 193 patients who were admitted for psychiatric treatment. All staff who had had sustained contact with or primary responsibility for the patient—attendants, nurses, psychiatrists, physicians, and psychologists—were asked to make judgments. Forty-one patients were alleged, with high confidence, to be pseudopatients by at least one member of the staff. Twenty-three were considered suspect by at least one psychiatrist. Nineteen were suspected by one psychiatrist *and* one other staff member. Actually, no genuine pseudopatient (at least from my group) presented himself during this period.

The experiment is instructive. It indicates that the tendency to designate sane people as insane can be reversed when the stakes (in this case, prestige and diagnostic acumen) are high. But what can be said of the 19 people who were suspected of being "sane" by one psychiatrist and another staff member? Were these people truly "sane," or was it rather the case that in the course of avoiding the type 2 error the staff tended to make more errors of the first sort—calling the crazy "sane"? There is no way of knowing. But one thing is certain: any diagnostic process that lends itself so readily to massive errors of this sort cannot be a very reliable one.

THE STICKINESS OF PSYCHODIAGNOSTIC LABELS

Beyond the tendency to call the healthy sick—a tendency that accounts better for diagnostic behavior on admission than it does for such behavior after a lengthy period of exposure—the data speak to the massive role of labeling in psychiatric assessment. Having once been labeled schizophrenic, there is nothing the pseudopatient can do to overcome this tag. The tag profoundly colors others' perceptions of him and his behavior.

From one viewpoint, these data are hardly surprising, for it has long been known that elements are given meaning by the context in which they occur. Gestalt psychology made this point vigorously, and Asch demonstrated that there are "central" personality traits (such as "warm" versus "cold") which are so powerful that they markedly color the meaning of other information in forming an impression of a given personality.

"Insane," "schizophrenic," "manic-depressive," and "crazy" are probably among the most powerful of such central traits. Once a person is designated abnormal, all of his other behaviors and characteristics are colored by that label. Indeed, that label is so powerful that may of the pseudopatients' normal behaviors were overlooked entirely or profoundly misinterpreted. Some examples may clarify this issue.

Earlier I indicated that there were no changes in the pseudopatient's personal history and current status beyond those of name, employment, and, where necessary, vocation. Otherwise, a veridical description of personal history and circumstances was offered. Those circumstances were not psychotic. How were they made consonant with the diagnosis of psychosis? Or were those diagnoses modified in such a way as to bring them into accord with the circumstances of the pseudopatient's life, as described by him?

As far as I can determine, diagnoses were in no way affected by the relative health of the circumstances of a pseudopatient's life. Rather, the reverse occurred: the perception of his circumstances was shaped entirely by the diagnosis. A clear example of such translation is found in the case of a pseudopatient who had had a close relationship with his mother but was rather remote from his father during his early childhood. During adolescence and beyond, however, his father became a close friend, while his relationship with his mother cooled. His present relationship with his wife was characteristically close and warm.

Apart from occasional angry exchanges, friction was minimal. The children had rarely been spanked. Surely there is nothing especially pathological about such a history. Indeed, many readers may see a similar pattern in their own experiences, with no markedly deleterious consequences. Observe, however, how such a history was translated in the psychopathological context, this from the case summary prepared after the patient was discharged:

> This white 39-year-old male... manifests a long history of considerable ambivalence in close relationships, which begins in early childhood. A warm relationship with his mother cools during his adolescence. A distant relationship to his father is described as becoming very intense. Affective stability is absent. His attempts to control emotionality with his wife and children are punctuated by angry outbursts and, in the case of the children, spankings. And while he says that he has several friends, one senses considerable ambivalence embedded in these relationships also....

The facts of the case were unintentionally distorted by the staff to achieve consistency with a popular theory of the dynamics of a schizophrenic reaction. Nothing of an ambivalent nature had been described in relations with parents, spouse, or friends. To the extent that ambivalence could be inferred, it was probably not greater than is found in all human relationships. It is true the pseudopatient's relationships with his parents changed over time, but in the ordinary context that would hardly be remarkable —indeed, it might very well be expected. Clearly, the meaning ascribed to his verbalizations (that is, ambivalence, affective instability) was determined by the diagnosis: schizophrenia. An entirely different meaning would have been ascribed if it were known that the man was normal.

All pseudopatients took extensive notes publicly. Under ordinary circumstances, such behavior would have raised questions in the minds of observers, as, in fact, it did among patients. Indeed, it seemed so certain that the notes would elicit suspicion that elaborate precautions were taken to remove them from the ward each day. But the precautions proved needless. The closest any staff member came to questioning these notes occurred when one pseudopatient asked his physician what kind of medication he was receiving and began to write down the response. "You needn't write it," he was told gently. "If you have trouble remembering, just ask me again."

If no questions were asked of the pseudopatients, how was their writing interpreted? Nursing records for three patients indicate that the writing was seen as an aspect of their pathological behavior. "Patient engages in writing behavior" was the daily nursing comment on one of the pseudopatients who was never questioned about his writing. Given that the patient is in the hospital, he must be psychologically disturbed. And given that he is disturbed, continuous writing must be a behavioral manifestation of that disturbance, perhaps a subset of the compulsive behaviors that are sometimes correlated with schizophrenia.

One tacit characteristic of psychiatric diagnosis is that it locates the sources of aberration within the individual and only rarely within the complex of stimuli that surrounds him. Consequently, behaviors that are stimulated by the environment are commonly misattributed to the patient's disorder. For example, one kindly nurse found a pseudopatient pacing the long hospital corridors. "Nervous, Mr. X?" she asked. "No, bored," he said.

The notes kept by pseudopatients are full of patient behaviors that were misinterpreted by well-intentioned staff. Often enough, a patient would go "berserk" because he had, wittingly or unwittingly, been mistreated by, say, an attendant. A nurse coming upon the scene would rarely inquire even cursorily into the environmental stimuli of the patient's behavior. Rather, she assumed that his upset derived from his pathology, not from his present interactions with other staff members. Occasionally, the staff might assume that the patient's family (especially when they had recently visited) or other patients had stimulated the outburst. But never were the staff found to assume that one of themselves or the structure of the hospital had anything to do with a patient's behavior. One psychiatrist pointed to a group of patients who were sitting outside the cafeteria entrance half an hour before lunchtime. To a group of young residents he indicated that such behavior was characteristic of the oral-acquisitive nature of the syndrome. It seemed not to occur to him that there were very few things to anticipate in a psychiatric hospital besides eating.

A psychiatric label has a life and an influence of its own. Once the impression has been formed that the patient is schizophrenic, the expectation is that he will continue to be schizophrenic. When a sufficient amount of time has passed, during which the patient has done nothing bizarre, he is considered to be in remission and available for discharge. But the label endures beyond discharge, with the unconfirmed expectation that he will behave as a schizophrenic again. Such labels, conferred by mental health professionals, are as influential on the patient as they are on his relatives and friends, and it should not surprise anyone that the diagnosis acts on all of them as a self-fulfilling prophecy. Eventually, the patient himself accepts the diagnosis, with all of its surplus meanings and expectations, and behaves accordingly.

The inferences to be made from these matters are quite simple. Much as Zigler and Phillips have demonstrated that there is enormous overlap in the symptoms presented by patients who have been variously diagnosed, so there is enormous overlap in the behaviors of the sane and the insane. The sane are not "sane" all of the time. We lose our tempers "for no good reason." We are occasionally depressed or anxious, again for no good reason. And we may find it difficult to get along with one or another person—again for no reason that we can specify. Similarly, the insane are not always insane. Indeed, it was the impression of the pseudopatients while living with them that they were sane for long periods of time—that the bizarre behaviors upon which their diagnoses were allegedly predicated constituted only a small fraction of their total behavior. If it makes no sense to label ourselves permanently depressed on the basis of an occasional depression, then it takes better evidence than is presently available to label all patients insane or schizophrenic on the basis of bizarre behaviors or cognitions. It seems more useful, as Mischel has pointed out, to limit our discussions to *behaviors*, the stimuli that provoke them, and their correlates.

It is not known why powerful impressions of personality traits, such as "crazy" or "insane," arise. Conceivably, when the origins of and stimuli that give rise to a behavior are remote or unknown, or when the behavior strikes us as immutable, trait labels regarding the *behaver* arise. When, on the other hand, the origins and stimuli are known and available, discourse is limited to the behavior itself. Thus, I may hallucinate because I am sleeping, or I may hallucinate because I have ingested a peculiar drug. These are termed sleep-induced hallucinations, or dreams, and drug-induced hallucinations, respectively. But when the stimuli to my hallucinations are unknown, that is called craziness, or schizophrenia—as if that inference were somehow as illuminating as the others.

THE EXPERIENCE OF PSYCHIATRIC HOSPITALIZATION

The term "mental illness" is of recent origin. It was coined by people who were humane in their inclinations and who wanted very much to raise the station of (and the public's sympathies toward) the psychologically disturbed from that of witches and "crazies" to one that was akin to the physically ill. And they were at least partially successful, for the treatment of the mental ill *has* improved considerably over the years. But while treatment has improved, it is doubtful that people really regard the mentally ill in the same way that they view the physically ill. A broken leg is something one recovers from, but mental illness allegedly endures forever. A broken leg does not threaten the observer, but a crazy schizophrenic? There is by now a host of evidence that attitudes toward the mentally ill are characterized by fear, hostility, aloofness, suspicion, and dread. The mentally ill are society's lepers.

That such attitudes infect the general population is perhaps not surprising, only upsetting. But that they affect the professionals—attendants, nurses, physicians, psychologists, and social workers—who treat and deal with the mentally ill is more disconcerting, both because such attitudes are self-evidently pernicious and because they are unwitting. Most mental health professionals would insist that they are sympathetic toward the mentally ill, that they are neither avoidant nor hostile. But it is more likely that an exquisite ambivalence characterizes their relations with psychiatric patients, such that their avowed impulses are only part of their entire attitude. Negative attitudes are there too and can easily be detected. Such attitudes should not surprise us. They are the natural offspring of the labels patients wear and the places in which they are found.

Consider the structure of the typical psychiatric hospital. Staff and patients are strictly segregated. Staff have their own living space, including their dining facilities, bathrooms and assembly places. The glassed quarters that contain the professional staff, which the pseudopatients came to call "the cage," sit out on every dayroom. The staff emerge primarily for caretaking purposes—to give medication, to conduct a therapy or group meeting, to instruct or reprimand a patient. Otherwise, staff keep to themselves, almost as if the disorder that afflicts their charges is somehow catching.

So much is patient-staff segregation the rule that, for four public hospitals in which an attempt was made to measure the degree to which staff and patients mingle, it was necessary to use "time out of the staff cage" as the operational measure. While it was not the case that all time spent out of the cage was spent mingling with patients (attendants, for example, would occasionally emerge to watch television in the dayroom), it was the only way in which one could gather reliable data on time for measuring.

The average amount of time spent by attendants outside of the cage was 11.3 percent (range, 3 to 52 percent). This figure does not represent only time spent mingling with patients, but also includes time spent on such chores as folding laundry, supervising patients while they shave, directing ward clean-up, and sending patients to off-ward activities. It was the relatively rare attendant who spent time talking with patients or playing games with them. It proved impossible to obtain a "percent mingling time" for nurses, since the amount of time they spent out of the cage was too brief. Rather, we counted instances of emergence from the cage. On the average, daytime nurses emerged from the cage 11.5 times per shift, including instances when they left the ward entirely (range, 4 to 39 times). Late afternoon and night nurses were even less available, emerging on the average 9.4 times per shift (range, 4 to 41 times). Data on early morning nurses, who arrived usually after midnight and departed at 8 a.m., are not available because patients were asleep during most of this period.

Physicians, especially psychiatrists, were even less available. They were rarely seen on the wards. Quite commonly, they would be seen only when they arrived and departed, with the remaining time being spent in their offices or in the cage. On the average, physicians emerged on the ward 6.7 times per day (range 1 to 17 times). It proved difficult to make an accurate estimate in this regard, since physicians often maintained hours that allowed them to come and go at different times.

The hierarchical organization of the psychiatric hospital has been commented on before, but the latent meaning of that kind of organization is worth noting again. Those with the most power have least to do with patients, and those with the least power are most involved with them. Recall, however, that the acquisition of role-appropriate behaviors occurs mainly through the observation of others, with the most powerful having the most influence. Consequently, it is understandable that attendants not only spend more time with patients than do any other members of the staff—that is required by their station in the hierarchy —but also, insofar as they learn from their superiors' behavior, spend as little time with patients as they can. Attendants are seen mainly in the cage, which is where the models, the action, and the power are.

I turn now to a different set of studies, these dealing with staff response to patient-initiated contact. It has long been known that the amount of time a person spends with you can be an index of your significance to him. If he initiates and maintains eye contact, there is reason to believe that he is considering your requests and needs. If he pauses to chat or actually stops and talks, there is added reason to infer that he is individuating you. In four hospitals, the pseudopatient approached the staff member with a request which took the following form: "Pardon me, Mr. [or Dr. or Mrs.] X, could you tell me when I will be eligible for grounds privileges?" (or " . . . when I will be presented at the staff meeting?" or " . . . when I am likely to be discharged?"). While the content of the question varied according to the appropriateness of the target and the pseudopatient's (apparent) current needs, the form was always a courteous and relevant request for information. Care was taken never to approach a particular member of the staff more than once a day, lest the staff member become suspicious or irritated. In examining these data, remember that the behavior of the pseudopatients was neither bizarre nor disruptive. One could indeed engage in good conversation with them.

The data for these experiments are shown in Table 1, separately for physicians (column 1) and for nurses and attendants (column 2). Minor differences between these four institutions were overwhelmed by the degree to which staff avoided continuing contacts that patients had initiated. By far, their most common response consisted of either a brief response to the question offered while they were "on the move" and with head averted, or no response at all.

The encounter frequently took the following bizarre form: (pseudopatient) "Pardon me, Dr. X. Could you tell me when I am eligible for grounds privileges?" (physician) "Good morning Dave. How are you today?" (moves off without waiting for a response).

It is instructive to compare these data with data recently obtained at Stanford University. It has been alleged that large and eminent universities are characterized by faculty who are so busy that they have no time for students. For this comparison, a young lady approached individual faculty members who seemed to be walking purposefully to some meeting or teaching engagement and asked them the following questions.

1. "Pardon me, could you direct me to Encina Hall?" (at the medical school: " . . . to the Clinical Research Center?").

Table 1

Self-Initiated Contact by Pseudopatients With Psychiatrists and Nurses and Attendants, Compared With Other Groups

Contact	Psychiatric hospitals		University campus (nonmedical)	University medical center Physicians		
	(1) Psychiatrists	(2) Nurses and attendants	(3) Faculty	(4) "Looking for a psychiatrist"	(5) "Looking for an internist"	(6) No additional comment
Responses						
Moves on, head averted (%)	71	88	0	0	0	0
Makes eye contact (%)	23	10	0	11	0	0
Pauses and chats (%)	2	2	0	11	0	0
Stops and talks (%)	4	0.5	100	78	100	90
Mean number of questions answered (out of 6)	*	*	6	3.8	4.8	4.5
Respondents (No.)	13	47	14	18	15	10
Attempts (No.)	185	1283	14	18	15	10

*Not applicable

2. "Do you know where Fish Annex is?" (there is no Fish Annex at Stanford).
3. "Do you teach here?"
4. "How does one apply for admission to the college?" (at the medical school: " ... to the medical school?").
5. "Is it difficult to get in?"
6. "Is there financial aid?"

Without exception, as can be seen in Table 1 (column 3), all of the questions were answered. No matter how rushed they were, all respondents not only maintained eye contact, but stopped to talk. Indeed, many of the respondents went out of their way to direct or take the questioner to the office she was seeking, to try to locate "Fish Annex," or to discuss with her the possibilities of being admitted to the university.

Similar data, also shown in Table 1 (columns 4, 5, and 6), were obtained in the hospital. Here too, the young lady came prepared with six questions. After the first question, however, she remarked to 18 of her respondents (column 4), "I'm looking for a psychiatrist," and to 15 others (column 5), "I'm looking for an internist." Ten other respondents received no inserted comment (column 6). The general degree of cooperative responses is considerably higher for these university groups than it was for pseudopatients in psychiatric hospitals. Even so, differences are apparent with the medical school setting. Once having indicated that she was looking for a psychiatrist, the degree of cooperation elicited was less than when she sought an internist.

POWERLESSNESS AND DEPERSONALIZATION

Eye contact and verbal contact reflect concern and individuation: their absence, avoidance and depersonalization. The data I have presented do not do justice to the rich daily encounters that grew up around matters of depersonalization and avoidance. I have records of patients who were beaten by staff for the sin of initiating verbal contact. During my own experience, for example, one patient was beaten in the presence of other patients for having approached an attendant and told him, "I like you." Occasionally, punishment meted out to patients for misdemeanors seemed so excessive that it could not be justified by the most radical interpretations of psychiatric canon. Nevertheless, they appeared to go unquestioned. Tempers were often short. A patient who had not heard a call for medication would be roundly excoriated, and the morning attendants would often wake patients with, "Come on, you m—— f——s, out of bed!"

Neither anecdotal nor "hard" data can convey the overwhelming sense of powerlessness which invades the individual as he is continually exposed to the depersonalization of the psychiatric hospital. It hardly matters *which* psychiatric hospital —the excellent public ones and the very plush private hospital were better than the rural and shabby ones in this regard, but again, the features that psychiatric hospitals had in common overwhelmed by far their apparent differences.

Powerlessness was evident everywhere. The patient is deprived of many of his legal rights by dint of his psychiatric commitment. He is shorn of credibility by virtue of his psychiatric label. His freedom of movement is restricted. He cannot initiate contact with the staff, but may only respond to such overtures as they make. Personal privacy is minimal. Patient quarters and possessions can be entered and examined by any staff member, for whatever reason. His personal history and anguish are available to any staff member (often including the "grey lady" and "candy striper" volunteer) who chooses to read his folder, regardless of their therapeutic relationship to him. His personal hygiene and waste evacuation are often monitored. The water closets may have no doors.

At times, the depersonalization reached such proportions that pseudopatients had the sense that they were invisible, or at least unworthy of account. Upon being admitted, I and other pseudopatients took the initial physical examination in a semipublic room, where staff members went about their own business as if we were not there.

On the ward, attendants delivered verbal and occasionally serious physical abuse to patients in the presence of other observing patients, some of whom (the pseudopatients) were writing it all down. Abusive behavior, on the other hand, terminated quite abruptly when other staff members were known to be coming. Staff are credible witnesses. Patients are not.

A nurse unbuttoned her uniform to adjust her brassiere in the presence of an entire ward of viewing men. One did not have the sense that she was being seductive. Rather, she didn't notice us. A group of staff persons might point to a patient in the dayroom and discuss him animatedly, as if he were not there.

One illuminating instance of depersonalization and invisibility occurred with regard to medications. All told, the pseudopatients were administered nearly 2100 pills, including Elavil, Stelazine, Compazine, and Thorazine, to name but a few. (That such a variety of medications should have been administered to patients presenting identical symptoms is itself worthy of note.) Only two were swallowed. The rest were either pocketed or deposited in the toilet. The pseudopatients were not alone in this. Although I have no precise records on how many patients rejected their medications, the pseudopatients frequently found the medications of other patients in the toilet before they deposited their own. As long as they were cooperative, their behavior and the pseudopatients' own in this matter, as in other important matters, went unnoticed throughout.

Reactions to such depersonalization among pseudopatients were intense. Although they had come to the hospital as participant observers and were fully aware that they did not "belong," they nevertheless found themselves caught up in and fighting the process of depersonalization. Some examples: a graduate student in psychology asked his wife to bring his textbooks to the hospital so he could "catch up on his homework"—this despite the elaborate precautions taken to conceal his professional association. The same student, who had trained for quite some time to get into the hospital, and who had looked forward to the experience, "remembered" some drag races that he had wanted to see on the weekend and insisted that he be discharged by that time. Another pseudopatient attempted a romance with a nurse. Subsequently, he informed the staff that he was applying for admission to graduate school in psychology and was very likely to be admitted, since a graduate professor was one of his regular hospital visitors. The same person began to engage in psychotherapy with other patients—all of this as a way of becoming a person in an impersonal environment.

THE SOURCES OF DEPERSONALIZATION

What are the origins of depersonalization? I have already mentioned two. First, are attitudes held by all of us toward the mentally ill—including those who treat them—attitudes characterized by fear, distrust, and horrible expectations on the other. Our ambivalence leads us, in this instance as in others, to avoidance.

Second, and not entirely separate, the hierarchical structure of the psychiatric hospital facilitates depersonalization. Those who are at the top have least to do with patients, and their behavior inspires the rest of the staff. Average daily contact with psychiatrists, psychologists, residents, and physicians combined ranged from 3.9 to 25.1 minutes, with an overall mean of 6.8 (six pseudopatients over a total of 129 days of hospitalization). Included in this average are time spent in the admissions interview, ward meetings in the presence of a senior staff member, group and individual psychotherapy contacts, case presentation conferences, and discharge meetings. Clearly, patients do not spend much time in interpersonal contact with doctoral staff. And doctoral staff serve as models for nurses and attendants.

There are probably other sources. Psychiatric installations are presently in serious financial straits. Staff shortages are pervasive, staff time at a premium. Something has to give, and that something is patient contact. Yet, while financial stresses are realities, too much can be made of them. I have the impression that the psychological forces that result in depersonalization are much stronger than the fiscal ones and that the addition of more staff would not correspondingly improve patient care in this regard. The incidence of staff meetings and the enormous amount of record-keeping on patients, for example, have not been as substantially reduced as has patient contact. Priorities exist, even during hard times. Patient contact is not a significant priority in the traditional psychiatric hospital, and fiscal pressures do not account for this. Avoidance and depersonalization may.

Heavy reliance upon psychotropic medication tacitly contributes to depersonalization by convincing staff that treatment is indeed being conducted and that further patient contact may not be necessary. Even here, however, caution needs to be exercised in understanding the role of psychotropic drugs. If patients were powerful rather than powerless, if they were viewed as interesting individuals rather than diagnostic entities, if they were socially significant rather than social lepers, if their anguish truly and wholly compelled our sympathies and concerns, would we not *seek* contact with them, despite the availability of medications? Perhaps for the pleasure of it all?

THE CONSEQUENCES OF LABELING AND DEPERSONALIZATION

Whenever the ratio of what is known to what needs to be known approaches zero, we tend to invent "knowledge" and assume that we understand more than we actually do. We seem unable to acknowledge that we simply don't know. The needs for diagnosis and remediation of behavioral and emotional problems are enormous. But rather than acknowledge that we are just embarking on understanding, we continue to label patients "schizophrenic," "manic-depressive," and "insane," as if in those words we had captured the essence of understanding. The facts of the matter are that we have known for a long time that diagnoses are often not useful or reliable, but we have nevertheless continued to use them. We now know that we cannot distinguish insanity from sanity. It is depressing to consider how that information will be used.

Not merely depressing, but frightening. How many people, one wonders, are sane but not recognized as such in our psychiatric institutions? How many have been needlessly stripped of their privileges of citizenship, from the right to vote and drive to that of handling their own accounts? How many have feigned insanity in order to avoid the criminal consequences of their behavior, and, conversely, how many would rather stand trial than live interminably in a psychiatric hospital—but are wrongly thought to be mentally ill? How many have been stigmatized by well-intentioned, but nevertheless erroneous, diagnoses? On the last point, recall again that a "type 2 error" in psychiatric diagnosis does not have the same consequences it does in medical diagnosis. A diagnosis of cancer that has been found to be in error is cause for celebration. But psychiatric diagnoses are rarely found to be in error. The label sticks, a mark of inadequacy forever.

Finally, how many patients might be "sane" outside the psychiatric hospital but seem insane in it—not because craziness resides in them, as it were, but because they are responding to a bizarre setting, one that may be unique to institutions which harbor nether people? Goffman calls the process of socialization to such institutions "mortification"—an apt metaphor that includes the processes of depersonalization that have been described here. And while it is impossible to know whether the pseudopatients' responses to these processes are characteristic of all inmates—they were after all, not real patients—it is difficult to believe that these processes of socialization to a psychiatric hospital provide useful attitudes or habits of response for living in the "real world."

SUMMARY AND CONCLUSIONS

It is clear that we cannot distinguish the sane from the insane in psychiatric hospitals. The hospital itself imposes a special environment in which the meanings of behavior can easily be misunderstood. The consequences to patients hospitalized in such an environment—the powerlessness, depersonalization, segregation, mortification, and self-labeling—seem undoubtedly countertherapeutic.

I do not, even now, understand this problem well enough to perceive solutions. But two matters seem to have some promise. The first concerns the proliferation of community mental health facilities, of crisis intervention centers, of the human potential movement, and of behavior therapies that, for all of their own problems, tend to avoid psychiatric labels, to focus on specific problems and behaviors, and to retain the individual in a relatively nonpejorative environment.

Clearly, to the extent that we refrain from sending the distressed to insane places, our impressions of them are less likely to be distorted. (The risk of distorted perceptions, it seems to me, is always present, since we are much more sensitive to an individual's behaviors and verbalizations than we are to the subtle contextual stimuli that often promote them. At issue here is a matter of magnitude. And, as I have shown, the magnitude of distortion is exceedingly high in the extreme context that is a psychiatric hospital).

The second matter that might prove promising speaks to the need to increase the sensitivity of mental health workers and researchers to the *Catch-22* position of psychiatric patients. Simply reading materials in this area will be of help to some such workers and researchers. For others, directly experiencing the impact of psychiatric hospitalization will be of enormous use. Clearly, further research into the social psychology of such total institutions will both facilitate treatment and deepen understanding.

I and the other pseudopatients in the psychiatric setting had distinctly negative reactions. We do not pretend to describe the subjective experiences of true patients. Theirs may be different from ours, particularly with the passage of time and the necessary process of adaptation to one's environment. But we can and do speak to the relatively more objective indices of treatment within the hospital. It could be a mistake, and a very unfortunate one, to consider that what happened to us derived from malice or stupidity on the part of the staff. Quite the contrary, our overwhelming impression of them was of people who really cared, who were committed and who were uncommonly intelligent. Where they failed, as they sometimes did painfully, it would be more accurate to attribute those failures to the environment in which they too, found themselves than to personal callousness. Their perceptions and behavior were controlled by the situation, rather than being motivated by a malicious disposition. In a more benign environment, one that was less attached to global diagnosis, their behaviors and judgments might have been more benign and effective.

NO

Robert L. Spitzer

ON PSEUDOSCIENCE IN SCIENCE, LOGIC IN REMISSION AND PSYCHIATRIC DIAGNOSIS

Some foods taste delicious but leave a bad aftertaste. So it is with Rosenhan's study, "On Being Sane in Insane Places" (Rosenhan, 1973a), which, by virtue of the prestige and wide distribution of *Science*, the journal in which it appeared, provoked a furor in the scientific community. That the *Journal of Abnormal Psychology*, at this late date, chooses to explore the study's strengths and weaknesses is a testament not only to the importance of the issues that the study purports to deal with but to the impact that the study has had in the mental health community.

Rosenhan apparently believes that psychiatric diagnosis is of no value. There is nothing wrong with his designing a study the results of which might dramatically support this view. However, "On Being Sane in Insane Places" is pseudoscience presented as science. Just as his pseudopatients were diagnosed at discharge as "schizophrenia, in remission," so a careful examination of this study's methods, results, and conclusions leads me to a diagnosis of "logic, in remission."

Let us summarize the study's central question, the methods used, the results reported, and Rosenhan's conclusions. Rosenhan (1973a) states the basic issue simply: "Do the salient characteristics that lead to diagnoses reside in the patients themselves or in the environments and contexts in which observers find them?" Rosenhan proposed that by getting normal people who had never had symptoms of serious psychiatric disorders admitted to psychiatric hospitals "and then determining whether they were discovered to be sane" was an adequate method of studying this question. Therefore, eight "sane" people, pseudopatients, gained secret admission to 12 different hospitals with a single complaint of hearing voices. Upon admission to the psychiatric ward, the pseudopatients ceased simulating any symptoms of abnormality.

The diagnostic results were that 11 of the 12 diagnoses on admission were schizophrenia and 1 was manic-depressive psychosis. At discharge, all of the patients were given the same diagnosis, but were qualified as "in remission."[1]

From Robert L. Spitzer, "On Pseudoscience in Science, Logic in Remission and Psychiatric Diagnosis: A Critique of 'On Being Sane in Insane Places,'" *Journal of Abnormal Psychology*, vol. 84 (1975), pp. 442–452. Copyright © 1975 by The American Psychological Association. Reprinted by permission.

Despite their "show of sanity" the pseudopatients were never detected by any of the professional staff, nor were any questions raised about their authenticity during the entire hospitalization.

Rosenhan (1973a) concluded: "It is clear that we cannot distinguish the sane from the insane in psychiatric hospitals" (p. 257). According to him, what is needed is the avoidance of "global diagnosis," as exemplified by such diagnoses as schizophrenia or manic-depressive psychosis, and attention should be directed instead to "behaviors, the stimuli that provoke them, and their correlates."

THE CENTRAL QUESTION

One hardly knows where to begin. Let us first acknowledge the potential importance of the study's central research question. Surely, if psychiatric diagnoses are, to quote Rosenhan, "only in the minds of the observers," and do not reflect any characteristics inherent in the patient, then they obviously can be of no use in helping patients. However, the study immediately becomes confused when Rosenhan suggests that this research question can be answered by studying whether or not the "sanity" of pseudopatients in a mental hospital can be discovered. Rosenhan, a professor of law and psychology, knows that the terms "sane" and "insane" are legal, not psychiatric, concepts. He knows that no psychiatrist makes a diagnosis of "sanity" or "insanity" and that the true meaning of these terms, which varies from state to state, involves the inability to appreciate right from wrong—an issue that is totally irrelevant to this study.

DETECTING THE SANITY OF A PSEUDOPATIENT

However, if we are forced to use the terms "insane" (to mean roughly showing signs of serious mental disturbance) and "sane" (the absence of such signs), then clearly there are three possible meanings to the concept of "detecting the sanity" of a pseudopatient who feigns mental illness on entry to a hospital, but then acts "normal" throughout his hospital stay. The first is the recognition, when he is first seen, that the pseudopatient is feigning insanity as he attempts to gain admission to the hospital. This would be detecting sanity in a sane person simulating insanity. The second would be the recognition, after having observed him acting normally during his hospitalization, that the pseudopatient was initially feigning insanity. This would be detecting that the currently sane never was insane. Finally, the third possible meaning would be the recognition, during hospitalization, that the pseudopatient, though initially appearing to be "insane," was no longer showing signs of psychiatric disturbance.

These elementary distinctions of "detecting sanity in the insane" are crucial to properly interpreting the results of the study. The reader is misled by Rosenhan's implication that the first two meanings of detecting the sanity of the pseudopatient to be a fraud, are at all relevant to the central research question. Furthermore, he obscures the true results of his study—because they fail to support his conclusion—when the third meaning of detecting sanity is considered, that is, a recognition that after their admission as "insane," the pseudopatients were not psychiatrically disturbed while in the hospital.

Let us examine these three possible meanings of detecting the sanity of the pseudopatient, their logical relation to the central question of the study, and the actual results obtained and the validity of Rosenhan's conclusions.

THE PATIENT IS NO LONGER "INSANE"

We begin with the third meaning of detecting sanity. It is obvious that if the psychiatrists judged the pseudopatients as seriously disturbed while they acted "normal" in the hospital, this would be strong evidence that their assessments were being influenced by the context in which they were making their examination rather than the actual behavior of the patient, which is the central research question. (I suspect that many readers will agree with Hunter who, in a letter to *Science* (Hunter, 1973), pointed out that, "The pseudopatients did *not* behave normally in the hospital. Had their behavior been normal, they would have walked to the nurses' station and said, 'Look, I am a normal person who tried to see if I could get into the hospital by behaving in a crazy way or saying crazy things. It worked and I was admitted to the hospital, but now I would like to be discharged from the hospital'" [p. 361].)

What were the results? According to Rosenhan, all the patients were diagnosed at discharge as "in remission."[2] The meaning of "in remission" is clear: It means without signs of illness. Thus, all of the psychiatrists apparently recognized that all of the pseudopatients were, to use Rosenhan's term, "sane." However, lest the reader appreciate the significance of these findings, Rosenhan (1973a) quickly gives a completely incorrect interpretation: "If the pseudopatient was

to be discharged, he must naturally be 'in remission'; but he was not sane, nor, in the institution's view, had he ever been sane" (p. 252). Rosenhan's implication is clear: The patient was diagnosed "in remission" not because the psychiatrist correctly assessed the patient's hospital behavior but only because the patient had to be discharged. Is this interpretation warranted?

I am sure that most readers who are not familiar with the details of psychiatric diagnostic practice assume, from Rosenhan's account, that it is common for schizophrenic patients to be diagnosed "in remission" when discharged from a hospital. As a matter of fact, it is extremely unusual. The reason is that a schizophrenic is rarely completely asymptomatic at discharge. Rosenhan does not report any data concerning the discharge diagnoses of the real schizophrenic patients in the 12 hospitals used in his study. However, I can report on the frequency of a discharge diagnosis of schizophrenia "in remission" at my hospital, the New York State Psychiatric Institute, a research, teaching, and community hospital where diagnoses are made in a routine fashion, undoubtedly no different from the 12 hospitals of Rosenhan's study. I examined the official book that the record room uses to record the discharge diagnoses and their statistical codes for all patients. Of the over 300 patients discharged in the last year with a diagnosis of schizophrenia, not one was diagnosed "in remission." It is only possible to code a diagnosis of "in remission" by adding a fifth digit (5) to the 4-digit code number for the subtype of schizophrenia (e.g., paranoid schizophrenia is coded as 295.3, but paranoid schizophrenia "in remission" is coded as 295.35). I therefore realized that a psychiatrist might intend to make a discharge diagnosis of "in remission" but fail to use the fifth digit, so that the official recording of the diagnosis would not reflect his full assessment. I therefore had research assistants read the discharge summaries of the last 100 patients whose discharge diagnosis was schizophrenia to see how often the term "in remission," "recovered," "no longer ill," or "asymptomatic" was used, even if not recorded by use of the fifth digit in the code number. The result was that only one patient, who was diagnosed paranoid schizophrenia, was described in the summary as being "in remission" at discharge. The fifth digit code was not used.

To substantiate my view that the practice at my hospital of rarely giving a discharge diagnosis of schizophrenia "in remission" is not unique, I had a research assistant call the record room librarians of 12 psychiatric hospitals, chosen catch as catch can.[3] They were told that we were interested in knowing their estimate of how often, at their hospital, schizophrenics were discharged "in remission" (or "no longer ill" or "asymptomatic"). The calls revealed that 11 of the 12 hospitals indicated that the term was either never used or, at most, used for only a handful of patients in a year. The remaining hospital, a private hospital, estimated that the terms were used in roughly 7 percent of the discharge diagnoses.

This leaves us with the conclusion that, because 11 of the 12 pseudopatients were discharged as "schizophrenia in remission," a discharge diagnosis that is rarely given to real schizophrenics, the diagnoses given to the pseudopatients were a function of the patients' behaviors and not of the setting (psychiatric hospital) in which the diagnoses were made. In fact, we must marvel that 11 psychiatrists all acted so rationally as to use at discharge the category of "in remission" or its equivalent, a category that is rarely used with real schizophrenic patients.

It is not only in his discharge diagnosis that the psychiatrist had an opportunity to assess the patient's true condition incorrectly. In the admission mental status examination, during a progress note or in his discharge note the psychiatrist could have described any of the pseudopatients as "still psychotic," "probably still hallucinating but denies it now," "loose associations," or "inappropriate affect." Because Rosenhan had access to all of this material, his failure to report such judgments of continuing serious psychopathology strongly suggests that they were never made.

All pseudopatients took extensive notes publicly to obtain data on staff and patient behavior. Rosenhan claims that the nursing records indicate that "the writing was seen as an aspect of their pathological behavior." The only datum presented to support this claim is that the daily nursing comment on one of the pseudopatients was, "Patient engaged in writing behavior." Because nursing notes frequently and intentionally comment on nonpathological activities that patients engage in so that other staff members have some knowledge of how the patient spends his time, this particular nursing note in no way supports Rosenhan's thesis. Once again, the failure of Rosenhan to provide data regarding instances where normal hospital behavior was categorized as pathological is remarkable. The closest that Rosenhan comes to providing such data is his report of an instance where a kindly nurse asked if a pseudopatient, who was pacing the long hospital corridors because of boredom, was "nervous." It was, after all, a question and not a final judgment.

Let us now examine the relation between the other two meanings of detecting sanity in the pseudopatients: the recognition that the pseudopatient was a fraud, either when he sought admission to the hospital or during this hospital stay, and the central research question.

DETECTING "SANITY" BEFORE ADMISSION

Whether or not psychiatrists are able to detect individuals who feign psychiatric symptoms is an interesting question but clearly of no relevance to the issue of whether or not the salient characteristics that lead to diagnoses reside in the patient's behavior or in the minds of the observers. After all, a psychiatrist who believes in a pseudopatient who feigns a symptom *is* responding to the pseudopatient's behavior. And Rosenhan does not blame the psychiatrist for believing the pseudopatient's fake symptom of hallucinations. He blames him for the diagnosis of schizophrenia. Rosenhan (1973b) states:

> The issue is not that the psychiatrist believed him. Neither is it whether the pseudopatient should have been admitted to the psychiatric hospital in the first place.... The issue is the diagnostic leap that was made between the single presenting symptom, hallucinations, and the diagnosis schizophrenia (or in one case, manic-depressive psychosis). Had the pseudopatients been diagnosed "hallucinating," there would have been no further need to examine the diagnosis issue. The diagnosis of hallucinations implies only that: no more. The presence of hallucinations does not itself define

the presence of "schizophrenia." And schizophrenia may or may not include hallucinations. (p. 366)

Unfortunately, as judged by many of the letters to *Science* commenting on the study (Letters to the editor, 1973), many readers, including psychiatrists, accepted Rosenhan's thesis that it was irrational for the psychiatrists to have made an initial diagnosis of schizophrenia as *the most likely condition* on the basis of a single symptom. In my judgment, these readers were wrong. Their acceptance of Rosenhan's thesis was aided by the content of the pseudopatients' auditory hallucinations, which were voices that said "empty," "hollow," and "thud." According to Rosenhan (1973a), these symptoms were chosen because of "their apparent similarity to existential symptoms [and] the *absence* of a single report of existential psychoses in the literature" (p. 251). The implication is that if the content of specific symptoms has never been reported in the literature, then a psychiatrist should somehow know that the symptom is fake. Why then, according to Rosenhan, should the psychiatrist have made a diagnosis of hallucinating? This is absurd. Recently I saw a patient who kept hearing a voice that said, "It's O.K. It's O.K." I know of no such report in the literature. So what? I agree with Rosenhan that there has never been a report of an "existential psychosis." However, the diagnoses made were schizophrenia and manic-depressive psychosis, not existential psychosis.

DIFFERENTIAL DIAGNOSIS OF AUDITORY HALLUCINATIONS

Rosenhan is entitled to believe that psychiatric diagnoses are of no use and therefore should not have been given to the pseudopatients. However, it makes no sense for him to claim that within a diagnostic framework it was irrational to consider schizophrenia seriously as the most likely condition without his presenting a consideration of the differential diagnosis. Let me briefly give what I think is a reasonable differential diagnosis, based on the presenting picture of the pseudopatient when he applied for admission to the hospital.

Rosenhan says that "beyond alleging the symptoms and falsifying name, vocation, and employment, no further alterations of person, history, or circumstances were made" (p. 251). However, clearly the clinical picture includes not only the symptom (auditory hallucinations) but also the desire to enter a psychiatric hospital, from which it is reasonable to conclude that the symptom is a source of significant distress. (How often did the admitting psychiatrist suggest what would seem to be reasonable care: outpatient treatment? Did the pseudopatient have to add other complaints to justify inpatient treatment?) This, plus the knowledge that the auditory hallucinations are of 3 weeks duration,[4] establishes the hallucinations as significant symptoms of psychopathology as distinguished from so-called "pseudohallucinations" (hallucinations while falling asleep or awakening from sleep, or intense imagination with the voice heard from inside of the head).

Auditory hallucinations can occur in several kinds of mental disorders. The absence of a history of alcohol, drug abuse, or some other toxin, the absence of any signs of physical illness (such as high fever), and the absence of evidence of distractibility, impairment in concentration, memory or orientation, and a negative neurological examination all make an organic psychosis extremely unlikely. The absence of a recent precipitating stress rules out a transient situational disturbance of psychotic intensity or (to use a nonofficial category) hysterical psychosis. The absence of a profound disturbance in mood rules out an effective psychosis (we are not given the mental status findings for the patient who was diagnosed manic-depressive psychosis).

What about simulating mental illness? Psychiatrists know that occasionally an individual who has something to gain from being admitted to a psychiatric hospital will exaggerate or even feign psychiatric symptoms. This is a genuine diagnostic problem that psychiatrists and other physicians occasionally confront and is called "malingering." However, with the pseudopatients there was no reason to believe that any of them had anything to gain from being admitted into a psychiatric hospital except relief from their alleged complaint, and therefore no reason to suspect that the illness was feigned. Dear Reader: There is only one remaining diagnosis for the presenting symptom of hallucinations under these conditions in the classification of mental disorders used in this country, and that is schizophrenia.

Admittedly, there is a hitch to a definitive diagnosis of schizophrenia: Almost invariably there are other signs of the disorder present, such as poor premorbid adjustment, affective blunting, delusions, or signs of thought disorder. I would hope that if I had been one of the 12 psychiatrists presented with such a patient, I would have been struck by the lack of other signs of the disorder, but I am rather sure that having no reason to doubt the authenticity of the patients' claim of auditory hallucinations, I also would have been fooled into noting schizophrenia as the most likely diagnosis.

What does Rosenhan really mean when he objects to the diagnosis of schizophrenia because it was based on a "single symptom"? Does he believe that there are real patients with the single symptom of auditory hallucinations who are misdiagnosed as schizophrenic when they actually have some other condition? If so, what is the nature of that condition? Is Rosenhan's point that the psychiatrist should have used "diagnosis deferred," a category that is available but rarely used? I would have no argument with this conclusion. Furthermore, if he had presented data from real patients indicating how often patients are erroneously diagnosed on the basis of inadequate information and what the consequences were, it would have been a real contribution.

Until now, I have assumed that the pseudopatients presented only one symptom of psychiatric disorder. Actually, we know very little about how the pseudopatients presented themselves. What did the pseudopatients say in the study reported in *Science*, when asked as they must have been, what effect the hallucinations were having on their lives and why they were seeking admission into a hospital? The reader would be much more confident that a single presenting symptom was involved if Rosenhan had made available for each pseudopatient the actual admission work-up from the hospital record.

DETECTING SANITY
AFTER ADMISSION

Let us now examine the last meaning of detecting sanity in the pseudopatients, namely, the psychiatrist's recognition, *after* observing him act normally during his hospitalization, that the pseudopatient was initially feigning insanity and its relation to the central research question. If a diagnostic condition, by definition, is always chronic and never remits, it would be irrational not to question the original diagnosis if a patient were later found to be asymptomatic. As applied to this study, if the concept of schizophrenia did not admit the possibility of recovery, then failure to question the original diagnosis when the pseudopatients were no longer overtly ill would be relevant to the central research question. It would be an example of the psychiatrist allowing the context of the hospital environment to influence his diagnostic behavior. But neither any psychiatric textbook nor the American Psychiatric Association's *Diagnostic and Statistical Manual of Mental Disorders* (American Psychiatric Association, 1968) suggests that mental illnesses endure forever. Oddly enough, it is Rosenhan (1973a) who, without any reference to the psychiatric literature, says: "A broken leg is something one recovers from, but mental illness allegedly endures forever" (p. 254). Who, other than Rosenhan, alleges it?

As Rosenhan should know, although some American psychiatrists restrict the label of schizophrenia to mean chronic or process schizophrenia, most American psychiatrists include an acute subtype. Thus, the *Diagnostic and Statistical Manual*, in describing the subtype, acute schizophrenic episode, states that "in many cases the patient recovers within weeks."

A similar straw man is created when Rosenhan (1973a) says,

> The insane are not always insane... the bizarre behaviors upon which their (the pseudopatients) behaviors were

allegedly predicated constituted only a small fraction of their total behavior. If it makes no sense to label ourselves permanently depressed on the basis of an occasional depression, then it takes better evidence than is presently available to label all patients insane or schizophrenic on the basis of behaviors or cognitions. (p. 254)

Who ever said that the behaviors that indicate schizophrenia or any other diagnostic category comprise the total of a patient's behavior? A diagnosis of schizophrenia does not mean that all of the patient's behavior is schizophrenic anymore than a diagnosis of carcinoma of the liver means that all of the patient's body is diseased.

Does Rosenhan at least score a point by demonstrating that, although the professional staff never considered the possibility that the pseudopatient was a fraud, this possibility was often considered by other patients? Perhaps, but I am not so sure. Let us not forget that all of the pseudopatients "took extensive notes publicly." Obviously this was highly unusual patient behavior and Rosenhan's quote from a suspicious patient suggests the importance it had in focusing the other patients' attention on the pseudopatients: "You're not crazy. You're a journalist or a professor (referring to the continual note-taking). You're checking up on the hospital." (Rosenhan, 1973a, p. 252)

Rosenhan presents ample evidence, which I find no reason to dispute, that the professional staff spent little time actually with the pseudopatients. The note-taking may easily have been overlooked, and therefore they developed no suspicion that the pseudopatients had simulated illness to gain entry into the hospital. Because there were no pseudopatients who did not engage in such unusual behaviors, the reader cannot assess the significance of the patients' suspicions of fraud when the professional staff did not. I would predict, however, that a pseudopatient in a ward of patients with mixed diagnostic conditions would have no difficulty in masquerading convincingly as a true patient to both staff and patients if he did nothing unusual to draw attention to himself.

Rosenhan presents one way in which the diagnosis affected the psychiatrist's perception of the patient's circumstances: Historical facts of the case were often distorted by the staff to achieve consistency with psychodynamic theories. Here, for the first time, I believe Rosenhan has hit the mark. What he described happens all the time and often makes attendance at clinical case conferences extremely painful, especially for those with a logical mind and a research orientation. Although his observation is correct, it would seem to be more a consequence of individuals attempting to rearrange facts to comply with an unproven etiological theory than a consequence of diagnostic labeling. One could as easily imagine a similar process occurring when a weak-minded, behaviorally-oriented clinician attempts to rewrite the patient's history to account for "hallucinations reinforced by attention paid to patient by family members when patient complains of hearing voices." Such is the human condition.

One final finding requires comment. In order to determine whether "the tendency toward diagnosing the sane insane could be reversed," the staff of a research and teaching hospital was informed that at some time during the following three months, one or more pseudopatients would attempt to be admitted. No such attempt was actually made. Yet approximately 10 percent of the 193 real patients were suspected by two or more staff members (we are not told how many made judgments) to be pseudopatients. Rosenhan (1973a) concluded: "Any diagnostic process that lends itself so readily to massive errors of this sort cannot be a very reliable one" (p. 179). My conclusion is that this experimental design practically assures only one outcome.

ELEMENTARY PRINCIPLES OF RELIABILITY OF CLASSIFICATION

Some very important principles that are relevant to the design of Rosenhan's study are taught in elementary psychology courses and should not be forgotten. One of them is that a measurement or classification procedure is not reliable or unreliable in itself but only in its application to a specific population. There are serious problems in the reliability of psychiatric diagnosis as it is applied to the population to which psychiatric diagnoses are ordinarily given. However, I fail to see, and Rosenhan does not even attempt to show, how the reliability of psychiatric diagnoses applied to a population of pseudopatients (or one including the threat of pseudopatients). The two populations are just not the same. Kety (1974) has expressed it dramatically:

If I were to drink a quart of blood and, concealing what I had done, come to the emergency room of any hospital vomiting blood, the behavior of the staff would be quite predictable. If they labeled and treated me as having a bleeding peptic ulcer, I doubt that I could argue convincingly that medical science does not know how to diagnose that condition. (p. 959)

(I have no doubt that if the condition known as pseudopatient ever assumed epidemic proportions among admittants to psychiatric hospitals, psychiatrists would in time become adept at identifying them, though at what risk to real patients, I do not know.)

ATTITUDES TOWARD THE INSANE

I shall not dwell on the latter part of Rosenhan's study, which deals with the experience of psychiatric hospitalization. Because some of the hospitals participated in residency training programs and were research oriented, I find it hard to believe that conditions were quite as bad as depicted, but they may well be. I have always believed that psychiatrists should spend more time on psychiatric wards to appreciate how mind dulling the experience must be for patients. However, Rosenhan does not stop at documenting the horrors of life on a psychiatric ward. He asserts, without a shred of evidence from his study, that "negative attitudes [toward psychiatric patients] are the natural offspring of the labels patients wear and the places in which they are found." This is nonsense. In recent years large numbers of chronic psychiatric patients, many of them chronic schizophrenics and geriatric patients with organic brain syndromes, have been discharged from state hospitals and placed in communities that have no facilities to deal with them. The affected communities are up in arms not primarily because they are mental patients labeled with psychiatric diagnoses (because the majority are not recognized as ex-patients) but because the behavior of some of them is sometimes incomprehensible, deviant, strange, and annoying.

There are at least two psychiatric diagnoses that are defined by the presence of single behaviors, much as Rosenhan would prefer a diagnosis of hallucinations to a diagnosis of schizophrenia. They are alcoholism and drug abuse. Does society have negative attitudes toward these individuals because of the diagnostic label attached to them by psychiatrists or because of their behavior?

THE USES OF DIAGNOSIS

Rosenhan believes that the pseudopatients should have been diagnosed as having hallucinations of unknown origin. It is not clear what he thinks the diagnosis should have been if the pseudopatients had been sufficiently trained to talk, at times, incoherently, and had complained of difficulty in thinking clearly, lack of emotion, and that their thoughts were being broadcast so that strangers knew what they were thinking. Is Rosenhan perhaps suggesting multiple diagnoses of (a) hallucinations, (b) difficulty thinking clearly, (c) lack of emotion, and (d) incoherent speech... all of unknown origin?

It is no secret that we lack a full understanding of such conditions as schizophrenia and manic-depressive illness, but are we quite as ignorant as Rosenhan would have us believe? Do we not know, for example, that hallucinations of voices accusing the patient of sin are associated with depressed affect, diurnal mood variation, loss of appetite, and insomnia? What about hallucinations of God's voice issuing commandments, associated with euphoric affect, psychomotor excitement, and accelerated and disconnected speech? Is this not also an entirely different condition?

There is a purpose to psychiatric diagnosis (Spitzer & Wilson, 1975). It is to enable mental health professionals to (a) communicate with each other about the subject matter of their concern, (b) comprehend the pathological processes involved in psychiatric illness, and (c) control psychiatric disorders. Control consists of the ability to predict outcome, prevent the disorder from developing, and treat it once it has developed. Any serious discussion of the validity of psychiatric diagnosis, or suggestions for alternative systems of classifying psychological disturbance, must address itself to these purposes of psychiatric diagnosis.

In terms of its ability to accomplish these purposes, I would say that psychiatric diagnosis is moderately effective as a shorthand way of communicating the presence of constellations of signs and symptoms that tend to cluster together, is woefully inadequate in helping us understand the pathological processes of psychiatric disorders, but does offer considerable help in the control of many mental disorders. Control is possible because psychiatric diagnosis often yields information of value in predicting the likely course of illness (e.g., an early recovery, chronicity, or recurrent episodes) and because for many mental disorders it is useful in suggesting the best available treatment.

Let us return to the three different clinical conditions that I described, each of which had auditory hallucinations as one of its manifestations. The reader will have no difficulty in identifying the three hypothetical conditions as schizophrenia, psychotic depression, and mania. Anyone familiar with the literature on psychiatric treatment will know that there are numerous well-controlled studies (Klein

& Davis, 1969) indicating the superiority of the major tranquilizers for the treatment of schizophrenia, of electroconvulsive therapy for the treatment of psychotic depression and, more recently, of lithium carbonate for the treatment of mania. Furthermore, there is convincing evidence that these three conditions, each of which is often accompanied by hallucinations, are influenced by separate genetic factors. As Kety (1974) said, "If schizophrenia is a myth, it is a myth with a strong genetic component."

Should psychiatric diagnosis be abandoned for a purely descriptive system that focuses on simple phenotypic behaviors before it has been demonstrated that such an approach is more useful as a guide to successful treatment or for understanding the role of genetic factors? I think not. (I have a vision. Traditional psychiatric diagnosis has long been forgotten. At a conference on behavioral classification, a keen research investigator proposes that the category "hallucinations of unknown etiology" be subdivided into three different groups based on associated symptomatology. The first group is characterized by depressed affect, diurnal mood variation, and so on, the second group by euphoric mood, psychomotor excitement....)

If psychiatric diagnosis is not quite as bad as Rosenhan would have us believe, that does not mean that it is all that good. What is the reliability of psychiatric diagnosis prior to 1972? Spitzer & Fleiss (1974) revealed that "reliability is only satisfactory for three categories: mental deficiencies, organic brain syndrome, and alcoholism. The level of reliability is no better than fair for psychosis and schizophrenia, and is poor for the remaining categories." So be it. But where did Rosenhan get the idea that

psychiatry is the only medical specialty that is plagued by inaccurate diagnosis? Studies have shown serious unreliability in the diagnosis of pulmonary disorders (Fletcher, 1952), in the interpretation of electrocardiograms (Davis, 1958), in the interpretation of X-rays (Cochrane & Garland, 1952; Yerushalmy, 1947), and in the certification of causes of death (Markush, Schaaf, & Siegel, 1967). A review of diagnostic unreliability in other branches of physical medicine is given by Garland (1960) and the problem of the vagueness of medical criteria for diagnosis is thoroughly discussed by Feinstein (1967). The poor reliability of medical diagnosis, even when assisted by objective laboratory tests, does not mean that medical diagnosis is of no value. So it is with psychiatric diagnosis.

Recognition of the serious problems of the reliability of psychiatric diagnosis has resulted in a new approach to psychiatric diagnosis—the use of specific inclusion and exclusion criteria, as contrasted with the usually vague and ill-defined general descriptions found in the psychiatric literature and in the standard psychiatric glossary of the American Psychiatric Association. This approach was started by the St. Louis group associated with the Department of Psychiatry of Washington University (Feighner, Robins, Guze, Woodruff, Winokur, & Munoz, 1972) and has been further developed by Spitzer, Endicott, and Robins (1974) as a set of criteria for a selected group of functional psychiatric disorders, called the Research Diagnostic Criteria (RDC). The Display shows the specific criteria for a diagnosis of schizophrenia from the latest version of the RDC.[5]

DIAGNOSTIC CRITERIA FOR SCHIZOPHRENIA FROM THE RESEARCH DIAGNOSTIC CRITERIA

1. At least two of the following are required for definite diagnosis and one for probable diagnosis:

   a. Thought broadcasting, insertion, or withdrawal (as defined in the RDC).

   b. Delusions of control, other bizarre delusions, or multiple delusions (as defined in the RDC), of any duration as long as definitely present.

   c. Delusions other than persecutory or jealousy, lasting at least 1 week.

   d. Delusions of any type if accompanied by hallucinations of any type for at least 1 week.

   e. Auditory hallucinations in which either a voice keeps up a running commentary on the patient's behaviors or thoughts as they occur, or two or more voices converse with each other (of any duration as long as definitely present).

   f. Nonaffective verbal hallucinations spoken to the subject (as defined in this manual).

   g. Hallucinations of any type throughout the day for several days or intermittently for at least 1 month.

   h. Definite instances of formal thought disorder (as defined in the RDC).

   i. Obvious catatonic motor behavior (as defined in the RDC).

2. A period of illness lasting at least 2 weeks.

3. At no time during the active period of illness being considered did the patient meet the criteria for either probable or definite manic or depressive syndrome (Criteria 1 and 2 under Major Depressive or Manic Disorders) to such a degree that it was a prominent part of the illness.

Reliability studies using the RDC with case record material (from which all cues as to diagnosis and treatment were removed), as well as with live patients, indicate high reliability for all of the major categories and reliability coefficients generally higher than have ever been reported (Spitzer, Endicott, Robins, Kuriansky, & Garland, in press). It is therefore clear that the reliability of psychiatric diagnosis can be greatly increased by the use of specific criteria. (The interjudge reliability [chance corrected agreement, K] for the diagnosis of schizophrenia using an earlier version of RDC criteria with 68 newly admitted psychiatric inpatients at the New York State Psychiatric Institute was .88, which is a thoroughly respectable level of reliability). It is very likely that the next edition of the American Psychiatric Association's *Diagnostic and Statistical Manual* will contain similar specific criteria.

There are other problems with current psychiatric diagnosis. The recent controversy over whether or not homosexuality per se should be considered a mental disorder highlighted the lack of agreement within the psychiatric profession as to the definition of a mental disorder. A definition has been proposed by Spitzer (Spitzer & Wilson, 1975), but it is not at all clear whether a consensus will develop supporting it.

There are serious problems of validity. Many of the traditional diagnostic categories, such as some of the subtypes of schizophrenia and of major affective illness, and several of the personality disorders, have not been demonstrated to be distinct entities or to be useful for prognosis or treatment assignment. In addition, despite considerable evidence supporting the distinctness of such conditions as schizophrenia and manic-depressive illness, the boundaries separating these conditions from other conditions are certainly not clear. Finally, the categories of the traditional psychiatric nomenclature are of least value when applied to the large numbers of outpatients who are not seriously ill. It is for these patients that a more behaviorally or problem-oriented approach might be particularly useful.

I have not dealt at all with the myriad ways in which psychiatric diagnostic labels can be, and are, misused to hurt patients rather than to help them. This is a problem requiring serious research which, unfortunately, Rosenhan's study does not help illuminate. However, whatever the solutions to that problem the misuse of psychiatric diagnostic labels is not a sufficient reason to abandon their use because they have been shown to be of value when properly used.

In conclusion, there are serious problems with psychiatric diagnosis, as there are with other medical diagnoses. Recent developments indicate that the reliability of psychiatric diagnosis can be considerably improved. However, *even with the poor reliability of current psychiatric diagnosis, it is not so poor that it cannot be an aid in the treatment of the seriously disturbed psychiatric patient.* Rosenhan's study, "On Being Sane in Insane Places," proves that pseudopatients are not detected by psychiatrists as having simulated signs of mental illness. This rather remarkable finding is not relevant to the real problems of the reliability and validity of psychiatric diagnosis and only serves to obscure them. A correct interpretation of his own data contradicts his conclusions. In the setting of a psychiatric hospital, psychiatrists are remarkably able to distinguish the "sane" from the "insane."

NOTES

1. The original article only mentions that the 11 schizophrenics were diagnosed "in remission." Personal communication from D. L. Rosenhan indicates that this also applied to the single pseudopatient diagnosed as manic-depressive psychosis.

2. In personal communication D. L. Rosenhan said that "in remission" referred to a use of that term or one of its equivalents, such as recovered or no longer ill.

3. Rosenhan has not identified the hospitals used in this study because of his concern with issues of confidentiality and the potential for ad hominem attack. However, this does make it impossible for anyone at those hospitals to corroborate or challenge his account of how the pseudopatients acted and how they were perceived. The 12 hospitals used in my mini-study were: Long Island Jewish-Hillside Medical Center, New York; Massachusetts General Hospital, Massachusetts; St. Elizabeth's Hospital, Washington, D.C.; McLean Hospital, Massachusetts; UCLA, Neuropsychiatric Institute, California; Meyer-Manhattan Hospital (Manhattan State), New York; Vermont State Hospital, Vermont; Medical College of Virginia, Virginia; Emory University Hospital, Georgia; High Point Hospital, New York; Hudson River State Hospital, New York, and New York Hospital-Cornell Medical Center, Westchester Division, New York.

4. This was not in the article but was mentioned to me in personal communication by D. L. Rosenhan.

5. For what it is worth, the pseudopatient would have been diagnosed as "probable" schizophrenia using these criteria because of 1(f). In personal communication, Rosenhan said that when the pseudopatients were asked how frequently the hallucinations occurred, they said "I don't know." Therefore, Criterion 1(g) is not met.

REFERENCES

American Psychiatric Association. *Diagnostic and statistical manual of mental disorders* (2nd ed.). Washington, D.C.: American Psychiatric Association, 1968.

Cochrane, A. L., & Garland, L. H. Observer error in interpretation of chest films: International Investigation. *Lancet*, 1952, 2, 505–509.

Davies, L. G. Observer variation in reports on electrocardiograms. *British Heart Journal*, 1958, 20, 153–161.

Feighner, J. P., and Robins, E., Guze, S. B., Woodruff, R. A., Winokur, G., & Munoz, R. Diagnostic criteria for use in psychiatric research. *Archives of General Psychiatry*, 1972, 26, 57–63.

Feinstein, A. *Clinical judgment*. Baltimore, Md.: Williams & Wilkins, 1967.

Fletcher, C. M. Clinical diagnosis of pulmonary emphysema—an experimental study. *Proceedings of the Royal Society of Medicine*, 1952, 45, 577–584.

Garland, L. H. The problem of observer error. *Bulletin of the New York Academy of Medicine*, 1960, 36, 570–584.

Hunter, F. M. Letters to the editor. *Science*, 1973, 180, 361.

Kety, S. S. From rationalization to reason. *American Journal of Psychiatry*, 1974, 131, 957–963.

Klein, D., & Davis, J. *Diagnosis and drug treatment of psychiatric disorders*. Baltimore, Md.: Williams & Wilkins, 1969.

Letters to the editor. *Science*, 1973, 180, 356–365.

Markush, R. E., Schaaf, W. E., & Siegel, D. G. The influence of the death certifier on the results of epidemiologic studies. *Journal of the National Medical Association*, 1967, 59, 105–113.

Rosenhan, D. L. On being sane in insane places. *Science*, 1973, 179, 250–258. (a)

Rosenhan, D. L. Reply to letters to the editor. *Science*, 1973, 180, 365–369. (b)

Spitzer, R. L., Endicott, J., & Robins, E. *Research diagnostic criteria*. New York: Biometrics Research, New York State Department of Mental Hygiene, 1974.

Spitzer, R. L., Endicott, J., Robins, E., Kuriansky, J., & Garland, B. Preliminary report of the reliability of research diagnostic criteria applied to psychiatric case records. In A. Sudilofsky, B. Beer, & S. Gershon (Eds.), *Prediction in psychopharmacology*, New York: Raven Press, in press.

Spitzer, R. L. & Fleiss, J. L. A reanalysis of the reliability of psychiatric diagnosis. *British Journal of Psychiatry*, 1974. 125, 341–347.

Spitzer, R. L., & Wilson, P. T. Nosology and the official psychiatric nomenclature. In A. Freedman & H. Kaplan (Eds.), *Comprehensive textbook of psychiatry*. New York: Williams & Wilkins, 1975.

Yerushalmy, J. Statistical problems in assessing methods of medical diagnosis with special reference to X-ray techniques. *Public Health Reports*, 1947, 62, 1432–1449.

CHALLENGE QUESTIONS

Classic Dialogue: Do Diagnostic Labels Hinder Treatment?

1. Would society be better off if there were no names (such as "normal" or "abnormal") for broad categories of behavior? Why, or why not?

2. Who would you consider best qualified to judge a person's mental health: a parent, a judge, or a doctor? Why?

3. If a person at any time displays symptoms of a mental disorder, even fraudulently, is it helpful to consider that the same symptoms of disorder may appear again? Why, or why not?

4. Is there any danger in teaching the diagnostic categories of mental behavior to beginning students of psychology? Explain.

On the Internet...

http://www.dushkin.com

Journal of Personality and Social Psychology

This site contains a description of the *Journal of Personality and Social Psychology,* the current issue's table of contents (with abstracts), and past tables of contents. Looking over the tables of contents should provide you with an overview of current topics of interest to social psychologists.

http://www.apa.org/journals/psp.html

Psychology of Religion Page

This site serves as a resource for the psychological aspects of belief and behavior. It starts with a general introduction to the psychology of religion and connects to other links related to religion's influence on people's lives.

http://www.gasou.edu/psychweb/psyrelig/psyrelig.htm

Society for the Study of Social Issues

This home page for the Society for the Study of Social Issues provides information about current research in social psychology as well as abstracts of issues of the *Journal of Social Issues.*

http://www.umich.edu/~sociss/

PART 7

Social Psychology

Social psychologists usually study the more "social" aspects of behavior, which include the influences of society upon the individual. One particularly controversial example is the question of whether or not pornography is harmful. Another example that is gaining more exposure is whether or not religious commitment can improve one's mental health. Both of these questions are addressed in this section.

■ Is Pornography Harmful?

■ Does Religious Commitment Improve Mental Health?

ISSUE 15

Is Pornography Harmful?

YES: Victor Cline, from "A Psychologist's View of Pornography," in D. E. Wildmon, ed., *The Case Against Pornography* (Victor Books, 1986)

NO: F. M. Christensen, from *Pornography: The Other Side* (Greenwood Press, 1990)

ISSUE SUMMARY

YES: Victor Cline, a professor emeritus of psychology and copresident of the seminar group Marriage and Family Enrichment, argues that pornography poses a great harm to viewers because it degrades women and desensitizes males to sexual violence.

NO: Professor of philosophy F. M. Christensen contends that there is little evidence that pornography is harmful and that pornography is only a scapegoat for other societal problems.

There is no denying that the amount of sexually explicit materials in our society has increased. Whereas movie directors and magazine photographers once feared photographing kisses and plunging necklines, they now do not hesitate to photograph simulated intercourse and nudity. Some consider this type of material pornography. Likewise, there is general agreement that the production of hard-core pornography has also increased. How does this affect our society? Does the proliferation of pornographic materials hurt people, particularly women and children?

In 1985 the U.S. Attorney General's Commission on Pornography, commonly referred to as the Meese commission, was appointed to answer these questions. In the course of the commission's work, many psychological studies were examined and many psychologists were consulted. Although the members of the commission did not agree unanimously on all the issues, they did conclude that pornography is harmful. Interestingly, a "shadow commission"—a citizen group that followed the commission to report on its theory and practice—immediately criticized this conclusion, claiming that it was politically motivated and that it ignored many important psychological investigations of the issues.

In the following selections, Victor Cline sides with and even adds to the Meese commission's findings. Cline argues that media portrayals of male aggression against women can have very harmful effects on women. He points to research documenting the potential harm of aggressive erotic materials to the male psyche, including studies on the effects of repeated exposure to sexual and violent materials. He believes that these studies show that viewing explicit sexual or violent material can decrease the inner controls that normally prevent violent behavior and increase the likelihood that an individual will act out what is viewed.

F. M. Christensen, in contrast, considers the various charges against pornography and concludes that there is little evidence confirming that it has ill effects. In refuting the charge that viewing pornography leads to wrongful behavior, Christensen argues that we assign too much power to the media. The media do not control our desires and actions, he asserts, but, as a form of media, pornography has nevertheless become a scapegoat for society's ills. Christensen concludes that society's problems related to sex and violence originate elsewhere.

POINT	COUNTERPOINT
• There is plenty of evidence that pornography is harmful.	• A careful interpretation of the evidence does not show any harm from pornography.
• Pornography creates a climate in which a rapist believes he is giving in to "natural urges."	• Sexual entertainment has little effect on a person's perceptions of reality.
• After repeated exposure to nonaggressive pornography, men show more callousness toward women.	• Pornography has become a scapegoat for the conflicts between men and women.
• Pornography can be a threat to marriages and families.	• Pornography can help to preserve marriages.

YES

Victor Cline

A PSYCHOLOGIST'S VIEW OF PORNOGRAPHY

VIOLENT CRIME ON INCREASE

The United States is by far the most violent country in the world compared with all of the other advanced societies. For example, the U.S. rape rate is many times higher than that of the United Kingdom. We have more homicides annually on just the island of Manhattan than those reported in all of England, Scotland, and troubled Ireland combined. Our homicide rate is ten times that of the Scandinavian countries. At the present time crimes of violence in the U.S. are increasing at four to five times the rate of population growth.

Behavioral scientists recognize that there are many causes for any violent act, and it behooves us to investigate and understand those key triggers or contributors—if we care at all about the kind of society we want for ourselves and our children. Many lines of evidence have pointed to media influences such as commercial cinema and television as being especially suspect; as presenting inappropriate models and instigations of violent and antisocial behavior, especially for our young.

MENTAL HEALTH STUDY BLAMES TV VIOLENCE

In reviewing all of the scientific evidence relating to the effect TV violence has on behavior, the National Institute of Mental Health in 1984 issued a ten-year-report that concluded that there is in deed "overwhelming evidence of a causal relationship between violence on television and later aggressive behavior."

Some long-term studies and cross national studies also indicate that this learned aggressive behavior is stable over time—the victims stay aggressive. It is by no means just a transient kind of effect.

The reviewers of the research at the National Institute of Mental Health also note the role that TV (and by implication, commercial cinema) play as sex educators for our children. TV contributes significantly to sex role

From Victor Cline, "A Psychologist's View of Pornography," in D. E. Wildmon, ed., *The Case Against Pornography* (Victor Books, 1986). Copyright © 1986 by SP Publications, Inc., Wheaton, IL 60187. Reprinted by permission.

socialization as well as shaping attitudes and values about human sexuality. Various studies suggest that in TV presentations sex is commonly linked with violence. Erotic relationships are seldom seen as warm, loving, or stable. When sex is depicted it is almost always illicit. It is rather rare to suggest or depict sexual relations between a man and a woman married and who love each other. This agrees with similar results from my own research on the content of commercial cinema conducted several years ago.

RAPE RATE GROWS 700 PERCENT

Aggression against women is increasingly becoming a serious social problem. This can be seen in the escalation of wife battering, sexual molestation of female children, and sexual assaults on adult females.

Examining empirical data on the incidence of this type of thing is risky. This is because nearly all statistics on rape, for example, tend to underreport its actual occurrence. Many women for reasons of shame, humiliation, embarrassment, or seeking to avoid further trauma do not report these experiences. Data from many sources indicates that police get reports on one in four attempted or actual rapes. And of those reported less than 5 percent result in prosecution and conviction. Since 1933 the increase in the rape rate in the U.S. is in excess of 700 percent (this is in relation to population growth —in actual numbers the increase is much greater).

This means that the chances of a woman being sexually attacked are seven times greater now than in 1933. This clearly indicates major changes in male attitudes about sexual aggressiveness toward women. Obviously, more men today have a lower esteem of women. Why should this be in an age such as ours when women are being heard and winning rights?

PORNOGRAPHY DEGRADES WOMEN

Feminists such as Susan Brownmiller, Diana Russell, Laura Lederer, and Kathleen Barry point to the fact that our culture influences men to regard women as things—to be used. They note, for example, that nearly all pornography is created by males for a primarily male audience. Most of it is hostile to women. There is much woman hatred in it. It is devoid of foreplay, tenderness, caring, to say nothing of love and romance. They see its main purpose to humiliate and degrade the female body for the purpose of commercial entertainment, erotic stimulation, and pleasure for the male viewer. This is perceived as creating a cultural climate in which a rapist feels he is merely giving in to a normal urge and a woman is encouraged to believe that sexual masochism is healthy liberated fun.

Susan Brownmiller states, "Pornography, like rape, is a male invention designed to dehumanize women."

Many of the men's magazines such as *Hustler* are filled with antifemale messages both overt and covert. The victims in most "hard R" slasher movies are women—it is they who are most often sexually assaulted, tortured, and degraded. The feminist's concern is that these films sexually stimulate men while at the same time pairing this erotic arousal with images of violent assaults on women. The possibility of conditioning a potential male viewer into deviancy certainly has to be considered here.

MEN CONDITIONED TO
SEXUAL DEVIATION

In a laboratory experiment using classical conditioning procedures at the Naudsley Hospital in London, England, Dr. Stanley Rachman conditioned a number of young males into being fetishists—a mild form of sexual deviation. A number of studies by such investigators as Davison, Bandura, Evans, Hackson, and McGuire suggest that deviant sexual fantasies through a process of masturbatory conditioning are related in many instances to later acted-out deviant sexual behavior. What happens here is that deviant sexual fantasies in the man's mind are paired with direct sexual stimulation and orgasm via masturbation. In this way the deviant fantasies acquire strong sexually arousing properties—which help sustain the sexual interest in the deviant behavior. Thus reinforced sexual imagery and thoughts (accompanied via masturbation) are a link in the acquisition and maintenance of new deviant sexual arousal and behavior. In the light of this, media portrayals of sex modeling male aggression against women logically can have a harmful effect on certain viewers. These portrayals, it would be concluded, facilitate deviant conditioning by providing new malignant fantasy material as well as increasing motivation for masturbatory experiences—leading to changes in the man's sexual attitudes, appetites, and behavior.

For example: A Los Angeles firm is currently marketing an 8mm motion picture film, available through the mails to anybody wishing it, which depicts two girl scouts in their uniforms selling cookies from door to door. At one residence they are invited in by a mature, sexually aggressive male who proceeds to subject them to a variety of unusual and extremely explicit sexual acts—all shown in great detail. This film is what is usually referred to as "hard-core" pornography. If the research of Rachman, McGuire, and others has any meaning at all, it suggests that such a film could potentially condition some male viewers, via masturbatory conditioning, into fantasies and later behavior involving aggressive sex with female minors.

Also, we might mention, that sex therapists have for years used carefully selected erotic material to recondition men with sexual deviations and help them out of their problems. In other words, the conditioning can go both ways using erotic materials. If all sexual deviations are learned, as psychologist Albert Bandura suggests, then one would assume that most deviations occur through "accidental conditioning"—which is exactly what many feminists have concerns about—especially as they see how they are treated in male-oriented media presentations.

At the present time in most urban areas of the U.S., there have arisen groups of women with concerns about what the media are doing to them—and especially about the social/sexual enculturation of males. Women Against Violence in Pornography and Media, based in San Francisco, is one example of this kind of group. Initially, their concerns were intuitive, moralistic, and emotional. They picketed various establishments—movie houses, adult bookstores, etc., selling or marketing highly sexist and antifemale materials—material that might tend to engender hate toward women. This includes the so-called "snuff films" in which women were supposedly murdered on-camera for the voyeuristic entertainment of male viewers.

However, in the last five years there has been a flood of well-done behavioral studies by researchers that appear to scientifically legitimize the concerns of these groups. These studies have repeatedly given documentation of potential harms to viewers of aggressive erotic materials, especially males.

These findings have been given very little attention by the popular press and are known only to a few scientists who are privy to the journals that these articles are showing up in. Thus, most ordinary citizens, journalists, as well as professionals in other disciplines, are not aware of these studies. For example, one of the editors of the *Utah Daily Chronicle* on March 1, 1985, in an editorial column discussing the cable TV bills before our state legislature, wrote, "Research has shown there is no demonstrable relationship between watching TV and increased aggressiveness . . . [and] regardless of what Utah legislators may believe, there is no scientific correlation between obscenity and antisocial conduct."

Both of these statements are totally incorrect. I am sure they were written as a result of ignorance, not as a conscious attempt at deception. In fact, quite ironically, on the day this editorial appeared, the Department of Psychology was sponsoring a widely publicized seminar featuring one of the nation's leading authorities on television effects, Dr. Raoul Huesmann, who discussed a pioneering 22-year study on the long-term negative effects of TV violence viewing.

WORLD'S MOST VIOLENT ADVANCED SOCIETY

I will not further belabor the issue of media violence and its potential negative effects on viewers. The evidence is really quite overwhelming on this issue. But let me briefly summarize what the literature suggests:

1. We are the most violent advanced society in the world.
2. We have the highest rates of media violence (in our entertainments) of any nation.
3. There are something like 20 years of behavioral studies linking exposure to media violence with violent behavior. These include both laboratory and field studies. And while there are many contributions to any particular violent act, I do not think that any fair reviewer of the literature can deny that the media are one important contributor to the violence problems in our society.

In my judgment repeated violence viewing also desensitizes the observer to the pathology in the film or material witnessed. It becomes with repeated viewing more acceptable and tolerable. We lose the capacity to empathize with the victim. Man's inhumanity to man (or woman) becomes a spectator sport. We develop and cultivate an appetite for it, no different than in early Rome, where people watched gladiatorial contests in which men fought to their deaths, dismembering their opponents' bodies. In other contests, others fought wild animals barehanded, eventually to be eaten alive. Again, a spectator sport. We become to some extent debased, even dehumanized, if you wish, by participating in these kinds of experiences. And, of course, approximations of what happened in the Roman arena nightly occur in some movie houses and on some TV screens —especially the cable variety where explicit violence is broadcast unedited. And usually—women are the victims.

INCREASING ASSAULTS IN MARRIAGE

Let us now move to the issue of linking aggressive pornography to increased aggressive behavior in marriage. It can be physical abuse, psychological abuse, or both. I see many couples in marital counseling. Violence between spouses is a common problem. Of course many women have learned to fight back. And this leads to an ever-escalating exchange of anger and hostility. Divorce usually doesn't solve the problem. If you don't know how to handle anger and aggressive feelings in one relationship, switching partners doesn't necessarily solve that problem for you in the next relationship.

There have been many experiments on aggressive pornography and its effects on consumers conducted by such capable investigators as Edward Donnerstein and Leonard Berkowitz at the University of Wisconsin; Neil Malamuth and James Check at the University of Manitoba; Dolf Zillman and Jennings Bryant at Indiana University; and Seymour Feshbach and his associates at UCLA.

SEXUAL AROUSAL, AGGRESSION LINKED

There has been a convergence of evidence from many sources suggesting that sexual arousal and aggression are linked or are mutually enhancing. Thus materials that are sexually exciting can stimulate aggressive behavior and, contrariwise, portrayals of aggression in books, magazines, and films can raise some people's levels of sexual arousal.

Thus it is not by accident that some four-letter words are frequently used in the context of an epithet or as part of a verbal attack on another.

Many theorists have noted the intimate relationship between sex and aggression —including Sigmund Freud, or more recently, Robert Stoler at UCLA who suggests that frequently it is hostility that generates and enhances sexual excitement.

A large number of research studies consistently and repetitiously keep coming to one conclusion—those subjects who are sexually aroused by strong erotic stimuli show significantly greater aggression than nonaroused controls.

The typical experiment will sexually arouse with pornographic stimuli a group of experimental subjects who will then be given an opportunity to punish a confederate with electric shock. Their aggressiveness will be compared to a neutral group who will have seen only a bland nonsexual film or reading material.

If the film combines both erotic *and* aggressive elements, this usually produces even higher levels of aggressiveness (as measured by the subjects' willingness to shock their partners at even higher and apparently more painful levels of shock intensity). If the erotic material is very mild—like pin-ups and cheesecake type photos—then it appears to have reverse effect on aggression—tending to dampen it.

In the situation of reading about or witnessing a filmed presentation of rape, if the female victim is seen as in great pain this can also have a dampening effect on aggressive arousal. It serves as an inhibitor. But if the portrayal showing the woman as finally succumbing to and enjoying the act (as is typical of most pornography), then the situation is reversed for males (but not females). It becomes very arousing. For men, the fantasy of a woman becoming sexually excited as a result of a sexual assault reverses any inhibitions that might have been initially mobilized by the coercive nature of the act and seeing the woman initially in pain.

This message—that pain and humiliation can be "fun"—encourages in men the relaxation of inhibitions against rape.

Doctors Gager and Schurr in their studies on the causes of rape note that a common theme in pornography is that women enjoy being raped and sexually violated. Sexual sadism is presented as a source of sexual pleasure for women. The Gager and Schurr studies note: "The pattern rarely changes in the porno culture.... After a few preliminary skirmishes, women invite or demand further violation, begging male masters to rape them into submission, torture, and violence. In this fantasy land, females wallow in physical abuse and degradation. It is a pattern of horror which we have seen in our examination of sex cases translated again and again into actual assaults."

UNIVERSITY STUDY SHOWS EFFECTS OF MOVIES

Going outside the laboratory, Neal Malamuth at the University of Manitoba sent hundreds of students to movies playing in the community. He wanted to see what the effects would be of their being exposed to films portraying sexual violence as having positive consequences. The movies they went to see were not pornography, but everyday "sex and violence" of the R-rated variety. The films included *Swept Away* (about a violent male aggressor and a woman who learns to crave sexual sadism; they find love on a deserted island). A second film, *The Get-*

away, tells about a woman who falls in love with the man who raped her in front of her husband, then both taunt the husband until he commits suicide.

A second group of students was assigned to see two control films, *A Man and a Woman*, and *Hooper*, both showing tender romance and nonexplicit sex. Within a week of seeing the films, Malamuth administered an attitude survey to all students who had participated in the experiment. The students did not know that the survey had anything to do with the films which they seen. Embedded within the survey were questions relating to acceptance of interpersonal violence and acceptance of such rape myths as "women enjoy being raped." Examples of questions asked also included: "Many women have an unconscious wish to be raped and may unconsciously set up a situation in which they are likely to be attacked."

The results of the survey indicated that exposure to the films portraying sexual violence significantly increased male subjects' acceptance of interpersonal violence against women. For females, the trend was in the opposite direction.

Dr. Malamuth concluded: "The present findings constitute the first demonstration in a nonlaboratory setting... of relatively long-term effects of movies that fuse sexuality and violence." And, of course, these were not hard-core pornography but rather R-rated type, edited films that have appeared on national commercial TV and unedited films shown on cable TV.

As I review the literature on media effects, it appears that in the areas of both sex and violence materials depicting these kinds of behaviors do several things: (1) they stimulate and arouse aggressive and sexual feeling—especially in males; (2) they show or instruct in detail *how* to do the acts—much of it antisocial; (3) when seen frequently enough have a desensitization effect which reduces feelings of conscience, guilt, inhibitions, or inner controls, the act is in a sense legitimized by its repetitious exposure; and finally, (4) there is increased likelihood that the individual will act out what he has witnessed.

Seymour Feshbach's research at UCLA has a direct bearing on this issue. After exposing a group of male college students to a sadomasochistic rape story taken from *Penthouse* magazine—telling of a woman's pleasure at being sexually mistreated—he asked these men if they would like to emulate what the rapist did to the woman. Seventeen percent said they would. When asked the same question but with the added assurance they would not get caught—51 percent indicated a likelihood of raping. This finding has been replicated in a number of other studies—though the percentages vary somewhat from research to research.

Doctors Edward Donnerstein and Neil Malamuth, in reviewing a large number of both field and laboratory experiments, found that exposure to media materials that mix both sex and violence causes six things to happen: (1) it sexually excites and arouses (especially) the male viewer; (2) it increases both his aggressive *attitudes* and *behavior*; (3) it stimulates the production of aggressive rape fantasies; (4) it increases men's acceptance of so-called rape myths (such as: "women ask for it"); (5) it produces a lessened sensitivity about rape (and increased callousness); and (6) it leads to men admitting an increased possibility of themselves raping someone—especially if they think they can get away with it.

PORNOGRAPHY REDUCES COMPASSION

What about exposure to nonaggressive erotic materials? Do these have any kind of effects on the consumer? Doctors Dolf Zillman and Jennings Bryant at Indiana University studied 160 male and female undergraduates who were divided into groups where they were exposed to: (1) massive amounts of pornography over a period of six weeks; (2) a moderate amount of pornography over that time period; and (3) no exposure over the same time period. Among their many findings were that being exposed to a lot of pornography led to a desensitization effect. The more they saw, the less offensive and objectionable it became to them. They also tended to see rape as a more trivial offense. They had an increasing loss of compassion for women as rape victims (even though no aggressive pornography was shown them).

Massive exposure to nonaggressive pornography clearly promoted sexual callousness in males toward women generally. This was measured by a scale where men agreed with such items as: "Pickups should expect to put out." Or, "If they are old enough to bleed, they are old enough to butcher" (referring to women).

The thrust of this presentation is to suggest that there is an abundance of scientific evidence suggesting social harms from some types of media exposure as has been previously discussed. The studies we have discussed are only illustrative. Many others have not been mentioned due to time limitations. Extensive documentation and lengthy bibliographies on this subject matter are available from the speaker on request.

CAN WE CONTROL PORNOGRAPHY?

We now come to the really hot issue—the bottom line. Does a community have a constitutional right through democratically enacted laws to censor or limit the public broadcast of these kinds of materials—because of their malignant nature? The recent controversy about the First Amendment of the Constitution? Where does or where can one draw the line? How bad or pathological does material have to be before it can be limited? Or should our position be: anything goes regardless of the consequences? Free speech is free speech.

Seymour Feshbach, the UCLA psychologist, states: "As psychologists, we would support community efforts to restrict violence in erotica to adults who are fully cognizant of the nature of the material and who choose knowingly to buy it. We are opposed to advertisements that have appeared in some popular magazines depicting sadomasochism; a recent fashion layout in *Vogue,* for instance, featured a man brutally slapping an attractive woman. We also oppose the practice of some therapists who try to help their patients overcome sexual inhibitions by showing them films of rape or by encouraging them to indulge in rape fantasies. Psychologists, in our judgment, ought not to support, implicitly or explicitly, the use and dissemination of violent erotic materials."

In reference to the First Amendment to our Constitution, we must recognize that today there are many kinds of democratically enacted prohibitions of speech and expression. These, of course, can be amended or repealed anytime we wish. Examples include libel, slander, perjury, conspiracy, false advertising, excitement to violence or speech that might create a "clear and present danger" such as yelling "Fire!" in a crowded theater. Still other examples include TV cigarette advertisements and also obscenity. In fact most of the people who went to jail in the Watergate scandal did so because of what they said—or for words they spoke (e.g., perjury and conspiracy).

In certain public broadcast mediums such as TV and radio, even obscene language can be proscribed without running afoul of the First Amendment.

At present, cable TV is the most controversial area about what is appropriate or inappropriate for broadcast. Currently there are virtually no restrictions on what can be aired. There are some channels in the U.S. broadcasting the roughest kind of hard-core pornography. There are others, including some in Utah, that are regularly broadcasting soft-core pornography mixed with violence. Last spring one of the local cable networks broadcast some 15 times *Eyes of a Stranger.* This film shows in explicit detail a young woman and her boyfriend being attacked by a sadist. He chops the boyfriend's head off, then proceeded to tear the girl's clothes off, strangle her, then rapes the dead body. The film continues with a series of attacks, rapes, and killings of other females. In my judgment this kind of programming, some of it in primetime, represents antisocial and irresponsible behavior on the part of the cable station owners.

Of course, there are many other similar type films which are being regularly broadcast. This is not an isolated incident. But along with this are films of great merit and quality which represent a major contribution to our cultural life as well as entertainment.

At present close to 30 percent of homes in the U.S. have cable. Industry analysts project that by 1985 this will be up to 50 percent and by the end of the decade 80–90 percent. This means that within a few years most all of us will have cable. This is not hard to understand when you consider that very shortly the cable networks will be able to outbid the regular networks for choice sporting events, fights, new Broadway musicals, etc. Even now all the latest movies come to cable before they reach regular commercial TV.

At present there is a double standard in television. The FCC (Federal Communications Commission) has control over the broadcast of appropriate materials by the regular commercial TV channels. They cannot air obscene or other objectionable material without threat of losing their licenses. Cable TV has no restrictions whatever. And, of course, cable firms are taking advantage of this. And there are some adults in our community who are delighted. Others are appalled and have concerns, especially about exposing their children to this kind of programming.

As with most controversial issues, there are no simple solutions which will please everybody. But somewhere a line must be drawn—if we care about the quality of life in our community. We have a right to protect ourselves in our own self-interest.

MEDIA SAVAGERY GROWS

George Elliot has commented: "If one is for civilization, for being civilized . . . , then one must be willing to take a middle way and pay the price for responsibility. To be civilized, to accept authority, to rule with order, costs deep in the soul, and not the least of what it costs is likely to be some of the sensuality of the irresponsible." Some have argued, as Elliot notes, that since guilt reduces pleasure in sex, the obvious solution is to abolish all sexual taboos and liberate pornography, which in turn would supposedly free the human spirit —and the body.

This is a cheery optimistic view, not unlike the sweet hopefulness of the old-fashioned anarchist who thought that all we had to do in order to attain happiness was to get rid of governments so that we might all express our essentially good nature unrestrained. But sexual anarchism, or the aggressive impulse turned loose, like political anarchism before it, is a "lovely" but fraudulent daydream. Perhaps, before civilization, savages were noble, but if there is anything we have learned in this century, it is that those who regress from civilization become ignoble beyond all toleration. They may aspire to innocent savagery, but what they achieve too often is brutality and loss of their essential humanity.

The issue of how we should deal with the savagery which continues to escalate in our media presentations is just as much your problem as mine. I have shared with you some of the consequences of its presence on our culture. But the solution has to be a shared one—if we really believe in democracy.

NO

F. M. Christensen

ALLEGED ILL EFFECTS FROM USE

[T]he belief that pornography is evil in itself is simply wrong. This leaves open the important question of whether it has effects on the user's attitudes or behavior that are harmful to anyone. Charges that this is so are continually being made, so... we will explore [a few aspects of] that issue [here]....

One particularly profound problem involves the issue of human agency. Now, some people are logically inconsistent in regard to this issue. In response to the suggestion that a violent criminal was made that way by a traumatic childhood, they invoke a notion of absolute free will: "His circumstances are not to blame; he *chose* to let them affect him!" But let the subject be something as comparatively minor as exposure to words or pictures, and suddenly the same people insist on a causal influence. The perennial debate over freedom of the will can hardly be discussed here. But one thing is perfectly clear from all the evidence: heredity and environment have a powerful influence on human behavior. The only room for rational debate is over whether that influence is total (deterministic) or not—and, once more, over just how much effect different types of causal factor exert....

THE DOMINO THEORY OF CHARACTER

The first of the claims we will discuss is usually expressed in vague generalities; it is basically the charge that use of pornography tends to produce all sorts of wrongful behavior. From the rhetoric some of its proponents employ, one would swear they believe sexual thoughts that are not strictly confined will create a desire to rush out and break windows or steal cars. It is as if they retained the primitive belief that individuals are motivated by only two basic desires—to do good or to do evil—rather than by a complex panoply of needs and emotions. In the minds of some, this idea seems to rest on the conviction that one sort of corruption just naturally leads to others. Few, if any, scientists take such ideas seriously today; "degeneracy theory," with its concept that physical, psychological, and moral defects are all bound together, was popular in the last century but died with the rise of psychology and scientific medicine. In the rest of the population, unfortunately, notions like this one linger on.

The more specific suggestion is sometimes made that "losing self-control" in regard to sex—as allegedly might be precipitated by the use of pornography—produces a general lack of self-discipline, hence a tendency toward selfish libertinism or worse. This sort of thinking has a long history. In Victorian times, married couples were advised to limit the frequency of their sexual activities strictly lest they lead to a weakening of the will and of general character. And the myth that sexual excess brought about the decline and fall of Rome has been around for centuries, having come down to us with those old suspicions about bodily pleasure. (Never mind the gladiators and slavery and brutal imperialism; sexual pleasure was Rome's real failing.) Part of what is involved in the thinking, evidently, is an inability to distinguish between the very specific matter of sexual "permissiveness" and the rejection of *all* restraints on behavior. Alternatively, it is a confusion between a strong interest in sex and a failure to care about any other sources of happiness, or else a tendency to be concerned only with one's own happiness or with the pleasures of the moment. Such tendencies are certainly bad; for example, a person or nation fixated on momentary satisfactions will lack the discipline to plan for and protect future happiness. But there is no reason to suppose that sexual desires are any more apt to have such consequences than are other strong desires.

... [I]t is revealing to point out the inconsistency between these concerns and the lack of fears associated with other needs and pleasures, say, those involving food, love, religious devotion, or the arts. How many are alarmed that our lack of eating taboos—so common in other cultures—will lead to a general obsession with the happiness of the moment? Perhaps we should ban the Wednesday food section in the newspaper, with its seductive pictures and emphasis on the pleasure of eating over its utilitarian function. How many suppose that getting great enjoyment from music or dance will lead to a general lack of self-discipline, or to a disregard for the welfare of others (say, of those who perform them)? The rhetoric about the perils of "pleasure-seeking" is remarkably selective in regard to which pleasures it notices. The real source of this belief, it seems clear, is the sexual anxiety with which so many are raised; it produces the fear that something terrible will happen if one should ever "let go."

The most important response to such charges, however, is that those who make them do not have a shred of genuine evidence. They have been accepted and repeated endlessly, like so many other cultural beliefs, without critical examination. In earlier times, when racism was more socially acceptable than it is now, mixing of the races was often alleged to have brought about the decline of Rome and other civilizations—on the basis of the same worthless *post hoc* reasoning.... Certain commentators have claimed to have evidence from one or two studies that reported finding a statistical association between exposure to sexual materials and juvenile delinquency in the United States. It could well be true that in this society, there has been a tendency for those who lack the traditional sexual attitudes to reject other social standards as well. The former is easily explained as a result of the latter, however: those who have been less well socialized into or have rebelled against the system as a whole will naturally be among the ones whose sexual behavior is less constrained. Alternatively, those whose needs have led them to break one social taboo will feel less threatened by other societal rules....

Of course, that a belief is held for bad reasons does not mean there are no good reasons for it. Nonetheless, it can be said without hesitation that the evidence available is strongly against the "domino theory" of character. One has only to consider the cross-cultural picture to begin to realize this, say, the promiscuous children and youth of Mangaia or the Trobriand Islands or the Muria villages, who grow up into hard-working adults who have internalized all of their society's moral standards. More generally, there is no indication that sexually positive cultures have greater amounts of antisocial behavior. In fact, one cross-cultural survey found significantly more personal crime in groups where premarital sex is strongly punished than in others. (The fact that the crime rate in permissive northern Europe is much lower than that in the United States may already be known to the reader—but beware of *post hoc* thinking.) The belief that gratifying sexual feelings tends somehow to turn into a general state of moral corruption, or even to damage one's capacity for self-discipline, is sheer superstition....

PERSONAL RELATIONSHIPS

A second variety of claim that pornography has ill effects is that its use tends to damage personal relationships between men and women. This charge takes several different forms, including some that are bizarre (e.g., the idea that many men prefer it to real women and hence will avoid relationships with them if given that option). The simplest of these allegations, however, just points out that numerous women are upset by their partners' interest in pornography, so that it becomes a source of conflict. Part of the problem here is jealousy: the mere biologically normal fact that the partner is attracted to other persons is threatening to some, even when it is all fantasy. But that is evidently not the main difficulty. Few men feel upset over their partners' interest in love stories, say, in soap operas, with their romantic hunks and adulterous love affairs. The real problem seems to be the woman's aversion to nudity and sexual openness.

That being so, this argument presupposes that pornography is hurtful rather than proving it. For it could equally well be said that it is the woman's prudishness, rather than the man's interest in pornography, that is "the real" source of the trouble; which it is would have to be argued for rather than just assumed. Mention to the feminists and religionists who employ this objection that women's liberation or religious devotion has broken up many relationships, and they will make the same basic point.... [M]oreover, it seems clear which one is the real culprit. In earlier years, the attitude that explicit sex is offensive to women led men to go off by themselves to watch "stag films"; what could have been an enjoyable shared experience became a source of alienation. Although female interest in such things might never approach that of males, the ones who divide the sexes are those who say, "My desires are noble and yours are nasty," not those who believe in the equal worth and dignity of the needs of both.

One special argument of this kind alleges that pornography harms relationships by its overemphasis on sex, and also by its underemphasis on companionship or romantic love. It is said to "teach men" to value the former too much and the latter too little. With its culture-bound and egocentric notions of how much emphasis is too much or too little, this claim ignores the possibility of keeping the sexes in harmony by teaching women to want sex in the same way. Its biggest error, however, lies in assigning to media depictions far more power to influence basic desires than is at all justified. As usual, those who make this claim express no similar beliefs about the persuasive powers of the constant barrage of love songs and love stories in all the entertainment media. If such exposure were really so effective, one would think, we would all be incurable love-junkies by now. In any case, there is certainly no lack of publicity promoting love and companionship in our society. Moreover, male sexuality is not detectably different in cultures without appreciable amounts of pornography; indeed, it is evidently very much the same the world over.

What really underlies this claim is an old problem: the unfortunate fact that, on average, men's and women's needs in regard to love/commitment and sex are not well matched. Unable—or perhaps just unwilling—to believe men could ultimately have such different needs than they themselves do, some women suppose it must be the different amount of stress on sex or love among men that does it. One common response is simply to deny that men are really different. For example, these women say men just *think* they have a strong need for sex because advertisers keep telling them they do. Others grant the reality of male sexual responses but do not want to believe they are natural. (Among feminists, this is just part of the wider conviction that

there are *no* innate differences between the sexes except anatomical ones.) Yet those who make both claims insist it is men who have been most affected by culture in this regard. Over and again, without offering any argument as to which is cause and which effect, they assert that men would not be so interested in sex, or so attracted to female bodies, if only there were not so much emphasis on those things in this society. Besides projecting their own responses onto male nature—responses that are themselves largely culture-conditioned—the women (and sometimes men) who make such claims are somehow blind to all the societal efforts to suppress male sexuality and promote female needs.

What is true is that a double standard is still taught to adolescents in our culture. But it is glaringly false to say that it encourages males to be sexual; it merely discourages them less. Consider the common charge that "this society" teaches young males they have to "score" to be real men, for example. In fact, you will not find this preached by any of the major socializing institutions, not by church, government, school, family, *or* the media. Even that small segment of the latter that celebrates sex overtly cannot really be said to do this—and it is standardly maligned and even banned by the society at large. The one place where such a thing is taught is in the peer groups of some young men as they themselves rebel against society's teaching on the subject, trying to justify their own needs and feelings. However all this may be, the point remains that pornography is not the cause of male sexuality. It has again become a scapegoat in connection with male-female conflicts whose real causes lie in biology, or at least much deeper in the socialization of men—or of women....

Some have claimed there is scientific evidence that standard pornography causes misperception of other people's sexual desires. In a certain type of experiment, volunteers are exposed to a presentation of some kind and then asked questions about their beliefs or attitudes. (A subterfuge is used to keep them from realizing the true purpose of the test.) In one version of this test, subjects who have been shown sexual materials indicated they regarded women (as well as men) as somewhat more sexually liberal than did subjects who had not been shown the materials. In itself, this is no evidence of misperception; the former might have been closer to the truth than the latter. In any case, the result is not in the least remarkable. A recent or extended experience of *any* kind looms large in one's consciousness. Hence just about any book or movie, *or real person* that one has recently met, would have a similar influence on one's other judgments, temporarily. For a more striking example, one who has just seen a scary movie is much more likely to look under the bed before retiring at night. The effect soon fades, however; it is swamped by that of subsequently encountered books or movies or real people. And most of the latter tend to promote the culture's current party line on sex, just as they do on other subjects. Except in unusual circumstances, the conclusion remains: sexual entertainment will have little effect on perceptions of reality.

A variant of this objection says that the ecstatic pleasure often portrayed in pornography will tend to make the readers or viewers disappointed with their own sexual experience and, hence, with their partners or their partners'

performance. (Although it is women who standardly complain about the latter, this new claim is usually framed in terms of male dissatisfaction.) It is not always clear whether those who present the argument believe ordinary tepid sex is really all that is possible—the half-hour orgasms of Mangaian women argue otherwise—or whether for some reason they just think it unwise to aspire to greater enjoyment. In any case, few people would be misled even by genuine exaggeration, which is an extremely common part of life. Does the hysterical euphoria of the consumers in commercials for hamburgers and soft drinks make anyone seriously expect them to taste different? Once again, the only reason for possibly being misled in the special case of sex is societally imposed ignorance. And it is people who use arguments like this one who often want to keep young people in that vulnerable state....

Most of the... claims about pornography's "effects" assume that too much stress on sex is dangerous to an intimate relationship. That can certainly be true, but the proper balance of emphasis between sex and other needs in that context is one that requires sensitive exploration, not dogma. In fact, those who give these fallacious arguments typically overlook the opposite problem. Surveys and clinical experience have long revealed that a high percentage of couples have unsatisfying sex lives. That is a major destroyer of relationships in itself. There are many reasons for this, but a serious one continues to be the sexual inhibition this society inculcates, with its *negative* stress on sex. Conversely,... countless women have discovered that sex could be a joy rather than a burden, and they have done so precisely by learning to become more sexually assertive and more adventurous in bed.

What is especially relevant to our purposes about the latter fact is that pornography has often aided in the process. Large numbers of people have reported that it has helped their sex lives and hence their relationships. In one survey of couples who went to sex movies together, for example, 42 percent made that claim. In her beautiful little book on female sexuality, *For Yourself*, Dr. Lonnie Barbach tells how women have overcome difficulty in getting sexually aroused, or in having orgasms, by learning to use fantasy and pornography. Indeed, it has become standard practice for therapists to use sex films to treat the sexual disabilities of individuals and couples. The ways in which they help are very revealing in light of what has just been discussed: they aid in overcoming inhibition, enhance arousal in preparation for sex, and introduce ideas and techniques that bring freshness to a stale routine. So far from harming intimate personal relationships, pornography can have the very opposite effect.

MARRIAGE AND THE FAMILY

A third general charge of social harm from pornography has been put forth, mostly by traditionalists. Its use is seen as a threat, not to love and personal relationships as such, but to marriage and the family. The basic claim is that by celebrating sex for its own sake, pornography entices people to leave or refrain from entering committed relationships—"Why be married if you can get sex without it?" —or else leads to their breakup by encouraging extramarital adventures that result in jealous conflicts. This is a seri-

ous charge indeed. The legalistic concern some have with marriage ceremonies is highly questionable; but the family, in its role of raising children, is of crucial importance. And divorce, with its adverse effects on children, has become increasingly common in recent decades. Such a large and complex topic can hardly be explored adequately here, but we can address two relevant questions: Is a positive attitude toward sex for its own sake necessarily a threat to marriage? And is pornography an appreciable factor in promoting that sort of attitude, hence itself such a threat?

The answer to the first question seems to be negative. For one thing, there have been many cultures with a stable family life and also an accepting attitude toward nonmarital sex. In fact, prior to the rise of the world religions and the empires that spread them, socially sanctioned premarital sex may well have been the cross-cultural norm. It has even been suggested that such behavior contributes to later marital stability by providing young people with experience on which to base a wiser choice of mate. In any case, it does not speak very well of marriage to suggest that, given a choice, people will reject it. As a matter of fact, most do have a strong inclination toward pair-bonding. Since they do not marry just for sex in the first place (and *shouldn't* do so), liberal sexual attitudes are not likely to dissuade them; only the timing is apt to be affected. In addition, there are many good reasons for not forcing young people to rush into marriage by making it the only way they can get sex.

As for the case of *extra*marital sex, where it has been socially sanctioned and controlled, it too has not been a serious threat to the stability of the family. It is true that jealousy is a powerful emotion. But it is also true that humans are far from being strictly monogamous in their feelings. Although our culture has traditionally taken jealousy as morally justified and condemned extramarital desires, others have done just the reverse: they have sought to mitigate the conflict between the two emotions by controlling the former more than the latter. And the anthropological reports indicate that they succeed rather well. It just may be, for all we know, that their system works better than ours in this respect. In fact, it can be argued that our unbending attitude toward sexual exclusivity contributes to marital breakup by creating unrealistic expectations. The offending party may not want such a break but feel it is necessary to satisfy other desires; and the offended one may fear loss of face in not avenging the act, or else think there must be something wrong with one of them or with the marriage for such a thing to have happened.

However all this may be, it is not the immediate question here. For us the issue is whether pornography is in any of the ways suggested a threat to the family in our culture. In spite of what many assume, it is far from obvious that it is. Indeed, it may be more likely to act as a "safety valve" for preventing marital breakup by providing a substitute way to satisfy nonmonogamous desires. Many cultures of the world have had special festival times and special locations in which the usual sexual taboos could be broken. (For just one example, consider the temple "prostitution" of the ancient Near East, in which all men and women took part.) The seeming value of such institutions in maintaining both monogamy and mental health has been noted by many students of the subject. The fact that such large numbers of strictly monogamous couples in the present time have come to use sexual entertainment together hints that it can serve the same purpose. Given the strong biological urge to have more than one sex partner, this may be an extremely important consideration.

Furthermore, pornography can help to preserve marriages by means of the positive effects listed earlier. As for the chance that it can also have the opposite effect, it might be suggested that romantic love stories present more of a danger to long-term pairing by awakening desires that many a marriage gone stale cannot satisfy. After all, falling in love with someone else is more likely to produce the wish for divorce than is a one-night stand. In any case, factors other than sexual fantasies have been vastly more influential in creating marital instability. The data indicate that such things as the following have been responsible for increasing divorce rates: greater independence for women (most female advocates of long-term commitment do not assail *this* causal factor), changes in laws and attitudes regarding divorce, unemployment and other financial troubles, and the greater mobility of the population, which has led to a loss of controls by the extended family and the community.

To really answer the question before us, however, we must consider the possible dynamics. Exactly how might pornography produce the allegedly destabilizing desires? Those who make the charge sometimes talk as if it is just a matter of arousing feelings that would not otherwise exist. But that is *their* fantasy, for biology can quite adequately do so. It does not take "outside agitators" like pornography to produce lust and wandering eyes. There is one thing, however, that pornography certainly can do, and that is to thwart attempts to suppress such feelings. Efforts to promote one moral point of view are indeed apt to be hampered when people are allowed to become aware of other views as genuine alternatives. This is just to say, however, that freedom and knowledge are an obstacle to attempts at thought control. "How're you gonna keep 'em down on the farm, after they've seen Paris?" asks an old song. It was not only the pill, but the loosening of restraints on sexual content in the media, that launched the reassessment of traditional sexual attitudes that occurred in the 1960s.

So there is a much broader point here that is very important. It is clear that formal and informal education—learning more about the world—tend to make people more tolerant and liberal in their views. For just one apparent example, surveys have revealed that half the readers of sex magazines are college educated, in contrast to a third of the readers of magazines in general. Ideologues, however, do not like such tolerance; what they are opposed to at bottom is the right of other people to make up their own minds. (From Moscow to Washington, they answer, "Don't *let* 'em see Paris.") But it cannot easily be argued that keeping people in ignorance of different ideas is best for them. As Carl Sagan pointed out in *Cosmos,* science has flourished at those times and places in history where there have been the greatest social openness and freedom. So it is for good reasons that we have our tradition of freedom of expression: aside from the great value of liberty itself, we have a better chance of discovering truth in a "free marketplace of ideas" than in conditions where only certain beliefs and attitudes may be extolled.

In particular, our best hope of working out the most viable social arrangement concerning sex and the family is to allow an open dialogue in which all human needs are given consideration. It is just as wrong to censor portrayals of alternative sexual lifestyles as it is to suppress those of different political or religious systems. In all likelihood, given the large range of human differences that exists, the best system in the present regard is a pluralistic one that allows individuals to discover the different modes of living that maximize their fulfillment. To rigidly impose the same kinds of relationships upon everyone (on homosexual and heterosexual, pair-bonder and non-pair-bonder and so forth) surely does not serve the best interests of individual people. And the common assumption that it is best for society as a whole is the product, not of a careful study of alternatives, but of the very prejudice that censors consideration of alternatives. Socially enforced error is self-perpetuating.

CHALLENGE QUESTIONS

Is Pornography Harmful?

1. How do you explain the increase of sexually explicit materials in our society? How does this affect our society?

2. Do you believe that today's more liberal attitudes toward sex have an effect on the incidence of rape, including date rape? Why, or why not?

3. Should policymakers pass legislation controlling or even banning pornography and other sexually explicit materials? Support your position.

4. Cline reports that viewing nonaggressive pornography can lead men to be more callous toward women. Do you agree? Do you think that other circumstances can lead to such attitudes? If so, what?

ISSUE 16

Does Religious Commitment Improve Mental Health?

YES: David B. Larson, from "Have Faith: Religion Can Heal Mental Ills," *Insight* (March 6, 1995)

NO: Albert Ellis, from "Dogmatic Devotion Doesn't Help, It Hurts," *Insight* (March 6, 1995)

ISSUE SUMMARY

YES: David B. Larson, president of the National Institute for Healthcare, maintains that religious commitment improves mental health and that spirituality can be a medical treatment.

NO: Albert Ellis, president of the Institute for Rational-Emotive Therapy, challenges Larson's studies and questions particularly whether a religious commitment of "fanatic" proportions is truly mentally healthy.

Before the modern forms of medicine and psychotherapy were ever formulated, many religious people were considered healers. The Judeo-Christian tradition and its literature are filled with claims about healing powers and reports of healing even psychological disorders. Part of the reason that these healing claims have been discounted is that some periods of history equated religious sin with psychological disorder. The people of these periods assumed that what we would now call "schizophrenia" and "depression" were really the results of sin or the indwelling of an evil spirit.

Recently, however, the healing claims of some religious people have gained a new hearing. Few of these people would contend that all psychological and emotional problems are simply sin or an evil spirit. But they caution us that although medical and living problems play an important role in psychological disorders, religious factors may also be influential. And although biological and psychological treatments have enjoyed some success, religious variables, such as spirituality, can also be important factors in alleviating mental or emotional problems. At the very least, they argue, this is an empirical rather than a religious question. Do religious factors, such as spirituality and religious commitment, improve one's mental health?

David B. Larson believes that this type of improvement has been demonstrated in numerous empirical studies. In the following selection, he presents research findings showing that spirituality is an effective treatment for drug and alcohol abuse and depression as well as an effective reducer of teen suicide and divorce. Larson explains how spirituality and religious commitment accomplish these results. Unfortunately, Larson says, psychologists' bias against religion has resulted in a continuing neglect of research on religious factors. Such bias has prevented therapists and policymakers from fully understanding the role of religion in health care. This, in turn, has deprived patients of a vital tool in coping with psychological disorders.

Albert Ellis, in contrast, questions how vital this "tool" really is. Ellis distrusts the objectivity of the studies that Larson cites. Nearly all the studies, he contends, were conducted by religious believers and published in religious journals. These people, according to Ellis, can hardly be considered to be dispassionate observers of "reality." Ellis also asserts that the more seriously people take their religious beliefs, the more fanatical they can become. Fanaticism, he suggests, is mentally and emotionally unhealthy. Therefore, the seriously religious—those who are committed and convinced—cannot be the psychologically healthy.

POINT	COUNTERPOINT
• The religiously committed report a higher rate of marital satisfaction than the nonreligious.	• Religious people are more likely than nonreligious people to respond in a socially desirable fashion.
• Many mental health professionals resist positive findings on religious people because of antireligious views.	• Many studies of religious people do not present a true picture of the mental health benefits of being religious.
• Religious people have a greater sense of overall life satisfaction than nonreligious people.	• Many religious people have a tendency to claim happier and less stressful lives than they actually have.
• Mental health status improves for those who attend religious services on a regular basis.	• There is a high degree of correlation between dogmatic religiosity and mental disorder.
• Studies show that religious commitment is the best predictor of a lack of substance abuse.	• Most of these studies are conducted by religious believers who are motivated to prove that religionists are healthier than nonreligionists.

YES

David B. Larson

HAVE FAITH: RELIGION CAN
HEAL MENTAL ILLS

If a new health treatment were discovered that helped to reduce the rate of teenage suicide, prevent drug and alcohol abuse, improve treatment for depression, reduce recovery time from surgery, lower divorce rates and enhance a sense of well-being, one would think that every physician in the country would be scrambling to try it. Yet, what if critics denounced this treatment as harmful, despite research findings that showed it to be effective more than 80 percent of the time? Which would you be more ready to believe—the assertions of the critics based on their opinions or the results of the clinical trials based upon research?

As a research epidemiologist and board-certified psychiatrist, I have encountered this situation time and again during the last 15 years of my practice. The hypothetical medical treatment really does exist, but it is not a new drug: It is spirituality. While medical professionals have been privately assuming and publicly stating for years that religion is detrimental to mental health, when I actually looked at the available empirical research on the relationship between religion and health, the findings were overwhelmingly positive.

Just what are the correlations that exist between religion and mental health? First, religion has been found to be associated with a decrease in destructive behavior such as suicide. A 1991 review of the published research on the relationship between religious commitment and suicide rates conducted by my colleagues and I found that religious commitment produced lower rates of suicide in nearly every published study located. In fact, Stephen Stack, now of Wayne State University, showed that non-church attenders were four times more likely to kill themselves than were frequent attenders and that church attendance predicted suicide rates more effectively than any other factor including unemployment.

What scientific findings could explain these lower rates of suicide? First, several researchers have noted that the religiously committed report experiencing fewer suicidal impulses and have a more negative attitude toward suicidal behavior than do the nonreligious. In addition, suicide is a less-acceptable alternative for the religiously committed because of their belief in a moral accountability to God, thus making them less susceptible than the nonreligious to this life-ending alternative. Finally, the foundational religious beliefs in an afterlife, divine justice and the possibility of eternal condemnation all help to reduce the appeal of potentially self-destructive behavior.

If religion can reduce the appeal of potentially self-destructive behavior such as suicide, could it also play a role in decreasing other self-destructive behavior such as drug abuse? When this question has been examined empirically, the overwhelming response is yes. When Richard Gorsuch conducted a review of the relationship between religious commitment and drug abuse nearly 20 years ago, he noted that religious commitment "predicts those who have not used an illicit drug regardless of whether the religious variable is defined in terms of membership, active participation, religious upbringing or the meaningfulness of religion as viewed by the person himself."

More recent reviews have substantiated the earlier findings of Gorsuch, demonstrating that even when employing varying measures of religion, religious commitment predicted curtailed drug abuse. Interestingly, a national survey of 14,000 adolescents found the lowest rates of adolescent drug abuse in the most "politically incorrect" religious group—theologically conservative teens. The drug-abuse rates of teens from more liberal religious groups rose a little higher but still sank below rates of drug abuse among nonreligious teens. The correlations between the six measures of religion employed in the survey and the eight measures of substance abuse all were consistently negative. These findings lead the authors of the study to conclude that the amount of importance individuals place

on religion in their lives is the best predictor of a lack of substance abuse, implying that "the (internal) controls operating here are a result of deeply internalized norms and values rather than fear ... or peer pressure." For teens living in a society in which drug rates continue to spiral, religion may not be so bad after all.

Just as religious commitment seems to be negatively correlated with drug abuse, similar results are found when examining the relationship between religious commitment and alcohol abuse. When I investigated this area myself, I found that those who abuse alcohol rarely have a strong religious commitment. Indeed, when my colleagues and I surveyed a group of alcoholics, we found that almost 90 percent had lost interest in religion during their teenage years, whereas among the general population, nearly that same percentage reported no change or even a slight increase in their religious practices during adolescence. Furthermore, a relationship between religious commitment and the nonuse or moderate use of alcohol has been extensively documented in the research literature. Some of the most intriguing results have been obtained by Acheampong Amoateng and Stephen Bahr of Brigham Young University, who found that whether or not a religion specifically proscribed alcohol use, those who were active in a religious group consumed substantially less than those who were not active.

Not only does religion protect against clinical problems such as suicide and drug and alcohol abuse, but religious commitment also has been shown to enhance positive life experiences such as marital satisfaction and personal well-being. When I reviewed the published studies on divorce and religious commitment, I found a negative relationship between church attendance and divorce in nearly every study that I located.

To what can these lower rates of divorce be attributed? Some critics argue that the religiously committed stay in unsatisfactory marriages due to religious prohibitions against divorce. However research has found little if any support for this view. In my review I found that, as a group, the religiously committed report a higher rate of marital satisfaction than the nonreligious. In fact, people from long-lasting marriages rank religion as one of the most important components of a happy marriage, with church attendance being strongly associated with the hypothetical willingness to remarry a spouse —a very strong indicator of marital satisfaction. Could these findings be skewed because, as is believed by some in the mental-health field, religious people falsify their response to such questions to make themselves look better? When the studies were controlled for such a factor the researchers found that the religiously committed were not falsifying their responses or answering in a socially acceptable manner and truly were more satisfied in their marriages.

Although the religiously committed are satisfied with their marriages, is this level of satisfaction also found in the sexual fulfillment of married couples? Though the prevailing public opinion is that religious individuals are prudish or even sexually repressed, empirical evidence has shown otherwise. Using data from *Redbook* magazine's survey of 100,000 women in 1975, Carole Tavris and Susan Sadd contradicted the longstanding assumption that religious commitment fosters sexual dysfunction. Tavris and Sadd found that it is the most religious women who report the greatest happiness and satisfaction with marital sex—more so than either moderately religious or nonreligious women. Religious women also report reaching orgasm more frequently than nonreligious women and are more satisfied with the frequency of their sexual activity than the less pious. Thus, while surprising to many, research suggests that religious commitment may play a role in improving rather than hindering sexual expression and satisfaction in marriage.

Not only has religious commitment been found to enhance sexual satisfaction, but overall life satisfaction as well. For example, David Myers of Hope College reviewed well-being literature and found that the religiously committed have a greater sense of overall life satisfaction than the nonreligious. Religion not only seems to foster a sense of well-being and life satisfaction but also may play a role in protecting against stress, with religiously committed respondents reporting much lower stress levels than the less committed. Even when the religiously committed have stress levels that are similar to the nonreligious, the more committed report experiencing fewer mental-illness problems than do the less committed.

Mental-health status has been found to improve for those attending religious services on a regular basis. Indeed, several studies have found a significant reduction in diverse psychiatric symptomatology following increased religious involvement. Chung-Chou Chu and colleagues at the Nebraska Psychiatric Institute in Omaha found lower rates of rehospitalization among schizophrenics who attended church or were given supportive aftercare by religious homemakers and ministers. One of my own studies confirmed that religious commitment can improve recovery rates as well. When my colleagues and I examined elderly women recovering from hip fractures, we found that those women with stronger religious beliefs suffered less from depression and thus were more likely to walk sooner and farther than their non-religious counterparts.

* * *

Yet, despite the abundance of studies demonstrating the beneficial effects of religious commitment on physical and mental health, many members of the medical community seem immune to this evidence. This resistance to empirical findings on the mental-health benefits of religious commitment may stem from the anti-religious views espoused by significant mental-health theorists. For example, Sigmund Freud called religion a "universal obsessional neurosis" and regarded mystical experience as "infantile helplessness" and a "regression to primary narcissism." More recently, Albert Ellis, the originator of rational-emotive therapy, has argued that "unbelief, humanism, skepticism and even thorough-going atheism not only abet but are practically synonymous with mental health; and that devout belief, dogmatism and religiosity distinctly contribute to, and in some ways are equal to, mental or emotional disturbance." Other clinicians have continued to perpetuate the misconception that religion is associated with psychopathology by labeling spiritual experiences as, among other things, borderline psychosis, a psychotic episode or the result of temporal-lobe dysfunction. Even the consensus report, "Mysticism: Spiritual Quest or Psychological Disturbance," by the Group for the Advancement of Psychiatry supported the long-standing view of religion as psychopathology; calling religious and mys-

tical experiences "a regression, an escape, a projection upon the world of a primitive infantile state."

What is perhaps most surprising about these negative opinions of religion's effect on mental health is the startling absence of empirical evidence to support these views. Indeed, the same scientists who were trained to accept or reject a hypothesis based on hard data seem to rely solely on their own opinions and biases when assessing the effect of religion on health. When I conducted a systematic review of all articles published in the two leading journals of psychiatry, the *American Journal of Psychiatry* and the *Archives of General Psychiatry*, which assessed the association between religious commitment and mental health, I found that more than 80 percent of the religious-mental health associations located were clinically beneficial while only 15 percent of the associations were harmful—findings that run counter to the heavily publicized opinion of mental-health professionals. Thus, even though the vast majority of published research studies show religion as having a positive influence on mental health, religious commitment remains at best ignored or at worst, maligned by the professional community.

The question then begs to be asked: Why do medical professionals seem to ignore such positive evidence about religion's beneficial effect on mental health? One possible source of this tension could lie in clinicians' unfamiliarity with or rejection of traditional religious expression. For example, not only do mental-health professionals generally hold levels of religious commitment that diverge significantly from the general population, but they have much higher rates of atheism and agnosticism as well. The most recent survey of the belief systems of mental-health professionals found that less than 45 percent of the members of the American Psychiatric Association and the American Psychological Association believed in God—a percentage less than half that of the general population. When asked whether they agreed with the statement, "My whole approach to life is based on my religion," only one-third of clinical psychologists and two-fifths of psychiatrists agreed with that statement—again, a percentage that is nearly half that of the U.S. population. Indeed, more than 25 percent of psychiatrists and clinical psychologists and more than 40 percent of psychoanalysts claimed that they had abandoned a theistic belief system, compared with just less than 5 percent of the general population reporting the same feelings.

Science is assumed to be a domain that progresses through the gradual accumulation of new data or study findings, yet the mental-health community seems to be stalled in its understanding of the interface between religion and mental health. If a field is to progress in its knowledge and understanding of a controversial issue such as religion, empirical data and research must be relied upon more than personal opinions and biases. At a time when the rising cost of health care is causing so much discussion in our country, no factor that may be so beneficial to health can be ignored. The continuing neglect of published research on religion prevents clinicians and policymakers from fully understanding the important role of religion in health care and deprives patients as well as themselves of improved skills and methods in clinical prevention, coping with illness and quality of care. The mental health establishment needs to begin to recognize that it is treating a whole person—mind, body and, yes, even spirit.

NO

Albert Ellis

DOGMATIC DEVOTION DOESN'T HELP, IT HURTS

According to the psychological studies cited by David Larson, religious believers have more satisfying marriages, more enjoyable sex lives, less psychological stress, less depression and less drug and alcohol abuse than nonreligious people. Do these studies present a "true" picture of the mental health benefits of being religious? Probably not, for several reasons. First, the scientific method itself has been shown by many postmodernists to be far from "objective" and unassailable because it is created and used by highly subjective, often biased individuals. Scientists are never purely dispassionate observers of "reality" but frequently bring their own biases to their experiments and conclusions.

Second, practically all the studies that Larson cites were conducted by religious believers; some were published in religious journals. Many of the researchers were motivated to structure studies to "prove" that religionists are "healthier" than nonreligionists and only to publish studies that "proved" this.

None of the studies cited—as I noted when I read many of them myself —eliminated the almost inevitable bias of the subjects they used. I showed, in two comprehensive reviews of personality questionnaires that were published in the *Psychological Bulletin* in 1946 and 1948 and in several other psychological papers, that people often can figure out the "right" and "wrong" answers to these questionnaires and consequently "show" that they are "healthy" when they actually are not. I also showed, in an article in the *American Sociological Review* in 1948, that conservative and religious subjects probably more often were claiming falsely to have "happier" marriages on the Burgess-Locke Marriage Prediction Test than were liberal and nonreligious subjects.

This tendency of conservative, religious, job-seeking and otherwise motivated individuals to overemphasize their "good" and deemphasize their "poor" behavior on questionnaires has been pointed out by a number of other reviewers of psychological studies. Because all these studies included a number of strongly religious subjects, I would guess that many of these religionists had a distinct tendency to claim to be happier, less stressful and less addictive personalities than a good clinician would find them to be. I believe that this is a common finding of psychologists and was confirmed by my reviews mentioned previously.

Although Larson has spent a number of years locating studies that demonstrated that religious believers are healthier than nonreligious subjects, a large number of researchers have demonstrated the opposite. Several other studies have found that people who rigidly and dogmatically maintain religious views are more disturbed than less-rigid religious followers. But all these studies, once again, are suspect because none of them seem to have eliminated the problem of the biased answers of some of their subjects who consciously or unconsciously want to show how healthy they are.

Larson points out that many psychologists are sure that religionists are more disturbed than nonreligionists in spite of their having no real scientific evidence to substantiate their opinions. He is largely right about this, in view of what I have already said. Nonetheless, some reasonably good data back up the views of these psychologists that devout religionists often are disturbed.

Antiabortion killers such as Paul Hill have demonstrated that fanatical beliefs can have deadly consequences. But lesser-known fanatical religious believers have used ruthless tactics to oppose such "enlightened" views as birth control, women's liberation and even separation of church and state. Some religious zealots have jailed, maimed or even killed liberal proponents of their own religions. Nobel laureate Naguib Mahfouz is still recovering from stab wounds inflicted by Muslim extremists last October near his home in Cairo. (Mahfouz, considered by many to be a devout Muslim, frequently has ridiculed religious hypocrisy in his work.) Indian-born author Salman Rushdie has lived for seven years under a death sentence pronounced by the late Ayatollah Khomeini. Rushdie explained to the *New York Times* that dissidents within the Muslim world become "persons whose blood is unclean and therefore deserves to be spilled."

Religious persecution and wars against members of other religions have involved millions of casualties throughout human history Islamic fundamentalists from North Africa to Pakistan have established, or done their best to establish, state religions that force all the citizens of a country or other political group to strictly obey the rules of a specific religious group.

People diagnosed as being psychotic and of having severe personality disorders frequently have been obsessed with religious ideas and practices and compulsively and scrupulously follow religious teachings.

The tragic, multiple suicides of members of the Switzerland-based Order of the Solar Temple last October is only the most recent illustration of an extremist religious cult which manipulated its adherents and induced some of them to harm and kill themselves.

Do these manifestations of religious-oriented fanaticism, despotism, cultism and psychosis prove that religious-minded people generally are more disturbed than nonreligious individuals? Of course not. Many—probably most—religionists oppose the extreme views and practices I have just listed, and some actually make efforts to counteract them. One should not conclude, then, that pious religiosity in and of itself equals emotional disturbance.

However, as a psychotherapist and the founder of a school of psychotherapy called rational emotive behavior therapy, I have for many years distinguished between people who hold moderate religious views and those who espouse devout, dogmatic, rigid religious attitudes. In my judgment, most intelligent and educated people are in the former group and temperately believe God (such as Jehovah) exists, that He or She created the universe and the creatures in it, and that we preferably should follow religious, ethical laws but that a Supreme Being forgives us fallible humans when we do not follow His or Her rules. These "moderate" religionists prefer to be "religious" but do not insist that the rest of us absolutely and completely always must obey God's and the church's precepts. Therefore, they still mainly run their own lives and rarely damn themselves (and others) for religious nonobservance. In regard to God and His or Her Commandments, they live and let live.

The second kind of religious adherents —those who are devout, absolutistic and dogmatic—are decidedly different. They differ among themselves but most of them tend to believe that there absolutely has to be a Supreme Being, that He or She specifically runs the universe, must be completely obeyed and will eternally damn all believers and nonbelievers who deviate from His or Her sacred commands.

Another devout and absolutistic group of people do not believe in anything supernatural, but do rigidly subscribe to a dogmatic, secular belief system— such as Nazism, Fascism or Communism —which vests complete authority in the state or in some other organization and which insists that nonallegiance or opposition to this Great Power must be ruthlessly fought, overthrown, punished and annihilated.

As an advocate of mental and emotional health, I have always seen "moderate" religious believers as reasonably sound individuals who usually are no more neurotic (or otherwise disturbed) than are skeptical, nonreligious people. Like nonbelievers, they are relatively open-minded, democratic and unbigoted. They allow themselves to follow and experience "religious" and "secular" values, enjoyment and commitments. Therefore, they infrequently get into serious emotional trouble with themselves or with others because of their religious beliefs and actions.

This is not the case with fanatical, pietistic religionists. Whether they are righteously devoted to God and the church or to secular organizations and cults (some of which may be atheistic) these extreme religionists are not open-minded, tolerant and undamning. Like nonreligious neurotics and individuals with severe personality disorders, they do not merely wish that other religionists and nonbelievers agree with them and worship their own Supreme Being and their churchly values. They insist, demand and command that their God's and their church's will be done.

Since the age of 12, I have been skeptical of anything supernatural or god-like. But I always have believed that undogmatic religionists can get along well in the world and be helpful to others, and I relate nicely to them. Many, if not most, of the mental-health professionals with whom I have worked in the field of rational emotive behavior therapy are religious. A surprisingly large number of them have been ordained as Protestant ministers, Catholic priests or nuns or Jewish rabbis. A few have even been fundamentalists! So some forms of psychotherapy and moderate religious belief hardly are incompatible.

The important question remains: Is there a high degree of correlation between devout, one-sided, dogmatic religiosity and neurosis (and other personality disorders)? My experience as a clinical psychologist leads me to conclude that there well may be. Some of the disturbed traits and behaviors that pietistic religionists tend to have (but, of course, not always have) include these:

A dearth of enlightened self-interest and self-direction. Pietistic religionists tend to be overdevoted, instead, to unduly sacrificing themselves for God, the church (or the state) and to ritualistic self-deprivation that they feel "bound" to follow for "sacred" reasons. They often give masochistic and self-abasing allegiance to ecclesiastical (and/or secular) lords and leaders. Instead of largely planning and directing their own lives, they often are mindlessly overdependent on religious-directed (or state-directed) creeds, rules and commandments.

Reduced social and human interest. Dogmatic religionists are overly focused on godly, spiritual and monastic interests. They often give greater service to God than to humanity and frequently start holy wars against dissidents to their deity and their church. Witness the recent murders by allegedly devout antiabortionists!

Refusal to accept ambiguity and uncertainty. In an obsessive-compulsive fashion, they hold to absolute necessity and complete certainty, even though our universe only seems to include probability and chance. They deny pliancy, alternative-seeking and pluralism in their own and other people's lives. They

negate the scientific view that no hypothesis is proved indisputably "true" under all conditions at all times.

Allergy to unconditional self-acceptance. Emotionally healthy people accept themselves (and other humans) unconditionally—that is, whether they achieve success and whether all significant others approve of them. Dogmatic religionists unhealthily and conditionally accept themselves (and others) only when their God, their church (or state) and similar religionists approve of their thoughts, feelings and behaviors. Therefore, they steadily remain prone to, and often are in the throes of, severe anxiety guilt and self-condemnation.

In rational-emotive therapy we show people that they "get" emotionally disturbed not only by early or later traumas in their lives but mainly by choosing goals and values that they strongly prefer and by unrealistically, illogically and defeatingly making them into one, two or three grandiose demands: (1) "I absolutely must succeed at important projects or I am an utterly worthless person"; (2) "Other people must treat me nicely or they are totally damnable"; (3) "Life conditions are utterly obligated to give me everything that I think I need or my existence is valueless."

When people clearly see that they are largely upsetting themselves with these godlike commandments, and when they convert them to reasonable—but often still compulsive—desires, they are able to reconstruct their disturbed thoughts, feelings and actions and make themselves much less anxious, depressed, enraged and self-hating and much more self-actualizing and happy.

Being a philosophical system of psychotherapy, rational emotive behavior therapy has much to learn from theological and secular religions. But individuals who choose to be religious also may learn something important from it, namely: Believe whatever you wish about God, the church, people and the universe. But see if you can choose a moderate instead of a fanatical form of religion. Try to avoid a doctrinal system through which you are dogmatically convinced that you absolutely must devote yourself to the one, only, right and unerring deity and to the one, true and infallible church. And try to avoid the certitude that you are God. Otherwise, in my view as a psychotherapist, you most probably are headed for emotional trouble.

CHALLENGE QUESTIONS

Does Religious Commitment Improve Mental Health?

1. Explain why Ellis feels that the data concerning the benefits of religion are not objective. Could his explanation be applied to other types of psychological research?

2. Ellis is the founder of a major school of psychotherapy— rational-emotive therapy. Find a description of this therapy, and discuss how Ellis's own nonreligious values might influence his formulation of this therapy.

3. If it were generally agreed that religious factors were beneficial for mental health, how might psychotherapists use these factors? What problems might a person encounter in employing these factors?

4. How does Ellis distinguish between those who adopt moderate forms of religion and those who adopt fanatical forms of religion? How is this distinction different from the distinction between those who consider their religion relatively superficially and those who take their religious beliefs seriously?

5. For the last few centuries, religion and science have been considered completely separate endeavors. How might this historical separation play into the controversy between Larson and Ellis?

On the Internet . . .

Communication and Gender
This site provides lessons from a course on communication and gender. It contains a great deal of information on gender issues.
http://cyberschool.4j.lane.edu/people/faculty/giesen/commg/Lessons/Lessons.htm

National Women's Resource Center
This site contains bibliographic databases with current citations to literature related to women's substance abuse and mental illness. *http://www.nwrc.org/*

New England Mindbody Institute's Women's Health Site
The New England Mindbody Institute's Women's Health program is devoted to helping women achieve and maintain peak levels of psychological, physical, and spiritual health and well-being. It covers topics from premenstrual syndrome and menopause to midlife psychology and marriage.
http://www.ne-mindbody.com/women.html

Progressive Women's Issues, Interests, and Information on the Internet
This site provides a list of Web links related to women's issues.
http://www.igc.org/igc/issues/women/index.html

Shattered Love, Broken Lives
This site is a selection of articles generated during the *Standard-Times's* 11-part survey of domestic violence. Topics include batterers, how women cope, and solutions to domestic violence.
http://www.s-t.com/projects/DomVio/content.HTML

WomensNet
WomensNet supports women's organizations worldwide by providing and adapting telecommunications technology to enhance their work.
http://www.igc.org/igc/womensnet/

PART 8

Women's Issues

Although what are often referred to as women's issues affect everyone, the women's movement has brought special attention and a special perspective to some issues. This is as true for psychology as it is for many other disciplines. At the same time, however, this attention and this perspective has been controversial in psychology. Some have argued, for instance, that this attention has meant an inattention to other psychological issues. Some have claimed, for example, that attention to wife beating—as a result of the women's movement—has led many psychologists to overlook the phenomenon of husband beating. Is this true? Has the women's movement biased psychological researchers to ignore important variables? Does the liberal perspective of this movement lead to a misinterpretation of psychological findings?

■ Are Women Violent Toward Their Male Partners?

■ Does Abortion Have Severe Psychological Effects?

ISSUE 17

Are Women Violent Toward Their Male Partners?

YES: Murray A. Straus, from "Physical Assaults by Wives: A Major Social Problem," in Richard J. Gelles and Donileen R. Loseke, eds., *Current Controversies on Family Violence* (Sage Publications, 1993)

NO: Demie Kurz, from "Physical Assaults by Husbands: A Major Social Problem," in Richard J. Gelles and Donileen R. Loseke, eds., *Current Controversies on Family Violence* (Sage Publications, 1993)

ISSUE SUMMARY

YES: In a review of the relevant research, sociologist Murray A. Straus contends that women are just as physically violent toward their partners as men are and that this violence is a serious social problem in need of further investigation and prevention.

NO: Feminist researcher Demie Kurz contends that family violence researchers like Straus misunderstand the context of inequality and male dominance in marriage and that this misunderstanding diverts attention away from the true social problem of power-driven violence against women.

Many people assume that a battered spouse is synonymous with a battered woman. That is, it is typically assumed that husbands are much more likely to engage in physical abuse of their spouses than wives are. This assumption originates from two quite different sources. The first is traditional stereotypes: Males are thought to be more physically aggressive in conflict, whereas females are considered to be more likely to talk through their problems with others.

The second source is feminism. Because males occupy positions of power, according to many feminists, their use of violence toward women has been implicitly and explicitly condoned by society. Many old laws, for example, allowed men to "chastise" and "correct" their wives. Many feminists believe that this type of societal atmosphere gives men permission to be physically abusive to their female partners. In this sense, both sources—traditional stereotypes and feminist theory—have furthered the notion that women rarely physically abuse their male partners.

Imagine the controversy, then, when Murray A. Straus reviewed the research on family violence and reported that this traditional notion is false. Specifically, Straus found not only that women are often physically violent toward their male partners but also that women are as violent toward their husbands as men are to their wives. Although previous explanations attributed most incidents of female violence to acts of self-defense, in the selection that follows, Straus contends that recent research indicates that women (not their husbands) often initiate the physical violence. For this reason, Straus asks that efforts to prevent violence *by* wives be added to efforts to prevent violence *to* wives.

In the second selection, Demie Kurz contends that the research reviewed by Straus is misleading and flawed. She feels that the researchers misinterpreted their findings because of poorly designed and ambiguous investigative questions. Furthermore, these researchers grounded their studies on faulty theoretical assumptions. Specifically, they disregarded the role of gender in marital relationships and, thus, were not appropriately sensitive to the male dominance that permeates such relationships. Kurz provides an alternative interpretation of these studies that acknowledges important gender issues in marital violence. As a result of this reinterpretation, she strongly disputes the notion that women are as violent toward their male partners as men are to their female partners.

POINT	COUNTERPOINT
• Research indicates that women are as physically violent toward their husbands as men are to their wives.	• This research is flawed because it does not attend to the male-dominated social climate that condones violence toward women.
• Responses to survey questions about isolated acts of violence show that men and women are equally violent toward their partners.	• Survey questions concerning isolated acts of violence ignore the numerous male acts of violence that preceded the violence in question.
• The notion that all female violence is perpetrated in self-defense is not supported by recent research, which shows that women often initiate the violence.	• Female violence is generally committed in self-defense because of inherent gender inequalities and male dominance in heterosexual relationships.
• Increased effort should be expended to prevent violence by women toward their husbands.	• A focus on female violence draws attention away from the institutionalized power differences between men and women.

YES
Murray A. Straus

PHYSICAL ASSAULTS BY WIVES: A MAJOR SOCIAL PROBLEM

The first purpose of this [selection] is to review research that shows that women initiate and carry out physical assaults on their partners as often as men do. A second purpose is to show that, despite the much lower probability of physical injury resulting from attacks by women, assaults by women are a serious social problem, just as it would be if men "only" slapped their wives or "only" slapped female fellow employees and produced no injury. One of the main reasons "minor" assaults by women are such an important problem is that they put women in danger of much more severe retaliation by men. They also help perpetuate the implicit cultural norms that make the marriage license a hitting license. It will be argued that, to end "wife beating," it is essential for women also to end the seemingly "harmless" pattern of slapping, kicking, or throwing things at male partners who persist in some outrageous behavior and "won't listen to reason."

The [selection] focuses exclusively on physical assaults, even though they are not necessarily the most damaging type of abuse. One can hurt a partner deeply—even drive the person to suicide—without ever lifting a finger. Verbal aggression may be even more damaging than physical attacks (Vissing, Straus, Gelles, & Harrop, 1991). This [selection] is concerned only with physical assaults because, with rare exception, the controversy has been about "violence," that is, physical assaults, by wives.

DEFINITION AND MEASUREMENT OF ASSAULT

The National Crime Panel Report defines *assault* as "an unlawful physical attack by one person upon another" (U.S. Department of Justice, 1976). It is important to note that neither this definition nor the definition used for reporting assaults to the Federal Bureau of Investigation (1989) requires injury or bodily contact. Thus if a person is chased by someone attempting to hit the individual with a stick or to stab the person, and the victim escapes, the attack is still a felony-level crime—an "aggravated assault"—even though the victim was not touched. Nevertheless, in the real world, the occurrence

From Murray A. Straus, "Physical Assaults by Wives: A Major Social Problem," in Richard J. Gelles and Donileen R. Loseke, eds., *Current Controversies on Family Violence* (Sage Publications, 1993). Copyright © 1993 by Sage Publications, Inc. Reprinted by permission. Notes and references omitted. Portions of this article are adapted from Murray A. Straus, "Physical Assults by Women Partners: A Major Social Problem," in M. R. Walsh, ed., *Women, Men, and Gender: Ongoing Debates* (Yale University Press, 1997).

of an injury makes a difference in what the police, prosecutors, and juries do. Consequently, injury will also be considered [here].

GENDER DIFFERENCES IN SPOUSE ASSAULT AND HOMICIDE RATES

National Family Violence Surveys

The National Family Violence Surveys obtained data from nationally representative samples of 2,143 married and cohabiting couples in 1975 and 6,002 couples in 1985 (information on the sample and methodology is given in Gelles & Straus, 1988; Straus & Gelles, 1986, 1990). Previously published findings have shown that, in both surveys, the rate of wife-to-husband assault was about the same (actually slightly higher) than the husband-to-wife assault rate (Straus & Gelles, 1986, 1990). However, the seeming equality may occur because of a tendency by husbands to underreport their own assaults (Dutton, 1988; Edleson & Brygger, 1986; Jouriles & O'Leary, 1985; Stets & Straus, 1990; Szinovacz, 1983). To avoid the problem of male underreporting, the assault rates were recomputed for this [selection] on the basis of information provided by the 2,994 women in the 1985 National Family Violence Survey. The resulting overall rate for assaults by wives is 124 per 1,000 couples, compared with 122 per 1,000 for assaults by husbands *as reported by wives*. This difference is not great enough to be statistically significant. Separate rates were also computed for minor and severe assaults. The rate of minor assaults by wives was 78 per 1,000 couples, and the rate of minor assaults by husbands was 72 per 1,000. The severe assault rate was 46 per 1,000 couples for assaults by wives and 50 per 1,000 for assaults by husbands. Neither difference is statistically significant. As these rates are based exclusively on information provided by women respondents, the near equality in assault rates cannot be attributed to a gender bias in reporting. . . .

Injury adjusted rates. Stets and Straus (1990) and Brush (1990) provide data that can be used to adjust the rates to take into account whether the assault resulted in an injury. Stets and Straus found a rate of 3% for injury-producing assaults by men and 0.4% for injury-producing assaults by women. Somewhat lower injury rates were found by Brush for another large national sample—1.2% of injury-producing assaults by men and 0.2% for injury-producing assaults by women. An "injury adjusted" rate was computed using the higher of the two injury estimates. The resulting rate of injury-producing assaults by husbands is 3.7 per 1,000 ($122 \times .03 = 3.66$), and the rate of injury-producing assaults by wives is much lower—0.6 per 1,000 ($124 \times .004 = 0.49$). Thus the injury adjusted rate for assaults by men is six times greater than the rate of domestic assaults by women.

Although the injury adjusted rates correspond more closely to police and National Crime Victimization Survey statistics, . . . there are several disadvantages to rates based on injury (Straus, 1990b, pp. 79–83), two of which will be mentioned. One of the disadvantages is that the criterion of injury contradicts the new domestic assault legislation and new police policies. These statutes and policies premise restraining orders and encourage arrest on the basis of attacks. They do not require observable injury.

Another disadvantage of using injury as a criterion for domestic assault is that injury-based rates omit the 97% of assaults by husbands that do not result in injury but that are nonetheless a serious social problem. Without an adjustment for injury, the National Family Violence Survey produces an estimate of more than 6 million women assaulted by a male partner each year, of which 1.8 million are "severe" assaults (Straus & Gelles, 1990). If the injury adjusted rate is used, the estimate is reduced to 188,000 assaulted women per year. The figure of 1.8 million seriously assaulted women every year has been used in many legislative hearings and countless feminist publications to indicate the prevalence of the problem. If that estimate had to be replaced by 188,000, it would understate the extent of the problem and could handicap efforts to educate the public and secure funding for shelters and other services. Fortunately, that is not necessary. Both estimates can be used, because they highlight different aspects of the problem.

Other Surveys of Married and Dating Couples

Married and cohabiting couples. Although there may be exceptions that I missed, *every* study among the more than 30 describing some type of sample that is not self-selective (such as community random samples and samples of college student dating couples) has found a rate of assault by women on male partners that is about the same as the rate of assault by men on female partners. The space available for this [selection] does not permit me to describe each of those studies, but they include research by respected scholars such as Scanzoni (1978) and Tyree and Malone (1991) and large-scale studies such as the Los Angeles Epidemi-

ology Catchment Area study (Sorenson & Telles, 1991), the National Survey of Households and Families (Brush, 1990), and the survey conducted for the Kentucky Commission on Women (Schulman, 1979).

The Kentucky study also brings out a troublesome question of scientific ethics, because it is one of several in which the data on assaults by women were intentionally suppressed. The existence of those data became known only because Hornung, McCullough, and Sugimoto (1981) obtained the computer tape and found that, among the violent couples, 38% were attacks by women on men who, as reported by the women themselves, had not attacked them. Some of the other studies that found approximately equal rates are cited in Straus and Gelles (1990, pp. 95–105).

Dating couples. Sugarman and Hotaling (1989) summarize the results of 21 studies that reported gender differences in assault. They found that the average assault rate was 329 per 1,000 for men and 393 per 1,000 for women. Sugarman and Hotaling comment that a "surprising finding ... is the *higher* proportion of females than males who self-report having expressed violence in a dating relationship" (p. 8; emphasis added). Moreover, other studies published since their review further confirm the high rate of assault by women in dating relationships (see, e.g., Pirog-Good & Stets, 1989; Stets & Straus, 1990).

Samples of "battered women." Studies of residents in shelters for battered women are sometimes cited to show that it is only their male partners who are violent. However, these studies rarely obtain or report information on assaults by women, and when they do, they ask only about self-defense. Pagelow's (1981) questionnaire, for example, presents respondents with a list of "factors responsible for causing the battering," but the list does not include an attack *by* the woman, therefore precluding finding information on female-initiated assaults. One of the few exceptions is in the work of Walker (1984), who found that one out of four women in battering relationships had answered affirmatively that they had "used physical force to get something [they] wanted" (p. 174). Another is the study by Giles-Sims (1983) that found that in the year prior to coming to a shelter, 50% of the women reported assaulting their partners, and in the six months after leaving the shelter, 41.7% reported an assault against a spouse. These assaults could all have been in self-defense, but Giles-Sims's case study data suggest that this is not likely. . . .

Spouse Homicide Rates

Homicide rates published by the FBI show that only 14% of homicide offenders are women (calculated from Federal Bureau of Investigation, 1989, unnumbered table at bottom of p. 9). However, the percentages of female offenders vary tremendously according to the relationships between offenders and victims. Female-perpetrated homicides of *strangers* occur at a rate that is less than a twentieth the male rate. The female share goes up somewhat for murders of *acquaintances.* As for murders of *family* members, women committed them at a rate that was almost half the rate of men in the period 1976–1979 and more than a third of the male rate during the period 1980–1984.

However, *family* includes all relatives, whereas the main focus of this [selection] is couples. Two recent gender-specific estimates of the rates for partner homicide indicate that wives murder male partners at a rate that is 56% (Straus, 1986) and 62% (Browne & Williams, 1989) as great as the rate of partner homicides by husbands. This is far from equality, but it also indicates that, in partner relationships, even when the assaults are so extreme as to result in death, the rate for wives is extremely high, whereas, as noted above, for murders of strangers the female rate is only a twentieth of the male rate.

SELF-DEFENSE AND ASSAULTS BY WIVES

In previous work I have explained the high rate of attacks on spouses by wives as largely a *response* to or a defense against assault by the partner (Straus, 1977, 1980); Straus et al., 1980). However, new evidence raises questions about that interpretation.

Homicide

For lethal assaults by women, a number of studies suggest that a substantial proportion are self-defense, retaliation, or acts of desperation following years of brutal victimization (Browne, 1987; Browne & Williams, 1989; Jurik, 1989; Jurik & Gregware, 1989). However, Jurik (1989) and Jurik and Gregware's (1989) investigation of 24 cases in which women killed husbands or lovers found that the victim initiated use of physical force in 10 (40%) of the cases. Jurik and Gregware's Table 2 shows that only 5 out of the 24 homicides (21%) were in response to "prior abuse" or "threat of abuse/death." Mann's (1990) study of the circumstances surrounding partner homicides by wives shows that many women who murder their spouses are impulsive, violent, and have criminal records. Jurik (1989) and Jurik and Gregware (1989) also report that 60% of the women they studied had previous arrests. The widely cited study by Wolfgang (1958) refers to "victim-precipitated" homicides, but the case examples indicate that these homicides include cases of retaliation as well as self-defense.

National Family Violence Survey

Wife-only violence. Of the 495 couples in the 1985 National Family Violence Survey for whom one or more assaultive incidents were reported by a woman respondent, the husband was the only violent partner in 25.9% of the cases, the wife was the only one to be violent in 25.5% of the cases, and both were violent in 48.6% of the cases. Thus a minimum estimate of violence by wives that is *not* self-defense because the wife is the only one to have used violence in the past 12 months is 25%. Brush (1990) reports similar results for the couples in the National Survey of Families and Households.

Perhaps the real gender difference occurs in assaults that carry a greater risk of causing physical injury—such as punching, kicking, and attacks with weapons. This hypothesis was investigated using the 211 wives who reported one or more instances of a "severe" assault. The resulting proportions were similar: both, 35.2%; husband only, 35.2%; and wife only, 29.6%.

The findings just reported show that regardless of whether the analysis is based on all assaults or is focused on dangerous assaults, about as many women as men attacked spouses who had *not* hit them during the one-year referent period. This is inconsistent with the self-defense explanation for the high rate of domestic assault by women. However, it is possible that, among the couples where both assaulted, all the women were acting in self-defense. Even if that unlikely assumption were correct, it would still be true that 25–30% of violent marriages are violent solely because of attacks by the wife.

Initiation of attacks. The 1985 National Family Violence Survey asked respondents, "Let's talk about the last time you and your partner got into a physical fight and [the most severe act previously mentioned] happened. In that particular instance, who started the physical conflict, you or your partner?" According to the 446 wives involved in violent relationships, their partners struck the first blows in 42.3% of the cases, the women hit first in 53.1% of the cases, and the women could not remember or could not disentangle who hit first in the remaining 3.1% of the cases.

Similar results were obtained by five other studies. Bland and Orne's (1986) study of marital violence and psychiatric disorder in Canada found that wives initiated violence somewhat more often than did husbands. Gryl and Bird (1989) found that "respondents in violent dating relationships indicated that their partners initiated the violence 51% of the time; they initiated it 41% of the time; and both were equally responsible 8% of the time." Saunders (1989) analyzed data on the sequence of events in the 1975 National Family Violence Survey and found that women respondents indicated that they struck the first blow in 40% of the cases. Henton, Cate, Koval, Lloyd, and Christopher (1983) found that "in 48.7%... of the relationships, the respondent perceived that both partners were responsible for 'starting' the violence" (p. 472). A large-scale Canadian study found that women struck the first blow about as often as men. However, as in the case of the Kentucky survey mentioned earlier, the authors have not published the findings, perhaps because they are not "politically correct." ...

CONTEXT AND MEANING

The number of assaults by itself, however, ignores the contexts, meanings, and consequences of these assaults. The fact that assaults by women produce far less injury is a critical difference. There are probably other important differences between men and women in assaults on partners. For example, a man may typically hit or threaten to hit to force some specific behavior on pain of injury, whereas a woman may typically slap a partner or pound on his chest as an expression of outrage or in frustration because of his having turned a deaf ear to repeated attempts to discuss some critical issue (Greenblat, 1983). Despite this presumed difference, both are uses of physical violence for coercion.

A meta-analysis of research on gender differences in aggression by Eagly and Steffen (1986) brings out a related difference in context and meaning. These researchers found no *overall* difference in aggression by men and women, but less aggression by women if the act would produce harm to the target. These and other differences in context, meaning, and motivation are important for understanding violence by women against partners, but they do not indicate the absence of assault by women. Nor do differences between men and women in the histories, meanings, objectives, and

consequences of assaults refute the hypothesis discussed below: that assaults by wives help legitimate male violence. Only empirical research can resolve that issue.

VIOLENCE BY WIVES INCREASES THE PROBABILITY OF WIFE BEATING

There seems to be an implicit cultural norm permitting or encouraging minor assaults by wives in certain circumstances. Stark and McEvoy (1970) found about equal support for a wife hitting a husband as for a husband hitting a wife. Greenblat (1983) found that both men and women are *more* accepting of wives hitting husbands than of husbands hitting wives. Data from the National Family Violence Survey also show more public acceptance of a wife slapping a husband than of a husband slapping a wife. Greenblat suggests that this is because "female aggressors are far less likely to do physical harm" (p. 247). These norms tolerating low-level violence by women are transmitted and learned in many ways. For example, even casual observation of the mass media suggests that just about every day, there are scenes depicting a man who makes an insulting or outrageous statement and an indignant woman who responds by "slapping the cad," thus presenting an implicit model of assault as a morally correct behavior to millions of women.

Let us assume that most of the assaults by wives fall into the "slap the cad" genre and are not intended to, and only rarely, cause physical injury. The danger to women is shown by studies that find that minor violence by wives increases the probability of severe assaults by husbands (Bowker, 1983; Feld & Straus, 1989;

Gelles & Straus, 1988, pp. 146–156). Sometimes this is immediate and severe retaliation. Regardless of whether that occurs, however, a more indirect and probably more important effect may be that such morally correct slapping acts out and reinforces the traditional tolerance of assault in marriage. The moral justification of assault implicit when a woman slaps or throws something at a partner for doing something outrageous reinforces his moral justification for slapping her when *she* is doing something outrageous, or when she is obstinate, nasty, or "not listening to reason" as he sees it. To the extent that this is correct, one of the many steps needed in primary prevention of assaults on wives is for women to forsake even "harmless" physical attacks on male partners and children. Women must insist on nonviolence from their sisters, just as they rightfully insist on it from men.

It is painful to have to recognize the high rate of domestic assaults by women. Moreover, the statistics are likely to be used by misogynists and apologists for male violence. The problem is similar to that noted by Barbara Hart (1986) in the introduction to a book on lesbian battering: "[It] is painful. It challenges our dream of a lesbian utopia. It contradicts our belief in the inherent nonviolence of women. And the disclosure of violence by lesbians... may enhance the arsenal of homophobes.... Yet, if we are to free ourselves, we must free our sisters" (p. 10). My view of recognizing violence by wives is parallel to Hart's view on lesbian battering. It is painful, but to do otherwise obstructs a potentially important means of reducing assaults by husbands—raising the consciousness of women about the implicit norms that are reinforced by a ritualized slap for outrageous behavior on the part of their partners.

It follows from the above that efforts to prevent assaults by husbands must include attention to assaults by wives. Although this may seem like "victim blaming," there is an important difference. Recognizing that assaults by wives are one of the many causes of wife beating does not justify such assaults. It is the responsibility of husbands as well as wives to refrain from physical attacks (including retaliation), at home as elsewhere, no matter what the provocation.

DENYING THE EVIDENCE

The findings showing approximately equal rates of partner assault by men and women have been greeted with disbelief and anger by some feminist scholars. There is a large literature which attempts to repudiate the findings. Most of these efforts fall into three categories: (1) criticism of the Conflict Tactics Scales, (2) criticism of the authors of such studies for ignoring the sexist structure of society, and (3) implicitly excusing violence by women by arguing that it must be understood in the context of male oppression.

Validity of the Conflict Tactics Scales

The fact that so many studies have found equal rates of assault has been blamed on deficiencies in the Conflict Tactics Scales (CTS), the instrument used in most of the studies. These critiques contain so many factual errors that the authors could not have examined the CTS firsthand. Because of space limitations I can give only three of the many alleged deficiencies. One example is the assertion that the CTS measures only violence used to settle a conflict and that it ignores purely malicious violence. On the contrary, the instructions ask respondents to describe what happens "when they disagree, get annoyed with the other person, or just have spats or fights because they're in a bad mood or tired or for some other reason." A second erroneous criticism is that the findings are questionable because men underreport their own violence. Although men do underreport, this could not have produced the statistics in this [selection] because they are based on data provided by women. Another example is the claim that the CTS gives a biased and limited picture of abuse of partners because it ignores verbal abuse. This is perhaps the most preposterous criticism because a measure of Verbal Aggression is one the CTS scales.

In addition to factual errors, there are conceptual errors. For example, it is claimed that the CTS is invalid because the continuum of violence in the scales is so broad that it fails to discriminate among the different kinds of violence. Rather, it is the broad continuum that enables one to differentiate cases of minor and severe violence. Perhaps the most important conceptual error is the belief that the CTS is deficient because it does not measure the consequences of physical assault (such as physical and emotional injury) or the causes (such as desire to dominate). This is akin to thinking that a spelling test is inadequate because it does not measure why a child spells badly, or does not measure possible consequences of poor spelling, such as low self-esteem or low evaluations by employers. The concentration of the CTS on acts of physical assault is deliberate and is one of its strengths. Only by having separate measures of assaults, injuries, and context can one, for example, show

that acts of violence by men result in more injury than when the same acts are committed by women (Stets & Straus, 1990; Straus, 1990a, 1990b).

Like all tests and scales, the CTS is not perfect. Nevertheless, numerous reviews by scholars who do not have a vested interest in blaming the messenger for the bad news agree that the CTS is the best available instrument (see, e.g., reviews by Grotevant & Carlson, 1989; Hertzberger, 1991.) Its use in many studies since 1973 has established its validity and reliability. New evidence on validity and reliability is published almost monthly by research scholars who are using the CTS in many countries. No other scale meets this standard. Finally, no matter what one thinks of the CTS, at least four studies that did not use the CTS also found roughly equal rates of violence by women.

Faulty Research Design Due to Ignoring Institutionalized Sexism

An indirect approach to discounting the findings on equal rates of assault is the claim that the theoretical approach of the studies is invalid because they ignore the sexist structure of society. Since my research has borne the brunt of this criticism, an examination of that research is appropriate. It shows that a paper I presented at a conference in 1973 was the sociological work that introduced most of the feminist explanations of couple violence (Straus, 1976). These feminist approaches include institutionalized male power, cultural norms legitimating male violence against women, and economic inequality between men and women that locks women into violent marriages. These contributions were widely cited until I published "politically incorrect" data on violence by women and was therefore excommunicated from feminist ranks. However, I remain one of the faithful, and have never accepted the excommunication. On the contrary, I have continued to research and write on these issues (see for example Coleman & Straus, 1986, Kolb & Straus, 1974; Straus, 1973, 1976, 1994, Straus et al., 1980; Yllö & Straus, 1990).

Excusing Assaults by Women

The third most popular mode of denying the bad news about assaults by female partners is to explain it away as the result of frustration and anger at being dominated by men. This is parallel to the excuses men give to justify hitting their partners, such as a woman's being unfaithful. In my opinion, parts of some critiques are justifications of violence by women in the guise of feminism. This is a betrayal of the feminist ideal of a nonviolent world. In addition, excusing violence by women and denying overwhelming research evidence may have serious side effects. It may contribute to undermining the credibility of feminist scholarship and contribute to a backlash that can also thwart progress toward the goal of equality between men and women.

CONCLUSIONS

Ending assaults *by* wives needs to be added to efforts to prevent assaults *on* wives for a number of reasons. Perhaps the most fundamental reason is the intrinsic moral wrong of assaulting a spouse, as expressed in the fact that such assaults are criminal acts, even when no injury occurs. A second reason is the unintended validation of the traditional cultural norms tolerating a certain level of violence between spouses. A third reason is the danger of escalation when wives

engage in "harmless" minor violence. Feld and Straus (1989) found that if the female partner also engaged in an assault, it increased the probability that assaults would persist or escalate in severity over the one-year period of their study, whereas if only one partner engaged in physical attacks, the probability of cessation increased. Finally, assault of a spouse "models" violence for children. This effect is as strong for assaults by wives as it is for assaults by husbands (Jaffe, Wolfe, & Wilson, 1990; Straus, 1983, 1992a; Straus et al., 1980).

It should be emphasized that the preventive effect of reducing minor assaults by wives has not been proven by the evidence in this [selection]. It is a plausible inference and a hypothesis for further research. Especially needed are studies to test the hypothesis that "harmless" assaults by wives strengthen the implicit moral justification for assaults by husbands. If the research confirms that hypothesis, it would indicate the need to add reduction of assaults by wives to efforts to end wife beating, including public service announcements, police arrest policy, and treatment programs for batterers. Such changes must be made with extreme care for a number of reasons, not the least of which is to avoid implying that violence by women justifies or excuses violence by their partners. Moreover, although women may assault their partners at approximately the same rate as men assault theirs, because of the greater physical, financial, and emotional injury suffered, women are the predominant victims (Stets & Straus, 1990; Straus et al., 1980). Consequently, first priority in services for victims and in prevention and control must continue to be directed toward assaults by husbands.

NO

Demie Kurz

PHYSICAL ASSAULTS BY HUSBANDS: A MAJOR SOCIAL PROBLEM

Are women violent toward men? This question has been asked repeatedly, particularly in recent years as the issue of domestic violence has gained national recognition. The women's movement, which brought the issue of battered women to public attention in the late 1970s, claims that it is men who are violent (Dobash & Dobash, 1992; Schechter, 1982; Tierney, 1982). Currently, advocates for battered women in many professions and organizations accept this analysis, and use it to promote change in the legal, medical, and social service responses to battered women (American College of Physicians, 1986; Attorney General's Task Force on Family Violence, 1984; Johnson, 1985; Koop, 1985).

However, among social scientists there has been a lot of controversy about the nature of violence in intimate relationships, particularly the question of whether women are violent toward men. A number of social scientists identify with the feminist tradition and argue that women are the victims of violence in relationships with men (Bowker, 1986; Breines & Gordon, 1983; Dobash & Dobash, 1979; Kurz, 1989; Loseke, 1992; Pagelow, 1981; Stanko, 1985; Wardell, Gillespie, & Leffler, 1983; Yllö & Bograd, 1988). These researchers claim that, historically, the law has promoted women's subordination and condoned husbands' use of force in marriage. Other social scientists, the "family violence" researchers, argue that the real problems are "spouse abuse" and "family violence" (see, e.g., Gelles, 1974; Gelles & Cornell, 1985; Gelles & Straus, 1988; McNeely & Robinson-Simpson, 1987; Schwartz, 1987; Shupe, Stacey, & Hazelwood, 1987; Steinmetz, 1977–1978; Stets, 1990; Stets & Straus, 1990; Straus, 1980a; Straus & Gelles, 1990; Straus, Gelles, & Steinmetz, 1980). These researchers believe that women as well as men are violent, and some claim that women "initiate and carry out physical assaults on their partners as often as men do."

This debate over men's and women's use of violence has significant consequences for popular and academic conceptions of battered women, and for social policy. How a problem is framed determines the amount of concern that is generated for that problem as well as the solutions that are proposed.

From Demie Kurz, "Physical Assaults by Husbands: A Major Social Problem," in Richard J. Gelles and Donileen R. Loseke, eds., *Current Controversies on Family Violence* (Sage Publications, 1993). Copyright © 1993 by Sage Publications, Inc. Reprinted by permission. References omitted.

Research findings influence whether the media and the public take battered women seriously, or whether they view them as equally blameworthy partners in "family violence." Feminists fear that a focus framing the problem as "spouse abuse" will lead to decreased funding for shelters, a diversion of resources to "battered men," and/or increased arrests of women in "domestic disputes" under mandatory arrest policies. More generally, feminists fear that a focus on "spouse abuse" diverts attention from the causes of violence against women—inequality and male dominance.

In this [section] I argue that the feminist point of view best explains the nature and the extent of violence between men and women in intimate relationships. Feminists argue that violence between intimates takes place within a context of inequality between men and women in marriage, whereas family violence researchers promote a gender-neutral view of power in intimate relationships. I will compare the evidence and theories presented by the proponents of each perspective, and I will argue that the family violence view is based on false assumptions about the nature of marriage and of equality between men and women.

A FEMINIST PERSPECTIVE ON VIOLENCE IN INTIMATE RELATIONSHIPS

Feminist researchers argue that women are the victims of male violence. They support their point of view with official crime statistics, data from the criminal justice system and hospitals, interviews with victims of battering and batterers, and historical evidence. Looking at such data, which, as Straus notes, are biased toward finding extreme victimization, it

is clear that women are overwhelmingly the victims of violence. The National Crime Victimization Survey of 1982 reported that 91% of all violent crimes between spouses were directed at women by husbands or ex-husbands, whereas only 5% were directed at husbands by wives or ex-wives (cited in Browne, 1987, p. 7). Analysis of these data over time provides similar results (Gaquin, 1977–1978; Schwartz, 1987). In their study of police records in Scotland, Dobash and Dobash (1979) found that when gender was known, women were targets in 94% and offenders in 3% of cases. Other studies based on data from the criminal justice system show similar results (Kincaid, 1982; McLeod, 1984; Quarm & Schwartz, 1985; Watkins, 1982).

Data on injury patterns confirm that it is women, not men, who sustain injuries in conflicts between males and females in intimate relationships. Brush (1990), in an analysis of data from the National Survey of Families and Households, found that women were significantly more likely to be injured than were men in disputes involving violent tactics. Berk, Berk, Loseke, and Rauma (1983), based on their examination of police records, conclude that in 95% of cases it is the woman who is injured and that, even when both partners are injured, the woman's injuries are nearly three times as severe as the man's. Data from hospitals show women to be overwhelmingly the injured parties (Kurz, 1987, 1990; McLeer & Anwar, 1989; Stark, Flitcraft, & Frazier, 1979). These data lead feminist researchers to reject the concept of "spouse abuse," the idea that women are equally as violent as men.

Feminists claim that the use of violence by men to control female intimates has long been condoned by major social institutions. The first law in the United

States to recognize a husband's right to control his wife with physical force was an 1824 ruling by the Supreme Court of Mississippi permitting the husband "to exercise the right of moderate chastisement in cases of great emergency" (quoted in Browne, 1987, p. 166). This and similar rulings in Maryland and Massachusetts were based on English common law, which gave a husband the right of "correction" of his wife, although he was supposed to use it in moderation.

> In 1871 wife beating was made illegal in Alabama. The court stated: The privilege, ancient though it be, to beat her with a stick, to pull her hair, choke her, spit in her face or kick her about the floor, or to inflict upon her like indignities, is not now acknowledged by our law.... the wife is entitled to the same protection of the law that the husband can invoke for himself. (quoted in Browne, 1987, p. 167)

A North Carolina court made a similar decision in 1874, but limited the kinds of cases in which the court should intervene:

> If no permanent injury has been inflicted, nor malice, cruelty nor dangerous violence shown by the husband, it is better to draw the curtain, shut out the public gaze, and leave the parties to forget and forgive. (quoted in Browne, 1987, p. 167)

Until recent legal reforms were enacted, the "curtain rule" was widely used by the legal system to justify its nonintervention in cases of wife abuse..

The law and the nature of marriage have changed dramatically since the early twentieth century; however, feminists claim that these institutions continue to condone violence against women. Although new laws have criminalized battering, we do not know whether these laws will be enforced (Buzawa & Buzawa, 1990; Kurz, 1992). A recent study suggests that even police who receive training in how to make a criminal response to battering cases may continue to view battered women as unfortunate victims of personal and social problems such as poverty and, in the absence of strong police department support, view arrests as low priority and not part of their "real" work (Ferraro, 1989). To the extent that these laws are not viewed seriously, the legal system will continue to treat battering as an individual problem, rather than as criminal behavior.

As for marriage, feminists argue that it still institutionalizes the control of wives by husbands through the structure of husband-wife roles. As long as women are responsible for domestic work, child care, and emotional and psychological support, and men's primary identity is that of provider and revolves around employment, the husband has the more important status and also controls the majority of decisions in the family. It is through such a system, coupled with the acceptance of physical force as a means of control, that, in the words of Dobash and Dobash (1979), the wife becomes an "appropriate victim" of physical and psychological abuse. Feminists argue further that the use of violence for control in marriage is perpetuated not only through norms about a man's rights in marriage, but through women's continued economic dependence on their husbands, which makes it difficult for wives to leave violent relationships. This dependence is increased by the lack of adequate child care and job training, which would enable women to get jobs with which they could support themselves.

Citing interview data from men and women that demonstrate that battering incidents occur when husbands try to make their wives comply with their wishes, feminist researchers believe that men still use violence as a way to control female partners. Based on data from interviews with 109 battered women, Dobash and Dobash (1979) demonstrate how, over the course of their marriages, batterers increasingly control wives through intimidation and isolation, findings confirmed by other interview studies (Pagelow, 1981; Walker, 1984). Violence, therefore, is just one of a variety of controls that men try to exercise over female partners; others are anger and psychological abuse (Adams, 1988; Dobash & Dobash, 1979; Mederos, 1987). Interviews with batterers show that men believe they are justified in their use of violence, particularly when their wives do not conform to the ideal of the "good wife" (see Adams, 1988; Dobash & Dobash, 1979; Ptacek, 1988).

Some researchers have also found that male dominance is a factor in other types of violence in the family. For example, Bowker, Arbitell, and McFerron (1988) found that 70% of wife beaters also physically abused their children; these researchers argue that the most important cause and context of child abuse is current abuse of a woman by a male intimate. They also found that the severity of wife beating predicted the severity of child abuse, and that the greater the degree of husband dominance, the greater the likelihood of child abuse. Similarly, Stark and Flitcraft (1985), in their review of medical records, found that children whose mothers were battered were more than twice as likely to be physically abused as were children whose mothers were not battered. They also believe that purposive violence by male intimates against women is the most important context for child abuse. Thus to understand and prevent child abuse it is important to consider that, among other factors, male dominance has a significant impact on fathers' treatment of children (Margolin, 1992).

Finally, feminists have shown how, in addition to the law and the family, a variety of institutions condone male dominance and reinforce battering on an ongoing, everyday basis. Some have demonstrated how this occurs through the labeling and processing of abused women by frontline workers who have the most contact with these women. Stark et al. (1979) argue that because of patriarchal medical ideologies and practices, health care practitioners fail to recognize battering and instead label battered women as having psychological problems. These researchers claim that the actions of health care workers serve to perpetuate battering relationships and argue that the medical system duplicates and reinforces the patriarchal structure of the family. In my own work, I have documented how individual staff in emergency rooms come to define battered women as not "true medical cases," but "social" ones, and feel they make extra work and trouble for medical practitioners (Kurz, 1987, 1990). Battered women who do not look like "typical victims" are frequently not recognized as battered and are sent back home, without any recognition of or attention to their battering.

Other studies address the issue of how violence against women is taught and reinforced in institutions such as the military (Russell, 1989) and sports (Messner, 1989). Sanday (1991) and others (e.g., Martin & Hanmer, 1989) have studied the ways in which fraternity practices and rituals, in promoting loyalty to a brotherhood of men, legitimate gang rape and other types of violence against women. Kanin (1984) suggests that the college date rapists he studied came from a more highly sexualized subculture than did non-date rapists.

FAMILY VIOLENCE RESEARCH AND THE FEMINIST CRITIQUE

In stark contrast to feminist researchers, family violence researchers focus on "spouse abuse," on women's as well as men's use of violence. They claim that women as well as men are perpetrators of physical violence (McNeely & Mann, 1990; McNeely & Robinson-Simpson, 1987; Steinmetz, 1977–1978; Steinmetz & Lucca, 1988), and some claim that women are as violent within the family as men (Stets & Straus, 1990; Straus & Gelles, 1986). In this section I argue that when researchers claim that women are as violent as men, they do so on the basis of faulty data and flawed assumptions about gender and the family.

Family violence researchers typically base their claims about women's use of violence on data collected using the Conflict Tactics Scales (CTS) (Straus, 1979), an instrument that requires respondents to identify conflict tactics they have used in the previous year. These range from nonviolent tactics (calm discussion) to the most violent tactics (use of a knife or gun). Using the CTS, family violence researchers find similar percentages of husbands and wives using violent tactics (e.g., Straus & Gelles, 1986; Straus et al., 1980). On the basis of these data, one family violence researcher concluded that there is a "battered husband syndrome" (Steinmetz, 1977–1978, 1987). Findings based on the CTS have been replicated

by a number of researchers both in the United States and abroad (Brinkerhoff & Lupri, 1988; Nisonoff & Bitman, 1979; Stets, 1990), including for dating relationships (Arias, Samios, & O'Leary, 1987; DeMaris, 1987; Lane & Gwartney-Gibbs 1985).

Straus cites findings from the 1985 National Family Violence Survey, based on women's responses to the Conflict Tactics Scales, that show that both wife and husband were violent in 48.6% of cases, the husband only was violent in 25.9% of cases, and the wife only was violent in 25.5% of cases. Straus concludes from these data that "regardless of whether the analysis is based on all assaults or is focused on dangerous assaults, about as many women as men attacked spouses who had *not* hit them during the one-year referent period." Citing other studies that show the same results, he concludes that these figures are "inconsistent with the self-defense explanation for the high rate of domestic assault by women."

Feminist researchers argue that the data showing that women are as violent as men, particularly data based on the Conflict Tactics Scales, are misleading and flawed (Berk et al., 1983; Breines & Gordon, 1983; Dobash & Dobash, 1979; Dobash, Dobash, Wilson, & Daly, 1992; Pleck, Pleck, Grossman, & Bart, 1977– 1978; Saunders, 1989). Feminists believe that the validity of the CTS is undermined because the continuum of violence in the scales is so broad that it fails to discriminate among different kinds of violence (Dobash & Dobash, 1979; Dobash et al., 1992; Stark & Flitcraft, 1985). For example, the CTS contains the item "bit, kicked, or hit with a fist." Thus a woman who bites is equated with a man who kicks or hits with a fist. Another item, "hit or tried to hit with an object," which is counted as severe violence, is similarly ambiguous. Critics also argue that the scale does not take into account self-defense.

In support of their position, feminists also point to the findings of studies in which women were asked about their use of violence. For example, Saunders (1988) found that in the vast majority of cases, women attributed their use of violent tactics to self-defense and fighting back. Emery, Lloyd, and Castleton (1989), in an interview study based on a small sample of women who were victims of dating violence, found that most of the women spoke of self-defense. Some women also spoke of using violence in frustration and anger at being dominated by their partners and in retaliation for their partners' violent behavior.

Further, feminists point out that the CTS focuses narrowly on counting acts of violence. Such a focus draws attention away from related patterns of control and abuse in relationships, including psychological abuse and sexual abuse, and does not address other means of nonviolent intimidation and domination, including verbal abuse, the use of suicide threats, and the use of violence against property, pets, children, or other relatives. Similarly, the conception of violence as a "conflict tactic" fails to convey the connection between the use of violence and the exercise of power.... Yllö argues that violence is better conceptualized as a "tactic of coercive control to maintain the husband's power."

In addition to their view that women commit as many violent acts as men, family violence researchers also claim that women initiate violence as frequently as men do. They draw this conclusion on the basis of responses to a question in the National Family Violence Survey about who initiated conflicts in the relationship. The National Family Violence Survey, based on the CTS, found that in 53% of cases wives reported that they hit first; their partners initiated the violence in 42% of cases. These findings have led family violence researchers to a new focus on women's use of violence. Even though husbands use more serious types of violence, these researchers now claim that violence by women against their husbands must be considered a serious problem.

Let us briefly examine the logic of the family violence position that women initiate violence as often as do men.... Straus [considers] occasions when a woman slaps a man. He refers to a "typical case" in which a woman uses acts of violence and assumes that a man who is acting like a "cad" has done something offensive to a woman: "Let us assume that most of the assaults by women fall into the 'slap the cad' genre and are not intended to, and only rarely, cause physical injury." He then focuses on the woman's "assaults" and goes on to argue that a woman who "slaps the cad" is in effect provoking her partner by providing him with a justification for hitting:

> Such morally correct slapping acts out and reinforces the traditional tolerance of assault in marriage. The moral justification of assault implicit when a woman slaps or throws something at a partner for something outrageous reinforces his moral justification for slapping her when *she* is doing something outrageous, or when she is obstinate, nasty, or "not listening to reason" as he sees it.

After claiming that assaults by wives are one of the "causes" of assaults by husbands, he concludes with a stern warning that all women must forsake violence:

> One of the many steps needed in primary prevention of assaults on wives is for women to forsake even "harmless" physical attacks on male partners and children. Women must insist on nonviolence from their sisters, just as they rightfully insist on it from men.

In a few sentences, Straus proceeds from women's defensive behavior to a focus on women as provoking the violence. What is wrong with this logic? Although eliminating violence should be a high-priority goal for all men, women, and children, this reframing of the issue puts the blame and responsibility for the violence on the woman. Targeting women's behavior removes the focus from what men might be doing to women. What does it mean that he is acting like a "cad"? Does this refer to unwanted sexual advances, belittling of the woman, verbal intimidation, drunken frenzy? Who is responsible here? Focusing on the woman's behavior provides support for typical excuses and justifications by batterers, such as "She provoked me to do this" (Ptacek, 1988).

Another problem with asking a single question about who initiated the violence is that it does not focus on the meaning and context of female violence against male partners. For example, there were no questions asked about women's motives for striking first. We know that male physical and sexual violence against women is often preceded by name-calling and other types of psychological abuse (Browne, 1987), and that women may view these behaviors as early warning signs of violence and hit first in hopes of preventing their partners from using violence (Saunders, 1989). Hanmer and

Saunders (1984) have noted that many women hit first because of a "well-founded fear" of being beaten or raped by their husbands or male intimates. Thus, even when women do initiate violence, it may very well be an act of self-defense.

In my view there are many reasons it would be better if we all could be nonviolent—it may well be true that violence provokes more violence. However, we must understand the power dynamics behind the use of violence in particular types of relationships—we must examine who feels entitled to use violence and why. The feminist perspective addresses these critical questions about the context of violence.

A brief examination of the theoretical perspective of family violence researchers shows the faulty assumptions that guide their interpretation of the data. As one would expect from their findings, as well as their use of the terms *family violence* and *spouse abuse*, family violence researchers take a family systems approach to analyzing husbands' and wives' use of violence. They believe that the origins of the problem of violence lie in the nature of the family, not in the relationship between husband and wife (Gelles, 1983; Gelles & Straus, 1988), and that violence affects all family relationships. According to Straus et al. (1980):

> A fundamental solution to the problem of wife-beating has to go beyond a concern with how to control assaulting husbands. It seems as if violence is built into the very structure of the society and family system itself. . . . It [wife beating] is only one aspect of the general pattern of family violence, which includes parent-child violence, child-to-child violence, and wife-to-husband violence. (p. 44)

Family violence researchers believe that violence in the contemporary American family is caused by a variety of social structural factors, including stresses from difficult working conditions, unemployment, financial insecurity, and health problems (see, e.g., Gelles & Cornell, 1985; Gelles & Straus, 1988; Straus et al., 1980). They also believe that husbands and wives are affected by wider social norms condoning violence as a means of solving conflict, and they see evidence of the cultural acceptance of violence in television programming, folklore, and fairy tales (Straus, 1980b), as well as in surveys showing widespread public acceptance of violence. Straus and his colleagues also cite sexism as a factor in family violence; although they believe men and women are equally violent, they believe women are more victimized by family violence because of "the greater physical, financial, and emotional injury" women suffer.

Proponents of the family violence perspective make some important points about the prevalence of violence in American society; however, from a feminist perspective, the family violence view is seriously flawed. Although cultural norms of violence and stressful living conditions may influence individuals' use of violence, these wider cultural norms and social conditions are mediated by the norms of particular institutions. In the case of the institution of marriage, norms promoting male dominance in heterosexual relationships and males' right to use force have a direct influence on behavior in marriage.

Family violence researchers do acknowledge male dominance when they argue that sexism is an important factor in domestic violence and that women are the ones who are most seriously hurt in battering relationships. However, from a feminist perspective, sexism is not just *a* factor in domestic violence. For feminists, gender is one of the fundamental organizing principles of society. It is a social relation that enters into and partially constitutes all other social relations and activities, and pervades the entire social context in which a person lives. Thus feminists criticize family violence researchers for equating "spouse abuse," elder abuse, and child abuse, because from that perspective women constitute just one group among a number of kinds of victims. Feminists believe that wife abuse should be compared with related types of violence against women, such as rape, marital rape, sexual harassment, and incest (Wardell et al., 1983), all of which are also products of male dominance.

Feminists argue that family violence researchers disregard the influence of gender on marriage and heterosexual relationships and see power in the family as a gender-neutral phenomenon. Family violence researchers claim that "violence is used by the most powerful family member as a means of legitimizing his or her dominant position" (Straus et al., 1980, p. 193). They believe that power can as equally be held by a wife as by a husband. They also argue that "even less powerful members of the family tend to rely on violence as a reaction to their own lack of participation in the family decision-making process" (Straus et al., 1980, p. 193).

This view of the exercise of power as gender-neutral misrepresents the nature of marriage as a partnership of equals. As discussed above, marriage has been and still is structured so that husbands have more power than wives. Men are the primary wage earners and women, as those responsible for child rearing and household work, do not typically have the same bargaining power as their husbands. Thus power is not gender-neutral; it is structured into the institution of marriage in such a way that women are disadvantaged.

To conclude, the basic assumptions of the family violence and feminist approaches to domestic violence are irreconcilable. Further, each group has voiced strong disagreements with the other. Family violence researchers argue that the legitimate sociological approach to the issue of violence in the family should be a "multicausal" one; they believe that the feminist approach is biased by a single-minded focus on gender (Straus, 1991). Further, family violence researchers criticize feminist work as "political" (Gelles, 1983; Straus, 1991) and charge that they have been harassed for studying violent women (Gelles & Straus, 1988, p. 106; Straus, 1991). They believe that findings about women's violence have been "suppressed" because they are not "politically correct." Such statements posit a conspiracy of feminists to keep the "truth" from being known, rather than an understanding that different theories and methods lead to different conclusions.

Feminists fear that the family violence approach will reinforce existing popular conceptions that women cause their own victimization by provoking their male partners. They fear that such views will lead to policy outcomes that are harmful to women. Family violence researchers acknowledge that their research has been used to provide testimony against battered women in court cases and to minimize the need for shelters (Gelles & Straus, 1988, p. 90; Straus & Gelles, 1986, p. 471), however, they argue that this is less "costly" than the "denial and suppression" of violence by women (Straus & Gelles, 1986, p. 471). The question is, Costly for whom?

Feminists are concerned that if funders come to believe that family violence is a "mutual" occurrence between "spouses," or that there is a "battered husband syndrome," there will be decreased support for shelters for battered women. Feminists also fear a diversion of resources to shelters for "battered men." A recent *New York Times* article on a proposed shelter for battered men cited Straus' work as providing evidence that women assault men (Lewin, 1992). Men's rights groups cite the "battered husband syndrome" when lobbying for custody and child support issues from a men's rights perspective (Ansberry, 1988; Fathers for Equal Rights Organization, 1988; McNeely & Robinson-Simpson, 1987).

Feminists also fear that the family violence perspective will reinforce the individualist bias in the field of counseling —that counselors will focus on clients' individual and personal problems without identifying the inequality between men and women that is the context for battering (Adams, 1988). They disagree with those family violence proponents who argue that violence is caused primarily by frustration, poor social skills, or inability to control anger (Hotaling, Straus, & Lincoln, 1990; Shupe et al., 1987; Steinmetz, 1987). Finally, feminists worry that a belief in "spouse abuse" or a "battered husband syndrome" will encourage police who operate under mandatory arrest statutes to arrest women in "domestic disputes."

CONCLUSION

In this [selection] I have argued that women are typically victims, not perpetrators, of violence in intimate relationships. I have shown how norms and practices of male dominance promote the use of violence by men toward female intimates. The proponents of the family violence perspective, in arguing that women are violent toward men, disregard gender and its determining role in structuring marital and other heterosexual relationships.

Data on the use of conflict tactics and acts of violence must be interpreted in the context of power differences in male-female relationships. Abstracted from their context, data on who initiates and uses violence promote faulty conclusions. To interpret violence in the family, we must understand how gender shapes the exercise of power in heterosexual relationships.

CHALLENGE QUESTIONS

Are Women Violent Toward Their Male Partners?

1. Kurz contends that women are victims of a male-dominated society. Do you agree with this view? Support your answer.

2. People do not always answer survey questions honestly. Why might a woman in an abusive relationship hesitate to answer questions about that relationship honestly?

3. Are physical assaults by a woman the same as physical assaults by a man? How might they be similar? How might they be different?

4. Straus asserts that physical violence by women is a major social problem. Do you agree? Interview someone who works in marital therapy, with battered women, or in some other related field and ascertain his or her opinion regarding this issue.

5. What could lead to violence in intimate relationships? What can therapists do to prevent this violence?

ISSUE 18

Does Abortion Have Severe Psychological Effects?

YES: Anne C. Speckhard and Vincent M. Rue, from "Postabortion Syndrome: An Emerging Public Health Concern," *Journal of Social Issues* (vol. 48, no. 3, 1992)

NO: Nancy E. Adler et al., from "Psychological Responses After Abortion," *Science* (April 6, 1990)

ISSUE SUMMARY

YES: Psychotherapists Anne C. Speckhard and Vincent M. Rue argue that abortion has serious psychological consequences for women, including what they term "postabortion syndrome" (PAS).

NO: Psychologists Nancy E. Adler et al. contend that severe negative psychological reactions following abortion are infrequent.

Despite the controversy that induced abortion regularly raises, the procedure is still performed frequently. Currently, almost one-quarter of all pregnancies in the United States are terminated by legal, induced abortion, which equals 1.6 million annual abortions. Twenty-four percent of American women who abort are teenagers, 57 percent are younger than 25 years old, and almost 80 percent of these women are unmarried. Most abortions are performed sometime during the first trimester (the first three months), but a small percentage —about 10 percent—are performed later on in the pregnancy, when the fetus is more developed. Regardless of when a woman chooses to terminate a pregnancy, what psychological effects might be attached to abortion?

For many people, the subject of abortion is not just a psychological issue; it is also a moral and political issue. Those who consider themselves pro-life often claim that women who abort suffer many negative effects. They view abortion as a trauma with many permanent consequences. Those who consider themselves pro-choice, on the other hand, usually argue that any negative effects of abortion are minimal. Indeed, from the pro-choice perspective, abortion offers relief from the stress of pregnancy and the burden of caring for an unwanted child.

In the selections that follow, Anne C. Speckhard and Vincent M. Rue describe the sociopolitical context of abortion research. They argue that "there is a reluctance to call attention to the negative effects of abortion for fear of providing support to anti-abortion groups." They criticize research showing few negative effects of abortion as methodologically flawed and not representative of most women who undergo abortions. Speckhard and Rue maintain that women suffer negative psychological consequences after undergoing abortion much more often than people believe and that, in fact, many women experience symptoms of postabortion syndrome (PAS), including flashbacks, "anniversary reactions," and guilt.

Nancy E. Adler and her colleagues, basing their conclusions on a review of what they feel are methodologically sound studies, argue that psychological distress for women is usually greatest *before* an abortion and that the actual incidence of severe negative responses to abortion is quite low. Adler et al. claim that "the weight of the evidence... indicates that legal abortion of an unwanted pregnancy in the first trimester does not pose a psychological hazard for most women." The authors also describe some of the risk factors that may contribute to any distress that is experienced following abortion, but they suggest that this distress reflects typical strategies for coping with normal life stress.

POINT	COUNTERPOINT
• Abortion is a stressor that often has severe negative consequences.	• Distress is generally greater before abortion; thus, abortion is a stress reliever.
• Some psychological consequences of abortion can be permanent.	• Any negative psychological consequences are infrequent and limited in duration.
• The research on the effects of abortion is methodologically flawed.	• Methodologically sound studies do exist.
• Certain groups of women are underrepresented in the available research.	• The amount of bias from underrepresentation is minor.
• Psychology needs postabortion recovery treatment centers.	• Counseling and support is more useful before abortion, when the stress is greatest.

YES

Anne C. Speckhard
and Vincent M. Rue

POSTABORTION SYNDROME: AN EMERGING PUBLIC HEALTH CONCERN

Elective abortion, the most common surgical procedure in the United States, continues to generate considerable moral, legal, medical, and psychological controversy. This article reviews the pertinent literature, defines and describes postabortion syndrome (PAS) as a type of Post-Traumatic Stress Disorder. . . .

In the United States, prior to the liberalization and legalization of abortion, permission for an abortion sometimes required psychiatric determination of individual psychopathology (Stotland, 1989). When abortion became decriminalized and liberalized in the U.S. in 1973, psychiatric indications for abortion were eliminated. Today the abortion decision is private and requires no evidence of psychological impairment. In fact, psychiatric illness may be a contraindication (Moseley, Follingstad, & Harley, 1981; Ney & Wickett, 1989; Zakus & Wilday, 1987). In the current context, it is paradoxical but possible that the decision to elect abortion can generate significant resulting psychosocial distress (Rue, 1986; Speckhard, 1987b).

Clinical reports and recent studies have indicated that men, women, families, and even health care providers can sometimes experience negative psychological responses following abortion that do not appear to be linked back to individual pathology (Michels, 1988; Rue, 1986, 1987; Selby, 1990; Speckhard, 1987a, 1987b; Stanford-Rue, 1986). On the other hand, when psychopathology is present preabortion, increasing evidence suggests that abortion does not ameliorate individual dysfunction, but may worsen it (DeVeber, Ajzenstat, & Chisholm, 1991; Mall & Watts, 1979; Ney & Wickett, 1989).

Other recent studies have reported, however, minimal negative outcomes and even relief following abortion (Adler et al., 1990; David, 1985; Major, Mueller, & Hildebrandt, 1985). Not usually examined however, is the question of whether abortion may function in a dual role—as both coping mechanism *and* stressor. While abortion may indeed function as a stress reliever by eliminating an unwanted pregnancy, other evidence suggests that it may also

From Anne C. Speckhard and Vincent M. Rue, "Postabortion Syndrome: An Emerging Public Health Concern," *Journal of Social Issues,* vol. 48, no. 3 (1992), pp. 95–106. Copyright © 1992 by The Society for the Psychological Study of Social Issues. Reprinted by permission.

simultaneously or subsequently be experienced by some individuals as a psychosocial stressor, capable of causing posttraumatic stress disorder (PTSD)—(Barnard, 1990; Rue, 1985, 1986, 1987; Selby, 1990; Speckhard, 1987a, 1987b; Vaughan, 1991). We suggest that this constellation of dysfunctional behaviors and emotional reactions should be termed "postabortion syndrome" (PAS).

SOCIOPOLITICAL CONTEXT OF ABORTION RESEARCH

Like the decision to abort, the scientific study of the stress effects of abortion does not occur in a vacuum. The politicization of abortion has significantly restricted scientific investigation of the effects of abortion, and has produced a profound interpersonal and interprofessional schism in American society, including media reporting biases and public misinformation (Shaw, 1990).

There is a reluctance to call attention to negative consequences of abortion for fear of providing support to antiabortion groups. Minimizing acknowledgment and discussion of postabortion trauma may result in women feeling abandoned by their counselors and isolated from other women experiencing similar difficulties. This may discourage women from revealing their postabortion feelings and may result in labeling women with emotional difficulties after their abortion as deviant and in need of psychotherapy (Lodl, McGettigan, & Bucy, 1985).

Ironically, the politicization of abortion research may be leading us to stigmatize and label women who experience postabortion stress as pathological. This would indeed be unfortunate given the many years of feminist-oriented research

that attempted to remedy the "a priori" definition of women who choose abortion as pathological. Neither should those who experience abortion as traumatic now be defined as pathological without first considering the potential of abortion to act as a trauma even for some healthy women. Steinberg (1989) has cautioned, "We must examine the impact on these women because their numbers are so great and because the political and social volatility of this issue locks so many of them into silence" (p. 483).

Additionally, there is a danger of professional denial concerning the negative effects of abortion (Mester, 1978). The prevailing opinion espoused by the American Psychological Association (APA) is characteristic of the position held by most national and international mental health associations—i.e., that abortion, "particularly in the first trimester, does not create psychological hazards for most women undergoing the procedure" (Fox, 1990, p. 843); that "psychological sequelae [complications or conditions resulting from the event] are usually mild and tend to diminish over time without adversely affecting general functioning"; and that "severe emotional responses are rare" (American Psychological Association, 1987, p. 25). In the authors' opinion, the APA's position is an unwarranted overgeneralization that cannot be logically supported because it is based on a body of research that is methodologically flawed. David (1987) acknowledged,

Regardless of personal convictions about abortion, there is general agreement that uncertainty persists about the psychological sequelae of terminating pregnancies. Inconsistencies of interpretation stem from lack of consensus regarding the symptoms, severity, and duration of mental disorder; from opinions based on individual case studies; and from the lack of a national reporting system for adequate follow-up monitoring.... The literature abounds with methodological problems, lack of controls, and sampling inadequacies.... (p. 1)

Similarly, Adler et al. (1990) cautioned consumers of abortion regarding the psychological health risks by noting that "no definitive conclusions can be drawn about longer effects," and that "women who are more likely to find the abortion experience stressful may be underrepresented in volunteer samples" (p. 43).

Having gone "on record" supporting abortion, it may now be difficult for these professional groups to be open to reexamining their position. This has certainly been true of the American Psychological Association in its abortion advocacy positions, clearly stated in its U.S. Supreme Court amicus curiae briefs (i.e., in *Thornburgh v. ACOG, Hartigan v. Zbaraz,* and *Hodgson v. Humphrey*). In our opinion, the APA has been correctly criticized for overly extending the weight of scientific authority with respect to its statements and generalizations regarding adolescents and abortion (Gardner, Sherer, & Tester, 1989). On balance, Wilmoth (1988) concluded, "The most scientific conclusion about the psychological sequelae of abortion would be that the research permits no conclusions" (p. 9).

In 1989, U.S. Surgeon General Koop reported on his findings from meetings with scientists and clinicians, and from reviewing over 250 articles pertaining to the health risks of abortion. He concluded, "all these studies were reviewed... the data do not support the premise that abortion does or does not cause or contribute to psychological problems" (Koop, 1989a, p. 2). Later Koop testified in the U.S. House of Representatives: "there is no doubt about the fact that there are those people who do have severe psychological problems after abortion" (Koop, 1989b, p. 232), and stated, "if you study abortion the way many people have and see how well women feel about their decision 3 months after the actual procedure, you can be very badly misled" (p. 241).

RECENT ABORTION RESEARCH

Some recent reviews of the literature corroborate Koop's assessment (APA, 1987; Huckeba & Mueller, 1987), though others do not (Adler et al., 1990). Rue, Speckhard, Rogers, and Franz (1987) made an empirical assessment of the literature presented to Surgeon General Koop, which included (a) clinical evidence describing PAS; (b) a systematic analysis by Rogers that quantified threats to validity in 239 postabortion studies; and (c) a meta-analysis by Rogers of the controlled studies. (Excluding the meta-analysis, these data were later refined and published by Rogers, Stoms, & Phifer, 1989). In the paper by Rue et al. (1987), after excluding anecdotal and review articles, there remained 13 postpartum control-group studies, which were meta-analyzed, and 31 prospective and 32 retrospective uncontrolled studies, which were systematically analyzed.

The incidence of 20 methodological shortcomings in the above-mentioned 76 studies is presented in Table 1. For instance, in 69 of 76 studies insufficient sample size was evident (an $N \leq 385$), and in 33 studies substantial sample attrition was evident. Of the total number of studies, 49% used no baseline measurement and 25% had unclear outcome

Table 1

Percentage of Methodological Shortcomings in Comparison, Prospective, and Retrospective Studies of Abortion

Limitations in studies	Comparison studies ($N = 13$)	Prospective studies ($N = 31$)	Retrospective studies ($N = 32$)	Total ($N = 76$)
Sample size ($N \le 385$)	77	94	94	91
Sample attrition	31	45	47	43
Selection bias	23	35	28	30
No baseline measurement	31	35	69	49
No demographics	8	19	19	17
Abortion granted on psychiatric grounds	69	52	47	53
History of psychiatric instability	54	65	34	50
No/low instrument reliability	8	35	41	33
No/low interrater reliability	38	19	6	17
Interviewer bias	23	39	56	43
Recall distortion	15	3	59	29
Indirect data	31	16	13	17
Incomplete data	38	52	44	46
Contradiction	0	29	16	18
Unclear outcome criteria	23	29	22	25
Recovery room follow-up	0	16	0	7
Follow-up varies	15	10	38	22
Concomitant sterilization	31	32	28	30
No incidence data	23	26	0	15
Multiple abortions	23	39	38	36

Note. Unpublished table from data set of James Rogers originally used in Rue et al. (1987). Data set later refined and published in Rogers, Stroms, and Phifer (1989).

criteria. The mean number of methodological shortcomings per uncontrolled study was 6.9. It was also found that those uncontrolled studies with the greatest methodological weaknesses were more likely to report higher rates of positive experiences after abortion (Rue et al., 1987)....

After considering (a) prospective and retrospective studies, (b) postpartum control-group studies, and (c) the study that appeared to have used the best methodology of the various investigations reviewed (David, Rasmussen & Holst, 1981), Rue et al. (1987) concluded the following: (1) that the abortion literature is largely flawed as to design and methodology, (2) that all psychological studies of abortion display some negative outcomes for at least a proportion of those women studied, (3) that the clinical literature and experience with postabortion trauma are convergent in suggesting the need for the diagnostic category of PAS, and (4) that the types of errors found in the many studies examined *underestimate* the negative responses to abortion.

After reviewing the conclusions of the authors, Dr. Koop directed that the paper by Rue et al. (1987) be peer reviewed by health scientists within the federal government. Various anonymous criticisms of it were later reluctantly and unofficially provided to us (the identity of these reviewers was subsequently revealed in a congressional hearing and published in the committee report; the published versions are cited here). Some of the reviewers' criticisms displayed considerable bias: "Abortion is a moral issue (although all may not agree on this point either) and it must be removed from academic exercises of proof and disproof" (Dever, 1989, p. 165). Other reviewers concurred with the authors "that the issue could have important implications for public health" (Kleinman, 1989, p. 157). Some reviewers objected to the appropriateness of the meta-analytic technique. Meta-analysis, however, is now widely used and generally accepted as a means to obtain a numerical estimate of the overall effect size of a particular variable on a defined outcome. Indeed, in 1988 the authors conducted a computer search of the psychological, medical, health, biological, sociological, and family relations abstracts from 1980 to 1988, and found 895 citations, including approximately 528 meta-analyses that were reported in article titles. More recently, Posavac and Miller (1990) conducted a meta-analysis of the literature on the psychological effects of abortion and concurred that existing research is flawed methodologically, and that comparison group designs may tend to show more negative outcomes for abortion.

Perhaps the methodologically best-designed study completed to date is the Danish study reported by David et al. (1981), and David (1985). In it, admissions to psychiatric hospitals were tracked for a three-month period after either delivery or abortion for all Danish women under the age of 50, and then compared with the three-month admission rate to psychiatric hospitals for all Danish women of similar age. The authors found, "at all parities, women who obtained abortions are at higher risk for admission to psychiatric hospitals than are women who delivered" (David, 1985, p. 155). For abortion women, the psychiatric admission rate was 18.4 per 10,000 compared to 12.0 for delivering women and 7.5 for all Danish women aged 15–49. Of even more concern were the findings pertaining to women who were divorced, separated, or widowed at the time of abortion or delivery. The corresponding rates of psychiatric admission were 63.8 per 10,000 for these women aborting vs. 16.9 for these women [undergoing] delivery.

Four points require emphasis regarding this study (David et al., 1981): (1) it was relatively short-term and provided no long-term assessment of differences between women who aborted vs. those who delivered; (2) it most likely underreported the incidence and degree of postabortion traumatization because women may often be in denial for a considerable period of time after their abortion...; (3) the outcome measure used was admission to a psychiatric hospital, the worst-case circumstance— one could expect substantial quantitative differences between these two groups if less-severe dependent variables like depressive symptomatology or outpatient treatment in psychotherapy were used; and (4) women who elected abortion at all ages, parities, and relationship strata (except women aged 35–39, those with five pregnancies, and those who were married) had higher rates of admission to psychiatric hospitals than women who delivered.

An example of a methodologically unsound study is one in which 60% of 247 women surveyed failed to complete the study protocol three weeks postabortion (Major et al., 1985). Yet the authors concluded that the majority of women felt relief postprocedure. They did, however, caution:

> Of course, the possibility that women who returned to the clinic for their checkup were coping more successfully three weeks later than women who did not return cannot be ruled out, because we were unable to contact the women who did not return. (p. 594)

This high attrition rate could be attributed to avoidant behavior due to an abortion trauma, and it conforms to the view that women who are more likely to find the abortion experience stressful may be underreported in volunteer samples (Adler et al., 1990).

In 1987, Reardon conducted an exploratory survey of 252 high-stress, postabortion women. Although nonrandomly chosen and self-selected from 42 states, his sample compared favorably to national incidence data on women obtaining abortions by age, family size, race, marital status, and number of previous abortions. He found the majority of respondents experienced some of 28 negative outcomes including the following: flashbacks (61%), anniversary reactions (54%), suicidal ideation (33%), feelings of having less control of their lives (78%), difficulty in maintaining and developing relationships (52%), first use or increased use of drugs (49%), and delayed onset of stress, with most reporting their worst reactions as occurring one year or more postabortion (62%).

Likewise, Speckhard (1987b) found that all of the 30 women in her self-selected descriptive sample had long-term grief reactions, some lasting for over five years. Participants were women who described themselves as experiencing high-stress reactions, recruited through referrals from clinicians and other participants. In structured telephone interviews, the majority reported feelings of depression (100%), anger (92%), guilt (92%), fears that others would learn of the abortion (89%), preoccupation with the aborted child (81%), feelings of low self-worth (81%), discomfort around small children (73%), frequent crying (81%), flashbacks (73%), sexual dysfunction (69%), suicidal thoughts (65%), and increased alcohol usage (61%). The majority of the women studied reported being surprised at such intense reactions to their abortions.

These studies, though done with small, nonrandom groups, show that high-stress postabortive women can be doubly stigmatized by themselves—first by their fear of sharing their abortion experiences with one another and/or being viewed as deviant, and second by feeling that their negative reactions are a sign of maladjustment to what appears a relatively simple, common, and benign procedure (Speckhard, 1987a, 1987b). Koop (1989b) noted that in U.S. government reproductive surveys, the rate at which women reported having had an abortion was only half that expected based on abortion statistics.

Assessing the impact of abortion on the psychological health of women and men may not be as simple as some have suggested. In her book, *Parental Loss of a Child*, Rando included a chapter on the loss from induced abortion. In it, Harris (1986) described three obstacles to the clinical identification of negative responses following abortion: (1) masking of emotional responses may occur both at the time of the abortion and in later contacts with professionals; (2) if grief persists, it may surface in disguised form and be expressed behaviorally or in psychosomatic complaints; and (3) if the caregiver has ambivalent or unresolved feelings about abortion, this may interfere with the accurate assessment of postabortion trauma and the establishment of trust and the ability to be patient and empathic. Because of the self-insulation associated with the abortion experience, it is important that the caregiver be aware of the potential for grief, and take the initiative in exploring the client's perceptions and reactions. Joy (1985) stressed the need to be alert to women who are requesting counseling for depression resulting from unresolved grief over a prior abortion, i.e., a delayed grief reaction.

Vaughan (1991) studied 232 women from 39 states who by self-report suffered stress, guilt, grief, depression, and anger, which were defined as symptoms of PAS. The sample was purposive and was recruited primarily through a national network of crisis pregnancy centers affiliated with the Christian Action Council. The mean length of time since the abortion was 11 years. Vaughan employed the technique of canonical correlation between antecedent variables and postabortion variables. She found the following: (1) two different profiles of anger, guilt, and stress; (2) postabortion, 45% of respondents reported negative feelings toward subsequent pregnancies, difficulty bonding, and obsessive thoughts of having a replacement child; (3) only 5.9% of those not married but in a relationship at the time of the abortion continued their relationship postabortion; (4) 24% of the postabortive women had medical problems perceived as having been caused by the abortion; (5) 36% were suicidal postabortion; (6) 42% indicated negative interaction with the abortion clinic staff and felt the counseling received there was misleading and deceptive—this dissatisfaction was significantly related to high anger and guilt scores; and (7) the onset of the symptoms suggested as indicative of PAS was often several years postprocedure.

Mattinson (1985) reported on case studies from the Tavistock Institute in London. She found that, for some patients, the existence of postabortion grief placed interpersonal relationships at risk. Delayed grief reactions causing interpersonal stress took many different forms. Some were mild but persistent; others of a more extreme nature were triggered many years later by a loss of a different nature. Sometimes husbands were more affected than wives.

The first study to use standardized outcome measures of PTSD compared to the diagnostic criteria for PAS developed by Rue was conducted by Barnard (1990). She randomly selected 984 women from a Maryland abortion clinic for a follow-up questionnaire. Interestingly, 60% apparently gave the wrong telephone number at the time of their abortion. After administering a 48-item questionnaire designed to measure PAS (the Impact of Event Scale) and the Millon Clinical Multiaxial Inventory, Barnard reported 45% of her sample of 80 women had symptoms of avoidance and intrusion, and 19% met the full diagnostic criteria for PTSD three to five years following an abortion. She also noted that 68% of these women had little or no religious involvement at the time of the abortion.

Even representatives of Planned Parenthood, an organization that has historically denied the legitimacy of postabortion traumatization and the idea that abortion involves a human death experience, has affirmed that

> women can have a variety of emotions following an abortion (grief, depression, anger, guilt, relief, etc.). It is important to give her the opportunity to air these feelings and be reassured that her feelings are normal. The counselor can also help by letting the woman know that a sense of loss or depression following an abortion is common, due to both the end of the pregnancy as well as the physical and hormonal changes that occur after a pregnancy is over. (Saltzman & Policar, 1985, p. 94)

Because there has never been a national epidemiological study of the psychological health risks of abortion in this country, it is impossible to estimate with any accuracy the incidence of negative abortion sequelae. Lodl et al. (1985) estimated a range of 10%–50% experiencing distress following abortion. A recent APA task force on women and depression (McGrath, Keita, Strickland, & Russo, 1990) concluded that "abortion's relative risk of mental disorder compared with other reproductive events has not been fully ascertained" (p. 12).

Symptoms of traumatization have also been documented in populations of women aborting for genetic reasons, suggesting that the wantedness of the pregnancy at the time of the abortion may not be the key issue in whether or not a woman is traumatized by her abortion, as some have suggested. In a study of couples who elected prostaglandin induction abortion for genetic reasons, i.e., fetal anomalies, Magyari, Wedehase, Ifft, and Callanan (1987) reported negative psychological sequelae in their sample. Interestingly, the psychological intervention protocol developed by Magyari et al.

(1987) for these parents of wanted children identified the following: (1) the need for grief counseling that is anticipatory in nature, individualized, and emphasizes the normalcy of feelings; and (2) facilitation of the mourning process by affirming the pregnancy and providing memories central to the grief process. The latter included the options of seeing or holding the fetus, knowing the sex of the fetus, viewing a photo of the fetus, and naming the fetus. The majority of couples elected to see their aborted offspring.

As is often the case with abortion for nongenetic reasons, common feelings in these couples after abortion for genetic reasons included relief and a sense of conclusion to the crisis. Yet Magyari et al. (1987) cautioned, "We tell them that they face a difficult time and that recovery may not be as smooth as their friends and family may assume it will be" (p. 78). At six to eight weeks postabortion, the intervention team discussed unmet grief reactions thus far and assisted the couple by discussing future events including anniversary reactions. Immediate reproductive replacement was discouraged and the couple was warned "not to pursue a subsequent pregnancy as a replacement for the lost child" (Magyari et al., 1987, p. 80). Even with this intervention protocol in operation, within one year of the abortion, two out of three couples were pregnant again, suggesting the existence of a "replacement child phenomenon." Peppers (1987) has corroborated that grief over a perinatal loss, including abortion can occur irrespective of the wantedness of the pregnancy. In his study, 80 women having abortions at a clinic in Atlanta completed a 13-item grief scale....

ABORTION EXPERIENCED AS A STRESSOR

"Researchers tend to agree that, at some level, abortion is a stressful experience for all women" (APA, 1987, p. 18). The American Psychiatric Association (1987), in its *Diagnostic and Statistical Manual of Mental Disorders* (3rd ed., rev.; DSM-III-R), listed abortion as an example of a psychosocial stressor, but has not included the category of PAS. As a psychosocial stressor, abortion may lead some women to experience reactions ranging from mild distress to severe trauma, creating a continuum that we conceptualize as progressing in severity from postabortion distress (PAD), to PAS, to postabortion psychosis (PAP).

The concept of PAS is in the formative stages of understanding and operationalization (Wilmoth, 1988). It took the American Psychiatric Association over a decade to officially recognize posttraumatic stress disorder (PTSD). PAD, PAS, and PAP may currently be making a similar transition, though none of them are currently recognized even as subtypes or examples in the DSM-III-R. The following definitions are proposed:

Postabortion Distress

PAD may be defined as the manifestation of symptoms of discomfort following an abortion, resulting from three aspects: (a) the perceived physical pain and emotional stress of the pregnancy and abortion; (b) the perception of a loss from the abortion (i.e., loss of a role, dream, relationship, parts or perception of self, potential life, etc.); and (c) the conflict in personality, roles, values, and relationships that results from a changed perception of the appropriateness of the abortion decision.

PAD might be categorized as an adjustment disorder when impairment in occupational functioning or in usual social activities occurs. In order for it to be considered an adjustment disorder, the onset of distress must occur within three months of the abortion and persist no longer than six months, and persistent reexperience of the abortion stressor cannot be present (American Psychiatric Association, 1987).

Postabortion Psychosis

PAP is suggested as a generic designation for major affective or thought disorders not present before an abortion, and directly and clinically attributable to the induced abortion. PAP is characterized by chronic and severe symptoms of disorganization and significant personality and reality impairment, including hallucinations, delusions, and severe depression. Decompensation occurs when the individual becomes aware of, overwhelmed by, and unable to communicate the feelings of guilt, grief, fear, anger, and responsibility for the traumatic death of her/his unborn child. Other manifestations may include intolerable levels of affect, self-condemnation, anxiety, and terror at feeling unable to face the trauma, and also paranoia about being found out. Although PAP is not a commonly encountered reaction to abortion traumatization, clinical evidence of it has been reported (Sim & Neisser, 1979; Spaulding & Cavenar, 1978; Speckhard & Rue, in press).

Postabortion Syndrome

PAS is proposed as a type of PTSD that is characterized by the chronic or delayed development of symptoms resulting from impacted emotional reactions to the perceived physical and emotional trauma of abortion. We propose four basic components of PAS as a variant of PTSD: (1) exposure to or participation in an abortion experience, i.e., the intentional destruction of one's unborn child,[1] which is perceived as traumatic and beyond the range of usual human experience; (2) uncontrolled negative reexperiencing of the abortion death event, e.g., flashbacks, nightmares, grief, and anniversary reactions; (3) unsuccessful attempts to avoid or deny abortion recollections and emotional pain, which result in reduced responsiveness to others and one's environment; and (4) experiencing associated symptoms not present before the abortion, including guilt about surviving.

The proposed diagnostic criteria for PAS... were developed from the diagnostic assessment of PTSD in the DSM-III-R (American Psychiatric Association, 1987). The course of PAS conforms to the diagnostic criteria for PTSD—i.e., the symptoms of reexperience, avoidance, and associated symptoms must persist more than one month, or the onset may be delayed (i.e., greater than six months after the abortion). Clinical experience suggests that spontaneous recovery from PAS is not characteristic. Although PAS is categorized here as a type of PTSD, additional diagnoses including anxiety, depressive, or organic mental disorder may concurrently be made.

More than an accidental grab bag of isolated symptoms, PAS is conceptualized here as a clustering of related and unsuccessful attempts to assimilate and gain mastery over an abortion trauma. The resulting lifestyle changes involve partial to total cognitive restructuring and behavioral reorganization.

Wilmoth, Bussell, and Wilcox (1991) argue that PAS is not a type of PTSD because abortion is volitional. Peterson, Prout, and Schwarz (1991) have pointed out, however, that there are situations when patients suffering with PTSD in fact have reasons to feel guilty. They identify among many pathological identifications a "killer self" (p. 90). We submit that the volitional nature of the abortion decision is largely responsible for the perceived degree of traumatization. On the other hand, some women with PAS perceive their abortions as less than totally volitional. Some women feel their abortion was coerced, forced, or the only option available to them (Luker, 1975), and others feel their consent was not informed (Reardon, 1987; Speckhard, 1987b). Moreover, the DSM-III-R does not preclude volitional stressors in the criteria for PTSD (e.g., divorce and accidental homicide). In fact, it clearly indicates that PTSD is apparently more severe and longer lasting when the stressor is of human design (American Psychiatric Association, 1987, p. 248). We hold that abortion, intentionally caused and yielding unintended consequences, is one such example.

CONCLUSION

The psychological impact of abortion trauma on women, men, and children is far more complex than previously realized. Flawed studies and political pressure have produced an informational deficit concerning postabortion trauma. It is essential that the aftereffects of abortion be thoroughly reexamined. Failure to do so may lead women into making decisions about abortion that could be detrimental to them, decisions lacking in informed consent and free choice. Even critics like Wilmoth (1988, p. 12) have conceded that "after further study, PAS may become an accepted diagnostic category."

In addition to the need for improved research on this topic, the authors believe there is a growing need for specialized postabortion recovery treatment models and services—for example, postabortion counseling centers, peer support groups, and educational workshops for both the general public and professionals. A growing need is evident; the resistance to this viewpoint, however, may be formidable.

NOTES

1. The term fetal or unborn child is used throughout this article to indicate the differing stages of development, embryo to fetus, at which abortion occurs. This term is used in deference to the perceptions of women and men distressed by the loss of their psychological attachment to what they often refer to as "our baby."

REFERENCES

Adler, E., David, H., Major, B., Roth, S., Russo, N., & Wyatt, G. (1990). Psychological responses after abortion. *Science, 248*, 41–44.

American Psychiatric Association. (1987). *Diagnostic and statistical manual of mental disorders* (3rd ed., rev.). Washington, DC: Author.

American Psychological Association (1987). *Research review: Psychological sequelae of abortion.* Unpublished testimony presented to the Office of the U.S. Surgeon General. Washington, DC: Author.

Barnard, C. A. (1990) *The long-term psychosocial effects of abortion.* Portsmouth, NH: Institute for Pregnancy Loss.

David, H. (1985). Post-abortion and post-partum psychiatric hospitalization. *Ciba Foundation Symposium, 115*, 150–164.

David, H. (1987). Post-abortion syndrome? *Abortion Research Notes, 16*, 1–6.

David, H., Rasmussen, N., & Holst, E. (1981). Post-partum and postabortion psychotic reactions. *Family Planning Perspectives, 13*, 88–91.

DeVeber, L., Ajzenstat, J., & Chisholm, D. (1991). Postabortion grief: Psychological sequelae of induced abortion. *Humane Medicine, 7*, 203–209.

Dever, G. (1989, March 16). A report on *The psychological aftermath of abortion:* An evaluation.

Written testimony submitted to the Human Resources and Intergovernmental Relations Subcommittee of the Committee on Government Operations, U.S. House of Representatives. In *Medical and psychological impact of abortion* (pp. 162–173). Washington, DC: U.S. Government Printing Office.

Fox, R. (1990). Proceedings of the American Psychological Association, Incorporated for the year 1989: Minutes of the annual meeting of the Council of Representatives. *American Psychologist, 45*, 817–847.

Gardner, W., Sherer, D., & Tester, M. (1989). Asserting scientific authority. *American Psychologist, 44*, 895–902.

Huckeba, W., & Mueller, C. (1987). *Systematic analysis of research on psycho-social effects of abortion reported in refereed journals 1966–1985.* Unpublished manuscript. Washington, DC: Family Research Council.

Kleinman, J. (1989, March 16). Written testimony submitted to the Human Resources and Intergovernmental Relations Subcommittee of the Committee on Government Operations, U.S. House of Representatives. In *Medical and psychological impact of abortion* (pp. 156–157). Washington, DC: U.S. Government Printing Office.

Koop, C. (1989a, January 9). Letter to President Ronald Reagan concerning the health effects of abortion. In *Medical and psychological impact of abortion* (pp 68–71). Washington, DC: U.S. Government Printing Office.

Koop, C. (1989b, March 16). Testimony before the Human Resources and Intergovernmental Relations Subcommittee of the Committee on Government Operations, U.S. House of Representatives. In *Medical and psychological impact of abortion* (pp. 193–203, 218, 223–250). Washington, DC: U.S. Government Printing Office.

Lodl, K., McGettigan, A., & Bucy, J. (1985). Women's responses to abortion: Implications for postabortion support groups. *Journal of Social Work and Human Sexuality, 3*, 119–132.

Magyari, P., Wedehase, B., Ifft, R., & Callanan, N. (1987). A supportive intervention protocol for couples terminating a pregnancy for genetic reasons. *Birth Defects, 23*, 75–83.

Mall, D., & Watts, W. (Eds.). (1979). *The psychological aspects of abortion.* Washington, DC: University Publications of America.

Major, B., Mueller, P., & Hildebrandt, K. (1985). Attributions, expectations and coping with abortion. *Journal of Personality and Social Psychology, 48*, 585–599.

Mattinson, J. (1985). The effects of abortion on a marriage. *Ciba Foundation Symposium, 115*, 165–177.

McGrath, E., Keita, G., Strickland, B., & Russo, N. (Eds.). (1990). *Women and depression: Risk factors and treatment issues.* Washington, DC: American Psychological Association.

Mester, R. (1978). Induced abortion in psychotherapy. *Psychotherapy and Psychosomatics, 30,* 98–104.

Michels, N. (1988). *Helping women recover from abortion.* Minneapolis: Bethany House.

Moseley, D., Follingstad, D., & Harley, H. (1981). Psychological factors that predict reaction to abortion. *Journal of Clinical Psychology, 37,* 276–279.

Ney, P., & Wickett, A. (1989). Mental health and abortion: Review and analysis. *Psychiatric Journal of the University of Ottawa Press, 14,* 506–516.

Peppers, L. (1987). Grief and elective abortion: Breaking the emotional bond? *Omega, 18,* 1–12.

Peterson, K., Prout, M., & Schwarz, R. (1991). *Post-traumatic stress disorder: A clinician's guide.* New York; Plenum.

Posavac, E., & Miller, T. (1990). Some problems caused by not having a conceptual foundation for health research: An illustration from studies of the psychological effects of abortion. *Psychology and Health, 5,* 13–23.

Rando, T. (Ed.). (1986). *Parental loss of a child.* Champaign, IL: Research Press.

Reardon, D. (1987). *Aborted women: Silent no more.* Chicago: Loyola University Press.

Rogers, J., Stomis, G., & Phifer, J. (1989). Psychological impact of abortion. *Health Care for Women International, 10,* 347–376.

Rue, V. (1985). Abortion in relationship context. *International Journal of Natural Family Planning, 9,* 95–121.

Rue, V. (1986, August). *Post-abortion syndrome.* Paper presented at Conference on Post-Abortion Healing, University of Notre Dame.

Rue, V. (1987, August). *Current trends and status of post-abortion syndrome.* Paper presented at Conference on Post Abortion Healing, University of Notre Dame.

Rue, V., Speckhard, A., Rogers, J., & Franz, W. (1987). *The psychological aftermath of abortion: A white paper.* Testimony presented to the Office of the Surgeon General, U.S. Department of Health and Human Services, Washington, DC.

Saltzman, L., & Policar, M. (Eds.). (1985). *The complete guide to pregnancy testing and counseling.* San Francisco: Planned Parenthood of Alameda/San Francisco.

Selby, T. (1990). *The mourning after: Help for post-abortion syndrome.* Grand Rapids, MI: Baker Book House.

Shaw, D. (1990). Abortion bias seeps into news. Investigative series. *Los Angeles Times.* July 1, pp. 1, A30, A50; July 2, pp. 1, A20; July 3, pp. 1, A22, A23; July 4, pp. 1, A28, A38.

Sim, M., & Neisser, R. (1979). Post-abortive psychoses: A report from two centers. In D. Mall & W. Watts (Eds.), *The psychological aspects of abortion* (pp. 1–14). Washington, DC: University Publications of America.

Spaulding, J., & Cavenar, J. (1978). Psychoses following therapeutic abortion. *American Journal of Psychiatry, 135,* 364–365.

Speckhard, A. C. (1987a). *Post-abortion counseling.* Portsmouth, NH: Institute for Pregnancy Loss.

Speckhard, A. C. (1987b). *Psycho-social stress following abortion.* Kansas City, MO: Speed & Ward.

Speckhard, A., & Rue, V. (in press). Complicated mourning: Dynamics of impacted post-abortion grief. *Pre- & Peri-natal Psychology Journal.*

Stanford-Rue, S. (1986). *Will I cry tomorrow: Healing post-abortion trauma.* Old Tappan, NJ: Fleming Revell.

Steinberg, T. (1989). Abortion counseling: To benefit maternal health. *American Journal of Law and Medicine, 15,* 483–517.

Stotland, N. (1989). Psychiatric issues in abortion, and the implications of recent legal changes for psychiatric practice. In N. Stotland (Ed.), *Psychiatric aspects of abortion* (pp. 1–16). Washington, DC: American Psychiatric Press.

Vaughan, H. (1991). *Canonical variates of post-abortion syndrome.* Portsmouth, NH: Institute for Pregnancy Loss.

Wilmoth, G. (1988). Depression and abortion: A brief review. *Population and Environmental Psychology News, 14,* 9–12.

Wilmoth, G., Bussell, D., & Wilcox, B. (1991). Abortion and family policy: A mental health perspective. E. A. Anderson & R. C. Hula (Eds.), *The reconstruction of family policy* (pp. 111–127). New York: Greenwood

Zakus, G., & Wilday, S. (1987). Adolescent abortion option. *Social Work in Health Care, 12,* 77–91.

NO

Nancy E. Adler et al.

PSYCHOLOGICAL RESPONSES
AFTER ABORTION

A review of methodologically sound studies of the psychological responses of U.S. women after they obtained legal, nonrestrictive abortions indicates that distress is generally greatest before the abortion and that the incidence of severe negative responses is low. Factors associated with increased risk of negative response are consistent with those reported in research on other stressful life events.

Abortion has been a legal medical procedure throughout the United States since the 1973 Supreme Court decision in *Roe v. Wade*, with 1.5 million to 1.6 million procedures performed annually. U.S. abortion patients reflect all segments of the population. In 1987, almost 60% of abortion patients were under 25 years of age. Most (82%) were not married, and half had no prior births. Nearly 69% of women obtaining abortions were white (1). Abortions are most often performed in the first trimester; the median gestational age is 9.2 weeks; 97% of abortions are performed by instrumental evacuation (2).

Although much literature exists on the psychological consequences of abortion, contradictory conclusions have been reached. Disparate interpretations are due in part to limitations of the research methods and in part to political, value, or moral influences. In this review of studies with the most rigorous research designs, we report consistent findings on the psychological status of women who have had legal abortions under nonrestrictive circumstances (3). This article is limited to U.S. studies; however, results from a study in Denmark are also relevant because of the existence of a uniform national population registration system not available in the United States (4).

RESPONSES AFTER ABORTION

Responses after abortion reflect the entire course of experiencing and resolving an unwanted pregnancy. Although there may be sensations of regret, sadness, or guilt, the weight of the evidence from scientific studies (3) indi-

From Nancy E. Adler, Henry P. David, Brenda N. Major, Susan H. Roth, Nancy F. Russo, and Gail E. Wyatt, "Psychological Responses After Abortion," *Science*, vol. 248 (April 6, 1990), pp. 41–44. Copyright © 1990 by The American Association for the Advancement of Science. Reprinted by permission.

cates that legal abortion of an unwanted pregnancy in the first trimester does not pose a psychological hazard for most women.

Descriptive studies have shown the incidence of severe negative responses after abortion to be low (5–10). After first-trimester abortion, women most frequently report feeling relief and happiness. In a study by Lazarus (5), 2 weeks after first-trimester abortions, 76% of women reported feeling relief, while the most common negative emotion, guilt, was reported by only 17%. Negative emotions reflecting internal concerns, such as loss, or social concerns, such as social disapproval, typically are not experienced as strongly as positive emotions after abortion (5–8). For example, Adler (6) obtained ratings of feelings over a 2- to 3-month period after abortion on Likert-type scales, with 5 representing strongest intensity. Mean ratings were 3.96 for positive emotions, 2.26 for internally based negative emotions, and 1.89 for socially based negative emotions.

Women show little evidence of psychopathology after abortion. For example, on the short form of the Beck Depression Inventory, scores below 5 are considered nondepressed (11). In a sample of first-trimester patients, Major et al. (9) obtained mean scores of 4.17 (SD* = 3.92) immediately after the abortion and 1.97 (SD = 2.93) 3 weeks later.

Measures used in most studies were not designed to assess psychopathology, but, rather, emotional distress within normal populations. These indicators show significant (12) decreases in distress from before abortion to immediately after and from before abortion or immediately after to several weeks later (9, 10). For

*[SD = standard deviation.—Ed.]

example, Cohen and Roth (10) found a drop in the depression subscale of the Symptom Checklist 90 (SCL-90) from a mean of 24.1 (SD = 11.8) at the time of arrival at a clinic to a mean of 18.4 (SD = 12.2) in the recovery room. Similar drops were shown on the anxiety scale of the SCL-90 and on the Impact of Events scale, an indicator of distress.

Only two studies compared responses after abortion with those after birth. Athanasiou et al. (13) studied women after early (suction) abortion, late (saline) abortion, and term birth. Starting with 373 women, researchers matched 38 patients in each group for ethnicity, age, parity, and marital and socioeconomic status. Thirteen to sixteen months after abortion or delivery, women completed the Minnesota Multiphasic Personality Inventory (MMPI) and the SCL. None of the groups had a mean score on any subscales of the MMPI above 70, the cutoff indicating psychopathology. Few differences among groups were shown (14), and the authors concluded that the three groups were "startlingly similar."

Zabin et al. (15) interviewed 360 adolescents seeking pregnancy tests and compared those who had negative results, those who were pregnant and carried to term, and those who were pregnant and aborted. All three groups showed higher levels of state (transient) anxiety at base line than they did 1 or 2 years later (for example, for the abortion group $\bar{X}$ = 74.6 at base line versus 45.6 and 43.6 at 1 and 2 years later). Two years after the initial interview, the abortion group showed, if anything, a more positive psychological profile than either of the other two groups. There were no differences on state anxiety, but the abortion group was significantly lower on trait anxiety than either of the other two groups, was higher on self-esteem than the negative pregnancy group, and had a greater sense of internal control than the childbearing group.

FACTORS RELATING TO PSYCHOLOGICAL RESPONSES

Although most women do not experience negative psychological responses after abortion, case studies document some negative experiences. Various aspects of the abortion experience may contribute to distress. Ambivalence about the wantedness of the pregnancy may engender a sense of loss. Conflict about the meaning of abortion and its relation to deeply held values or beliefs, perceived social stigma, or lack of support may also induce negative reactions.

The decision process. The greater the difficulty of deciding to terminate a pregnancy, the more likely there will be negative responses after abortion (6–8, 16). For example, Adler (6) found that the difficulty of deciding to abort, reported several days before abortion, was positively associated with the experience of negative emotions reflecting loss 2 to 3 months after abortion ($r = 0.37$), but was not related to a statistically significant extent to the experience of positive emotions or of negative emotions reflecting social disapproval.

Although most women do not find the decision to abort difficult, some do (16), and it appears to be more difficult for women seeking termination later in pregnancy. Whereas only 7% of 100 first-trimester patients studied by Osofsky *et al.* (17) reported initial indecision and 12% reported difficulty in deciding about abortion, corresponding figures among 200 second-trimester patients were 36 and 51%. Women undergoing second-trimester abortions also report more emotional distress after abortion than do those terminating first-trimester pregnancies (17–19).

Women who perceive more support for the decision to abort are more satisfied with their decision (7, 20). Those with fewer conflicts over abortion are also more satisfied; in a sample of adolescents, Eisen and Zellman (21) found that satisfaction with the decision 6 months after an abortion was associated with a favorable opinion of abortion in general as well as for themselves.

The more a pregnancy is wanted and is viewed as personally meaningful by the woman, the more difficult abortion may be. Major *et al.* (9) found that among 247 first-trimester abortion patients, women who described their pregnancy as being "highly meaningful" compared to those who found their pregnancy to be less personally meaningful reported more physical complaints immediately after the abortion and anticipated more negative consequences. Three weeks after the abortion, women who had indicated having had no intention to become pregnant scored significantly lower on the Beck Depression Inventory ($\bar{X} = 1.68$, SD = 2.33) than did the minority of women who had at least some intention to become pregnant ($\bar{X} = 3.71$, SD = 5.03).

In summary, women who report little difficulty in making their decision, who are more satisfied with their choice, and who are terminating pregnancies that were unintended and hold little personal meaning for them show more positive responses after abortion. Women with negative attitudes toward abortion and who perceive little support for their decision have more difficulty deciding about abortion. These factors may also contribute to delay in obtaining abortions (19), potentially subjecting women to the greater stress of second-trimester procedures (17–19).

Perceived social support. Perceived social support can buffer some adverse effects of stressful life events (22). However, social support is complex. Support for having the abortion needs to be differentiated from support in general; the former is associated with more favorable outcomes; the latter may not be.

Women with greater support for their abortion from parents and the male partner generally show more positive responses after abortion (8, 23, 24). Intimacy with and involvement of the male partner was a significant predictor of emotional reaction in two samples (8). Together with satisfaction with the decision and the woman's initial emotional response to becoming pregnant, partner support accounted for almost 40% of the variance in psychological response 2 to 3 weeks after abortion. Moseley et al. (24) found that having negative feelings toward one's partner, making the abortion decision alone, and experiencing opposition from parents were associated with greater emotional distress on the Multiple Affective Adjective Check List both before a first-trimester abortion and immediately after. However, Robbins (25) found that single women who maintained a strong relationship with their partner reported more negative change on the MMPI 6 weeks after abortion and more regret 1 year later than those whose relationships deteriorated.

In a study of actual social support, Major et al. (9) recorded whether women were accompanied to the clinic by a male partner. Out of 247 women, 83 were accompanied. Compared to unaccompanied women, those with partners were younger and expected to cope less well beforehand; women who were more distressed about the abortion may have expressed a greater need for their partners to accompany them. Accompanied women were significantly more depressed and reported more physical complaints immediately after abortion than unaccompanied women. Differences in depression after abortion remained after controlling for age and coping expectations, but they did not remain in a 3-week follow-up of a subset of women.

Coping processes and expectancies. Generalized positive outcome expectancies and situation-specific coping expectancies and processes have been linked to a variety of health-relevant outcomes (26). Major et al. (9) found that among abortion patients, those who expected to cope well scored lower on the Beck Depression Inventory than those with more negative expectations ($\bar{X} = 2.98$, SD $= 3.04$ versus $\bar{X} = 5.93$, SD $= 4.41$, respectively). Those expecting to cope well also showed more positive mood, anticipated fewer negative consequences, and had fewer physical complaints both immediately after abortion and 3 weeks later.

Cohen and Roth (10) examined coping styles and levels of anxiety and depression before and immediately after abortion. As noted earlier, anxiety and depression decreased significantly from before the abortion to afterwards for all women, but those who used approach strategies (for example, thinking about the procedure, talking about it) showed a greater decrease in anxiety from before to after abortion than those not using these strategies. Women who used denial scored significantly higher in depression and anxiety than did those who did not deny.

LIMITATIONS OF RESEARCH AND FUTURE DIRECTIONS

Although each study has methodological shortcomings and limitations, the diversity of methods used provides strength in drawing general conclusions. Despite the diversity, the studies are consistent in their findings of relatively rare instances of negative responses after abortion and of decreases in psychological distress after abortion compared to before abortion. However, weaknesses and gaps found among studies provide challenges for future research.

First, samples of well-defined populations and information on subjects who choose not to participate are needed. Studies have sampled women from specific clinics or hospitals. Both public and private clinics have been used, and samples have varied in their ethnic and socioeconomic character. Women whose abortions are performed by private physicians are not represented; they are estimated to be about 4% of women having abortions (27).

Of more concern is the necessary use of volunteers, which can introduce bias if women who agree to participate in research differ from those who do not on characteristics linked to more positive or negative outcomes. An analysis of studies that provide data on characteristics of research participants versus the population from which the sample was drawn suggests that women who are more likely to find the abortion experience stressful may be underrepresented in volunteer samples. However, the amount of bias introduced by this underrepresentation appears to be minor and unlikely to influence the general conclusions (28).

Second, the timing of measurement has been limited. Many studies lack base-line date from before the abortion. We know of no studies with data collected before the pregnancy, making it impossible to control for variables that may be associated with the initial occurrence of the pregnancy and which could influence responses after abortion. One of the best predictors of a woman's psychological status after abortion is likely to be her functioning before the occurrence of the unwanted pregnancy (29). Former Surgeon General C. Everett Koop has called for a prospective study of a nationally representative sample of women of childbearing age (30). Such a study would address both issues of representativeness and of base-line measurement.

Timing of assessment after abortion has also been limited. Some studies obtained measures within a few hours after the procedure, while the woman was still in the clinic. Responses at this time may not be indicative of longer term response. A few studies have obtained measures a few weeks or months after abortion; the longest follow-up is 2 years. Therefore, no definitive conclusions can be drawn about longer term effects. Although individual case studies have identified instances in which individuals develop severe problems that they attribute to an earlier abortion experience (31), the number of such cases is comparatively small. Moreover, research on other life stresses suggests that women who do not experience severe negative responses within a few months after the event are unlikely to develop future significant psychological problems related to the event (32). Longer term studies are needed to confirm this observation and to ascertain the influence of other life events attributed retrospectively to the abortion experience.

Finally, in studying psychological responses after abortion, it is important to separate the experience of abortion from the characteristics of women seeking abortion and from the context of resolving an unwanted pregnancy. A useful comparison would be women who carry an unwanted pregnancy to term and surrender the child for adoption; this would control both for the unwantedness of the pregnancy and the experience of loss. The study by Athanasiou et al. (13) matched women who were terminating pregnancies with those carrying to term on key demographic variables, but they were not matched on "wantedness" of the pregnancy. Similarly, the comparison used in the Danish study (4) for women aborting their pregnancies was women carrying to term, most of whom were likely to be delivering wanted pregnancies. One would expect more adverse outcomes for women carrying unwanted pregnancies to term (33).

A number of questions can be addressed without a comparison group. Theoretically grounded studies testing conditional hypotheses about factors that may put women at relatively greater risk for negative responses are particularly important. Such studies can address critical questions about the nature of the abortion experience and its aftermath, and can point the way to interventions if needed.

CONCLUSION

Scientific studies on psychological responses to legal, nonrestrictive abortion in the United States suggest that se-vere negative reactions are infrequent in the immediate and short-term aftermath, particularly for first-trimester abortions. Women who are terminating pregnancies that are wanted and personally meaningful, who lack support from their partner or parents for the abortion, or who have more conflicting feelings or are less sure of their decision beforehand may be at relatively higher risk for negative consequences.

Case studies have established that some women experience severe distress or psychopathology after abortion and require sympathetic care. As former Surgeon General C. Everett Koop testified before Congress regarding his review of research on psychological effects of abortion, such responses can be overwhelming to a given individual, but the development of significant psychological problems related to abortion is "minuscule from a public health perspective" (34).

Despite methodological shortcomings of any single study, in the aggregate, research with diverse samples, different measures of response, and different times of assessment have come to similar conclusions. The time of greatest distress is likely to be before the abortion. Severe negative reactions after abortions are rare and can best be understood in the framework of coping with a normal life stress.

NOTES

1. S. K. Henshaw and J. Silverman, *Fam. Plann. Perspect.* **20**, 158 (1988).

2. S. Henshaw, *ibid.* **19**, 5 (1987); C. Tietze and S. K. Henshaw, *Induced Abortion: A World Review* (Alan Guttmacher Institute, New York, 1986); E. Powell-Griner, *Mon. Vital Stat.* **36** (no. 5), 1 (1987).

3. Studies included in this article had to meet the following three criteria: (i) the research was empirical and based on a definable sample; (ii) the sample was drawn from the United States; and (iii) the women studied had undergone abortions under legal and nonrestrictive conditions (for example, women did not have to qualify for the procedure on the basis of threat to physical or mental health). These criteria allow for maximal generalizability to U.S. women under current conditions.

4. Through the use of computer linkages to national abortion and birth registers, the admissions register to psychiatric hospitals was tracked for women 3 months after abortion (n = 27,234) or delivery (n = 71,370) and for all women 15 to 49 years of age residing in Denmark (n = 1,169,819). To determine incidence rates, only first admissions to psychiatric hospitals were recorded, excluding women who had been admitted within the 15 previous months. The key finding was that for both never-married women and currently married women, the psychiatric admission rate after pregnancy was roughly the same for abortions or deliveries—about 12 per 10,000 compared to 7 per 10,000 for all women of reproductive age. Among the much smaller group of separated, divorced, or widowed women, those who had terminated pregnancies (which perhaps were originally intended) experienced a fourfold higher admissions rate (64 per 10,000) than the group of separated, divorced, or widowed women who delivered (17 per 10,000). However, because there may be a bias against hospitalizing a new mother, particularly if she is nursing, the relative psychological risk of delivery may be underestimated [H. P. David, N. Rasmussen, E. Holst, *Fam. Plann. Perspect.* 13, 88 (1981)].

5. A. Lazarus, *J. Psychosom. Obstet. Gynaecol.* 4, 141 (1985).

6. N. E. Adler, *Am. J. Orthopsychiatry* 45, 446 (1975).

7. J. D. Osofsky and H. Osofsky, *ibid.* 42, 48 (1972).

8. L. R. Shusterman, *Soc. Sci. Med.* 13A, 683 (1979).

9. B. Major, P. Mueller, K. Hildebrandt, *J. Pers. Soc. Psychol.* 48, 585 (1985). Means for 3-week follow-up interviews reported here do not match means published in the original article. Due to an error in the original publication, standard deviations were reported instead of means, but all tests of significance were accurate. The correct means are reported here.

10. L. Cohen and S. Roth, *J. Hum. Stress.* 10, 140 (1984).

11. A. T. Beck and R. W. Beck, *Postgrad. Med.* 52, 81 (1972).

12. In this article, significance is used in terms of statistical significance and may not represent clinically significant changes or associations.

13. R. Athanasiou, W. Oppel, L. Michaelson, T. Unger, M. Yager, *Fam. Plann. Perspect,* 5, 227 (1973).

14. The only statistically significant differences found were as follows: (i) women who had experienced term birth scored higher on the paranoia subscale of the MMPI ($\bar{X}$ = 61.7, SD = 14.6) than did women in either abortion group ($\bar{X}$ = 58.9, SD = 12.2 for suction patients and $\bar{X}$ = 54.6, SD = 9.4 for saline patients) and (ii) suction abortion patients reported fewer somatic complaints on the SCL ($\bar{X}$ = 10.6, SD = 8.0) than either the saline abortion or delivery patients ($\bar{X}$ = 14.7, SD = 8.1 and $\bar{X}$ = 14.8, SD = 9.3, respectively).

15. L. S. Zabin, M. B. Hirsch, M. R. Emerson, *Fam. Plann. Perspect.* 21, 248 (1989).

16. M. B. Bracken, *Soc. Psychiatry* 13, 135 (1978).

17. J. D. Osofsky, H. J. Osofsky, R. Rajan, D. Spitz, *Mt. Sinai J. Med.* 42, 456 (1975).

18. J. B. Rooks and W. Cates, Jr., *Fam. Plann. Perspect.* 9, 276 (1977); N. B. Kaltreider, S. Goldsmith, A. Margolis, *Am. J. Obstet. Gynecol.* 135, 235 (1979).

19. M. Bracken and S. Kasl, *ibid.* 121, 1008 (1975).

20. M. B. Bracken, L. V. Klerman, M. Bracken, *ibid.* 130, 251 (1978).

21. M. Eisen and G. L. Zellman, *J. Gen. Psychol.* 145, 231 (1984).

22. S. Cohen and T. A. Wills, *Psychol. Bull.* 98, 310 (1985); R. C. Kessler and J. D. McLeod, *Social Support and Health,* S. Cohen and S. L. Syme, Eds. (Academic Press, Orlando, FL, 1985), pp. 219–240.

23. M. B. Bracken, M. Hachamovitch, G. Grossman, *J. Nerv. Ment. Dis.* 158, 154 (1974).

24. D. T. Moseley *et al., J. Clin. Psychol.* 37, 276 (1981).

25. J. M. Robbins, *Soc. Probl.* 31, 334 (1984).

26. M. F. Scheier and C. S. Carver, *J. Pers.* 55, 169 (1987); A. Bandura, *Psychol. Rev.* 84, 191 (1977).

27. S. K. Henshaw, J. D. Forrest, J. Van Vort, *Fam. Plann. Perspect.* 19, 63 (1987).

28. N. E. Adler, *J. Appl. Soc. Psychol.* 6, 240 (1976); E. W. Freeman, *Am. J. Orthopsychiatry* 47, 503 (1977).

29. E. C. Payne, A. R. Kravitz, M. T. Notman, J. V. Anderson, *Arch. Gen. Psychiatry* 33, 725 (1976); E. M. Belsey, H. S. Greer, S. Lal, S. C. Lewis, R. W. Beard, *Soc. Sci. Med.* 11, 71 (1977).

30. C. E. Koop, letter to R. W. Reagan, 9 January 1989.

31. A. C. Speckhard, *The Psycho-Social Aspects of Stress Following Abortion* (Sheed and Ward, Kansas City, MO, 1987).

32. C. B. Wortman and R. C. Silver, *J. Consult. Clin. Psychol.* 57, 349 (1989).

33. One may also find more adverse consequences for the children born as a result of unwanted pregnancy [H. P. David, Z. Dytrych, Z. Matejcek, V. Schuller, *Born Unwanted: Developmental Effects of Denied Abortion* (Springer, New York, 1988)].

34. Committee on Government Operations, House of Representatives, *The Federal Role in Determining the Medical and Psychological Impact of Abortions on Women*, 101st Cong., 2d sess., 11 December 1989, House Report 101-392, p. 14.

35. This article is based on a review conducted by a panel convened by the American Psychological Association. The authors were members of the panel. We thank J. Gentry and B. Wilcox for contributions to the manuscript and G. Markman and A. Schlagel for manuscript preparation.

CHALLENGE QUESTIONS

Does Abortion Have Severe Psychological Effects?

1. If someone you know were considering terminating a pregnancy, what advice would you offer? Why?

2. What potential problems do you see in research on abortion effects? How would you design an experiment to minimize these problems?

3. Is abortion a moral, psychological, or political issue? What is the basis of your conclusion? How does this answer affect your position regarding whether abortion is harmful or not?

4. What are the strengths and weaknesses of Speckhard and Rue's proposal that postabortion syndrome occurs in some women following abortion?

CONTRIBUTORS TO THIS VOLUME

EDITOR

BRENT SLIFE is a clinical psychologist and a professor of psychology at Brigham Young University in Provo, Utah. A fellow of the American Psychological Association, he has authored over 80 articles and books, his most recent being *What's Behind the Research: Discovering Hidden Assumptions in the Behavioral Sciences* (Sage Publications, 1995), which attempts to make accessible to students the many conceptual issues of psychology. Recently voted Teacher of the Year at Brigham Young, he is also editor of the *Journal of Theoretical and Philosophical Psychology* and serves in editorial capacities on the *Journal of Mind and Behavior* and *Theory and Psychology*. He received his Ph.D. from Purdue University, where he and Joseph Rubinstein, coeditor of the first seven editions of *Taking Sides: Clashing Views on Controversial Psychological Issues*, began the dialogue approach to psychology that is the basis of this volume.

STAFF

David Dean   List Manager
David Brackley   Developmental Editor
Juliana Poggio   Associate Developmental Editor
Rose Gleich   Administrative Assistant
Brenda S. Filley   Production Manager
Juliana Arbo   Typesetting Supervisor
Diane Barker   Proofreader
Lara Johnson   Graphics
Richard Tietjen   Publishing Systems Manager

AUTHORS

ALAN C. ACOCK is a professor in and chair of the Department of Human Development and Family Sciences at Oregon State University in Corvallis, Oregon.

NANCY E. ADLER is a professor in the Department of Psychology at the University of California, San Francisco.

NANCY C. ANDREASEN is a doctor in the Mental Health Clinical Research Center of the University of Iowa Hospitals and Clinics and College of Medicine.

J. MICHAEL BAILEY is an associate professor of psychology at Northwestern University in Evanston, Illinois. His main research interests focus on the genetics and environment of sexual orientation, on which he has published dozens of journal articles and book chapters. He earned his Ph.D. in psychology from the University of Texas.

ELIZABETH BALDWIN is a research ethics officer for the American Psychological Association's Science Directorate. Her work involves a broad range of research ethics issues, including those relating to the use of animals in research. She has also worked at the Congressional Research Service in the Division of Science Policy. She holds a B.A. in biology, an M.S. in entomology, and an M.A. in science, technology, and public policy.

ELLEN BASS is a nationally recognized counselor, lecturer, and professional trainer who works with survivors of child sexual abuse.

DIANA BAUMRIND is a research psychologist and the principal investigator for the Family Socialization and Developmental Competence Project of the University of California's Institute for Human Development in Berkeley, California. She has contributed numerous articles to professional journals and books, and she is on the editorial board for *Developmental Psychology*. She is also the author of *Child Maltreatment and Optimal Caregiving in Social Contexts* (Garland Publishing, 1995).

ALAN D. BOWD is a professor of educational psychology and director of the School of Education at Lakehead University in Thunder Bay, Ontario, Canada. He received an M.A. in psychology from the University of Sydney and a Ph.D. in educational psychology from the University of Calgary. His main interest is in the ethical treatment of animals, and his published research has focused on the development of beliefs and attitudes about animals during childhood.

BRANDON S. CENTERWALL is an assistant professor of epidemiology in the School of Public Health and Community Medicine at the University of Washington in Seattle, Washington.

ZACK Z. CERNOVSKY is an associate professor of psychiatry in the Department of Psychology at the University of Western Ontario in London, Ontario, Canada.

ANDREW CHRISTENSEN is a professor of psychology at the University of California, Los Angeles. He is coauthor, with Neil S. Jacobson, of *Integrative Couple Therapy: Promoting Acceptance and Change* (W. W. Norton, 1996).

F. M. CHRISTENSEN is a professor in the Department of Philosophy at the University of Alberta in Edmonton, Alberta, Canada.

VICTOR CLINE is a professor emeritus of psychology at the University of Utah in Salt Lake City, Utah. His research interests include media effects and person perception issues.

H. S. COHEN is a physician in general practice based in the Netherlands.

LEE COLEMAN is a psychiatrist in Berkeley, California, and a critic of the role of mental health professionals in legal settings. His current research interests focus on false accusations of child sexual abuse.

LAURA DAVIS is an expert on healing from child sexual abuse and a nationally recognized workshop leader.

PATRICK H. DeLEON is a psychologist and a lawyer.

DAVID H. DEMO is an associate professor in the Department of Sociology at Virginia Polytechnic Institute and State University in Blacksburg, Virginia. His research focuses on the influences of family structure and family relations on parents and children.

ALBERT ELLIS, founder of rational-emotive therapy, is president of the Institute for Rational-Emotive Therapy, located in New York City. He received his Ph.D. in clinical psychology from Columbia University, and he has authored or coauthored more than 600 articles and over 50 books on psychotherapy, marital and family therapy, and sex therapy, including *Why Some Therapies Don't Work: The Dangers of Transpersonal Psychology* (Prometheus Books, 1989), with Raymond Yaeger.

SEYMOUR FISHER is a professor of psychology and coordinator of research training in the Department of Psychiatry and Behavioral Sciences at the University of New York Health Science Center at Syracuse. He has published 16 books and approximately 200 scientific papers. His scholarly work has focused on such areas as body image, sexual behavior, the validity of psychoanalytic theory, the psychodynamics of comedians, and the efficacy of psychotropic drugs.

ROGER P. GREENBERG is a professor in and head of the Division of Clinical Psychology, as well as director of psychology internship training, at the State University of New York Health Science Center at Syracuse. His more than 150 publications and presentations include the award-winning books *The Scientific Credibility of Freud's Theories and Therapy* (Columbia University Press, 1985) and *A Critical Appraisal of Biological Treatments for Psychological Distress: Comparisons With Psychotherapy and Placebo* (Lawrence Erlbaum, 1989), both coauthored with Seymour Fisher.

STEVEN C. HAYES is a professor in the Department of Psychology at the University of Nevada in Reno, Nevada. He is editor of *Rule-Governed Behavior: Cognition, Contingencies, and Instructional Control* (Plenum Press, 1989) and coeditor of *Acceptance and Change: Content and Context in Psychotherapy* (Context Press, 1994).

ELAINE HEIBY is a professor in the Department of Psychology at the University of Hawaii at Manoa.

HERBERT HENDIN is executive director of the American Suicide Foundation in New York City and a professor of psychiatry at New York Medical College. He is a graduate of the Columbia University Psychoanalytic Center, where he also taught for 15 years. He recently completed a study of assisted suicide and euthansia in the United States and the Netherlands.

NEIL S. JACOBSON is a professor of psychology at the University of Washington in Seattle, Washington. His research interests include behavior, marital therapy, depression, and family therapy. He is coauthor, with John M. Gottman, of *When Men Batter Women: New Insights into Ending Abusive Relationships* (Simon & Schuster, 1998).

GERALD KLERMAN (d. 1992) was a professor of psychiatry at Cornell Medical College. He also taught at Harvard University and Yale University, and he was the administrator for the Alcohol, Drug Abuse, and Mental Health Administration under President Jimmy Carter.

PETER D. KRAMER is a psychiatrist and the author of *Moments of Engagement: Intimate Psychotherapy in a Technological Age* (W. W. Norton, 1989).

DEMIE KURZ is codirector of the Department of Sociology at the University of Pennsylvania in Philadelphia, Pennsylvania. She is the author of *For Richer, for Poorer: Mothers Confront Divorce* (Routledge, 1995).

DAVID B. LARSON is an assistant secretary of planning at the Department of Health and Human Services in Washington, D.C.

TERRY R. McGUIRE is an associate professor of biological sciences at Rutgers University in Piscataway, New Jersey. He is coeditor, with Jerry Hirsch, of *Behavior-Genetic Analysis* (H. Ross Publishing, 1982).

STANLEY MILGRAM (1933–1984) was an experimental social psychologist and a professor of psychology at the Graduate School and University Center of the City University of New York. He is especially well known for his series of controversial investigations regarding obedience to authority, which were performed at Yale University from 1960 to 1963. His publications include *Obedience to Authority: An Experimental View* (Harper & Row, 1975).

RICHARD C. PILLARD is director of the Family Studies Laboratory at the Boston University School of Medicine.

D. L. ROSENHAN (b. 1929) is a professor of law and psychology at Stanford University and a social psychologist whose focal concern has been clinical and personality matters. He has also been a faculty member at Princeton University, the University of Pennsylvania, and Swarthmore College.

VINCENT M. RUE is codirector of the Institute for Pregnancy Loss in Portsmouth, New Hampshire.

J. PHILIPPE RUSHTON is a John Simon Guggenheim Fellow and a professor of psychology at the University of Western Ontario in London, Ontario, Canada. He holds a Ph.D. and a D.Sc. from the University of London, and he is a fellow of the American Association for the Advancement of Science and of the American, British, and Canadian Psychological Associations. He is the author of *Race, Evolution, and Behavior* (Transaction Publishers, 1995).

VICTOR D. SANUA is an adjunct professor of psychology at St. John's University in New York City. He is the editor of *Fields of Offerings: Studies in Honor of Raphael Patai* (Fairleigh Dickinson University Press, 1983). He earned his

B.A. at American University and his M.A. and Ph.D. at Michigan State University.

MARTIN E. P. SELIGMAN is a professor in the Department of Psychology at the University of Pennsylvania and is well known for his formulation of the learned helplessness model. A member of the APA's Public Education Campaign Advisory Task Force, Seligman has published over 15 books, including *What You Can Change and What You Can't: The Complete Guide to Successful Self-Improvement* (Alfred A. Knopf, 1994) and *Helplessness: On Depression, Development, and Death* (W. H. Freeman, 1992).

KENNETH J. SHAPIRO is executive director of Psychologists for the Ethical Treatment of Animals and editor of the academic biannual *Society and Animals*. His background is in clinical psychology, phenomenological psychology, and intellectual history. He has published scholarly work in phenomenological psychology, developing and applying methods for the study of both human and nonhuman animals.

BRIAN SIANO is a writer and researcher based in Philadelphia, Pennsylvania. His column "The Skeptical Eye" appears regularly in *The Humanist*.

ANNE C. SPECKHARD is a clinician, a researcher, and a consultant practicing in Alexandria, Virginia, who has consulted on several postpartum stress research projects.

ROBERT L. SPITZER is affiliated with the New York State Psychiatric Institute in New York City. He is a former chairman of the American Psychiatric Association and its Task Force on Nomenclature and Statistics.

MURRAY A. STRAUS is a professor of sociology and codirector of the Family Research Laboratory at the University of New Hampshire in Durham, New Hampshire. He has held academic appointments at Cornell University, the University of Minnesota, the University of Wisconsin, and Washington State University, as well as at universities in England, India, and Sri Lanka. He has published over 150 articles and 15 books, including *Beating the Devil Out of Them: Corporal Punishment in American Families*, coauthored with Denise A. Donnelly (Lexington Books, 1994).

JUDITH S. WALLERSTEIN is an internationally recognized authority on the effects of divorce on children and their parents. Her current research interests focus on successful marriage. Before her retirement, she was executive director of the Center for the Family in Transition —a research, training, and clinical center in Corte Madera, California, which she founded in 1980—and a senior lecturer in the School of Social Welfare at the University of California, Berkeley. She is coauthor, with Sandra Blakeslee, of *Second Chances: Men, Women, and Children a Decade After Divorce* (Ticknor & Fields, 1989). She received a Ph.D. in psychology from Lund University in Sweden in 1978.

JACK G. WIGGINS, JR., is a member of the board of trustees for the American Psychological Foundation.

RICHARD N. WILLIAMS is a member of the psychology department at Brigham Young University.

ROBERT WRIGHT is senior editor of *The New Republic* and the author of *The Moral Animal: The New Science of Evolutionary Psychology* (Pantheon Books, 1994).

INDEX